THE CAMBRIDGE
COMPANION TO

ᴍ SHEPARD

...ᵍhts have exerted as much influence on the contempo-
rᵃ ...ᵉpard. His plays are performed on and off Broadway and
...ᵉgional American theatres. They are also widely performed
...ᵢ Europe, particularly in Britain, Germany, and France, finding
...ᵖular and scholarly audience. In this collection of seventeen original
...ₛ, American and European authors from different professional and aca-
...ᵉmic backgrounds explore the various aspects of Shepard's career – his plays,
poetry, music, fiction, acting, directing, and film work. The volume covers the
major plays, including *Curse of the Starving Class*, *Buried Child*, and *True
West*, as well as other lesser known but vitally important works. A thorough
chronology of Shepard's life and career, together with biographical chapters,
a note from the legendary Joseph Chaikin, and an interview with the playwright, give a fascinating first-hand account of an exuberant and experimental
personality.

THE CAMBRIDGE
COMPANION TO
SAM SHEPARD

EDITED BY
MATTHEW ROUDANÉ
Georgia State University

CAMBRIDGE
UNIVERSITY PRESS

PUBLISHED BY THE PRESS SYNDICATE OF THE UNIVERSITY OF CAMBRIDGE
The Pitt Building, Trumpington Street, Cambridge, United Kingdom

CAMBRIDGE UNIVERSITY PRESS
The Edinburgh Building, Cambridge CB2 2RU, UK
40 West 20th Street, New York, NY 10011-4211, USA
477 Williamstown Road, Port Melbourne, VIC 3207, Australia
Ruiz de Alarcón 13, 28014 Madrid, Spain
Dock House, The Waterfront, Cape Town 8001, South Africa

http://www.cambridge.org

First published 2002

Printed in the United Kingdom at the University Press, Cambridge

Typeface Sabon 10/13 pt.   *System* LATEX 2$_\varepsilon$ [TB]

A catalogue record for this book is available from the British Library

Library of Congress Cataloguing in Publication data
The Cambridge Companion to Sam Shepard / edited by Matthew Roudané.
p.   cm.
Includes bibliographical references and index.
ISBN 0 521 77158 7 (hbk) – ISBN 0 521 77766 6 (pbk)
1. Shepard, Sam, 1943 – Handbooks, manuals, etc.   2. Dramatists, American –
20th century – Biography – Handbooks, manuals, etc.   I. Title: Companion to
Sam Shepard. II. Roudané, Matthew Charles, 1953 –   III. Cambridge University Press.
PS3569.H394 Z65   2002
812'.54 – dc21
[B]   2001043211

ISBN 0 521 77158 7 hardback
ISBN 0 521 77766 6 paperback

For SUSAN and NICKOLAS

CONTENTS

ACKNOWLEDGMENTS

I would like to thank Robert Sattelmeyer, who chairs the Department of English, and Ahmed Abdelal, Dean of the College of Arts and Sciences at Georgia State University, for supporting my research over the years. Del Hamilton and Faye Allen of 7 Stages Theatre in Atlanta deserve thanks as well. Hamilton and Allen, who have acted in and directed numerous Shepard plays for two decades, introduced me to Joseph Chaikin, and our conversations were invaluable. When I told Chaikin I wanted to interview Shepard for this volume, he wrote to the playwright on my behalf. Meeting with Chaikin was an honor, and I am grateful for his telling me much about his collaborative work with Shepard. I thank Bill Coco, Scott Robinson and Jonah Zeiger, for their help. Thanks go to my graduate research assistants, Veda Laxmi Khulpateea, Laura Carter, and Sabina L. Muller, who assisted with the final preparation of the manuscript. Thanks, too, to Katie Wheeler. Working with the contributors to this volume has been a pleasure; it's been a delight to work with, once again, Sarah Stanton and her colleagues at Cambridge University Press, and Margaret Berrill deserves special thanks for her careful copyediting.

I am grateful for the help of Judy Boals, Shepard's agent, who patiently answered my many questions and passed along several key requests to Shepard. Thanks to Shepard and his publishers for permission to quote from his work.

I especially want to express my gratitude to Sam Shepard. After years of seeing his plays, writing about them, and trying to teach them well to my many students, it was a great inspiration to meet him for our interview. He has been enormously helpful throughout the production of this book. He was also kind enough to share with me a manually typed version of *The Late Henry Moss*, which gave me the chance to offer some speculative thoughts on this drama at the end of the *Companion*.

Finally, as always, much thanks to my wife, Susan Ashley.

I would like to acknowledge permission to quote from the following copyright material:

From *Simpatico*. Copyright 1995, Sam Shepard. By permission of Vintage Books, a division of Random House.

From *States of Shock, Far North, Silent Tongue*. Copyright 1993, Sam Shepard. By permission of Vintage Books, a division of Random House.

From *Cruising Paradise*. Copyright 1995, Sam Shepard. By permission of Vintage Books, a division of Random House.

From *Seven Plays* (*Buried Child, Curse of the Starving Class, The Tooth of Crime, La Turista, Tongues, Savage Love, True West*). Copyright 1986, Sam Shepard. By permission of Bantam Books, a division of Random House.

From *Fool for Love and Other Plays* (*Angel City, Geography of a Horse Dreamer, Action, Cowboy Mouth, Melodrama Play, Seduced, Suicide in B-Flat*. Copyright 1984, Sam Shepard. By permission of Bantam Books, a division of Random House.

From *The Late Henry Moss*. Copyright 2000, Sam Shepard. By permission of Sam Shepard.

From *Man Fly*. Copyright 1975, Sam Shepard. By permission of Sam Shepard.

NOTES ON CONTRIBUTORS

SUSAN C. W. ABBOTSON currently teaches at Rhode Island College and has published *The Student Companion to Arthur Miller* (2000), as well as articles in various journals on Miller, August Wilson, and Nick Park's *Wallace and Gromit* films.

THOMAS P. ADLER, Professor of English and Department Head at Purdue University, has taught dramatic literature since 1970. He has published five books and over sixty articles on a wide range of modern British and American playwrights, including essays on Miller, Williams, and Hellman for three other Cambridge Companion volumes. His next book will be a study of the plays of Tom Stoppard and David Hare.

CHRISTOPHER BIGSBY is Professor of American Studies at the University of East Anglia. He has published more than twenty-five books on British and American culture, including *Confrontation and Commitment: A Study of Contemporary American Drama 1959–1966* (1967), *Albee* (1969), *The Black American Writer* (1969), *The Second Black Renaissance* (1980), *A Critical Introduction to Twentieth-Century American Drama* (1982–85), *David Mamet* (1985), *Modern American Drama 1945–2000* (2000), and, as editor, *Contemporary English Drama* (1981), *Arthur Miller and Company* (1990), and *The Portable Arthur Miller* (1995). His most recent book is *Contemporary American Playwrights* (2000). Bigsby is co-editor, with Don Wilmeth, of the three-volume (1998, 2000) *The Cambridge History of American Theatre*. He is also the author of three novels: *Hester* (1994), *Pearl* (1995), and *Still Lives* (1996).

STEPHEN J. BOTTOMS is a lecturer in Theatre Studies at the University of Glasgow, Scotland, where he specializes in contemporary American theatre and performance art. He is the author of *The Theatre of Sam Shepard: States of Crisis* (1998) and *Albee: Who's Afraid of Virginia Woolf?*, both for Cambridge University Press, and of several widely published articles. His piece for this volume draws on his extensive original research into the history of the 1960s Off-Off-Broadway movement, which forms the basis of a forthcoming book. He also writes, directs, and performs with the Glasgow-based Flexible Deadlock theatre company.

JOHAN CALLENS is a research associate of the Fund for Scientific Research (Flanders), affiliated with the Free University of Brussels (VUB), where he teaches American literature and theatre. He is the author of *Double Binds: Existentialist Inspiration and Generic Experimentation in the Early Work of Jack Richardson*

(1993), *Acte(s) de Présence: Teksten over Engelstalig theatre in Vlaanderen en Nederland* (1996), and *From Middleton and Rowley's "Changeling" to Sam Shepard's "Bodyguard": A Contemporary Appropriation of Renaissance Drama* (1997). Among his more recent editions are a double Shepard issue of *Contemporary Theatre Review* (1998) and an English-language issue of *Degrés* on intermediality in the performing arts (2000). He serves on the editorial boards of the *European Journal of American Culture* and the Flemish theatre quarterly *Documenta*.

JOSEPH CHAIKIN is one of America's leading directors, actors, and producers within the alternative theatre world. The winner of six Obie Awards, including the Obie's first Lifetime Achievement Award in 1977, Chaikin is the founder of the Open Theatre, the Winter Project, and the Other Theatre. His collaborations with Shepard include *Joseph Chaikin and Sam Shepard: Letters and Texts, 1972–1984* (edited by Barry Daniels), *Tongues, Savage/Love, The War in Heaven*, and *When the World was Green: A Chef's Fable*. He has also published the influential *The Presence of the Actor*. As a member of the Living Theatre, he acted in Jack Gelber's *The Connection* in 1959, and his involvement in American theatre since then has influenced a whole generation of playwrights.

JOHN M. CLUM is Professor of English and Professor of the Practice of Drama at Duke University. Recent books include *Something for the Boys: Musical Theatre and Gay Culture* and *Still Acting Gay: Male Homosexuality in Modern Drama*, both from St. Martin's Press, and a new anthology: *Asking and Telling: Gay Drama for the Millennium*. He is the author of numerous essays on twentieth-century American playwrights. John Clum is also a playwright whose works have been produced in theatres around the United States.

DAVID J. DeROSE is a Professor of English and Drama at Saint Mary's College of California where he recently served as Director of the MFA Creative Writing Program. He is the former Director of the Theatre Studies Program at Yale University and holds a PhD in Dramatic Art from University of California, Berkeley. His many writings on contemporary American theatre include *Sam Shepard* (1992).

ANN C. HALL is currently serving as Chair of the English Division at Ohio Dominican College and President of the Harold Pinter Society. She hosted the "Pinter in London" conference with participants from over ten countries. Speakers included Pinter, Ronald Harwood, Michael Billington and others. She has written *A Kind of Alaska: Women in the Plays of O'Neill, Pinter, and Shepard* and edited *Delights, Dilemmas, and Desires: Essays on Women and the Media*, as well as numerous essays on modern drama.

LESLIE KANE is Professor of English at Westfield State College. She is the author of *The Language of Silence: The Unspoken and the Unspeakable in Modern Drama* and *Weasels and Wisemen: Ethics and Ethnicity in the Works of David Mamet*. She has edited *David Mamet: A Casebook, Israel Horowitz: A Collection of Critical Essays, "Glengarry Glen Ross": Text and Performance*, and *David Mamet in Conversation*. President of the David Mamet Society and co-editor of the *David Mamet Review*, Kane's work has appeared in *The Printer Review, American Drama, Theatre* Journal, *The Yearbook on English Studies*, and collections of essays.

KIMBALL KING, Professor of English at the University of North Carolina at Chapel Hill, is co-editor of the *Southern Literary Journal* and has written books on Thomas Nelson Page and Augustus B. Longstreet. His primary field of interest is contemporary British and American drama and he is the author of *Twenty British Playwrights* (1977), *Ten Irish Playwrights* (1979), *Ten American Playwrights* (1982), *Sam Shepard: A Casebook* (1988), and *Hollywood on Stage: Playwrights Evaluate the Culture Industry* (1998). Currently he is General Editor for Garland Publishing of two series: Casebooks on Modern Drama and Studies in Modern Drama.

CARLA J. MCDONOUGH is Associate Professor of English at Eastern Illinois University where she specializes in modern drama. She is the author of the book *Staging Masculinity: Male Identity in Contemporary American Drama* (1997), as well as numerous articles or book chapters about Sam Shepard, David Mamet, David Rabe, Adrienne Kennedy, and Christina Reid.

BRENDA MURPHY is Professor of English at the University of Connecticut. She is the author of *Congressional Theatre: Dramatizing McCarthyism on Stage, Film, and Television* (1999), *Miller: Death of a Salesman* (1995), *Tennessee Williams and Elia Kazan: A Collaboration in the Theatre* (1992), and *American Realism and American Drama, 1880–1940* (1987), and the editor of the *Cambridge Companion to American Women Playwrights* (1999) and *A Realist in the American Theatre: Selected Drama Criticism of William Dean Howells* (1992).

MARC ROBINSON is the author of *The Other American Drama* and editor of *The Theatre of Maria Irene Fornes* and *Altogether Elsewhere: Writers on Exile*. He teaches at Yale College, where he is the Director of Theatre Studies, and at the Yale School of Drama.

MATTHEW ROUDANÉ is Professor of English at Georgia State University in Atlanta, where he specializes in American drama. He has published *Understanding Edward Albee* (1987), *Conversations with Arthur Miller* (1987), *American Dramatists* (1989), *"Who's Afraid of Virginia Woolf?": Necessary Fictions, Terrifying Realities* (1990), *Public Issues, Private Tensions: Contemporary American Drama* (1993), *Approaches to Teaching Miller's "Death of a Salesman"* (1995), *American Drama Since 1960: A Critical History* (1996), and *The Cambridge Companion to Tennessee Williams* (1997). Some of his more recent work appears in Don Wilmeth and Christopher Bigsby's *The Cambridge History of American Theatre*, vol. III (2000). Roudané is editor of the *South Atlantic Review*. He served as a dramaturg for 7 Stages Theatre in Atlanta, where he worked with Joseph Chaikin, who directed Edward Albee's *A Delicate Balance* (2002).

SAM SHEPARD has written nearly fifty plays, eleven of which have won Obie Awards. His first plays, *Cowboys* and *The Rock Garden*, were produced in 1963 by Theatre Genesis in New York City. For several seasons he worked with Off-Off-Broadway theatre groups, including La MaMa and Caffe Cino. From 1975 to 1983, he was Playwright in Residence at San Francisco's Magic Theatre. In 1979 he was awarded the Pulitzer Prize for Drama for *Buried Child*, and in 1984 he gained an Oscar nomination for his performance in *The Right Stuff*. His screenplay for *Paris, Texas* won the Palme d'Or award at the 1984 Cannes Film Festival, and he wrote and directed the film *Far North* in 1988. He was elected to the American Academy of Arts and Letters in 1986. In 1992, he received the Gold Medal for Drama from the Academy and was inducted into the Theatre Hall of Fame in 1994. He has appeared in over thirty films, including *Days of Heaven, Francis, Country, Crimes of the Heart, Steel Magnolias, Voyager, The Pelican Brief, Hamlet,* and *The Pledge.* His drama *When the World Was Green: A Chef's Fable,* written with his long-time collaborator, Joseph Chaikin, and commissioned by 7 Stages Theatre in Atlanta, premiered at the Olympics Arts Festival in 1996 and then opened in New York as part of the Signature Theatre Company's season devoted to his work. He wrote and directed his last play of the twentieth century, *The Late Henry Moss,* in 2000.

LESLIE A. WADE is Associate Professor at Louisiana State University's Department of Theatre. A doctoral graduate of the University of California at Santa Barbara, Wade has presented his work at national and international theatre conferences and has published essays in numerous journals, including *Theatre Studies, Text and Performance Quarterly, Theatral Annuaire, Journal of Dramatic Theory and Criticism, Theatre Symposium,* and *Western European Stages.* His book *Sam Shepard and the American Theatre* was published by Greenwood Press (1997). He serves on the editorial board of *Theatre History Studies.* Recipient of a Louisiana State Arts Council's fellowship in playwriting, Wade has also received writing awards from the Association for Theatre in Higher Education, the Los Angeles Arts Council, and the American College Theatre Festival. He has twice directed the grant-project "Native Voices and Visions," a script-writing competition for Louisiana playwrights. Wade currently serves as the LSU Theatre Department's director of graduate studies and co-director of LSU in London.

CHRONOLOGY

1943   November 5: Samuel Shepard Rogers, named Steve, is born, Fort Sheridan, Illinois.

1949   Starts school in South Pasadena, California.

1961   Graduates high school and begins training in animal husbandry.

1963   Moves to New York and finds work as a busboy at the Village Gate nightclub in Greenwich Village. Changes name to Sam Shepard.

1964   October 10: *Cowboys* and *The Rock Garden* premiere at Theatre Genesis (dir. Ralph Cook).
November 23: *Up to Thursday* premieres at the Village South Theatre, under the sponsorship of Edward Albee's Playwrights Unit (dir. Charles Gnys).

1965   February 10: *Dog* and *Rocking Chair* premiere at Café La MaMa (dir. John Banks).
April 16: *Chicago* premieres at Theatre Genesis (dir. Ralph Cook).
September: *4-H Club* premieres at the Cherry Lane Theatre with the backing of the Playwrights Unit (dir. Charles Gnys).
November 16: *Icarus's Mother* premieres at Caffe Cino (dir. Michael Smith).

1966   January 20: Premiere of *Red Cross* at Judson Poets' Theatre (dir. Jacques Levy).
Spring: *Fourteen Hundred Thousand* premieres at the Firehouse Theatre, Minnesota (dir. Sydney Schubert Walter). The play is later filmed for National Educational Television (dir. Tom O'Horgan).

1967   *Five Plays* is published by Bobbs-Merrill.
March 4: *La Turista* premieres at the American Place Theatre (dir. Jacques Levy).
May 18: *Melodrama Play* premieres at Café La MaMa (dir. Tom O'Horgan).
November: *Cowboys #2* premieres at the Mark Taper Forum in Los Angeles (dir. Edward Parone).
December 26: *Forensic and the Navigators* premieres at Theatre Genesis (dir. Ralph Cook).

1968   Begins work on a screenplay for Antonioni's *Zabriskie Point*. He soon resigns and begins touring as a drummer with Holy Modal Rounders, with whom he records *The Moray Eels Eat the Holy Modal Rounders* (Elektra).

1969   June 17: Kenneth Tynan's musical *Oh! Calcutta* premieres at the Eden Theatre, New York, and includes the final scene of Shepard's play *The Rock Garden*.

November: Shepard weds O-Lan Johnson at St. Mark's Church.

December 26: *The Unseen Hand* premieres at La MaMa Experimental Theatre Club (dir. Jeff Bleckner).

1970   January: US premiere of *The Holy Ghostly* at the McCarter Theatre, Princeton, NJ, in a production by Tom O'Horgan's New Troupe, after touring in 1969 with La MaMa troupe.

March 12: *Operation Sidewinder* premieres at Lincoln Center for the Performing Arts (dir. Michael Schultz).

May: Jesse Mojo Shepard is born.

July: *Shaved Splits* premieres at La MaMa ETC (dir. Bill Hart).

1971   Shepard briefly separates from O-Lan to live with Patti Smith at the Chelsea Hotel.

March 4: *The Mad Dog Blues* premieres at Theatre Genesis (dir. Robert Glaudini).

April 29: *Cowboy Mouth*, written with Patti Smith (dir. Glaudini) and *Back Bog Beast Bait* (dir. Tony Barsha) premiere at the American Place Theatre. *Cowboy Mouth*, with Shepard in the leading role, closes after one performance when Shepard inexplicably leaves.

Summer: Shepard and family move to London.

1972   July 17: *The Tooth of Crime* premieres at the Open Space Theatre, London (dir. Charles Marowitz).

Joseph Chaikin's Open Theatre, New York, presents *Nightwalk*, a collaborative work including textual contributions by Shepard.

1973   July: BBC Television airs *Blue Bitch*.

Shepard's prose collection *Hawk Moon* is published.

The Tooth of Crime premieres in the US. Staged by Richard Schechner's Performance Group, the production is surrounded by controversy.

1974   February 21: *Geography of a Horse Dreamer*, directed by Shepard, premieres at the Royal Court Theatre Upstairs, London.

March 25: *Little Ocean* premieres at the Hampstead Theatre Club, London (dir. Stephen Rea).

Summer: The Shepards leave London for California.

October: *Action* opens at the Royal Court Theatre Upstairs (dir. Nancy Meckler).

1975   April 15: *Action* and *Killer's Head*, the latter starring a young Richard Gere, have their US premiere in a double bill at the American Place Theatre (dir. Nancy Meckler). The same program, directed by Shepard, opens at the Magic Theatre, San Francisco, shortly thereafter.

Fall: Shepard joins Bob Dylan's *Rolling Thunder Review Tour* as the writer of a proposed screenplay.

1976   July 2: *Angel City* premieres at the Magic Theatre (dir. Shepard).

October 15: *Suicide in B-Flat* debuts at the Yale Repertory Theatre (dir. Walt Jones).

October 22: *The Sad Lament of Pecos Bill on the Eve of Killing His Wife* opens at the Bay Area Playwrights' Festival (dir. Robert Woodruff).

1977   March 18: *Inacoma* premieres at the Magic Theatre. The performance is developed by a company of actors and musicians and directed by Shepard.

April 21: *Curse of the Starving Class* premieres at the Royal Court Theatre (dir. Nancy Meckler).

Rolling Thunder Logbook published.

Director Jacques Levy acquires Shepard's manuscript, *Jackson's Dance*, wishing to stage the 1972 play about painter Jackson Pollock at the Public Theatre. Pollock's widow Lee Krasner refuses to give the necessary legal permission.

1978   April: Premiere of *Seduced* at the Trinity Square Repertory Theatre, Providence, RI (dir. Jack Gelber).

June 7–11: *Tongues* begins a limited run at the Magic Theatre with Shepard and Joseph Chaikin appearing in it.

June 27: *Buried Child* opens at the Magic Theatre (dir. Robert Woodruff).

Summer: Shepard makes his film debut in Terrence Malick's *Days of Heaven*.

1979   June 7: *Jacaranda* premieres at St. Clement's Church, New York. The performance includes a Daniel Nagrin dance piece and libretto by Shepard.

September 5: *Savage/Love* premieres at the Eureka Theatre Summer Festival, San Francisco.

Buried Child wins the Pulitzer Prize for Drama.

1980   July 10: *True West* premieres at the Magic Theatre (dir. Robert Woodruff). The play moves to New York's Public Theatre, but the shift is marred by clashes with producer Joseph Papp.

Shepard appears in the film, *Resurrection* (dir. Daniel Petrie).

1981   O-Lan Shepard and the Overtone Theatre construct *Supersititions* from pieces in *Motel Chronicles*.

Shepard appears in the film *Raggedy Man* (dir. Jack Fisk).

1982   *Motel Chronicles*, a prose collection, published.

Steppenwolf Theatre in Chicago revives *True West*. John Malkovich plays Lee to Gary Sinise's Austin. A film of this production, directed by Sinise, appears on Public Broadcasting Service television the following year.

While filming *Frances* (dir. Graeme Clifford), Shepard begins a relationship with the film's star, Jessica Lange.

1983   February 8: *Fool for Love* premieres at the Magic Theatre (dir. Shepard).

Shepard acts in the movie, *The Right Stuff* (dir. Philip Kaufman), for which he receives an Oscar award nomination as Best Supporting Actor.

Shepard and Lange move to Santa Fe, New Mexico.

1984   March: Shepard's father, Sam Rogers, dies.

July: Divorce from O-Lan is finalized.

Paris, Texas, a Shepard screenplay directed by Wim Wenders, is released and wins Palme d'Or at the Cannes Film Festival.

While working in Massachusetts with Shepard and others, Chaikin suffers a stroke. Shepard writes *The War in Heaven* with Chaikin while he convalesces.

Shepard and Lange appear in *Country* (dir. Richard Pearce).

1985   January 8: *The War in Heaven* premieres on WBAI radio.

December 5: *A Lie of the Mind* premieres at New York's Promenade Theatre (dir. Shepard). Wins New York Drama Critics Circle Award for Best Play.

Robert Altman's film version of *Fool for Love* is released with Shepard as Eddie and Kim Basinger as Mary.

1986   Shepard and Lange move to Scottsville, Virginia.

The pair appears together in the film *Crimes of the Heart*, adapted from the Beth Henley play (dir. Bruce Beresford).

"Brownsville Girl," a song written by Shepard and Bob Dylan, appears on Dylan's album, *Knocked Out Loaded*.

Shepard is elected to the American Academy of Arts and Letters.

1987   *Esquire* Magazine publishes "True Dylan," an interview with Dylan conducted by Shepard and presented as a one-act play.

Shepard appears in the film *Baby Boom* (dir. Charles Shyer).

1988   Shepard, in Minnesota, directs his screenplay *Far North*. Lange appears in the film.

1989   Shepard appears as Dolly Parton's husband in Herb Ross's film *Steel Magnolias*.

1990   Shepard appears in *Bright Angel* (dir. Michael Fields), a movie adaptation of Richard Ford's short story collection *Rock Springs*.

1991   April 30: The premiere of *States of Shock* at the American Place Theatre (dir. Bill Hart).

Shepard acts in the movie *Defenseless* (dir. Martin Campbell), and lands the lead role in Volker Schlöndorff's *Voyager*

1992   Shepard directs another of his screenplays, *Silent Tongue*, in New Mexico.

The film *Thunder Heart* (dir. Michael Apted), in which Shepard plays a part, is released.

The American Academy of Arts and Letters awards Shepard the Gold Medal for Drama.

1993   Shepard appears in Alan J. Pakula's movie, *The Pelican Brief*, based on a John Grisham novel of the same title.

1994   Shepard's mother dies.

Shepard appears in *Safe Passage* (dir. Robert Allan Ackerman) with Susan Sarandon.

Film version of *Curse of the Starving Class* (dir. J. Michael McClary) is released.

November 1: *Simpatico* premieres at the Joseph Papp Public Theatre (dir. Shepard).

Shepard is inducted into the Theatre Hall of Fame.

1995   October 4: The Steppenwolf Theatre premieres a revised version of *Buried Child* (dir. Sinise). This version moves to Broadway in 1996.

Shepard and Lange move their family to Minnesota.

Shepard acts in the movies *The Streets of Laredo* (dir. Joseph Sarjent) and *The Good Old Boys* (dir. Tommy Lee Jones).

1996   *Cruising Paradise*, an account of Shepard's experiences starring in Volker Schlöndorff's film, *Voyager*, is published.

July 19: *When the World Was Green: A Chef's Fable*, written with and directed by Chaikin, premieres at the Olympics Arts Festival during the games in Atlanta.

November: The Signature Theatre Company of New York dedicates a season to Shepard's plays. The festivities open with the premiere of a revised version of *The Tooth of Crime*. With the added subtitle, *Second Dance*, this new version replaced Shepard's original score with music and lyrics by T-Bone Burnett.

Horton Foote's screenplay *Lily Dale* is filmed (dir. Peter Masterson) with Shepard appearing in the film.

1997   Shepard appears in the movie *The Only Thrill* (dir. Peter Masterson).

1998   February 10: *Eyes for Consuela* opens at the Manhattan Theatre Club at City Center Stage II in New York City (dir. Terry Kinney, starring David Straithaim and Daniel Faraldo).

July 8: The PBS series, Great Performances, airs a special on Shepard entitled *Sam Shepard: Stalking Himself*. The program includes a view of eight of Shepard's plays and is followed by a screening of the filmed production of *True West*.

The Magic Theatre in San Francisco renames one of its stages the Sam Shepard Theatre.

2000   Shepard acts in a film version of his *Simpatico* (dir. Matthew Warchus).

March 9: Opening of a revival of *True West* at the Circle in the Square Theatre, New York (dir. Matthew Warchus).

Shepard plays the ghost of Hamlet's father in a film adaptation of *Hamlet* (dir. Michael Almereyda).

November 14: *The Late Henry Moss* opens at the Magic Theatre, San Francisco. The play, directed by Shepard, stars James Gammon, Sean Penn, Nick Nolte, Woody Harrelson, Cheech Marin, and Sheila Tousey.

2001   Appears in the film *The Pledge*, starring Jack Nicholson and Sean Penn, who also directed.

September 5: The Signature Theatre Company stages the New York City premiere of *The Late Henry Moss*, directed by Joseph Chaikin.

MATTHEW ROUDANÉ

Introduction

Sam Shepard conferred upon the American stage its postmodernity in the 1960s. Of course he was not the *only* one to do so, but he interjected a youthful, exuberant, and experimental voice that extended our appreciation of a postmodern aesthetic. In the 2000s, Shepard continues experimenting with dramatic form and structure. He traverses the borders of faith, logic, and social coherence to reconnoiter a mythic and cultural terrain filled with uncertainty and the near-absence of love. His is a Zolaesque world, a malevolent universe in which a sense of bafflement and loss prevail. As Baylor says in *A Lie of the Mind* (1985), "We're all gonna get clobbered when we least expect it."[1] Contextualized within a narrative history of the American theatre, seeing characters "clobbered" on stage is hardly unique. From Susan Glaspell and Eugene O'Neill to Edward Albee and Adrienne Kennedy, American playwrights have presented a rich, if disturbing, series of physical, psychological, and moral assaults. Still, within the works of many twentieth-century American playwrights – Arthur Miller's *The Crucible* (1953), O'Neill's *Long Day's Journey into Night* (1956), Lorraine Hansberry's *A Raisin in the Sun* (1959), Marsha Norman's *Getting Out* (1977), Tony Kushner's companion plays, *Angels in America* (parts One and Two, 1991, 1992), and Margaret Edson's *Wit* (1999) – there is more often than not an implied sense of recovery, or some epiphanic coming to terms with one's self and culture. Or if it is too late for a John Proctor or Mary Tyrone, perhaps the spark of recognition transpires within the audience. For many American dramatists, confrontation triggers catharsis, catharsis insight, and that insight becomes a still point whose defining moment, itself, is the mechanism for a transcendent awareness, signaling the first step toward a spiritual recovery of the self.

Locating such affirmative textures within Shepard's theatre is difficult. Perhaps impossible. To be sure, there emerge momentary glimpses of hope, and Shepard's works in text and performance can be wildly funny. *True West* (1980), a play whose humor energizes the performance, sparkles during its absurdist, vaudevillian moments: when a baffled Lee discovers that there are ten Melly Fergusons living in Bakersfield; when Lee finally finds the pen in the trashed-out kitchen; and when their mother returns from Alaska and urges her sons to go see Picasso, whom she thinks will make a personal appearance at a museum in Los Angeles. On the other hand, a sadness pervades *True West* and most of Shepard's other plays, a sadness that dissolves into a sense of menace, then uncertainty. This decline finds its expression in the deeply problematic nature of loving relationships between men and women, as seen in *Fool for Love* (1983) and *Eyes for Consuela* (1998), or between parents and their children, as seen in *Curse of the Starving Class* (1977) or *Buried Child* (1979), or between brothers and fathers, as in *The Late Henry Moss* (2000). In Sam Shepard's entropic world, the primal family unit – whose members seem to be on some grand cosmic disconnect – is trapped within its own lies of the mind. Perhaps this explains why, when I asked if there were hints of hope and positive reconnection in such recent work as *When the World Was Green: A Chef's Fable* (1996) and in selected tales from *Cruising Paradise* (1996), Shepard replied, "I think hope and hopelessness are intimately connected, and I don't believe in one or the other. In a way I prefer hopelessness to hope. I think there's more hope in hopelessness."[2] Indeed, Shepard's heroes find themselves caught within a terrible binary of hope and hopelessness, struggling with their own distorted versions of objective reality, and trying to survive in an American landscape warped by its own deflected myths, generational schisms, and wayward sense of Manifest Destiny. Thus his characters typically exist in some ongoing "state of shock."

During the year Shepard saw his first plays staged, 1964, traditional notions of community, global boundaries, and citizenship were, once again, reinventing themselves. The Beatles and the Rolling Stones released their first albums (as they used to be called). The Space Race was on – as was the Cold War. With Kennedy's assassination, the escalating war in Southeast Asia, and the emerging civil rights movement, the objective yielded to the subjective, the once verifiable to the ineffable. Competing narratives were no longer limited to Joseph Heller's novel, *Catch-22* (1961), Edward Albee's play, *Who's Afraid of Virginia Woolf?* (1962), or Stanley Kubrick's film, *Dr. Strangelove or: How I Learned to Stop Worrying and Love the Bomb* (1964). Such narratives animated the streets, as race riots and antiwar protests soon would play counterpoint to a hope for national unity. Apocalypse now was a distinct possibility. American hegemony, in brief, was disappearing. And more than most, it seemed, Shepard was alive to and responsible for much of the theatrical revolution that interwove theatrical text with social context. His was, above all, an intensely voracious and fresh voice. It was, moreover, a voice that defined the private fears of the individual and the public disorders of a nation.

However one wishes to politicize his plays, though, Shepard's characters seem less concerned with social change and more fixed, at best, on discovering some genuine force in a world filled with shattered families and the iconography of popular culture. They are figures propelled by an inchoate inertia and preoccupied with merely surviving. Movie stars, cowboys, rock musicians, Hollywood agents, military personnel, mobsters, and drifters enact their repressed anxieties and depressed lives amidst the alluvia of a postmodernist set and setting. His plays take place in shabby motels and in suburbia, with empty refrigerators, '57 Chevys, rock-and-roll music, nearby shopping malls or deserts defining an arid world devoid of comfort. Within such a world his characters struggle, unsuccessfully, to find some authentic force. It is as if the quest, itself, becomes an all-consuming preoccupation. As Lee says in *True West*, "What I need is somethin' authentic. Somethin' to keep me in touch."[3]

In the summer of 1963, Shepard, a 19-year-old engaged in an on-the-road adventure from his California home, wound up in New York City and quickly immersed himself in, and soon became the unofficial star of, the alternative theatre scene. Thirty-seven years later he recalled,

> Looking back on it [Off-Off-Broadway], it was quite an extraordinary tapestry of atmospheres...It was really amazing to be a kid there. It was the most fortunate thing for somebody who wanted to write plays. It was absolute luck that I happened to be there when the whole Off-Off-Broadway movement was starting. I arrived there in '63 and by '64 Off-Off-Broadway was kicking out. It was just a great time for a writer.[4]

He proved to be an energetic new playwright, one sometimes unable to control his creative energies. Later in his career Shepard would carefully rewrite his scripts, but the early plays seem to be products of an imagination on hyper-drive. There was, apparently, little interest in revision. Still, it was soon clear that, as Shepard worked to transform craft into art, there was a singularly original talent emerging. He proved receptive to international innovations in drama, and his earliest plays, from *The Rock Garden* (1964) and *Up to Thursday* (1964) to *The Holy Ghostly* (1970) and *Back Bog Beast Bait* (1971), reflect such receptivity. The earlier plays tend to be brief, nonrealistic pieces, often filled with fantastic twists of narrative and lacking closure. Traditional versions of plot, character, and linearity find little place in the playwright's early works. Echoing Shepard's reaction against the Establishment, his plays were rebellions against traditional notions of dramatic form and structure. From Samuel Beckett, whose *Waiting for Godot* (1952) influenced his aesthetic principles, Shepard imported for his *Cowboys* (1964) and *Chicago* (1965) a sense of the absurd, an implied futility in any logical connection between words, actions, and deeds.

As his career developed, Shepard, probably unconsciously, benefited from other European absurdists. There is, in the plays he writes, a Pinteresque sense of tragicomedic menace. Like Peter Handke, Shepard is not afraid to call attention to the artificiality of the theatre, allowing him to move more readily from the real to the dream, from the familiar realistic props and settings to a symbolic and even mythic representation. One sees a Pirandellian playfulness that darkens as his own postmodern characters search for their identities. At times it is as if he drew from Antonin Artaud the power of the sacred, the violent, and the myth. Although little evidence exists to suggest that Shepard turned specifically to these international figures for inspiration, as a young, emerging artist living in the Village, his work could hardly help but be imbued with international artistic crosscurrents. Today Shepard also marvels at the aesthetic brilliance of fiction from others, including a Russian, an Irishman, and a Mexican (Anton Chekhov, Frank O'Connor, and Juan Rulfo). Perhaps this explains why Shepard based his *Eyes for Consuela* on Octavio Paz's short story "The Blue Bouquet."

On native ground, Shepard learned from the free associative forms of Beat poetry. He embraced the improvisational aspects of a free language, of a word-play liberated from rigid structures of meter and logical coherence. The poetry of Lawrence Ferlinghetti and Allen Ginsberg appealed to his verbal imagination, as did Jack Kerouac's "oceanic" prose in *On the Road* (1957). A rock musician who would later become a film star, Shepard was also drawn to the improvisational forms of jazz music. From Albee, he saw the incendiary power implicit in heated repartee, and he shared with Albee both a disdain and a distrust of Broadway (though, ironically, both dramatists would ultimately make successful transitions to Broadway). In the later 1960s, Joseph Chaikin recalled recently, Shepard used to drop in on rehearsals at the Open Theatre, watching performers work on their transformational acting techniques.[5] Such experiences opened new creative possibilities for Shepard as he continued with astonishing rapidity to move his instinctive experimentalism from the page to the stage. Although "we really didn't work together until *Tongues* . . . at the Magic Theatre, and that was in the seventies . . . I used to go to rehearsals [at the Open Theatre in the mid-sixties] just to sit there and listen to Joe and watch him. He was so eloquent about what he was looking for in the actor. And what he was looking for was completely different from what was going on at the time . . . Suddenly Joe opened up this whole new territory . . ."[6]

Once gaining entrance into this new territory, Shepard came of age as a writer during the 1970s and mid-1980s with such plays as *The Tooth of*

Crime (1972), *Action* (1974), *Curse of the Starving Class, Buried Child* (1978), *True West, Fool for Love*, and *A Lie of the Mind*. While Shepard's nonrealism was in many respects reaching its apex in 1978 with *Seduced* (a nonrealism, of course, that he would never fully abandon), as early as 1974 he voiced an interest in developing a more realistic theatre. "I'd like to try a whole different way of writing now, which is very stark and not so flashy and not full of a lot of mythic figures and everything, and try to scrape it down to the bone as much as possible," he said. For Shepard it was to be a realism, "but not the kind of realism where husbands and wives squabble and that kind of stuff."[7] His remarks slightly mislead. Men and women "squabble" in most of his later plays, with fighting intensifying in *Fool for Love* and reaching a (de)crescendo in *A Lie of the Mind*. Yet his comments do indicate a modified realism that informed the later plays. Beginning in 1977 with *Curse of the Starving Class*, and extending through *Buried Child, True West*, and *Fool for Love*, Shepard experimented with a modified realism, a form that also drove his work in the 1990s: *States of Shock* (1991), *Simpatico* (1994), *When the World Was Green*, and *Eyes for Consuela*. In terms of plots, characterizations, and language, these plays were closer to realistic performances than the works of the 1960s and earlier 1970s. A closer correspondence between the spoken word and its intended meaning grew. *Action*, though richly symbolic, sometimes followed a cause-and-effect pattern. Questions of coherence and believability were no longer unanswerable, but plot resolutions were hardly to be found. The mystery remained, especially in context of the family, but the rendering of the staged realities was less radical than in, say, a production like *Operation Sidewinder* (1970).

Shepard's commitment to dramatic excellence has yielded thus far eleven Obie Awards, a Pulitzer Prize, and numerous other accolades. He is, for many, the preeminent playwright of the postwar American theatre. The distinguishing marks of Shepard's dramas lie in his unique use of language, myth, music, and predatory characters. Although he shows, in the some fifty plays he has written to date, a rich variety of performative styles and cultural concerns, his central subject is often the American family. Victims and victimizers, the pursued and the pursuer vie for a metaphorical, psychological, and spiritual space in his plays. Meanwhile, options slowly diminish. There are no real survivors, no remissions of pain. Spaces open up which prove unbridgeable. Necessity rules. Irony is constantly reborn from the frustrated desires of those who obey compulsions they would wish to resist. And yet there is "a fire in the snow" (*Lie of the Mind* 131), there is a fractured poetry, there is an energy and a passion to the lives of those whose demons he stages. There is an intensity, a resonance, and a power which lift them above their social insignificance, just as the plays and prose fictions themselves never compromise with the banality of surfaces. He is a myth-maker who deconstructs myths, a storyteller aware of the coercive power of story. He is, finally and incontrovertibly, a poet of the theatre who himself discovers poetry in the broken lives which are the subjects of his plays, and in the broken society which they inhabit. However one wishes to see Shepard – as writer, musician, director, screen star, cowboy, and so on – it is clear that he has inscribed himself and his characters into a larger script, a script that contributes to the rhetoric of nationhood, and to a fuller understanding of what more richly constitutes the "Americanness" of American drama.

NOTES

1 Sam Shepard, *A Lie of the Mind* (New York: New American Library, 1987), 100. Page references in parentheses within the text are to this edition.
2 Matthew Roudané, "Shepard on Shepard: an Interview," 5 May 2000. See chapter 3, 75.
3 Sam Shepard, *True West*, in *Sam Shepard: Seven Plays* (New York: Bantam Books, 1981), 56.
4 "Shepard on Shepard," chapter 3, 65.
5 Conversations with Joseph Chaikin, 15 March and 28 March 2000.
6 "Shepard on Shepard," chapter 3, 74.
7 Kenneth Chubb, et al., "Metaphors, Mad Dogs, and Old Time Cowboys: Inter-view with Sam Shepard" (1974), reprinted in Bonnie Marranca (ed.), *American Dreams: The Imagination of Sam Shepard* (New York: Performing Arts Journal Publications, 1981), 208.

I

CHRISTOPHER BIGSBY

Born injured: the theatre of Sam Shepard

It is around forty years since Sam Shepard drifted across the continent from California to New York, leaving behind a psychologically damaging family situation, escaping a town that "grew out of nothing and nowhere."[1] Sam Shepard is a drifter by nature. It is in the blood. Like his father (who worked for the military) before him, he has moved from place to place: from California to New York to London, to the Southwest, to Virginia, to Minnesota. He has, in the past, drifted from playwriting to music, to acting, to screenwriting, to directing. He even exchanged one name for another (Rogers for Shepard), refusing to be defined. In his plays, if not his life, it is a losing game. As a character in *Simpatico* remarks, "I've changed my name... and nothing came of it. I've moved all over the place. I was in Texas for a while... Arizona. Nothing came from any of it. I've just got – further and further – removed."[2] But, then, that sense of removal – from other people, from a rooted surrounding, from the self – is a central concern of a writer whose plays explore the American psyche at a time of failed dreams and lost visions. He himself, meanwhile, is always anxious to move on, to explore new frontiers of experience. Now that impulse is reflected in his desire to try his hand at everything from rodeo riding to movie acting.

When he set out from California in 1963, his vehicle of choice was the theatre, as he joined a drama group performing along the blue highways of a country in which rock-and-roll was reshaping the psyche of a new generation, defining the rhythms of a culture turning its back on the supposed solidities of the Eisenhower years. When he arrived in New York he found himself in the middle of a rapidly transforming social and cultural world, and in a decade in which the performing self (as social construct, radical gesture, personal statement) would become a central metaphor and the theatre, therefore, for a brief while, a crucial arena.

This was not, of course, the theatre of Broadway, encysted, as it seemed to be, in the politics of materialism, compromised, as it was assumed to be, by its bourgeois clientele, and dedicated to supposedly outmoded models of drama. The new paradigms were Samuel Beckett, such Off-Broadway successes as Edward Albee's *The Zoo Story* and Jack Gelber's *The Connection*, and, beyond that, the emerging experiments in performance art. Indeed, even Off-Broadway had begun to seem both expensive and over-formal in its use of theatrical space. Now new "theatres" had sprung up in church halls, lofts, basements, and cafés, theatres anxious to allow young writers to experiment. Plays written one day could be performed the next. This was not, at first, a world of opening nights, newspaper reviews, and fashionable audiences, though there was a new coterie and the *Village Voice* became if not a midwife then the supplier of an occasional bunch of flowers. Art was no longer to bear the weight of solemn exegesis. It was to be a vibrant gesture, a surreal epiphany, a communal rite sufficient in and of itself. And it was here, specifically at Theatre Genesis, that Sam Shepard began a career that was to lead to a cascade of Obie Awards and, eventually, to a Pulitzer Prize. Yet, forty years later, it was as if he had acquired classic status almost by stealth. He remains in some sense a part of the counter-culture, even though the counter-culture has long since expired. He is an original, a major force in the theatre without ever notching up the kind of extended run once thought necessary to such status, without ever storming Broadway (except in a revival of *Buried Child* and *True West*), without, indeed, writing the kind of plays that audiences, critics, or readers could readily explain to others or themselves.

His early plays were surreal fragments, brittle images. Slowly these were extended and given a narrative spine, as in *The Tooth of Crime* (1972) and *Geography of a Horse Dreamer* (1974). Later came disturbing family plays (*Curse of the Starving Class*, 1977, *Buried Child*, 1978), in which violence was an ever-present possibility, and others in which the relationship between men and women was seen as profoundly problematic (*Fool for Love*, 1983, *A Lie of the Mind*, 1985). Meanwhile, male relationships were explored for what they could tell us about shifting power systems and the fragile boundaries of identity (*The Tooth of Crime*, *True West*, 1980, *Simpatico*, 1994). And behind such concerns was an engagement with America, with its myths, its failed utopianism, its spiritual attenuation, an engagement which hints at a conservative radicalism as he challenges America with its rhetoric of innocence. But behind that, in turn, lies a deeper concern and a more ancient point of fracture for, as Simms says in *Simpatico*, "It was all decided generations ago ... Faceless ancestors" (109). Indeed, it is tempting to feel that the real loss, and loss is Shepard's central theme, the loss which broke the connection with nature, which divided men and women, which separated language from truth, occurred at the moment of the fall. As a character says in *States of Shock* (1991), "No way of knowing the original moment. Abraham maybe ... Judas. Eve."[3] Betrayal is as basic a theme to Shepard as

8

it is to Arthur Miller. Sam Shepard's myths, in other words, are of greater antiquity than those of the Republic whose decline he laments, the sense of loss more profound than that inspired by the decay of puritanism into pragmatism or the rise of Sodom on the desert plains.

Tennessee Williams thought of himself as a radical rather than the southern Gothicist he was too often assumed to be. He saw his work as a social, moral, and even political critique of an America "sick with neon," in which power and money destroyed the artist, the emotionally vulnerable, the dissenter from national myths of appropriation, enabling materialism and exclusionary politics. Sam Shepard, whose first play was modeled on Williams's drama, is a poet of the Southwest, lamenting the loss of a rural world, but he, too, offers a radical, if oblique, critique of his society, from *Operation Sidewinder* (1970) – which counterposed an out-of-control military machine with Native Americans still in touch with the cosmos – to *States of Shock* and *Silent Tongue* (1992) which, in turn, seem to do much the same. Nuclear war (*Chicago* 1965), the death of the Black Panthers, the Gulf War (*States of Shock*), and, in *When the World Was Green* (1996), Bosnia, all find indirect expression in his work though, with the exception of *States of Shock*, this is not the starting point of his work; however, you could say of him, as Arthur Miller said of Tennessee Williams, "there is a radical politics of the soul as well as of the ballot box and the picket line."[4] In a 1984 interview he explained that "you take two characters and you set them in motion. It's very interesting to follow this thing that they're on... it's like getting on a wild horse."[5] His are not, certainly early in his career, heavily plotted plays serving a social or political objective. The metaphor, though, is as interesting as the description of process. The wild horse speaks to a spontaneity and freedom but it also suggests nostalgia for what is increasingly lost.

Indeed, as his career developed it became clear that his is an America that has lost touch with its own visions, in which myths have become fantasies, family units have collapsed, language is broken, metaphors pulled apart, natural rhythms dislocated. In interview he approvingly recalled the title of Bob Dylan's song, "Everything is Broken." His comment, "It's a great tune,"[6] is, in effect, an ironic acknowledgment of one of his own major themes. His is a society in moral free fall, a world in which men and women, apparently programmed to respond to different needs, circle one another warily, no longer sure of their roles, compelled by a passion with the power to destroy.

Implicit in his work is a sense of lost unity, of the severing of that connection between individuals once established through shared values, beliefs, the rhythms of the natural world, "ancient stuff," by which he seems to mean a sense of community deeper than family or nation, transcending the moment. In part that is a product of the modern, slowly obscuring the landscape, tightening a ligature on the free self and the organic community, though he, himself, could find a haunting beauty equally in the call of a whippoorwill or a '57 Chevy. But it goes a good deal deeper than this. His is a world in which things fall apart. The desire for connection remains, an echo of lost harmonies, but cutting across this is a debilitating violence, a personal and cultural anarchy. Somewhere in the past lies a disruptive trauma, so that his characters all live in a state of shock. At times he is tempted to locate that moment historically. It is World War II, from which men returned no longer able to relate to the women they had left behind ("those midwestern women from the forties suffered an incredible psychological assault, mainly by men who were disappointed in a way they didn't understand. While growing up I saw that assault over and over again, and not only in my own family. These were men who came back from the war, had to settle down, raise a family and send the kids to school – and they just couldn't handle it").[7] That date clearly has biographical force, more especially in the work of a man whose plays repeatedly draw on the details of his own life, his relationship with his father, and even the women in his own life ("when it comes right down to it... what you're really listening to in a writer is... his ability to face himself").[8] But he offers other dates for the disorienting violence that he dramatizes, the disturbing caesuras in experience, which relate to something more than autobiographical truths or to twentieth-century alienations, the entropic force of the modern.

In talking about *States of Shock*, inspired by an all-too contemporary event – the Gulf War – he recalled his visit to the Pine Ridge Indian Reservation in South Dakota, as Air Force jets flew overhead, a place where he saw displayed "the most devastated culture in America." Two years later, in his film *Silent Tongue*, he offered a commentary on the fate of a people literally and figuratively raped by a society whose Manifest Destiny seemed to be to expand across a continent without understanding the nature of the land ("Americans have lost compassion for their own country"),[9] the people they encounter ("we're haunted by the Native American religiousness, the true religiousness of a people who were in harmony with their environment, which we're completely out of touch with"),[10] or the fantasies they sell to themselves as a character sells snake oil to the gullible, trading humanity for hard cash ("It says something," he has said of *Silent Tongue*, "about Americans. There's a cure somewhere and the cure resides in some kind of magic potion, a miracle. The gullibility of it is incredible").[11]

His characters are driven less by a sense of genuine destiny, since, to Shepard, "character is... destiny. It's like the structure of our bones, the blood that runs through our veins,"[12] than by an unfocused sense of need born out of an awareness of loss: "People who have a profound hunger for anything – the hunger for drugs, the hunger for sex – this hunger is a direct response to a profound sense of emptiness and aloneness, maybe, or disconnectiveness."[13] The fracture in experience which has produced this sense of personal and cultural bereavement, as if something had, indeed, died, has its American style and tone, as it does its historical roots, but the loss is more primal. Here it is worth quoting Shepard at length on the question of myth, since it is the collapse of an underlying sense of continuity, reaching back beyond the corrosion of familial and societal bonds, which is at stake; and it was, in his view, myth that provided something of the cement that once held disintegrating forces in place, which generated the stories, the metaphors, within which it was possible to move with confidence, a coherence now missing along with the ur-narratives which gave it substance:

> The traditional meaning of myth, the ancient meaning of myth, is that it served a purpose in our life. The purpose has to do with being able to trace ourselves back through time and follow our emotional self. Myth served as a story in which people could connect themselves in time to the past. And thereby connect themselves to the present and the future . . . it acted as a thread in culture. And that's been destroyed . . . It doesn't exist anymore. All we have is fantasies about it. Or ideas that don't speak to our inner self at all . . . myth not only connects you and me to our personal families, it connects us to the family of generations and generations of races and people, tribes, the mythology of ancient people. The same with the American Indians – they were connected to their ancestors, people they never knew but are connected to through myth, through prayer, through ritual, through dance, music, all of those forms that lead people into a river of myth. And there was a connecting river, not a fragmented river . . . It's gone . . . contemporary efforts will fail. They have to be connected to ancient stuff.[14]

The tongue is severed, the ritual is abandoned, the music no longer sounds, except, perhaps, in the theatre, which itself offers a series of stories, and which, in Shepard's case, still finds a place for music, a theatre resonating, pulling together the fragments, reconnecting the pieces, though his own suspicion of endings implies a coexistent fear of a completion which in turn may imply stasis. Describing his approach to play-writing he says, "I think of it more like music. If you play an instrument and you meet somebody else who plays an instrument, and the two of you sit down and start to play music, it's really interesting to see where that music goes . . . It might not go anywhere you thought it would go."[15] However, for a man whose own life has at times seemed like a road movie, there is a tension between an imagery of resolution and one of restless change and that tension is evident both in his sense of the relationship between the sexes (at one moment signifying a redemptive unity and at another inevitable discord) and his own fascination with the self as still center and site of deep division.

It is tempting to hear something of that mystic and snake-oil seller Georgei Gurdjieff behind some of his statements, not least because Shepard has been fascinated by the ideas of a man whose stress on "ancient stuff," myths and rituals expressive of an underlying sense of unity behind the surface alienations and fractures of contemporary life, chimes so directly with his own. And given his own concerns with the spiritual debilitations of the modern world, its radical dislocations, how would he not be drawn to a Greek–Armenian writer of plays, searcher for spiritual locations, admirer of Native American rituals (albeit now degraded) and of the *Thousand and One Nights* as harmonizing text, who taught that modern man is suffering from a form of split personality and who founded an Institute for the Harmonious Development of Man? Interest, however, is not influence and Shepard has no need of a guru to facilitate his analysis of a contemporary malaise, no interest, indeed, in acknowledging that such an analysis is the starting point, as opposed to the implication, of his drama which he sees as born out of its own procedures, images, dialogue, character, rhythms.

There is, however, another writer with whom Shepard would have felt *simpatico*, a man whose poetry he read at his father's funeral: Lorca. Like Shepard, he learned his craft in part from acting and directing, from in-volvement in the practical realities of theatre production. He also, at times, embraced a radical politics, though his work was ineluctably the product of a poetic sensibility. For the fact is that the father with whom Shepard had such a fraught relationship, who was the source of withering violence and a model of disabling familial relationships, had also introduced him to the work of a poet/playwright with whom he would seem to have much in common. Indeed, while his father's example provided a warning of the disintegrative power of alcohol and violence, of an alienation so strong that it drove him to the very margin of social life and the brink of psychological disintegration, he was also the man who took time to read Lorca's poems, in Spanish, to his young son. Sam Shepard Rogers Sr. was a divided man and the inheritance he passed to his son was a double one.

Shepard is interested in the elemental. His plays may be littered with the surface detritus of a temporary society, but they also dig deeper. In the words of Edward Albee's *Who's Afraid of Virginia Woolf?* they seek to press down through the skin and the bone to the marrow. That is both their subject and their method. His characters are neurotically hypersensitive. They exist at the extreme of the emotional spectrum where character is pressed in the direction of archetype. They bear the wounds of their passion, of a love and a violence that are disturbingly fused. And the impact on the audience is itself emotional, visceral. Sometimes, as in *Fool for Love* or *States of Shock*, that is achieved through a literal amplification, through sound effects or music which resonates the action; more often it is a product of plays that invite the observer to sidestep the rational. He sets himself to enter the "depths of a certain emotional territory."[16] Indeed the word "emotion" recurs in his vocabulary, as, incidentally, it did in Lorca's ("I sincerely believe," said Lorca, "that the theatre is, nor can it be anything other than, emotion and poetry in its words, in its action and in its gestures").[17] Thus, Shepard has said of the power of music, which he frequently deploys in his work, that it can "bring the audience to terms with an emotional reality."[18] He has said of poetry that it derives from the fact that "language can occur out of an emotional context."[19] The political consciousness, particularly in his early work, comes, he explains, "from the emotional context that you were moving in."[20] But, by the same token, "this emotional thing goes a long way back,"[21] while he is interested in ideas only as they are expressed in and through "the body, the emotions."[22] As he has insisted, "if emotions that come up during a play call up questions, or seem to remind you of something that you can't quite put your finger on, then it starts to get interesting." These are "mythic emotions," and myth "speaks to everything at once, especially the emotions."[23] This is the territory that he occupies; this is the arena of his drama. Music, poetry, myth, language under pressure, moments of passion and violence, combine to address the audience at a level beyond the simply rational. This is not the emotional terrorism of some 1960s performance theatre groups, staging an assault on positivism and a mechanistic world and, indeed, sometimes the persons of the audience, in the name of the body, sanctifying the irrational and the Dionysian, but an attempt to acknowledge and address the extent to which we experience the world on the pulse. And, though again Lorca is more of a parallel than a direct influence, passion, violence, poetry, music, a sense of "ancient stuff," are all to be found in his work.

Lorca was a product of a particular region of Spain (the countryside near Granada). He had a powerful sense of the land and of a geography of the soul. He saw this as threatened by a modern world whose rhythms were not those of nature. In his *Poeta en Nueva York* he lamented those who had lost touch with the natural world, who lived dislocated lives and inhabited an alien environment of buildings which had no relationship to the land on which they stood. The only salvation lay in the music of Harlem, cutting through to another level of existence, in a people imprisoned by prejudice but still in some sense in touch with a world responsive to something more than materialism. It lay in the celebratory chants, the inclusive lists, of a Walt Whitman, singing an America in which all people seemed to belong to a shared human enterprise and a wider natural and spiritual realm. Shepard, whose own prose pieces – *Hawk Moon* (1981), *Motel Chronicles* (1982), *Cruising Paradise* (1996) – show a fondness for a Whitmanesque listing of people, places, objects, likewise draws his inspiration from a particular part of America – the Southwest – and, like Lorca, sees music, both literal and in terms of rhythmic structure, as central to his plays. Like Lorca, too, his plays are fascinated by the destabilizing power of passion, the sense that love is a disease creating a sense of dis-ease. They, too, blend the lyrical and the threatening.

Lorca spoke of creating a poetry "that will flow like blood when you cut your wrists, a poetry that has taken leave of reality,"[24] as, in his 1996 rewrite of *The Tooth of Crime*, Shepard has Crow hold out his arm and invite Hoss to slit his wrist, to make him bleed in a work stained with a poetry that takes us beyond the real. Lorca spoke of the "black sounds,"[25] the elemental qualities that he sought to articulate. Shepard's dramatic poetry also bleeds, while his desire to take leave of reality (and he has frequently spoken of his dissatisfaction with realism) is also frequently expressed through "black sounds." It is tempting, indeed, to suggest that Shepard reaches for that same tragic sense of life that is to be found in a writer whose radical politics never obscured his awareness of a deeper current running through human affairs. It is true that Shepard also admires Samuel Beckett, whose ironies might seem inimical to the tragic sensibility, and his early plays are plainly not without absurdist influence (or, indeed, like Lorca's early work, surrealist influence), but for all the ironic observation in *Simpatico* (which, in an early version, had an epigraph from Beckett – "You're on earth. There's no cure for that" – and in which a character observes that, "It's too late for sleeping and waking and sleeping and waking. I've been doing that all my life and it hasn't helped" [84]) – he seems concerned with something more than an ironic presentation of cosmic irony, of individuals as the victims of an indifferent god or their own self-defeating rationality. The line from *Simpatico*, however, should alert us to another quality that Shepard shares with Lorca: humor.

As Lorca observed, "The Theatre is a school of pain and laughter."[26] Of his rewrite of *Buried Child*, for the 1996 Broadway production, Shepard insisted that

> What triggered a lot of the rewriting was that I saw these weird actors and a director who intuitively understood the humor that couches the tragedy, and I wanted to reinforce that . . . You can't possibly do this thing as a Eugene O'Neill play. I've seen it done over and over again in a macabre, stone-faced, methodical quasi-tragic form, and it's deadly.[27]

One of Lorca's characters was Buster Keaton, in his work a child-killer. Keaton was likewise a figure admired by Shepard, who has also expressed his admiration for Stan Laurel, and he takes great pleasure in the slapstick elements in a number of his plays, including *True West* and the otherwise disturbing *States of Shock*. But where slapstick plays with the idea of anarchy, in the work of both Lorca and Shepard there is a darker dimension, a genuine loss of control.

Even the iconography of Lorca and Shepard is similar – the man on horseback, the land, a man and a woman confronting one another within an emotional space. When Lorca reached for an image to describe the relationship between things and ideas he insisted that "They have their own place and their own orbits; but metaphor joins them through the imagination taking a high fence on horseback," a process which "may often seem violent."[28] Shepard's imagination takes that same leap. He also, I suspect, feels with Lorca, "The terrible nostalgia for a lost life / And the fatal sentiment of having been born too late."[29] Certainly that would seem evident in the repeated lament that some formal unity, some inner coherence, has been eroded, that entropy seems a governing principle ("The motion animal breaks down . . . / The winged animal begins to swing in lower circles / Not looking for prey / Just preying not to crash / In Science talk it's called entropy").[30]

In *Blood Wedding* the Fiancée describes herself as "a burnt woman," seared by a passion over which she has no control, attracted to a man characterized by violence. Shepard's plays are full of such burnt women and men whose violence seems to be drawn from the same well as their passion, from *Curse of the Starving Class* through *Fool for Love* and *Paris, Texas* (1984) to *A Lie of the Mind*. He scarcely needed Lorca to discover this subject. Quite aside from personal experience it was, it seemed to him, a central fact of American life, celebrated in national myths of the pioneering male and sentimentally lamented by Country and Western music. But Lorca, who described his own poetry as "a conscious rocket of dark light, let off among the dull and torpid,"[31] provides a persuasive parallel for work which evidences that same "dark light," that same desire to stir the spirit.

Shepard is capable of a studied lyricism in his work – not merely in the metaphors which shine out from the fragments which make up *Motel Chronicles* and *Cruising Paradise*, but in the poetry of the aphasic monologues of those who reach for a communicative language but end up communicating primarily through the broken rhythms of their speech. "Stammering is the native eloquence of us fog people,"[32] observes a character in O'Neill's *Long Day's Journey into Night*, and in a sense it is, too, of many of Shepard's characters for whom language lags behind feeling, or is shattered by violence, who no longer feel part of the social world that generated that language. He is a poet in Cocteau's sense when he observed that

> The action of my play is in images, while the text is not: I substitute a "poetry of the theatre" for "poetry in the theatre." Poetry in the theatre is a piece of lace which it is impossible to see at a distance. Poetry of the theatre would be coarse lace; a lace of ropes, a ship at sea . . . The scenes are integrated like the words of a poem.[33]

Shepard's is a "poetry of the theatre." There are, to be sure, startling images offered – the eagle and the cat in *Curse of the Starving Class*, the flames in the snow in *A Lie of the Mind* – but the poetry lies as much in the structure of plays which seek rhymes in terms of characters who mirror one another, scenes whose juxtapositions themselves create metaphors, breathtaking, indeed impossible, leaps in time and space to be bridged only by the imagination, dialogue generated out of its own rhythms ("You begin to learn an underlying rhythmic sense in which things are shifting all the time . . . There's a kind of dialogue that's continually shifting and moving, and each time it creates something new . . . It could be just the shifts of attitudes, the shifts of ideas, where one line is sent out and another one comes back").[34] These are the visible tracery of ropes which constitute Shepard's poetry. This is the man who in *Motel Chronicles* speaks of seeing "language leaping across the room."[35] Sometimes he catches it in mid-flight, as if it had detached itself from sender and receiver and was compelling precisely because of its inner structure, its attenuated quality, its dislocation from social context.

His early plays were often surreal images, unrevised jazz scats of language, intriguing metaphors which he chose not to interrogate for meaning. A product of the Off-Off-Broadway movement, he valued spontaneity, the authenticity of feeling. He filled his plays with figures from modern myth: rock stars, movie stars, almost as if he were projecting himself along the lines of his own desires. Architects have a word for those paths which people instinctively follow in distinction from those provided by literal-minded and rational designers. They are called lines of desire. Shepard's theatre is a little like that. It follows lines of desire.

Looking back twenty years later he was inclined if not entirely to dismiss this early work then to see it as a product of the times and of his state of mind, which "wasn't the best." As he has said, "You end up with a kind of cavorting . . . But it doesn't satisfy you . . . I didn't know how to write a play . . . That's what happens – if you don't know how to ride a motorcycle, you crash a lot. They were 'fun' to do, they had a lot of energy in them . . . but . . . I wouldn't *stand* by them."[36] The most self-deprecating of playwrights, he is disinclined to express satisfaction with any but a very few of his works. Nonetheless, while these early plays are, indeed, often little more than visual and verbal collages, pulses of language delivered by figures whose two-dimensionality was a function of their origins in popular culture, they do hint at the power of a playwright then experimenting freely with the component elements of his craft. He certainly distrusted the implications of characters who entered the stage with a history, a coherent psychology, as he also distrusted the idea of a rational plot. Revelation had less to do with the gradual exposure of concealed truths than with the moment by moment generation of startling images.

Describing his approach to theatre, he explained that a character "appears out of nowhere in three dimensions and speaks...to something or someone else, or even to himself, or even to no one. I'm talking now about an open-ended structure where anything could happen as opposed to a carefully planned and regurgitated event which, for me, has always been as painful as pissing nickels."[37] Ideas, he insisted, emerged from plays and not the other way around. Language, meanwhile, had an almost magical, incantatory quality with the power to disturb the body chemistry, evidence for which he saw in the language, even in translation, of Native Americans, yet another example of his tendency to see in their world a key to something perhaps irremediably lost from mainstream America, except, possibly, through the electric immediacy of popular culture and music. Rock-and-roll, for him, was a form of contained violence but also a means of accessing the emotions directly. In *The Tooth of Crime*, revised in the late 1990s, he staged a play in which a character called Crow (a word which he had identified in his discussion of Native American language as having a particular power) uses music and words as weapons, and stages a battle which became even more murderous in the revised version.

Having traveled to England in the early 1970s in the belief that this was becoming the Mecca of rock-and-roll, he wrote *Geography of a Horse Dreamer* which, for all its English setting, seemed to address what would become an increasing concern, the corruption of an instinctual world (a character named for Buffalo Bill Cody, who can dream the winners of horse-races, is kidnapped to serve the interests of gangsters) and the loss of a sense of mystery. In some ways *Simpatico* would express a similar sense that something was coming to an end as horse-racing again becomes the subject of tawdry criminality, not least because the thoroughbred horse, now simply the source of profit for those who cynically switch one similar-looking horse for another, has a bloodline that can be traced back into the distant past. It is a connection to "ancient things," smashed by those for whom the past – as history or myth – has no meaning. The crime in *Simpatico* is not one against the Racing Commission or the punters, though an implied contract is thereby abrogated, one of many broken in Shepard's plays (contracts between fathers and sons, men and women, people and the environment which they inhabit). It is a crime against continuity. It is a smashing of the chain which locates us in time.

It was while in England, however, that he met the director Peter Brook, who suggested that his work would benefit from a greater concern for character. It was an observation that was to shift the center of gravity of his work. It was not that he was going to turn into Arthur Miller overnight but that it increasingly seemed to him that there needed to be some centripetal force in work which had previously been akin to a pin-wheel, with sparks flying randomly out into space. Convinced that "I'd been writing for ten years in an experimental maze – poking around, fishing in the dark," he felt that he "wasn't going anywhere. I felt I needed an aim in the work versus the instinctive stuff . . . I started with character, in all its complexities." As he observed,

> when you start to be more honest, and nail down the truth of the moment, you see that anything *can't* happen . . . A character can turn over a table or jump out the window . . . and you could get away with it, but what happens if you absolutely nail yourself to the truth of the moment? He can only go this way, she can only do that.[38]

But these characters were not to be realist constructions. They were real in the sense that those in a Pinter play are real, and Pinter plainly exists somewhere in the shadows of Shepard's work. They bear the impress of intense emotions. They are deformed by passions that flood their being. They reach for a meaning that seems closed to them, at times barely able to articulate their feelings or acknowledge the deconstructive forces that seem to define them. It was a shift in emphasis in his work that eventually, as he confessed, "led me to the family."[39]

For the most part his characters move through a world in which nothing is permanent. They have no hold on experience, no real purpose or direction. They live on the edge not in the existential sense that meaning resolves itself on boundaries but to the degree that they see nothing but what immediately confronts them. They have no peripheral vision. They inhabit the present and even here they focus only on the emotional reality of what confronts them. They see as a heat-seeking camera does, in primary colors. Their eyes are drawn to the heat. They are obsessives. Beyond the bars, motels, and rented rooms which they inhabit lies the desert blackness or simply space. They bear the scars of the past but cannot penetrate its mysteries, feel no connection with it. The future is of no interest. "Where have we been all this time," asks a figure in *Hawk Moon*, "what happens between the past and the future?" (*Motel Chronicles and Hawk Moon* 131) The present seems to bear witness to a secret unacknowledged pain, a wound acquired in a past to which his characters no longer have full access. By the same token they are not the product of a national dream, leaning into the future, awaiting the epiphany of meaning. None of them has the least interest in climbing aboard the celestial railroad to wealth or to an identity that is the product of making, doing, striving, unless it be the kidnappers in *Geography of a Horse Dreamer* or Carter in *Simpatico*, disguising himself with the products of theft and fraud.

They march to a different drummer, the percussive pulse of rock-and-roll or the sad laments of Country and Western songs with their regrets for lost happiness and broken relationships. Nor, however, are they rebels consciously challenging America's values, its age-long confusion of the material and the spiritual, as if there were, indeed, some connection between movement and progress, high achievement and God's good grace. His characters are wanderers who never sink their roots securely into one time or place. They are quite literally deracinated. They have no history they care to embrace, no destination better than another. They live on instinct, victims not of a disregarding social world, on whose margins they seem content to live, or of cosmic ironies, which leave them looking for order in a disordered universe, but of the feelings which sweep through them. They register a sense of loss, of emptiness, abandonment, even betrayal, and seek to fill that space with violence or love, each infiltrating the other until it seems virtually impossible to separate them. They inhabit a discard world in which everything seems disposable, including relationships. Such transformations as they undergo, as they exchange roles, as genders merge, as they blend, fuse, transmute, are an expression of alternative possibilities already contained within themselves rather than gifted to them by a culture in which nothing, finally, seems permanent or even lasting.

Thus, his 1976 play, *Angel City*, is set in a Los Angeles slowly disintegrating from a series of urban catastrophes, a play in which he voices a lament which runs throughout his work as he identifies: "The ambition to transform valleys into cities. To transform the unknown into the known without really knowing. To make things safe. To beat death. To be victorious in the face of absolute devastation."[40]

Until this point in his career Shepard had made little impact on mainstream America, while compelling admiration in those drawn to Off-Off-Broadway, but he now found himself regarded as more accessible, particularly when *Curse of the Starving Class* was followed by *Buried Child*, which won the Pulitzer Prize. These plays seemed to place the family at the center of attention, though, in the case of *Buried Child*, in a way which related less to the moral and social dilemmas highlighted by Arthur Miller than to Eugene O'Neill's *Desire Under the Elms*, in one direction, and Harold Pinter's *The Homecoming* in the other; that is to say it combined the brutal self-referentiality of the former, in its concern with incest, infanticide, and hermeticism, with the oblique ironies and physical threat of the latter. However, for Shepard, the family has other connotations. It carries a twin threat. It is the site of betrayed love – the grandfather, Dodge, warns his grandson's girl friend, "You think just because you propagate they have to love their offspring. You never see a bitch eat her puppies?"[41] – yet it also carries the risk of a contaminating inheritance, that son will become father, a curse be handed on. Dodge's own son, Tilden, tries to walk away into the desert and, like Travis, in Shepard's screenplay for Wim Wenders's film *Paris, Texas*, loses his language: "I was alone. I thought I was dead...I thought I was dying but I just lost my voice" (78). He returns and his language is restored, but so, too, is his inheritance. It is not a link he can break. He is trapped again. Only the young girl escapes, according to Dodge on a search for some way to fill the void that brings men and women together, that sends people wandering in search of meaning: "you're all alike you hopers. If it's not God then it's a man. If it's not a man then it's a woman. If it's not a woman then it's the land or the future of some kind. Some kind of future" (109). The past, however, is equally ironic, represented, as it is, by a buried baby, the product of an incestuous relationship. That moral connection between man and the soil, part of American myth, now renders up only the remains of former passions.

It was a play, however, that still had elements of the earlier Shepard and when he came to revise it they were precisely the elements that he chose to excise or clarify. Just as he now confessed to some embarrassment at having a character in *Curse of the Starving Class* appear carrying a slaughtered lamb ("I don't drag dead animals onstage anymore") so he came to regard "a guy with one leg whose wooden leg is being used to beat somebody over the head" as "too grotesque."[42] He no longer wanted anything in the play to be gratuitously mysterious and felt that he had not sufficiently explored the character of Vince, the young man who returns to the family home.

It should be said that Shepard himself resists the notion that he was offering an analysis of the American family:

> That's ridiculous. I mean that's not fair or unfair to read that into my plays. It just seems an incomplete, a partial way of looking at the play. People get off on tripping out on these social implications of the play and how that matches up to contemporary America. And that's okay. But that's not why I'm writing plays.[43]

His own interest lies elsewhere. However, the family, in *Curse of the Starving Class*, *Buried Child*, *True West*, and *A Lie of the Mind*, does become the location of passion, an imminent violence, and a sense of things in near-terminal decay. As Weston, the father in *Curse of the Starving Class*, observes:

> I kept trying to piece it together. The jumps. I couldn't figure out the jumps, from being born to growing up, to droppin' bombs, to having kids, to hittin' bars, to this. It all turned on me somehow. It all turned around on me. I kept looking for it out there somewhere. And all the time it was right inside this house.[44]

And, indeed, Shepard himself has grudgingly acknowledged that the family had, against his own instincts, become if not his subject then the environment of his drama. As he said,

> I always did feel a part of that tradition but *hated* it. I couldn't stand those plays that were all about the "turmoil" of the family. And then all of a sudden I realized, well, that was very much a part of my life, and maybe that has to do with being a playwright, that you're somehow ensnared beyond yourself.[45]

It is very tempting, indeed, though he himself would reject the notion on the grounds of his argument with its realism, to see something of O'Neill's *Long Day's Journey into Night* as an essential part of that tradition which he resists but feels ensnared in, at least with respect to the rhythm of attraction and repulsion which defines its progress, the rapid shifts between love and anger, the hermetic, containing, claustrophobic, annihilating quality of the family unit, capable of great damage and yet, occasionally, compassion. When Travis, in *Paris, Texas*, drives off into the desert, leaving behind the wife he has injured and to whom he is powerfully drawn, he does so out of a love whose other side is redemptive. There is not much redemption in the early Shepard, except, perhaps, through the very vitality, surreal humor, and structural élan of the plays in performance, but it is an element that has become more significant. Perhaps, like O'Neill, it simply took him a long time to lay his personal ghosts.

In the end Shepard came to feel that if the family was the source of a disintegrative pressure, of contradictory needs and defining tensions, it was also where he could eventually look for those connections, that sense of unity, whose lack he constantly laments. Besides, the family is itself a connection with the world beyond its parameters: "What does not have to do with family? There isn't anything . . . Even a love story has to do with family. Crime has to do with family. We all come out of each other – everyone is born out of a mother and a father, and you go on to be a father. It's an endless cycle."[46]

Despite his ambivalence, the decision to engage the family seems effectively not only to have unlocked autobiographical elements, which fueled first *Curse of the Starving Class* and, later, *Paris, Texas, Fool for Love, A Lie of the Mind*, and, in a very different direction, *Far North* (1988), but to have offered a route into a wider world of signification as schisms in the family resonate seismic disturbances in the self and the culture ("far off you could hear the sound of America cracking open and crashing into the sea" [*Hawk Moon* 12]). However, though his next play, *True West*, concerned two brothers and their mother, and certainly raised questions about the collapse of myth into fantasy, once again this was not what Shepard himself chose to stress. To him, a key aspect of the work had to do with the discovery and elaboration of a musical structure. As he explained,

> I like to look at the language and the inner rhythms of the play, and all that to me is related to music directly. In *True West* there are coyote sounds and crickets...And the dialogue is musical...I think it's very related to music, the whole rhythmic structure of it. Rhythm is the delineation of time in space, but it only makes sense with silences on either side of it.[47]

Paradoxically, this may explain why he has a fondness for sets surrounded by darkness. This is the visual equivalent of the containing silences. It, too, is the delineation of time in space.

This is perhaps to say no more than that there is a difference between the writer's explanation of methodology, what he sees as the generating force and structural principles of his work, and what audiences, drawn to character, responsive to action, anxiously struggling to decode the occasionally gnomic, see as an emerging theme. Nonetheless, it is a useful reminder that in part what those same audiences are responding to is the rhythm of those encounters, what O'Neill, in relation to the bruising confrontations in *Long Day's Journey into Night*, described as battles, battles which, in Shepard's case, are not simply within the family or between the paired individuals who so often constitute his dramatic unit, but within a self which is inherently divided along fault lines which separate opposing sensibilities (*True West, Simpatico*) or genders (*Fool for Love, A Lie of the Mind*).

However, while suggesting that his plays often lack a plot, he accepts that they do have themes and those themes do seem to be to do with male violence, a fragmenting social world, the decay of relationships, the loss of an organic connection between man and his environment, the attenuation of the link with a past whose rituals and stories once created a harmony disrupted and dislocated in the modern world. There is, for example, he insists, "no such thing as the West anymore! It's a dead issue!"[48] Hence the title *True West* was entirely ironic. *True West* took him back again to the Los Angeles of

Angel City, and a Hollywood reprocessing that same myth as two brothers clash over a script set in a mythic west. Vaguely reminiscent of Nathanael West's *The Day of the Locust*, a novel for which Shepard has expressed his admiration, this ends with a similar spasm of violence as the brothers seem to step into their own script as they do into one another's persona, exchanging roles as the play progresses. The West has always had a special significance to Shepard:

> I just feel like the West is much more ancient than the East . . . Wyoming, Texas, Montana and places like that . . . you really feel this ancient thing about the land . . . That it's primordial . . . it's this thing about space. No wonder these mysterious cults in Indian religion sprang up . . . It has to do with the relationship between the land and the people . . . It's much more physical and emotional to me.[49]

It is that elemental force, that relationship, that sense of mystery that seems to be betrayed by those who turn it into marketable products (*True West*, *Silent Tongue*), who parody it (*A Lie of the Mind*), or who corrupt it (*Simpatico*). At some level, however, *True West*, like many of his plays, stages a confrontation, "following these two guys, blow by blow, just following them, trying to stick with them and stick with the actual moment by moment thing of it."[50] He has described his participation in a rodeo in the same terms and, indeed, has spoken of the rodeo as having more drama than a hundred plays. What interests him as a writer is taking risks; what compels audiences is much the same. A rodeo is not "about" anything, except a man and a horse, the imminent risk of violence, the skill with which, moment by moment, the rider maintains his balance. It is entirely focused on itself. It is a mythic, an archetypal battle. The audience, meanwhile, responds viscerally. Their reaction is physical and emotional. For a brief while they are rooted in something that transcends the moment precisely because it concerns a contest with a history that traces back into myth. They recognize a kind of poetry and grace which emerges from the form, the structure, the confrontation itself. And that is how Shepard's plays work.

The rodeo, however, is essentially male and even as metaphor carries implications against which he would eventually work, for in a culture whose myths are so resolutely masculine there is something manifestly incomplete about this as an expression of behavior, values, meaning.

Shepard's fascination with male violence had its roots in his own family life as much as in the culture which in many ways seemed to generate it. "Machismo," he explained, "may be an evil force but what in fact is it? . . . I was a victim of it, it was part of my life, my old man tried to force on me a notion of what it was to be 'a man.' And it destroyed my dad. But you can't avoid facing it."[51] As Shepard told Matthew Roudané,

> I grew up in a condition where the male influences around me were primarily alcoholics and extremely violent and, at the same time, like lost children, not knowing how to deal with it. Instead, they were plunked down on the desert not knowing how they got there. And slowly they began receding further and further and further away – receding from the family, receding from society.[52]

That father is a brooding presence in *Fool for Love*, though he has also said of that play that he was determined "to write some kind of confrontation between a man and a woman as opposed to just men…I wanted to try to take the leap into a female character which I had never really done. I felt obliged to, somehow." At the same time he confessed that "it's hard for a man to say he can speak from the point of view of a woman. But you make the attempt."[53] Like the character in Pinter's *Old Times*, who is simultaneously present and absent, the old man is an expression of the tension between the principal characters, in this case, as he suggested, a man and a woman, though two who trace their roots to this mysterious man. In Shepard's play, however, he is also an embodiment of the betrayals, the deep ambivalence of the male. *Fool for Love* is in part about the close relationship between love and violence but at its heart is a mystery, slowly resolved, about the nature of the identity of the two lovers who turn out to be half-brother and -sister. Speaking of *Buried Child*, but with relevance to *Fool for Love*, Shepard has said that he regards the question of identity as of central importance. "Who in fact are we? Nobody will say we don't know who we are, because that seems like an adolescent question – we've passed beyond existentialism…Give me a break! There are things at stake here – things of the soul and the heart."[54] Both the central characters contain their father's identity, as they share part of one another. They contain the masculine and the feminine, May being capable of violence and Eddie of tenderness. In a sense, then, *Fool for Love* is as concerned with exploring the nature of the self as with acknowledging what seems to be the unbridgeable gulf between men and women, the conflicting needs of those who seek security and those who yearn to move on.

A Lie of the Mind intensifies this exploration, its opening stage direction effectively delineating the psychological and emotional terrain which Shepard enters: "Impression of huge dark space and distance between the two characters with each one isolated in his own pool of light." With music underscoring certain monologues and providing bridges between scenes, music "with an American backbone,"[55] the play is set, an epigraph from H. L. Mencken implies, in a wild place where people settled for no better reason than that they had become exhausted. They act out frontier myths at the level of parody.

But at the center of the action are a man and a woman who come close to annihilating one another, that annihilation being born out of the passion that defines and contains them. As a second epigraph, from the poet César Vallejo, implies, they are caught in the paradoxes of emotion, as they are in the ironies of gendered response: "Something identifies you with the one who leaves you, and it is your common power to return: thus your greatest sorrow. Something separates you from the one who remains with you and it is your common slavery to depart: thus your meagerest rejoicing."

Like *Paris, Texas*, the play opens when a spasm of male brutality has already occurred. Beth has suffered brain damage from Jake's physical assault on her; she has been stunned into a silence ended by her hesitant reentry into language. But in effect both their sensibilities are broken open in this play. They become mirror images in a work of echoes (scenes are paralleled, words repeated by different characters, physical actions duplicated). It is a play that explores the conflicting needs and behaviors of men and women, a play in which, as in Hemingway's short stories and early novels, love is a disease whose fever may bring with it a deceptive blush of health, and even a moment of assonance, but which leaves you "worse off than before you caught it" (92). But, beyond that, it is a play in which he explores a divided self whose incompletions are a clue both to the need to reach out and to the failure of such gestures. Jake and Beth are gender archetypes but they also contain elements of the opposite gender. As Shepard has said,

> You know in yourself, that the female part of oneself as a man is, for the most part, battered and beaten up and kicked to shit just like some women in relationships. The men themselves batter their own female part to their own detriment. And it became interesting from that angle – as a man, what is it like to embrace the female part of ourself that you have historically damaged for one reason or another.[56]

Beth is an actress who Jake suspects of allowing performance to blend into actuality in terms of her sexuality and there is, perhaps, a concern here for the degree to which roles – gender roles, social roles – are performed, as the other characters in the play seem to act out cultural scenarios which are little more than the remnants of a discarded and unexamined history.

Once again, he is interested in identity. In 1980 he had said that what he found most valuable was not place, since, after all, he is one of nature's wanderers, but "other people" because it was "through other people you can find a recognition of each other."[57] Yet in *A Lie of the Mind* that definition is not only bought at a price, it is complicated by the mystery which lies at the heart of the self and therefore of that interaction designed in part to gift identity.

His 1988 movie, *Far North*, seemed to suggest that in some senses the erosion of male identity had reached a point at which women moved to the center of the culture, the film opening with a man failing to control a horse and moving on to a hospital full of men drained of power. Set "here in the frontier...the far north of America,"[58] its central male figure is a man "born injured" (82), unable to assert his will. In flashback the family home had been full of muscular men. Now the men we see are aging while the glimpses of the nearby city we are offered are of an abandoned neighborhood, "a wide broken flat top road" and buildings that are "a shambles, mostly boarded up, broken windows, peeling paint, and caved-in roofs" (97). There is, it seems, no longer access to the past. Both men and women are now uncertain of their roles. The women have no husbands, and no easy relationship to one another (a daughter is uncontrollable, the mother suffering from Alzheimer's); the men have no function. Nonetheless, Shepard has said that he is beginning to feel that "the female side knows so much more than the male side. About childbirth. About death. About where it's at,"[59] and, indeed, one of the women is pregnant. The film ends, however, as the supposed patriarch of the family walks, rather than rides, his horse over a hill, a gesture which echoes the ending of other Shepard works but which is now purely ironic. Something has ended. It is by no means clear what is being born.

While shooting *Silent Tongue*, Shepard placed bets on the nearby racecourse. In *Motel Chronicles* he wrote about betting at Santa Anita. Horses have always been part of his life, from the time when he worked at the tracks in his youth to his involvement in rodeos. They are part of the connective tissue which still links men to the natural world. To taint that with criminality is thus an offense against something more than the law, as was apparent in his 1994 play, *Simpatico*.

Simpatico was, in part, written on the steering-wheel of a truck on a hundred-mile drive to Los Angeles: "On Highway 40 West or some of those big open highways, you can hold the wheel with one hand and write with the other. It's a good discipline, because sometimes you can only write two or three words at a time before you have to look back at the road, so those three words have to count."[60] The two characters at the heart of the play were familiar figures to Shepard who had made several false starts with them over the years. "There were," he has explained, "these two characters I'd been thinking about for quite a while, and when I got to L.A. it seemed like I had a one-act play. Then another character popped up; suddenly there were two acts. And out of that second act, a third. It took me a year to finish."[61] There is something appropriate about this description of a play improvised out of a journey, generating its own forward momentum (in *The Tooth of Crime*, Hoss is advised: "The road's what counts. Just look at the road. Don't worry about where it's going"),[62] and written as he passes through settlements strung along a freeway insofar as *Simpatico* opens in Cucamonga, one of a series of towns along the San Bernadino Freeway which includes Duarte, where Shepard was raised, and Azusa.

In *The Unseen Hand* (1969) he describes Azusa as "a real place. A real town," before insisting on its unreality. These are not, he suggests, so much towns as places where people lose the will to go on, as they did in *A Lie of the Mind*. Azusa is "a collection of junk. Mostly people." Many of its inhabitants live in trailer camps. It is "a temporary society that became permanent," a "dead end."[63] Growing up in Duarte Shepard had no greater ambition than buying a car and heading out. Such towns were, he says, "a jumping off place" with "a kind of junk magic."[64] Shepard's America is what Willy Loman described himself as being, "kind of temporary,"[65] and it is this fact that establishes the ironies which leave characters looking for permanent relationships in a country whose old values have been betrayed or simply discarded.

Just down the road lies the City of the Angels, Los Angeles, once authentically rooted in Western ideas and ideals, but now surrendered to something more than the temporary. It has become a "sprawling, demented snake . . . its fanged mouth wide open, eyes blazing, paralysed in a lunge of pure paranoia" (*Motel Chronicles* 97). In *Cruising Paradise* he speaks of "one of the last Spanish-style stations left on the Santa Fé Trail. Now its windows are all smashed out, framed by brick and fractured stucco. Dried pigeon-shit drops across the words Casa Del Desiento."[66] There is a powerful sense of a failed dream, of a coherent world run to seed, leaving the individual stranded, stripped of a real history and deprived of a role which might have been suspect, deriving, as it did, from a compromised myth, but which at least gave him a purchase on the world: "This sense of failure runs very deep – maybe it has to do with the frontier being systematically taken away . . . I can't put my finger on it [but] you don't have to look very far to see that the American male is on a very bad trip."[67] But it is not just the far West. In *Motel Chronicles* he talks of "Poor Texas / Carved into / Like all the rest" (24). His characters are hardly less carved into. Their identities are insecure. They blend into one another, exchange roles, assume disguises, divide, change their names. As Shepard himself said of the men in *Curse of the Starving Class*, *Buried Child*, and *True West*, "you spent the whole play trying to figure out what these men were about, who had no idea themselves."[68]

His characters live discontinuous lives. Some connection has been broken between themselves and the past (mythic and historical), between themselves and their families, their lovers, even the language they speak. Experience comes in fragments. Emotions flare up and quixotically turn into their opposites. America itself seems deracinated. Myths have devolved into fantasies. Communities have become no more than the serendipitous gatherings of strangers. Landmarks are sand-blasted away or suffocated in the detritus of a society in which nothing seems worth retaining, and beauty is seen less in the natural sweep of the land than in the tail-fin of a '57 Chevy or the functionalism of a weapon. His is a world of distant echoes, of narratives that have lost their point, individuals who have simplified their lives out of anxiety or passion. These are so many Gatsbys viewing life through a single window, blinded by the brightness of an obsession, reinventing themselves so that the very idea of identity becomes suspect.

These are not, for the most part, plays in which chronology has authority. Their rhythms are not determined by the clock. Place becomes an irrelevance both because towns seem interchangeable and because the true space they inhabit is psychological. Language, meanwhile, is little more than a kind of phatic communion, the words mattering less than tone, volume, rhythm. It is an exchange in which lexical meaning defers to other kinds of communication – a gestural language, a language scattered with gnomic images. Language is a weapon, a deceit, a lament.

His characters are, in their essence, solitary. There is a force-field around them, something profoundly intransitive about their relationships. They often communicate hesitantly or imperfectly as if loath to let go of language, to reveal themselves. And when they fall victim to love the object of that love is symbolically, and often literally, a mirror image of the self. He may have regretted introducing the theme of incest into *Fool for Love* but the hermeticism which that implies is to be found elsewhere in his work. People are versions of one another, transform, colonize those who are the object of their passion. Just as Shepard detected elements of his father in himself, so his characters often share something more than a genetic marker. There is self-love and self-hatred in them, externalized in terms of their relationship to others.

The figures in his fiction, meanwhile, drift. Lacking a real history they substitute nostalgia but less for people than the '32 Ford, the '45 Dodge, the '48 Chrysler sedan, the '57 Bel Air, the '58 Impala and, interestingly, nothing much later. Lacking a sense of direction they repeat the numbers of highways: South 201, South 306, Highway 608, Route 96. They carry a "mangled map of Utah" (*Motel Chronicles* 85). His stories and autobiographical fragments are littered with the names of gas stations – Exxon, Conoco, Texaco, Shell – and fast-food outlets: Quick Stop, Dennys, Happy Chef, Dairy Queen. They are filled with people staring blankly at flickering television screens, usually watching cartoons or sitcoms. His characters live in hotels, rented apartments, cinder-block motels "ninety miles from nowhere" (*Cruising Paradise* 135–6) and pass through streets replete with discarded doughnut boxes, beer cans, cigarette packs, products of a culture on the move, speeding in fast cars, living on fast food, moving on. "There *are* no communities," we are told in *Cruising Paradise*. Relationships are arbitrary and passing. Permanence is short-lived. "They lived together for five years straight," says the narrator of a story called "Pure Accident" (110). The temporary is permanent: "it's not temporary either. It's forever. / What is? / The loss" (102). Shepard thus speaks of a figure who suffered from "a long lostness that traveled way back inside him" (21). Yet even the banal can render up meaning. The Whitmanesque impulse survives, at least for Shepard, no stranger to driving across the American continent: "Without a partner. Completely alone. Relentless driving. Driving until the body disappears, the legs fall off, the eyes bleed, the hands go numb, the mind shuts down, and then, suddenly something new begins to appear" (159).

Simpatico is not a play in which the plot has a great deal of significance and perhaps the question asked by one of the characters – "Who was it decided to do away with all the plots?" (56) – is a sly indication of this. When his characters do, as here, attempt to plot their lives that plot unravels in the face of entropic forces structured into their very beings. We encounter them when the psyche is already breaking under the strain. Vinnie threatens to expose a criminal conspiracy of which he has been a part by offering evidence to its principal victim, Simms, but since he has no interest in vengeance and no desire to restore himself to his lost position the threat disappears. His partner in crime, who has hugely benefited from it and secured himself from betrayal by regular payments to Vinnie, should now be restored to his former condition. But in fact nobody seems secure in anything, least of all their identities. Two of them – Vinnie and Simms – have assumed names. Vinnie's would-be girlfriend, Cecilia, feels that she has "lived a dozen different lives" (39), while Vinnie and Carter effectively exchange places like the figures in *True West*. Neither is anyway what he once was. Vinnie's accusation, levelled at Carter – "like your seedy past is long forgot. Might never really have taken place. Might have actually belonged to a different man. A man so remote and dead to you that you've lost all connection" (21) – is not entirely implausible since they have both consciously remodeled themselves, turned into actors performing their lives. They are no longer continuous with their former selves. As Shepard himself has said, "Identity is a question for everybody in the play... Some are more firmly aligned with what they are, and who they think they are. To me, a strong sense of self isn't believing in a lot. Some people might define it that way, saying 'He has a strong sense of himself.'

But it's a complete lie."[69] As Simms, the target of the conspiracy, asks, "How many lives can a man live . . . within this *one*?" (61). However many that is, Carter is about to add another one, announcing that he is going to change his own name, making him the third of the four characters to do so.

For Shepard, identity is not a stable state. As he has said, "you see somebody, and you have an impression of that person from seeing them – the way they talk and behave – but underneath many, many different possibilities could be going on . . . It's not as though you started out with a character who suddenly developed into another character . . . Everybody's like that."[70] That transmutation occurs in *Simpatico* and as Vinnie and Carter change places so fears and anxieties suddenly break through to the surface. "I feel there are territories within us," Shepard has said, "that are totally unknown. Huge, mysterious and dangerous territories. We think we know ourselves, when . . . We have all these galaxies inside of us."[71]

The action of *Simpatico*, part of which is prefigured in a story, written in 1989 and published in *Cruising Paradise*, takes place not in Cucamonga itself but "on the outskirts." The apartment is "very sparse," its walls "absolutely bare," the plastic shower curtain "sun-bleached." Outside is a "black space. No trees. No buildings. No landscape of any kind. Just black." Shepard is emphatic in his negatives. His descriptions seem to unmake themselves, as do his characters who are less than they seem. They are, as Vinnie says, on "the edge of nowhere" (19), and since anonymity and pretense are what he and the other characters are about, this is their natural location. Indeed Vinnie lives here precisely because anonymity is a requirement. However, as he confesses, "I just got – further and further – removed" (33). He is, as Cecilia remarks, "a loner," or, as Carter observes, "separate, I mean – remote" (37). But, then, so are they all, as is the victim of their conspiracy, Simms, now ensconced in a similarly marginal community and living alone under a false name.

Beyond his window, too, is "blackness." His armchair is "faded." Just as Vinnie had been described as wearing "dark slacks," and being "very rumpled," so Simms wears dark slacks while "Everything is rumpled and worn" (53). And not, it seems, for these characters alone, for though Simms seems to have found some kind of peace, reconnecting himself through his work with equine bloodlines, he is solitary at the end of the play while Carter's belief that he can start again is met by Vinnie's assurance that "Those days are over . . . Give it up" (131). Everything is rumpled, bleached, worn out. The play ends as Vinnie leaves, Carter lies, child-like, in a blanket, and the phone rings. Who is on the phone? We never learn, but only one person has phoned here in the course of the play: Simms. If it were to be him then his apparent peace of mind might itself be no more than a performance.

That ambiguity hangs over Shepard's work. He acknowledges the betrayals, the disturbing caesuras in experience, the pressures that work to annihilate the characters who he chooses to locate on the very margins of a society which has lost touch with its own animating principles. Just beyond the windows of the temporary habitations in which they exist is a darkness, a desert terrain, which drives them back on a self too fragile and insecure to offer meaning. The necessities that compel them, and that appear to make them pure victims, seem to destroy the very consolations they seek, negate the relationships which are the primary focus of their lives. Yet, against this Shepard balances moments of consonance, glimpses of harmony. The possibility of redemption is not excluded. In *Savage/Love* (1979) both aspects of the title have force but, as the voice says, "Maybe I'm lost/Until now."[72] Connection is still possible, and not only between two separate selves but between the self and the world, for as the Speaker says in the final words of *Tongues* (1978), "Today the tree bloomed without a word./Tonight I'm learning its language."[73] As Shepard remarked, on the verge of the 1980s, "I certainly don't want to depress the hell out of people, but I think you've got to go through the night to get to the day, and I haven't gone all the way through the night yet."[74] He has still not gone all the way through that night but there is, perhaps, a fire in the snow.

NOTES

1 Sam Shepard, "Preface" to *Action and The Unseen Hand: Two Plays* (London: Faber and Faber, 1975).

2 Sam Shepard, *Simpatico: A Play in Three Acts* (London: Methuen, 1995), 33. Page references in parentheses within the text are to this edition.

3 Sam Shepard, *States of Shock; Far North; Silent Tongue: A Play and Two Screenplays* (New York: Vintage Books, 1993), 44.

4 Quoted in Christopher Bigsby, *Modern American Drama: 1945–1990* (Cambridge University Press, 1992), 37.

5 Amy Lippman, "Rhythm and Truths: An Interview with Sam Shepard," *American Theatre*, 1.1 (April 1984): 11.

6 Carol Rosen, "Silent Tongues: Sam Shepard's Exploration of Emotional Territory," *Village Voice*, 4 August 1992, 37.

7 Mona Simpson, Jeanne McCulloch, Benjamin Howe, "The Art of Theatre XII: Sam Shepard," *The Paris Review*, 142 (Spring 1997): 209.

8 Michael VerMeulen, "Sam Shepard: Yes, Yes, Yes," *Esquire* 93 (February 1980): 86.

9 Rosen, "Silent Tongues," 38.

10 Quoted in Stephen J. Bottoms, *The Theatre of Sam Shepard: States of Crisis* (Cambridge University Press, 1992), 252.

11 Rosen, "Silent Tongues," 38.

12 Ibid., 37.

13 Ibid., 35.

14 Ibid., 35.

15 Lippman, "Rhythm and Truths," 11.

16 Stephen Fay, "Renaissance Man Rides Out of the West," *Sunday Times Magazine*, 26 August 1984, 19.

17 Reed Anderson, *Federico Garcia Lorca* (London: Macmillan, 1984), 68.

18 Bonnie Marranca (ed.), *American Dreams: The Imagination of Sam Shepard* (New York: Performing Arts Journal Publications, 1981), 201.

19 Kenneth Chubb, et al., "Metaphors, Mad Dogs, and Old Time Cowboys: Interview with Sam Shepard" (1974), reprinted in Marranca, *American Dreams*, 207.

20 Chubb, "Metaphors, Mad Dogs," 195.

21 Ibid., 196.

22 Sam Shepard, "Language, Visualization, and the Inner Library" (1977), reprinted in Marranca, *American Dreams*, 217.

23 Ibid., 217.

24 Quoted in Manuel Duran (ed.), *Lorca: A Collection of Critical Essays* (Englewood Cliffs: Prentice-Hall, 1962), 6.

25 Duran, *Lorca*, 47.

26 Ibid., 155.

27 Don Shewey, *Sam Shepard* (New York: Da Capo Press, 1997), 238–39. Page references in parentheses within the text are to this edition.

28 Duran, *Lorca*, 43.

29 Ibid., 78.

30 Sam Shepard, *Hawk Moon* (New York: Performing Arts Journal Publications, 1981), 56. Page references in parentheses within the text are to this edition.

31 Duran, *Lorca*, 49.

32 Eugene O'Neill, *Long Day's Journey into Night* (New Haven: Yale University Press, 1956), 154.

33 Duran, *Lorca*, 172.

34 Simpson, et al., "The Art of Theatre XII," 223.

35 Sam Shepard, *Motel Chronicles and Hawk Moon* (London: Faber and Faber, 1985), 31. Page references in parentheses within the text are to this edition.

36 Jennifer Allen, "The Man on the High Horse," *Esquire*, November 1998, 148.

37 Shepard, "Language, Visualization," 214.

38 Allen, "Man on the High Horse," 148.

39 Ibid.

40 Sam Shepard, *Angel City and Other Plays* (London: Faber and Faber, 1978), 32.

41 Sam Shepard, *Buried Child, Seduced, Suicide in B-Flat* (New York: Urizen Books, 1979), 112. Page references in parentheses within the text are to this edition.

42 VerMeulen, "Sam Shepard," 80.

43 Lippman, "Rhythm and Truths," 9.

44 Sam Shepard, *Curse of the Starving Class* in *Sam Shepard: Seven Plays* (London: Faber and Faber, 1985), 194.

45 Allen, "Man on the High Horse," 148.

46 Ibid., 143.

47 Lippman, "Rhythm and Truths," 11.

48 Sam Shepard, *True West* in *Sam Shepard: Seven Plays* (London: Faber and Faber, 1985), 35. Page references in parentheses within the text are to this edition.

49 Lippman, "Rhythm and Truths," 10.

50 Ibid., 11.

51 Bottoms, *Theatre of Sam Shepard*, 16–17.

52 Matthew Roudané, "Shepard on Shepard: an Interview," chapter 3, 71.

53 Shewey, *Sam Shepard*, 142.

54 Stephanie Coen, "Things at Stake Here," *American Theatre*, 13 (September 1996): 28.

55 Sam Shepard, *A Lie of the Mind* (New York: New American Library, 1987), 92. Page references in parentheses within the text are to this edition.

56 Rosen, "Silent Tongues," 36.

57 VerMeulen, "Sam Shepard," 86.

58 Sam Shepard, *States of Shock; Far North; Silent Tongue* (New York: Vintage Books, 1993), 74. Page references in parentheses within the text are to this edition.

59 Kevin Sessums, "Geography of a Horse Dreamer," *Interview*, September 1988, 73.

60 Shewey, *Sam Shepard*, 226.

61 Simpson, et al., "Art of Theatre XII," 219.

62 Sam Shepard, *The Tooth of Crime*, in *Sam Shepard: Seven Plays*, 227.

63 Sam Shepard, *The Unseen Hand*, in *Action and The Unseen Hand* (London: Faber and Faber, 1975), 71.

64 Quoted in prefatory material to *Simpatico*, unpaginated.

65 Arthur Miller, *Death of a Salesman* (New York: Penguin, 1998), p. 36.

66 Sam Shepard, *Cruising Paradise* (New York: Vintage Books, 1977), 154–55. Page references in parentheses within the text are to this edition.

67 Michiko Katukani, "Myths, Dreams, Realities – Sam Shepard's America," *New York Times*, 29 January 1984, 2.26.

68 Rosen, "Silent Tongues," 36.

69 Shewey, *Sam Shepard*, 228.

70 Chubb, "Metaphors, Mad Dogs," 197.

71 Shewey, *Sam Shepard*, 167.

72 Barry Daniels (ed.), *Joseph Chaikin and Sam Shepard, Letters and Texts, 1972–1984* (New York: Theatre Communications Group, 1994), 96.

73 Ibid., 93.

74 VerMeulen, "Sam Shepard," 86.

2

STEPHEN J. BOTTOMS

Shepard and Off-Off-Broadway: the unseen hand of Theatre Genesis

Critical studies of Sam Shepard's plays frequently acknowledge the importance of the Off-Off-Broadway movement of the 1960s in providing the context and the impetus for Shepard to begin his career as a playwright. This semi-underground theatre scene, which found its home in the cafés, churches, lofts, and basements of New York's Greenwich Village and East Village districts, was an intrinsic part of the counter-cultural mood of the period. These alternative venues operated by a kind of do-it-yourself spirit of invention and improvisation, and initially their only funding source for plays was the money collected by passing a hat around the audience at the end of each show. The free admission policy maintained by all the key venues until the turn of the decade meant that playwrights and directors were relieved of commercial pressures and conventions: thus, for many in the movement, there was a conscious rejection of existing theatrical forms, and an attempt to forge an alternative theatre which was at once more community-based and more genuinely experimental.

It was in this context that Shepard first developed as a playwright. In 1964, his first two plays, *Cowboys* and *The Rock Garden*, premiered at Theatre Genesis, an Off-Off-Broadway venue based at St. Mark's in the Bowery, an episcopalian church in the East Village at 2nd Avenue and 10th Street. He continued to be based there until 1971, when Shepard and his young family left New York to start a new life in England (just as Off-Off-Broadway itself, in changing economic circumstances, was mutating into something less spontaneous and more institutionalized, simply in order to survive). That seven-year period was for Shepard the most prolific of his entire career, as he responded to the movement's seemingly insatiable demand for new material by turning out eighteen one-act plays and three two-act plays (to number only those which were actually produced). Shepard had plays presented at all of the key Off-Off-Broadway venues – itself a distinction shared by only one other writer, H. M. Koutoukas – and eventually at more "legitimate" theatres such as the subscription-funded American Place. He also collaborated in numerous ways with actors, directors, and other writers whom he encountered on the alternative circuit. This was, as Shepard himself wrote in 1985, "a playwright's heaven... The only impulse was to make living, vital theatre which spoke to the moment."[1]

Unquestionably, then, Shepard's work would never have developed and grown as it did in these crucial early years of his career without the opportunities and stimuli provided by the Off-Off-Broadway context. And yet studies of his plays – including my own book, *The Theatre of Sam Shepard* – generally provide very little understanding of the circles Shepard was working in at this time, and their impact on his writing. The primary reason for such oversights is, undoubtedly, the fact that Off-Off-Broadway itself has been largely neglected as a subject for historical research and critical analysis, and this is nowhere more true than in the case of Theatre Genesis. Despite being widely recognized as one of the most significant and prolific Off-Off-Broadway venues, alongside the Caffe Cino, Café La MaMa, and the Judson Poets' Theatre, Genesis is by far the most under-documented of this four some. Where the other three have all at one time or another since the 1960s been subjected to exhibitions, retrospective journalism, and some (albeit cursory) academic analysis, Genesis has been all but forgotten. In this chapter, I have sought to rectify this situation somewhat. Having already attempted, in *The Theatre of Sam Shepard*, a detailed textual analysis of Shepard's early plays, my goal here is to complement that work by providing some more clues as to the context in which they were written.[2] Drawing on the wider research which I have been conducting into the Off-Off Broadway movement, and on original interviews with several of Shepard's colleagues, I have sought to sketch out some of the key features of the work of Theatre Genesis, in order that the development of his writing within that environment, and indeed after leaving it, can be better appreciated.

Before continuing, it is perhaps necessary to stress just how important a role Theatre Genesis played in Shepard's early career. A small, black-box-style studio theatre in a converted upstairs hall at St. Mark's, the venue produced not only that first double bill of *Cowboys* and *The Rock Garden*, but also the premieres of *Chicago* (1965), *Forensic and the Navigators* (1967), and *The Mad Dog Blues* (1971). Although Shepard distributed his output widely among different theatres throughout the 1960s, only Ellen Stewart's Café La MaMa could equal this figure of premiering five of his plays – including, most notably, *Melodrama Play* (1967) and *The Unseen Hand* (1969). Significantly, though, even those Shepard plays appearing outside Theatre Genesis itself more often than not featured Genesis regulars among the key members of the cast and crew: *The Unseen Hand*, for instance, premiered with Lee Kissman and Beeson Carroll in the key roles of Blue Morphan and

Willie the Space Freak. Kissman had been acting at Genesis ever since he originated the role of the Boy in *The Rock Garden*, and had also appeared in *Chicago*, *Forensic and the Navigators*, *Up to Thursday* (Playwrights Unit, 1964), and *Red Cross* (Judson Poets' Theatre, 1966). He also went on to star as the gun-toting revolutionary Geez in *Shaved Splits* at La MaMa in 1970, in a production directed by Genesis-based actor–director Bill Hart. Beeson Carroll, having also appeared in *Forensic*, went on to feature in *The Mad Dog Blues* and *Back Bog Beast Bait* – a 1971 production at Wynn Handman's American Place Theatre staffed almost entirely by Genesis regulars and directed by Shepard's fellow Genesis playwright, Tony Barsha. Such cross-referencing could go on and on. Even Shepard's two-act extravaganza *Operation Sidewinder*, produced with the full resources of Lincoln Center behind it in 1970, starred Barbara Eda Young as Honey, the female lead: Young, who had effectively trained herself as an actress through five years of regular work at Theatre Genesis, was here making her début in "legitimate" professional theatre.

It is a mark of Shepard's dependence on and trust for his Genesis colleagues that he insisted on their prominent presence in so many of his plays, wherever they were being presented. For him, Theatre Genesis was a creative home in many more ways than the merely physical. Shepard was an integral member of the community of like-minded playwrights, directors, and actors which developed at St. Mark's during this period – a community spirit perhaps most clearly demonstrated when Shepard married Genesis actress O-Lan Johnson in the church in 1969, in a double wedding with actor–playwright Walter Hadler and his stage-manager bride, Georgia. When one begins to examine Shepard's early work alongside the plays of his Genesis colleagues, all kinds of common interests and affinities become apparent – just as an analysis of the early work of the predominantly gay group of playwrights working regularly at Caffe Cino also reveals many common thematic threads and theatrical methods. The Off-Off-Broadway movement was, in effect, a loose assembly of artistic communities, each related to but also distinct from the others.

Foundations

Theatre Genesis was the last of the four key Off-Off-Broadway venues to appear on the scene. Caffe Cino, Judson Poets' Theatre, and La MaMa had presented their first full productions in 1960, 1961, and 1962 respectively, but Genesis did not inaugurate its own work until that first double bill of Shepard plays in October 1964. By that time, the emergence of small-scale, noncommercial theatre all over lower Manhattan was a recognized phenomenon, and Genesis set itself up in direct response to the wealth of new playwriting talent that had begun to appear. From its inception, Genesis had a more self-conscious, programmatic approach to the nurturing of its writers than did any of the other venues. Rather than simply providing a stage and a time slot, as did Cino and La MaMa, artistic director Ralph Cook had very clear objectives in mind for Theatre Genesis; as was reflected in his very choice of title ("artistic director" was an industry term never adopted by or applicable to Joe Cino, Ellen Stewart, or Judson's Al Carmines, in their more ad hoc programming practices). The performance space itself was also more "theatre-like" than those elsewhere on the scene: rather than mounting plays on a platform stage in a café, as at Cino and La MaMa, or in the undisguised meeting rooms of a church, as with the Poets' Theatre at Judson Memorial Church, Genesis prided itself on its dedicated studio space. Tiny as it was (no more than about thirty by thirty-five feet), this so-called "black cube" nevertheless lent itself to many different experiments in stage and audience configuration.

The relatively "professional" appearance of Genesis's work was not, however, matched by any sense of carcerist self-promotion on the part of Cook and his colleagues. Indeed, of all the key Off-Off venues, Genesis showed the least inclination, during the 1960s, to push its work toward transfers to commercial, Off-Broadway productions. A major part of the reason for the venue's relative obscurity in documentations of this period surely lies in its very lack of interest in showing itself off to the wider world. Rather, Cook's concern was for the theatre to serve not its own interests, but the needs of its immediate community in the Bowery. Just as the Judson Poets' Theatre saw itself as part of the church's ministry to its local area, so Theatre Genesis was first and foremost a part of St. Mark's mission to its parish. However, where Judson was surrounded by the relatively affluent and artistically sophisticated community of Washington Square and the wider Greenwich Village area, St. Mark's was located in a run-down area riddled with social problems from homelessness to drug and alcohol abuse. Thus, from the outset, Genesis subscribed less to the "art for art's sake" ethos of Judson Poets' Theatre than to a sense of social and political mission which became integral to the work produced there.

In relation to Sam Shepard's work, these factors might at first seem oddly unrelated. Shepard clearly has succeeded in promoting himself and his work to wider audiences, and he does not normally spring to mind as one of America's more "politically engaged" dramatists. Certainly he had little time for the more purist, isolationist elements of Ralph Cook's approach, and – unlike most of the other Genesis-based playwrights – was not shy about pursuing productions at other venues in order to raise his public profile. Following the production of *Cowboys* and *The Rock Garden*, which were hailed by *Village Voice* critic Michael Smith as "a pair of provocative and generally original plays," Shepard quickly succeeded in securing productions at Edward Albee's new-writing workshop, the Playwrights Unit (*Up to Thursday* in November 1964, and *4-H Club* in September 1965), at La MaMa (*Dog* and *Rocking Chair*, February 1965), at Caffe Cino (*Icarus's Mother*, November 1965), and at Judson (*Red Cross*, January 1966).[3] Thus, in a little over a year since his first plays were staged, the 23-year-old Shepard had covered all of the important bases then available to him. In December 1965, in the first feature article about the emerging scene to appear in the *New York Times*, Elenore Lester named him as "the generally acknowledged 'genius' of the Off-Off-Broadway circuit," thereby ensuring that Shepard would henceforth be regarded with rivalry and a certain resentment by many of his fellow Off-Off playwrights.[4] Yet if Shepard's career instincts placed him somewhat at odds with the Theatre Genesis ethos (at this time only the Cino-based Lanford Wilson was pursuing production options with the same gusto), the style and attitude of his playwriting was, nonetheless, closely consistent with Ralph Cook's developing artistic vision. Indeed, when *Icarus's Mother* opened to generally unenthusiastic responses at Caffe Cino in 1965, some saw its failure as indicative of the absence of Theatre Genesis regulars in the cast or crew. "The acting styles and everything were all wrong," Barbara Young remembers: "I thought 'that's not Sam! This is the wrong production!'"[5]

If Shepard's plays seemed to "belong" most at Genesis, it was in large part because of his personal affinity with Ralph Cook. A native of California and a former bit-part actor in Hollywood Westerns, Cook had what actor–playwright Walter Hadler describes as "a kind of cowboy mind," which clearly appealed to Shepard: "Sam had grown up in California, and they hit it off."[6] Cook had been born in 1928, and was a good deal older than the playwrights he nurtured, but as such became something of a mentor and even father-figure for many of them (much as Ellen Stewart became "la mama"). Certainly Shepard – who had recently run away from a troubled family background – viewed him in this manner during his early career. The two men had met at the Village Gate nightclub, where Cook was head waiter and Shepard a busboy. Having recently been appointed "lay minister to the arts" at St. Mark's, Cook was looking for new playwrights to produce there, and Shepard's plays proved ideal for his purposes because they seemed so fresh and raw. This was a young man, relatively uneducated in theatre or literature, who was finding his way intuitively as a writer, and Cook seems to have perceived a kind of authenticity in this. Shepard's was, in effect, the voice of a kid off the local streets, and as such *Cowboys* and *The Rock Garden* seemed ideal to launch a theatre program whose purpose was, in part, "to help reopen communications between church and community."[7]

Although Cook regarded himself as an atheist, he had been attracted to St. Mark's in the first place because of the outreach work which Michael Allen, the newly elected pastor of the church, had initiated. Faced with a decline in numbers in the church's primarily white, middle-class congregation, Allen had made it his priority to establish social programs for the local community, which was a largely blue-collar, multi-ethnic mix of whites, African Americans, Puerto Ricans, and Ukrainians. When Cook had asked Allen if he could run an acting workshop for local youths, and possibly establish a theatre program, Allen had enthusiastically agreed. However, the first production presented at St. Mark's, in July 1964, was a pre-packaged, touring production of *Study in Color*, a play by Malcolm Boyd designed for presentation in churches. Cook had hated it, and had resolved in future to present only those plays which he thought both artistically valid and socially relevant in some way. *Cowboys* and *The Rock Garden* fit this bill, and became the first Genesis production proper, primarily because of their honesty and directness. The first play, which was apparently a fairly direct translation to the stage of the playful street antics of Shepard and his friend Charles Mingus III (who used to wander lower Manhattan as a kind of anarchic double act, adopting comic voices and dodging traffic), was seen as capturing both the energy and disaffection of the area's large, and largely disenfranchised, youth population, brought up on 1950s platitudes and television serials. "Their basic mood is exhaustion bordering on despair," *Voice* critic Michael Smith wrote of the play's two young male characters, "but from it they rouse themselves into bursts of wild energy, alternately joyous and desperate, in which they impersonate Wild West heroes surrounded by marauding Indians and relish in memory the sensate details of breakfast."[8]

If *Cowboys* depicted a couple of young people trying to create roles for themselves, *The Rock Garden* summarized what they were fleeing from. In a triptych of simple domestic scenes, Shepard depicted the banality and tedium of life in an archetypal, middle-American family home – complete with white picket fence. ("The writing is beautifully controlled," Smith noted, "and conveys the overpowering boredom of the situation without being boring for a moment.") In the crucial, climactic moment, the Boy at the centre of this family effects a kind of personal revolt against its repressive mediocrity by launching into an impassioned, vividly detailed monologue on the joys of rough sex, which prompts his father – in a superbly understated final image – to fall off his chair. It was this speech which brought immediate notoriety to the production and the new theatre, which was condemned for promoting obscenities in a church building. Yet Pastor Allen himself, in a move indicative of his ministry's priorities, publicly spoke back in support of the play, pointing out that it was more "Christian" to use offensive language in pursuit of truth than to use decent language in defense of conventionalized lies. *The Rock Garden*, Allen recalls in retrospect, "was really an attack on the pornography of American life," and for him represented exactly the kind of social and spiritual conscience which St. Mark's stood for. "One day Sam and I were talking," Allen notes: "I said to him, 'one day you will be recognized as America's greatest Christian playwright.' He responded that he hoped that would be true."[9]

This first production at Theatre Genesis was staffed almost entirely by a core group which Allen had gathered from amongst his friends and associates at the Village Gate – including actors Lee Kissman, Kevin O'Connor, and Stephanie Gordon (daughter of the nightclub's hostess). As a result of the success and notoriety of the Shepard bill, however, the theatre quickly began to attract the interest of others, and particularly of other would-be playwrights, who began submitting scripts by the dozen. Ralph Cook's selection policy for new plays was, however, considerably more rigorous than that adopted at venues such as Caffe Cino and Café La MaMa, where a new production had to be mounted every week or two so as not to drive away regular customers. Cook's insistence on producing new work only when he thought a play had something worthwhile to say meant that Theatre Genesis had a much more erratic schedule, often going two or even three months without a new production. The regularly pumping heart of the Genesis operation was, instead, the weekly Monday night playreading workshop, in which participating actors would read scripts submitted by aspiring writers. Those plays which caught Cook's attention in this context might go on to be mounted as full productions.

Through his selections, Cook gradually began to develop at Genesis a preference for what he called "a deeply subjective kind of realism" – a description which further underlined his affinity with Shepard's work.[10] By grounding his early plays in recognizable, everyday realities but distorting and abstracting these images through the application of a very personal, subjective vision, Shepard had begun to develop a kind of raw, neo-expressionist theatre which had clear antecedents in the European avant-garde work of Beckett, Genet, and Pinter, but which was also unmistakably American in tone and subject. Particularly important here was Shepard's freely spontaneous, rhythmic use of theatrical language, which was immediately acknowledged by critics as his most distinctive gift, and which allowed his characters to give voice to vividly imagistic monologues which seemed to spring, uncensored, from the wilder regions of the mind. Shepard's acknowledged influences here were the "beat" writing of Ginsberg and Kerouac, the action painting of Pollock, and the improvisational jazz of Charlie Parker, Ornette Coleman, and Charles Mingus II (father of his friend), all of which were enthusiasms shared by Cook, which greatly influenced his own choices of material to direct. Meanwhile, the establishment of the St. Mark's Poetry Project in 1965, as a sister organization to Theatre Genesis, proved to be another important factor in underlining the venue's distinctive bent, with its readings becoming a lightning rod for young, beat-influenced poets who fell over themselves to have their work heard in the presence of regular attenders including Gregory Corso, Rick Sanders, and Allen Ginsberg himself. If Judson Memorial Church, through its theatre, dance, and gallery programs, had established itself as the home of cool, witty mixed-media work in the neo-Dadaist vein, St. Mark's increasingly established an identity as the place where the writer's voice could be expressed with uncensored passion and directness.

A landmark production in helping to clarify the distinct approach of Theatre Genesis during this formative period was the April 1965 double bill of Shepard's *Chicago* with Lawrence Ferlinghetti's *The Customs Collector in Baggy Pants*. Unlike many other such bills which could be seen on the Off-Off-Broadway circuit (Shepard's *Red Cross*, for example, was bizarrely paired up with Theo Barnes's Japanese-inflected adaptation of *Antigone* at Judson Poets'), there was a consistency and clarity in the relationship between the two plays and their productions. Both the Shepard and the Ferlinghetti pieces are essentially rhythmically driven monologues (although *Chicago* also has a number of subsidiary characters), and both cleverly manipulate the use of direct address to the audience. As such, they mirror intriguingly the increasingly theatrical feel of the St. Mark's poetry readings (Ferlinghetti, of course, was himself a celebrated poet, of the San Francisco beat school). "The reading of the poems became a kind of performance art," explains Genesis playwright Murray Mednick:

> there was a kind of presentational quality to the language which I think we [in Theatre Genesis] were very influenced by. We had a similar attitude toward language, which has to do with a feeling about the spoken word as an almost shamanistic act – incantatory, ritualistic – as opposed to the theatrical [dialogue] tradition . . . We had a very high estimation of the idea of the word itself coming through the medium of the actor.[11]

Fellow playwright Tony Barsha likewise notes that "incantation" became such an integral part of the Genesis approach that "it became a necessity" even in the most dialogue-based plays: "there came a moment when the monologue had to come in. It had to be a revelatory monologue, a scatalogical monologue, a monologue of entropy, whatever."[12] In short, such verbal flights became as "necessary" to the Genesis aesthetic as the solo improvisation was to jazz performance.

The basic structure of both *Chicago* and *The Customs Collector* is one of gradual intensification in the monologuist's mood, from playfully ludicrous beginnings toward an eruption of near-hysterical anxiety by the end. In Ferlinghetti's piece, this is achieved partly by the sheer breathlessness of the actor after delivering an increasingly frantic seven-page monologue which literally has not a single period or pause anywhere in the text.[13] *Chicago* is more rhythmically complex, ebbing and flowing like the sea into which the inhabitants of Stu's story finally walk, but the effect is all the more disquieting for that: Shepard's use of humor is the more deft, and his attention to small, telling details the more precise, so it is in the steadily darkening accumulation of its comic–grotesque observations that the play's impact lies. A smelly, over-populated train journey gives way to a beach scene, a wild orgy of sand and sperm, a frantic attempt to make smothering rugs, and finally a ritual drowning by suicide. *Chicago*, like much of Shepard's early work, is difficult to make rational sense of, but through rhythm and image it conjures a vivid sense of a "subjectively real" trip to the dark side of the mind, to a nightmare world which Stu appears – finally – to crave escape from, as he leaps from the bathtub he has been confined in throughout the play and exhorts the audience to embrace life: "Breathing, ladies and gentlemen . . . it's fantastic!"[14] The ominous knocking of a policeman's nightstick from behind the audience as the lights fade clearly implies that, whatever Stu fears, it is not so easily escaped.

Tellingly, the juxtaposition with Ferlinghetti's play seemed to clarify something of the nature of Stu's anxiety. The customs collector, characterizing the location as the ladies' restroom on the "lifeboat full of flush toilets we call civilization" (79), and his listeners as "all the women I have ever loved and known" (85), asks – at first threateningly and finally desperately – for them to return to him the jewels they have stolen, "the twin gems" and "the great King of Diamonds" (81). The castration terror so obviously underlying this piece (and so beloved of the beat movement in general) throws into relief Stu's obvious anxiety over Joy's plans to go out of town on a job, and thus leave him alone in his (womb-like?) bathtub: despite his impish creativity, he seems impotently stranded there. Thus this double bill, taken together, clearly indicated a developing concern at Theatre Genesis with exploring the underside of a specifically *masculine* subjectivity – a concern which could at times, all too easily, spill over into a misogynistic depiction of women as the threatening "other," but which could also, in the best instances, be deeply revealing and even cathartic in the honesty of its confrontation with repressed male fears.

This production was also, very importantly, distinguished by a very sparing approach to staging. The only set item in *Chicago* is that free-standing bathtub, while *The Customs Collector* – continuing the bathroom theme – requires only a short row of toilet-cubicle doors. Pared-down settings of this sort were common in the spatially and financially constrained Off-Off-Broadway theatres, but the black-box studio at Theatre Genesis allowed single set items like this to stand out against a uniform background with an unusual clarity of focus. Shepard and Cook had undoubtedly learned from their experiences with *Cowboys* and *The Rock Garden*: the former play had successfully used an almost bare stage, while the latter had been criticized for the unconvincing attempt to construct a "realistic" domestic environment using theatrical flats. Thus they were, with *Chicago* in particular, moving toward the use of a single, distilled theatrical image, a "found object" which would act as the visual anchor for the play's flights of rhythmic, imagistic language. This was a method which Shepard was to use again and again in subsequent years (other notable "single images" including the trashed 1951 Chevrolet around which *The Unseen Hand* revolves, and the "evil-looking black chair" of *The Tooth of Crime*). As Murray Mednick points out, "[we found that] you could use a certain kind of visual symbology . . . to great effect in a small space. We were really interested in discovering iconographic usages: what would have the resonance of an icon, a newly discovered icon, so that you can communicate directly to the audience's subconscious? That's partly what Ralph meant by subjective realism."

It should be noted, perhaps, that not all of the "realism" in the early days of Theatre Genesis was particularly "subjective." Leonard Melfi's *Birdbath*, for example, which proved particularly popular with audiences in 1965, was a fairly conventionally realistic depiction of a late-night encounter between two strangers, distinguished primarily by its blend of tenderness and underlying psychological tension. Melfi, however, moved on from Theatre Genesis after a series of productions that year, pursuing the greater chance of a commercial breakthrough offered by working at La MaMa. Meanwhile, other figures whose instincts fit better with the evolving Genesis approach began to find their way to the venue. Murray Mednick, for example, a poet before he was a playwright (and a member of the St. Mark's Poetry Project), was first attracted to Theatre Genesis by Ferlinghetti's name, to see the *Chicago* double bill. Greatly struck by the standard of the performances (and particularly that of former Living Theatre actor Warren Finnerty, who played both Ferlinghetti's customs collector and the silent, threatening policeman in *Chicago*), Mednick shortly afterward submitted a short play of his own, *The*

Box, for consideration at the Monday night playreadings. It was given a full production in December 1965. The following April, Genesis premiered *The Pattern* and *The Trunk*, two plays by Tony Barsha, another self-confessed beatnik who was living in a dingy apartment across the street. Prior to discovering Genesis, Barsha confesses, "I didn't know what the fuck I was doing [with myself]. I was totally lost. Alienated youth!" For him and Mednick, Cook's vision for the theatre came as a kind of salvation, giving them a focus for their energies they had previously lacked, and they became key members of the Genesis set-up, working there almost exclusively until the early 1970s.

Creative exchanges

If Shepard himself had been fairly promiscuous in touting his work around the Off-Off-Broadway scene during the first year or so of his career, he too was attracted back to Genesis by this gradual evolution of a community of like-minded writers and actors. Part of the appeal was no doubt the simple fact that the Genesis affiliates were unique among the various Off-Off-Broadway groupings in being predominantly and unapologetically heterosexual men. ("It was a bunch of guys, and their babes, and their drugs," Barsha quips, at least half-seriously.) Shepard was not shy of gay company, but he was clearly most at home with "the Genesis boys," as they became generally known. More significantly still, Genesis was increasingly providing Shepard with fresh ideas and inspiration on a creative level. If it had been his work which had initially helped define the theatre's aesthetic, that debt was repaid plentifully. By 1966, Shepard's initial outpouring of one-act plays was starting to dry up, and even his admirers had begun to accuse him of simply repeating the same "stylistic trick" of spontaneous game-playing and rhythmic monologues, rather than further developing his initially intriguing instinct for implicit social comment. "Some of his outpourings are so gratuitous as to be tiresome," Michael Smith commented in his review of *Red Cross*: "style if simply repeated turns into empty formalism... It is time for [Shepard] to stop only exercising his technique and begin applying it to matters of more consequence."[15] As the context surrounding Shepard, both locally and nationally, began to change significantly in the latter part of the 1960s, he himself seems to have felt the need for a shift of emphasis.[16] Interaction with his Theatre Genesis colleagues aided him significantly in his search for fresh directions, and the impact of two key productions with which he was not directly involved is particularly worth emphasizing here. Tom Sankey's *The Golden Screw* (September 1966) and Murray Mednick and Tony Barsha's *The Hawk* (October 1967) are still remembered as being among the definitive Theatre Genesis productions because, as the Caffe

Cino-based playwright Robert Patrick stresses, "they were so perfectly realized, both of them: very good plays, brilliantly done. They stand out because they were so very typically Theatre Genesis. They were very political, very rebellious, very serious."[17]

The Golden Screw seems quite flat to read on the page now, but at the time it was the first play to articulate the growing counter-cultural distrust of "the system" through the medium of musical theatre.[18] The play's structure was simple: a series of sketches depicting aspiring musicians being systematically "screwed over" by the record industry (which stands, implicitly, for capitalist America in general) is interspersed with a series of folk–rock songs in sub-Dylan mode, performed by Sankey himself and his band, the Inner Sanctum. The show ended with a quiet but pointed "fuck you," breathed by Sankey into his microphone while staring straight at the audience (trite as that may now sound, its impact was electrifying at the time). The entire play, however, was felt to add up to something far greater than the sum of its various parts: "it is more than the first successful folk–rock musical," commented the *New York World Journal Tribune*, "its implications are as chilling for the audience (who are the ultimate victims) as for the performers. *The Golden Screw* shows why the odds against a vital American pop are so great, and why even undergrounds become industrial. It is tightly wound into a series of stunning vignettes and the music provides jolting irony."[19] Sankey's play proved so popular with audiences that in February 1967 it became the first Theatre Genesis show to move to a commercial, Off-Broadway run – albeit short-lived – and the songs were recorded as a soundtrack album (the ironies here go without saying). Given the impact of *The Golden Screw*, it is surely more than mere coincidence that, in May 1967, La MaMa premiered Shepard's own first attempt at a play with live rock songs, *Melodrama Play*. Shepard had his own personal reasons for this innovation – joining a band himself being one of them.[20] Yet the parallels between *Melodrama Play* and *The Golden Screw* are unavoidable; it too is an ironically satirical swipe at the recording industry and the way it enslaves its contractees to commercial pressures (literally, in this case), and it too plays on Bob Dylan's recent, groundbreaking shift from acoustic folk to electric rock as a key reference point. An uneven, rather awkward piece of work, it proved considerably less successful than Sankey's play with audiences and critics, but it nonetheless initiated Shepard's significant shift toward experiments with live rock music in his plays of the late 1960s and early 1970s: the immediate impact on audiences of electrified instruments played in tiny sweatbox theatres became an integral element of his work during this period, even as his writing style altered to accommodate more driving, rock-style language rhythms.

Mednick and Barsha's *The Hawk* provided equally significant inspiration for Shepard, but unlike *The Golden Screw* is a play which still rewards detailed textual scrutiny.[21] One of the earliest successful attempts to develop and structure a serious play from collaborative improvisation, it signaled the extent to which the Theatre Genesis "gang" had acquired a coherent artistic trajectory, independent of (if complementary to) the work of either Cook or Shepard. During the summer of 1967, Mednick (as writer), Barsha (as director), and a group of eight Genesis actors (including Lee Kissman, Barbara Young, O-Lan Johnson, and Walter Hadler) sequestered themselves on a farm in Pennsylvania to work on developing improvisational acting techniques drawn from a variety of sources. However, this group differed from other such companies of the time in that, under Mednick and Barsha's guidance, they prioritized the writerly questions of language and dramaturgical structure as much as they did actorly spontaneity. Gradually, a ritualistic narrative format developed for the piece, in which the Hawk, a heroin dealer, systematically murders a series of female junkies of varying social backgrounds, by deliberately overdosing them (issues such as violence against women and class difference are embedded in the fabric of the piece). Taking a short sequence of Mednick's rhythmic poetry as a kind of repetitive refrain after the death of each victim, the group developed a strikingly solid shape for the piece reminiscent of the classic jazz structure in which variations on the same basic melody are interspersed with sections of free improvisation. In this case, the repeated text frames and focuses a sequence of improvised monologues in which the actors had a free hand to deliver certain plot and character information in whatever manner seemed to "fly" on a given night. Hailed as a near-perfect fusion of the distinct skills of writer, director, and actors, *The Hawk* stunned Genesis audiences and also went on to an Off-Broadway transfer. There it failed utterly and closed within days, simply because the show's canny exploitation of the particular, stark dynamics of the Genesis space – intimate actor–audience relations, bare black stage featuring just three metal chairs, monologic address to the audience interspersed with highly physicalized action and mime – proved untranslatable to the existing commercial context. (The mainstream press were simply bewildered by the lack of set and the "vulgar" language.) Yet many who witnessed the Genesis original, such as critic Ruby Cohn, recall it as one of the single most impressive productions of the 1960s.

The Hawk's success at Genesis was followed, just two months later in December 1967, by Shepard's own first attempt at a script developed through collaborative improvisation. The five-strong cast of *Forensic and the Navigators* included three members of the *Hawk* collective (Kissman, Hadler, and Johnson). Working together with Ralph Cook as director, they expanded on a sketched-out treatment for the play which Shepard brought into rehearsal. For a writer whose approach prior to this had always been rigidly text-led, this was a significant departure (he had characteristically refused to alter a word of his scripts in rehearsal, believing – with Kerouac – that the first, most spontaneous draft is always the most "authentic"). The text of *Forensic*, written up after the fact, clearly indicates its Theatre Genesis origins: this is the first of Shepard's texts to specify "black space" as the basic setting, and calls for a striking, almost ceremonial furniture lay-out featuring two swivel chairs at either end of a white-draped table bearing a peace pipe (157). Although this, like *Melodrama Play*, is one of Shepard's less satisfying scripts (memorable chiefly for the hilarious Rice Krispies routine developed with O-Lan – written into the script as Oolan), his changing attitude toward the production process proved to be ongoing, as he began writing more elaborate theatrical effects into his scripts while allowing directors and casts more freedom to come up with their own answers to the resulting staging challenges.

Forensic and the Navigators, like *Melodrama Play*, had more pronounced social overtones than most of Shepard's previous work; a factor also indicative of the broader Genesis influence. It deals in cartoon fashion with a plot to free prisoners from an oppressive regime, which is bungled when the regime's enforcers arrive to exterminate them. These ideas are underdeveloped, but were taken up more effectively in subsequent plays. So too was another feature of *Forensic* which seems to have owed something to *The Hawk*. The lead characters, Forensic and Emmet, appear on one level to be two sides of the same divided consciousness, a blond cowboy-type and a dark-haired Indian-type (ego and shadow, yin and yang) who discuss "switching sensibilities" so as to disguise themselves and throw their hunters off the scent (158–59). This was Shepard's first, sketchy attempt at exploring the doppelganger theme (although it had also been vaguely alluded to in *Melodrama Play*, via the brothers Drake and Duke Durgens), a central thread of his work which runs all the way through *The Tooth of Crime* (1972) and *True West* (1980) to *Simpatico* (1994). *The Hawk*, however, is the clearest encapsulation of the theme in a Theatre Genesis play, with the Hawk himself shadowed everywhere by his mysterious "Double," who mirrors him visually, echoes his ritualistic "litany," and abets him in his murders. According to Murray Mednick, ideas concerning double nature, split consciousness and mirrored personalities fascinated many of the Genesis regulars, who discussed at length concepts such as Jung's ego and shadow dichotomy, Artaud's notion of the theatre and its double, and classic variations on the double theme such as those in Dostoyevsky and Edgar Allan Poe's story "William Wilson." As Mednick remarks, "we knew we were quoting this stuff. And the audience knew that we knew. There was a shared pleasure in that." Another prime example of this trend was Walter Hadler's first play for Theatre Genesis, *Solarium* (June 1968), in which a dirty, raggedy figure played by Beeson Carroll persuades a smart figure in golfing clothes (Michael Brody, another Genesis regular) to keep an eye on his grandmother's house while he goes off to visit the golf course himself. The twist, as Hadler himself summarizes it, is that "the guy gets trapped. It's an interesting reversal, very eerie in a certain kind of way, because the women don't notice the switch." The obvious parallels between this scenario and later Shepard plays including *True West* (in which Lee, not Austin, gets to play golf with Saul) and *Simpatico* (in which the wealthy Carter winds up helplessly immured in the hovel-like home of the destitute Vinnie) are probably coincidental. Nevertheless, what is clear is that such ideas were common currency at Theatre Genesis during the later 1960s, and that Shepard's subsequent, near-obsessive extrapolation of the double theme owes much to the seeds sown during his time there.

Trash aesthetics

The sense of group cohesion and mission at Genesis had in fact become so pronounced by the later sixties that the original, open-door policy for new playwrights was replaced by an exclusive commitment to the work of the resident group. Between April 1967 and April 1971 – when Adrienne Kennedy's *A Lesson in Dead Language* appeared, the month after Shepard's final Genesis show, *The Mad Dog Blues* – only Hadler (seven plays), Mednick (three plays and two collaborative projects), Barsha (two plays and two collaborations), Lee Kissman (one play), Joel Oppenheimer (director of the St. Mark's Poetry Project; one play), and Shepard himself (two plays) had new work produced there.[22] Meanwhile, all but two of the eight new Shepard plays produced elsewhere also had Genesis regulars in key production positions (the exceptions being *Melodrama Play* and *The Holy Ghostly*, both directed by Tom O'Horgan using his own permanent troupe). "We were kind of a group, kind of an alliance," Mednick explains: "we had a search in common: we all seemed to be looking for something submerged in the American language that could be half-unearthed." Genesis plays during this period typically foregrounded aspects of specifically American iconography and mythology, whether through more or less oblique references to the nation's history, or through the manipulation of imagery from contemporary popular culture – from cowboys to Coke bottles. It is no coincidence, therefore, that Shepard's work between 1967 and 1972 uses such imagery more consistently and insistently than at any other period in his career. As a group, Walter Hadler notes, the Genesis writers had discovered that

we in some ways had similar [life] experiences, and we had a certain kind of affection for the country's history. Not nationalism. But we were interested in exploring the mythic elements in that history, rather than sneering at them. Most
other groups working at the time had an attitude about anything American
being lesser or by its own definition something uninteresting, uncultured. But
we were allowed the luxury of investigating our own psychic... horror? pleasure? madness? Whatever: we were trying to get that into the plays. And that
was the great gift from Ralph to us.

The group's fascination with exploring different dimensions of the American
psyche, and – in particular – the nature of American violence, was easy to
caricature, not least because their work was at times perceived as merely
indulging a butch, cowboy-style masculinity. Indeed, onstage and off, the
reverence in which the group held the memory of Jackson Pollock seemed
at times to involve mimicking the kind of alcohol-fueled macho posturing
for which Pollock was notorious. *Village Voice* critic Arthur Sainer admired
much of the work produced at Theatre Genesis, but describes it as typically
consisting of characters "slamming doors and screaming and shooting up
and killing each other."[23] Similarly, Cino playwright William Hoffman, while
stressing that "I *loved* their work," nevertheless refers to the shows at Genesis
as "ballscratchers, testosterone plays."[24]

This side of the work is perhaps most clearly indicated by the rather unsettling frequency with which working firearms were on show at St. Mark's.
Tony Barsha recalls how, for his January 1967 play *Smash*, "I wanted a
nice sound of a gun," and tracked down a supplier which rented weapons to
movie companies: "I got a .38 or a .32 with a blank round in it, and used it in
this one play, but then everyone started writing plays with guns in them and
renting these guns." Shepard's first such piece was *Melodrama Play*, in which
Peter shoots Dana in the head at point blank range, and by 1970, with *Shaved
Splits*, he had Geez blasting sub-machine-gun rounds out of a window. The
array of gleaming, phallic weaponry which Becky Lou unpacks at the beginning of *The Tooth of Crime* (1972; written shortly after leaving New York
for England) is now the best-known manifestation of a gun fetishism which
emerged as one of the more questionable features of the Theatre Genesis
"aesthetic." "Each play had more guns in it," Barsha remembers, "until finally Walter Hadler did a play, *The Water Works at Lincoln* [1969], with an
entire arsenal of shotgun, automatic rifle, magnums and rifles." At a pivotal
moment in this piece, a group of redneck hunters turned their weapons on
the audience – using the stage pretense that they were a lake full of ducks –
and opened fire with blanks. This was perhaps the most extreme example
of what Barsha calls the Genesis instinct "to go after the audience, to sort
of grab hold of your spine and shake you." In this instance, though, with

terrified spectators literally diving under the seats, many felt that Hadler had gone too far. "It was at a point where that was enough," Barbara Young remarks: "that's enough of showing you have balls!"

In fairness to Hadler, though, it should be pointed out that – within the context of *The Water Works at Lincoln* – the shotgun sequence actually makes perfect sense.[25] Far from being gratuitously excessive, the play is a deeply serious, often curiously muted reflection on the American landscape which – like numerous Genesis plays of the period – combines a kind of Beckettian existential bleakness with abstract but nonetheless biting social–political metaphors. Two long-haired, working-class revolutionary types find themselves in a private park estate somewhere in the midwest, where the gates close at 5.15 PM prompt, and helicopter gunships with searchlights open fire on whichever members of the public are left inside. Within this estate, between dodging salvos of gunfire, this distinctly repellent, un-heroic duo encounter various bizarre figures including the gang of rednecks who decide to subject them to a kangaroo court trial and a lynching. Hadler, who freely admits to coming from a "hick" background, seems here to be confronting the dearth of role types available to working-class whites in America: whether revolutionary or reactionary, all seem trapped within this park where nature is neatly manicured and always somebody else's property. The weaponry, considered in this context, has a metatheatrical shock value which relates directly to the concerns of the play: by having his actors turn their shotguns on the audience, he can be seen as confronting his spectators not just with blank rounds but with their own fear of potential redneck violence, of a specifically American "return of the repressed."

There is a clue here to the pivotal concerns of much of the work at Theatre Genesis during the late 1960s: the group's social–political instincts and their interests in American mythology, machismo, and violence frequently fused together into agitated and yet poignant, "subjectively realistic" representations of the world as perceived by disenfranchised, working-class (or simply "underclass") males. If other parts of the Off-Off-Broadway movement were vitally important in terms of allowing the more open, uninhibited expression of gay and female voices on stage (thereby laying significant foundations for the development of explicitly gay-oriented and feminist theatre groups in the 1970s), Genesis was equally revolutionary at this time in its unapologetic promotion of a still-more-unfashionable "white trash" perspective. As such, though, their work was often uncomfortable precisely because it flew in the face of received wisdom. As Jim Goad recently underlined in his extraordinary book *The Redneck Manifesto: How Hillbillies, Hicks and White Trash Became America's Scapegoats* (1997), the mainstream American media and the liberal intelligentsia alike have tended mercilessly to caricature working-class whites as "cartoon people," as "rifle-totin', booger-eatin', beer-bellied swine flesh. Skeeter-bitten, ball-tuggin', homo-hatin', pig-fuckin', daughter-gropin' slugs."[26] The history of poor whites, which has included indentured servitude and other forms of severe exploitation preventing "self-realization," has often been ignored or forgotten. "These days, we hardly ever see the redneck as anything *but* a caricature," Goad points out: "The trailer park has become the media's cultural toilet, the only acceptable place to dump one's racist inclinations," and as a result "a whole vein of human experience, of potential literature, is dismissed as a joke."[27]

Theatre Genesis, however, chose to mine that "vein" in developing some of its most important material, and Sam Shepard was no exception to the rule. Although his plays were generally considered both funnier and less politically confrontational than those of Mednick or Hadler (who was well-read in the work of Marx, Lenin, and Kim Il Sung), his turn toward depicting the ephemera of American pop culture in the later 1960s was nevertheless indicative of his own attempt to confront and explore a cultural background which he had previously avoided facing. "He's white trash," Tony Barsha remarks bluntly: "that's what he comes from. He was just doing what came naturally, from his gut." Likewise, Shepard's embracing of the emotional force of rock-and-roll was – in his own words – a rejection of the "urban sophistication" of jazz, and an attempt to get "back to a raw gut kind of American shitkicker thing."[28] It is in this period that his characters begin wearing cowboy boots (all the better for kicking with), and existing in a blurred region somewhere between the worlds of the Hollywood Western and the Southern Californian landscapes familiar from his youth – be they the "trailer park towns" of the Los Angeles hinterlands or the desert lying beyond.

The Holy Ghostly, which premiered in January 1970, takes place in the latter setting, and – even given its more fantastical elements involving Native American folklore – is particularly revealing in terms of Shepard's attempts to confront his own background. In his most clearly autobiographical piece since *The Rock Garden*, he here dispenses with that play's lower-middle-class domesticity, dominated as it is by a matriarchal female, and deals primarily with a solitary father-figure, Pop, who takes pride in his "dirt farmer" heritage, and cherishes the rough, "ornery" language which he associates with it (this dichotomy of the mother-figure as a more civilizing, bourgeois influence and the spectre of the "old man" as a white trash desert rat recurs, most tellingly, as a central element of *True West*). Pop, who turns out to be "Stanley Hewitt Moss the sixth," just as Shepard's father was Samuel Shepard Rogers the sixth, tries to make his son, Ice (formerly Stanley Hewitt Moss the seventh), feel guilty for changing his name and abandoning his roots, by appealing to memories such as the two of them as "blood broth-ers," going "out in that jeep late at night and flash[ing] the headlights on them jackrabbits. Blastin' them damn jackrabbits all up against the cactus" (184). Pop also reminds Ice at length of the family's past struggles: using details based directly on the Rogers family background (many of which he recycles, in different ways, in *Buried Child*), Shepard presents Pop as the son of a struggling dairy farmer who wound up selling Hershey bars door to door, and as a survivor of the Great Depression who had to go to work young as a shophand to help support his entire family (185). Ice remains unmoved by all this, even describing Pop as "the oppressor's cherry" for refusing to see the way he has allowed himself to be exploited: "we don't see things eye to eye on certain political opinions," Pop acknowledges (187). And yet there is a sense that, on one level, the whole play is driven by Shepard's own need to come to terms with, and perhaps exorcize, the unsettling pride in brute masculinity (as a means of survival?) which his redneck father apparently drummed into him from birth: "Machismo may be an evil force," Shepard remarked in 1986, "but what in fact is it? . . . I know what this thing is about because I was a victim of it, it was a part of my life, my old man tried to force on me a notion of what it was to be a 'man.'"[29]

If *The Holy Ghostly*'s emphasis on inherited masculinity makes it a par-ticularly important precursor of Shepard's later, family plays, other work of the late sixties confronts questions of lower-class marginalization even more directly. *The Unseen Hand* (1969), arguably Shepard's most complete and effective piece of this period, concerns itself centrally with the limitations faced by the socially excluded. Its location is the town of Azusa, which lies adjacent to Duarte, where Shepard spent his adolescence, and was clearly chosen for its too-cute town slogan: "Everything from A to Z in the USA." Within the context of a play, the phrase implies aspirations to presenting a kind of latter day *Our Town* universality. Azusa, though, as Shepard himself made clear in a 1973 article on the play, is a million miles from Thornton Wilder's unmistakably middle-class, small-town paradise:

> These towns are obsessions of mine because of their accidentalness . . . People who couldn't make it in the big city just drove away from it. They got so far and just quit the road. Maybe some just ran out of gas. Anyhow, they began to nest in these little valleys. Lots of them lived in trailer camps . . . It was a temporary society that became permanent. Everybody still had the itch to get on to something better for themselves but found themselves stuck. It was a car culture for the young. For the old it was just a dead end.[30]

These ideas are summed up superbly in the iconographic opening image of *The Unseen Hand*, which presents a wrecked 1951 Chevrolet convertible, surrounded by garbage, lying adjacent to a busy highway (which Shepard takes pains to describe as being indicated via a combination of constant taped sound and a looped, sweeping headlight effect across the stage). Here we find Blue Morphan, an old man for whom this is clearly his own, private "dead end," talking endlessly to himself in a "slightly drunk," drawling monologue which evokes a world of railroad crossings, teenage hot-rod drivers, and Bob's Big Boys. The sheer length of this speech suggests an attempt to focus in on the image of Blue's socially marginalized aloneness as a kind of existential condition, in the Beckettian sense. It also functions to ground the rest of the play in Blue's subjective reality – indicating the possibility that the bizarre and impossible events which follow are simply a projection of his imagination. That idea is reinforced by the fact that the play ends in the same way, with another muted, rambling monologue: now, however, it is Blue's smarter, neater brother Sycamore who is marooned in the car, a change which suggests yet another "sensibility switch" like the one in Hadler's *Solarium*.

Whether or not the play is merely Blue/Sycamore's "projection," all its characters clearly function as variants on the ruling theme of white trash dislocation and disenfranchisement. Willie the Space Freak, for example, whose strange arrival first interrupts Blue's reverie, is ostensibly a refugee from a sci-fi movie, exiled from "Nogoland," on a planet in another galaxy. At the same time, though, his redneck credentials are established soon after entering when he notes, quite incidentally while sitting in the Chevy, that "we used to shoot deer and strap them over the hood" (7).[31] Subsequently, there is a clear sense that Willie's detailed descriptions of Nogoland stand as a bizarre metaphor for the United States: "the Silent Ones of the High Commission" run things from "the Capitol" in "the northeastern sector," while "huge refineries and industrial compounds" fill the middle of the country (22). Nogoland, Willie makes clear, is kept working by a race of prisoners – of whom he is one – who have been genetically modified from "fierce baboons": the Silent Ones "wanted an animal to develop that was slightly subhuman," and thus developed the Unseen Hand, a brand on the prisoners' foreheads which "curtail[s] our natural reasoning processes . . . Whenever our thoughts transcend those of the magicians, the Hand squeezes down and forces our minds to contract into non-preoccupation" (8).

All of this can be seen as alluding playfully to Jim Goad's stereotype of subhuman poor white trash – "gap-toothed, inbred, uncivilized, violent and hopelessly DUMB."[32] Yet Shepard also flips the idea on its head through Willie's insistence that the prisoners are actually "super-human entities with capacities for thoughts and feelings far beyond that of our captors" (8). These are, Willie tells Blue, "people, like you or me, with a strange history and stranger powers," powers which "could work for the good of mankind if allowed to unfold into their natural creativity." Under the oppression of the Hand, however, the prisoners "will surely work for evil, or worse, they will turn [their power] on themselves and commit a horrible mass suicide" (17). Willie's clearest example of such evil is "the Lagoon Baboon," a flesh-eating monster inhabiting "the Southland," which can perhaps be read as an oblique reference to the stereotypically bigoted poor whites of the American deep South.

However, the most vivid depiction which the play offers of the "Unseen Hand" controlling and warping its victims' minds comes in the form of an earthling – the nameless "Kid." Appearing dressed in a high school cheerleading outfit with his pants humiliatingly pushed down around his ankles, he bellows through a megaphone at his offstage oppressors who "think you're all so fuckin' bitchin' just 'cause your daddies are rich! Just 'cause your old man gives you a fuckin' Corvette for Christmas and a credit card!" (14). The Kid's resentment at the disadvantages created by his relative poverty threatens to erupt into violence ("we're gonna burn your fuckin' grandstand to the ground"), and it seems telling that Shepard developed on this kind of class-based high school gang rivalry as the background in which Hoss, in *The Tooth of Crime*, first discovered his potential as a "cold killer": "This was a class war. These were rich white kids from Arcadia who got T-Birds and deuce coups for Xmas from Mommy and Daddy . . . Soon as I saw that I flipped out. I found my strength. I started kickin' shit, man."[33] The Kid, however, on hearing of Willie and Blue's plans for freeing the Nogoland prisoners, becomes not a street thug but a revolutionary ringleader, and launches into a lengthy and detailed disquisition on tactics for a guerrilla-led terrorist uprising (25–26). Then, in another typically abrupt, disorienting character turnabout, Shepard presents the Kid as being helplessly enslaved to the values and trivial pleasures of an ultra-conservative, small-town America. The polar opposite choices in Hadler's *Water Works*, of resorting to either revolutionary or reactionary violence, are thus rolled into one schizophrenic ball of contradictions. "I'll kill you all!" the Kid screams at his erstwhile companions in conspiracy:

> I'll kill you! This is my home! Don't make fun of my home. I was born and raised here and I'll die here! I love it! That's something you can't understand! I love Azusa! I love the foothills and the drive-in movies and the bowling alleys and the football games and the drag races and the girls and the donut shop . . . and the Safeway Shopping Center and the freeway and the pool hall and the Bank of America . . . [etc.] (27)

Shepard, like Hadler, presents all this without attempting to offer any kind of answer to the serious questions underlying his deceptively playful scenario. Willie conjures Blue's brothers Sycamore and Cisco out of the past and rejuvenates Blue himself, thus creating a trio of Wild West cowboy outlaws whom he hopes will help him take on the Silent Ones: "if you came into Nogoland blazing your six-guns they wouldn't have any idea how to deal with you" (8). There seems to be an ironic appeal here to the Hollywood image of the cowboy rebel as working-class hero (a theme particularly apparent in the poignant 1963 Kirk Douglas movie *Lonely Are the Brave*, which Shepard was later to reference explicitly in *True West*). Yet this is clearly not a serious solution on Shepard's part to the social ills he has alluded to. Likewise, when Willie finally claims to have freed the Nogo prisoners, after exorcistically reciting the Kid's entire "I love Azusa" speech backwards, this is nothing more than a fantasy climax to the narrative. A hail of coloured ping-pong balls falls from the sky to signify the prisoners' liberation in a surreal *coup de théâtre* typical of the Genesis climax (similar stunts conclude *The Water Works at Lincoln*, *Forensic and the Navigators*, and Mednick's *The Hunter* [1968], to name but three). Yet the unalterable "reality" of the social situation is subtly acknowledged in the play's closing moments, as the brothers decide to absorb themselves into the economic system rather than attempting to take it on as outlaws: "we could sit it out...I could get me an office job...Settle down with a nice little pension...Get me a car maybe" (31). With Sycamore alone in the Chevy at the end, as Blue was at the outset, it is clear that little has changed.

Shepard, then, shared with his Theatre Genesis colleagues both an interest in obliquely addressing socio-political problems through his plays in this period, and a deep-rooted skepticism toward the conventionally touted solutions. "It was bullshit," Mednick remarks bluntly of the revolutionary rhetoric popular in the late 1960s: "I think we knew that the chances of it happening were slim to none." Hadler agrees, stressing that "part of our heritage as Americans was to distrust Europe – its philosophies and hysterias and its various forms of government." Marxist notions of revolution thus cut little ice with the Genesis group, who tended to look at the very idea of overthrowing the bourgeoisie as inherently bourgeois. Shepard's own skepticism toward top-down political change is neatly summarized in *The Unseen Hand* by Blue, in his (fictional) description of recent political history: "then they change the government from capitalism to socialism because the government's afraid of a full-blown insurrection. Then they have a revolution anyhow and things stay exactly like they was" (16).

The upshot of the Genesis group's political diagnosis, then, was a kind of deep, existential fatalism. Beckett's sense that there is "nothing to be done" to remedy the human condition tended to be fused with a sense of implacable, unalterable social injustice. This is visible again in Shepard's wildly comic nightmare vision of revolution, *Shaved Splits* (1970), in which Geez, the redneck insurrectionist from East Los Angeles, finally acknowledges that, for all his efforts, he is trapped in "dead end city": his vividly poetic description of the thrashing for life of a deer caught by a huntsman's bullet summarizes his own sense of helplessness. (In Geez's description, the subsequent skinning of the deer is clinical and bloodless and "very neat.")[34] Such bleak perspectives led to the Genesis playwrights being accused by some of nihilism.[35] Yet for others – as Robert Pasolli pointed out in a *Village Voice* feature on the work of Shepard, Mednick, and Hadler – their "dark diagnoses" of "incurable ills" seemed distinctly more plausible than "the implied prescriptions of many of their [contemporary playwriting] colleagues. [They] reflect our deep suspicion that what is wrong with our lives is so fundamental, yet so elusive, that we can do nothing to set it right." For Pasolli, the appeal of Shepard's work in particular lay in the underlying honesty of its vision: "[his] plays are autobiographical episodes abstracted through dramatic images of loss, fear and isolation."[36]

Exodus

The sad irony here is that, even as the "subjective realist" playwriting approach fostered by Ralph Cook was reaching its full fruition in plays such as those discussed, Cook himself was asking that the Genesis writers come up with something more prescriptive. A man with a previous history of mental problems, by 1970 he was again going "off the deep end" (to use Hadler's pained phrase): one dimension of this was that, in the spirit of the times, he began demanding politically propagandist work from his playwrights rather than the personal, ambiguous visions previously encouraged. Acting as a group, Mednick, Hadler, and Shepard (with the tacit support of Barsha and the others) asked Cook to step down, and took on the directorship of Theatre Genesis as a triumvirate. The new regime, however, found itself plagued with problems, not least of which was the fact that – almost at the same time – St. Mark's itself had seen a coup of its own, with Pastor Allen being forcibly removed from office by a revolt of the increasingly politicized congregation, which led to the installation of David Garcia as the new pastor. Garcia and his wife had extreme left-wing views, and helped make the church a working base for groups including the Black Panther Party and the Up Against the Wall Motherfuckers (both of which advocated armed insurrection). "He was

OK," Hadler recalls of Garcia as a person, "but it's a little bit difficult to run an artistic institution out of a political, pre-digested view of how things should be."

Against this backdrop, it is perhaps understandable that Shepard lost interest in exploring political issues even obliquely. His final play for Theatre Genesis, *The Mad Dog Blues* (1971), is essentially a fairly shallow jaunt through the detritus of American folklore, traditional and modern: "it was when Sam was writing the American myth," Barsha remarks dismissively, "because he'd been reading I guess that he was the American myth writer ... It was his bad period." *The Mad Dog Blues* is interesting chiefly for its treatment of the tensions in the disintegrating central relationship between Kosmo and Yahoodi, which – aside from being yet another variation on the "double" theme – was a thinly disguised depiction of Shepard's love–hate relationship with Murray Mednick. "We were like brothers," Mednick recalls, and that bond is more than apparent in the play. Yet given that Mednick was struggling with heroin addiction at this time, and finding it harder to have his work published than Shepard, the latter's depiction of Yahoodi as a "morbid little nihilistic junkie" (265), who is jealous of Kosmo's success as a rock star, was perhaps too close to the bone for comfort.

The production of *The Mad Dog Blues* also caused tensions because a larger-than-usual proportion of the theatre's operating budget was spent on an atypically elaborate set for it, with raked staging taking up most of the studio's floor space. Barsha claims that, as a result, he was forced to take his own play, *The Tragedy of Homer Stills*, into a production at La MaMa, because Genesis did not have the money left to stage it. The rights and wrongs of such disputes are impossible to verify now, but what is clear is that the once-close Genesis alliance was starting to fall a part over money and programming priorities, now that three of the playwrights were themselves in charge. These problems were exacerbated by the increasing incestuousness of the relationships between company members, and the bitterness being generated as a result. When the American Place Theatre presented the almost entirely Genesis-staffed double bill of Shepard's *Cowboy Mouth* and *Back Bog Beast Bait* in April 1971, just a month after *The Mad Dog Blues* had appeared, Shepard cast himself in the former play alongside its co-author Patti Smith, with whom he had been conducting a very public affair, while his wife O-Lan appeared in the latter piece. She was at that point involved with Robert Glaudini, director of *Cowboy Mouth*. O-Lan had been cast as Gris-Gris by *Beast Bait* director Tony Barsha despite the fact that Murray Mednick's then-girlfriend had originally been given the role: Mednick had apparently attacked Shepard physically over this turnabout. "The whole thing was imploding," Barsha puts it succinctly. It seems hardly surprising

that, following the opening performance, Shepard disappeared without saying where he was going, and *Cowboy Mouth* had to be cancelled, leaving
Beast Bait to run by itself. Shortly afterward, he and O-Lan reconciled their
differences and left New York for England in an attempt to make a fresh
start. Following their departure, in a bid to bring some much-needed structure to the Genesis organization, critic and playwright Michael Smith was
drafted in to replace Shepard in the triumvirate. By 1974, however, both he
and Mednick had had enough and quit, sensing that both the venue and the
movement as a whole were beyond resuscitation. Walter Hadler was left to
run what was left of Theatre Genesis until 1978, when it finally shut up
shop following a damaging fire at St. Mark's.

Acts of the Apostles

The years which Shepard had spent based at Theatre Genesis proved influential on his subsequent career in numerous respects. For example, after he
returned from England in 1974, to set up home in the San Francisco Bay
area, St. Mark's contacts such as poet–playwrights Lawrence Ferlinghetti
and Michael McClure (author of *The Beard*) were very important in helping him resettle. Indeed it was McClure who introduced Shepard to John
Lion, artistic director of the Magic Theatre, with whom he struck up a relationship not dissimilar from that he had shared with Ralph Cook. Their
association provided Shepard with a new theatrical home where he found,
once again, the kind of creative environment conducive to developing new
directions for his work. Between 1975 and 1983, Shepard wrote some of
his most famous plays, including *Buried Child*, *True West*, and *Fool for
Love*, all of which premiered at the Magic's small theatre in San Francisco's
Fort Mason complex. During the same period, Shepard also spent several
summers participating, as a playwriting teacher, in the Padua Hills Playwriting Festival near Los Angeles. The Festival, which had been established
by Murray Mednick in a conscious attempt to provide the kind of mentor-
ing role for young writers which Ralph Cook had provided for the Genesis
group, proved very important in the development of a new generation of playwrights and theatre-makers, from John Steppling to David Henry Hwang.
(Other Off-Off-Broadway veterans on the teaching staff included Maria
Irene Fornes and Shepard himself.)

Ralph Cook's influence appears also to have been felt by Shepard as he
began to attempt directing his own plays during the 1970s and '80s. Cook
is remembered, by all who knew him, as a director whose approach to new
writing was to avoid – as far as possible – imposing any vision of his own over
that of the playwright. Indeed, he was so "hands off" as to sometimes give

the impression that the playwrights were directing their plays *through* him. "That's what they liked about him," notes Tony Barsha: "It was almost like he didn't know what he was doing, except that he knew exactly what he was doing... He had the right people around him, and they'd start giving him all these ideas, and he'd say, 'Oh, we'll take that, we'll take that...' Ralph was very good at that." Shepard, who had always greatly appreciated Cook's treatment of his work, apparently underestimated just how much skill was involved in such an approach: during his first attempt at directing one of his own plays (the London premiere of *Geography of a Horse Dreamer* in 1974), he took the hands-off approach so literally that, according to actor Bob Hoskins, he seemed to think that playing poker and visiting the greyhound racetrack would give his actors all the information necessary to perform the play as he saw it. He was, of course, proved wrong, and learned some difficult lessons as a result, but in developing as a director he continued to follow Cook's lead, seeking to draw performances *from* his actors rather than imposing his own ideas for a play *on* them. "He absolutely gave you space," Barbara Young remembers of Cook's approach to actors: "If you were in trouble and you went to him, he'd say, 'You can do it! That's why you're playing this part!' I would be in tears, because I wanted him to give me the solution, but he'd force me to find the solution: he helped me to find myself as an actress." Similarly, Shepard is praised by actors as a director who will not – in Ed Harris's words – "let you off the hook," but insists that they apply their own skills and intelligence to find the best way to approach their roles.[37] "He does not even like to block a play," notes James Gammon, who appeared in Shepard's productions of *A Lie of the Mind* (1985) and *Simpatico* (1994): "I've never worked with a director who gave actors as much freedom as Sam."[38] Since 1983, Shepard has directed the premiere productions of almost all his new plays – two notable exceptions being *States of Shock* (1991) and *The Tooth of Crime: Second Dance* (1996), which were both handled by his old Theatre Genesis colleague, Bill Hart.

The most significant legacy of Shepard's time at St. Mark's, however, is surely there in his writing. Simply on the level of staging, for example, his plays continue to demonstrate a perennial fascination with the possibilities of placing simple set elements in relief against stark blackness, rather than "realistic" clutter: "The windows look out into black space," read the opening stage directions to *Simpatico*: "No trees. No buildings. No landscape of any kind. Just black."[39] More importantly, Cook's notion of pursuing "a deeply subjective kind of realism" appears to have provided Shepard with the grounding he needed to develop, in the 1970s, toward a style of dramaturgy which was at once more conventionally realistic than his previous work – in terms of depicting recognizable domestic environments – and yet still deeply subjectivized. Reality in Shepard's work is never an unproblematic given, but a site contested by the warring perspectives of his different characters, many of whom appear – as in the "double" pairings of Lee and Austin in *True West*, or Eddie and May in *Fool for Love* – to represent different sides of the writer's own consciousness.[40]

Perhaps most telling of all is Shepard's continued insistence on mixing existential or metaphysical concerns, over the nature of human identity and being, together with socio-cultural concerns over the specific ills facing Americans, in distinctively American circumstances. That approach was, as has been noted, typical of the Theatre Genesis aesthetic as it developed during the later 1960s in particular. Moreover, it strikes me that a consideration of Shepard's work in relation to this formative context is particularly beneficial in drawing attention to the often-neglected class dimensions of his plays. If the Genesis playwrights were driven, in part, by a concern with dramatizing the "dead ends" in which white, lower-class men in particular found themselves, that concern is equally apparent in much of Shepard's later work. The "white trash" theme is unfashionable, which perhaps explains why it tends to be recognized more in parodies of Shepard's work than in critical commentaries, but it is inescapably apparent, in one way or another, in most of his major plays. For example, the "two guys" pairings in both *True West* and *Simpatico* are partly defined by a sense of the artificial social barriers between them steadily breaking down. In the former play, Austin seems to fall prey to a kind of gnawing guilt at having attempted to deny his upbringing and assimilate himself into a comfortably bourgeois lifestyle, even as Lee confesses that his posturing pride in his lower-class status is simply a front for a deep-rooted sense of failure and helplessness: "I'm livin' out there [on the desert] because I can't make it here."[41] Shepard's often-criticized remarks that there is "something very moving [about] American violence" need to be considered in relation to this underlying awareness of the way that social inequity breeds a sense of impotence. The violence with which he is concerned "has to do with humiliation. There's some hidden, deep-rooted thing in the Anglo male American that has to do with inferiority, that has to do with not being a man . . . This sense of failure runs very deep."[42] This is a perspective which cultural commentators are only now starting to catch up with. In 1999, for example, feminist writer Susan Faludi published *Stiffed: The Betrayal of the Modern Man*, which strongly emphasizes a sense of the near-universal frustration felt by ordinary, working class men at their inability to realize the dreams of individual fulfillment which America promises.

This chapter has sought to draw attention to some of the key respects in which Sam Shepard's early work helped to define the emerging aesthetic of Theatre Genesis, and in which his work, in turn, developed further as a result of the inspiration he received from the community of like-minded theatre-makers which evolved at St. Mark's. As I have sought to show, a critical awareness of the work of Theatre Genesis during the 1960s can help to contextualize and cast fresh light on Shepard's own plays, both at that time and in the decades since. There is, I would argue, much work still to be done in this area. In closing, though, I would stress that there is also much to be gained from studying the plays of Shepard's Theatre Genesis colleagues *in their own right*. The comparative obscurity of the venue, taken together with Shepard's personal insistence on promoting himself elsewhere simultaneously, helps to explain why his work is remembered and studied where the plays of Mednick, Barsha, Hadler, and others remain largely unpublished and forgotten. Yet without in any way taking away from Shepard's achievements, I would argue that the work of his colleagues is worthy of standing comparison with the best of his plays from the 1960s and early '70s. Indeed, Murray Mednick believes that – given the clear overlap of concerns and techniques developed by the Genesis playwrights – the growth of Shepard's fame since that time has led to a certain distortion of critical perspective: "he's taken too much of the credit . . . He's become an icon, [but] there are some first class playwrights that have been neglected." While professional jealousy may well play a part in Mednick's sentiments, he nevertheless has a point. Among "companions to Sam Shepard," that which you hold in your hands is only one of many that deserve further scrutiny.

NOTES

1 Sam Shepard, "Introduction" to his *The Unseen Hand and Other Plays* (New York: Bantam Books, 1986), x.

2 Cf. Stephen J. Bottoms, *The Theatre of Sam Shepard: States of Crisis* (Cambridge University Press, 1998), chapters 1 and 2.

3 Michael Smith, "Theatre: *Cowboys* and *The Rock Garden*," *Village Voice*, 19 November 1964.

4 Elenore Lester, "The Pass the Hat Circuit," *New York Times*, Magazine section, 5 December 1965, 100.

5 Barbara Eda Young in an unpublished interview with the author, New York City, 18 February 1997. Michael Smith, who directed *Icarus's Mother* at the Cino, acknowledged the mistakes he made in an introduction to the play in Shepard's anthology, *Five Plays* (Indianapolis: Bobbs-Merrill, 1967), 26–28.

6 Walter Hadler in an unpublished interview with the author, New York City, 24 February 1997. Subsequent quotations taken from this source.

7 Michael Smith, "Introduction" to Nick Orzel and Michael Smith (eds.), *Eight Plays from Off-Off-Broadway* (Indianapolis: Bobbs-Merrill, 1966), 11.

8 Smith, "Theatre." (The text of *Cowboys* is unpublished, but is described in detail by David J. DeRose, who acquired the only extant manuscript from Ralph Cook, in his book *Sam Shepard* [New York: Twayne, 1992].)

9 The Very Reverend J. C. Michael Allen, in a letter to the author dated 25 August 1995.

10 Ralph Cook, "Theatre Genesis," in *Eight Plays from Off-Off-Broadway*, 94.

11 Murray Mednick in an unpublished interview with the author, Los Angeles, 14 January 1997. Subsequent quotations all from this source.

12 Tony Barsha in an unpublished interview with the author, Los Angeles, 17 January 1997. Subsequent quotations all from this source.

13 See Lawrence Ferlinghetti, *Unfair Arguments with Existence* (New York: New Directions, 1963), 79–85.

14 Sam Shepard, *The Unseen Hand and Other Plays* (New York: Bantam Books, 1986), 59. Unless otherwise indicated, page references in parentheses within the text are to this edition.

15 Michael Smith, "Theatre Journal," *Village Voice*, 27 January 1966. It is worth noting that, in retrospect, Smith now recalls Judson's *Red Cross* as one of the outstanding productions of the entire Off-Off-Broadway era, and his estimation of the play as one of Shepard's best is shared by many other critics. At the time, though, in the immediate context of Shepard's other recent output, Smith was not the only person frustrated by it.

16 Cf. Bottoms, *Theatre of Sam Shepard*, 60–65.

17 Robert Patrick in an interview with the author, Los Angeles, 13 January 1997.

18 *The Golden Screw* is anthologized in Robert J. Schroeder (ed.), *The New Underground Theatre* (New York: Bantam Books, 1968).

19 Richard Goldstein, "Turn of *The Golden Screw*," *New York World Journal Tribune*, 12 February 1967, 23.

20 Cf. Bottoms, *Theatre of Sam Shepard*, 65–68.

21 *The Hawk* is anthologized in Albert Poland and Bruce Mailman (eds.), *The Off-Off-Broadway Book* (Indianapolis: Bobbs-Merrill, 1972).

22 For a full listing of Genesis productions from 1964 to 1972, see Poland and Mailman, *Off-Off-Broadway*, xlii–xliii.

23 Arthur Sainer in an unpublished interview with the author, New York City, 15 September 1995.

24 William M. Hoffman in an unpublished interview with the author, New York City, 14 September 1995.

25 *The Water Works at Lincoln* remains unpublished. A 28-page manuscript was kindly supplied to me by Hadler himself.

26 Jim Goad, *The Redneck Manifesto* (New York: Simon and Schuster, 1997), 16.

27 Ibid.

28 Shepard interviewed by Pete Hamill, "The New American Hero," *New York*, 16 (5 December 1983): 80.

29 Shepard interviewed by Jonathan Cott, "The *Rolling Stone* Interview: Sam Shepard," *Rolling Stone*, 18 December 1986–1 January 1987, 172.

30 Sam Shepard, "Azusa is a Real Place," *Plays and Players*, 20.8 (May 1973), special insert, 1.

31 The image of a dead deer strapped to the front of vehicles is recurrent in Shepard's work: see, for example, his 1988 film *Far North*, when Bertrum is almost run down by a hunter's car.

32 Goad, *The Redneck Manifesto*, 15.

33 See Shepard's *The Tooth of Crime* in *Sam Shepard: Seven Plays* (London: Faber and Faber, 1985), 224.

34 Sam Shepard, *Shaved Splits*, in *The Unseen Hand and Other Plays* (Indianapolis: Bobbs-Merrill, 1971), 198.

35 This was a term applied to Mednick in particular: "Murray Mednick is nihilistic philosophically as well as dramaturgically. His plays deny all existing principles, values or institutions" (Robert J. Schroeder, introducing his edited play collection *The New Underground Theatre*, viii).

36 Robert Pasolli, "The Theatre of the Hung-up," *Village Voice*, 19 December 1968.

37 Ed Harris quoted by Ben Brantley, "Sam Shepard: Storyteller," *New York Times*, 13 November 1994, H26.

38 James Gammon quoted by Nan Robertson, "The Multi-Dimensional Sam Shepard," *New York Times*, 21 January 1986, C15.

39 Sam Shepard, *Simpatico* (London: Methuen, 1995), 3.

40 Cf. Bottoms, *Theatre of Sam Shepard*, 191–92.

41 Shepard, *Sam Shepard: Seven Plays*, 49.

42 Shepard interviewed by Michiko Kakutani, "Myths, Dreams, Realities – Sam Shepard's America," *New York Times*, 29 January 1984, B26.

3

MATTHEW ROUDANÉ

Shepard on Shepard: an interview

Our conversation took place on 5 May 2000, in St. Paul, Minnesota, a city not far from where Shepard lives on a horse farm with Jessica Lange and their children. Exactly on time, casually dressed, and eager to get to business, Shepard exuded a quiet and slightly restless presence. He was ready, so we sat down and immediately launched into an afternoon's talk. Unpretentious and charismatic, clearly aware of and yet slightly uncomfortable with his celebrity status, Shepard enjoyed discussing some of the key issues that have longed engaged his imagination. Like so many of his own characters, Shepard is a storyteller. What is probably not so apparent in reading this interview, though, is the energy, the voice, the animated quality of Shepard's talk. He would sometimes stare right in my eyes, big hands moving, while commenting on his plays and American culture. His humor seemed genuine, self-effacing, or ironic, depending on the point he was emphasizing. Shepard, who granted the interview exclusively for this *Companion*, was enormously helpful. Afterwards he even sent me a working copy of his latest play, though it was still several months before its premiere. Throughout he was thoughtful and carefully selected his words, often laughing at himself when recounting the private or professional situations he has found himself in over a four-decade career in the theatre, and implicitly acknowledging that his life as a playwright, film star, director, and musician has been a chaotically amazing journey.

ROUDANÉ: Let's start with a few questions about the beginning of your career. You've mentioned that Theatre Genesis was a kind of artistic home for you. What was it like to be a teenager arriving from California and finding himself caught up in the burgeoning Off-Off-Broadway theatre scene?

SHEPARD: It was just amazing. Theatre Genesis always felt like home base, really, because that's where I started, and it had a very different feel from all the other theatres. Each one of those theatres back then was very individual, although it was all called Off-Off-Broadway. They each had their own particular identity, and it depended directly on who was running it and who were the body of people involved. Looking back on it, it was quite an extraordinary tapestry of atmospheres. La MaMa was very different from the Judson Poets' Theatre and from Caffe Cino. But I guess the church – St. Mark's – really felt like home base, but it was a center for many different things besides theatre: there was poetry, there was jazz, there was dance, there was painting, sculpture, so it was kind of a magnet for the East Side. And also because it was on the East Side, this made it really very different from way over in the West Village by Caffe Cino, which was a little tiny cave. It was a really amazing time to be a kid there. It was the most fortunate thing for somebody who wanted to write plays. I just dropped down out of nowhere. It was absolute luck that I happened to be there when the whole Off-Off-Broadway movement was starting. I arrived there in '63 and by '64 Off-Off-Broadway was kicking out. It was just a great time for a writer.

ROUDANÉ: I've always wondered what you meant in the "Introduction" to *The Unseen Hand and Other Plays* when you suggest that the plays in that volume (i.e. many of your 1960s works) can't be fully appreciated unless contextualized within the time and place they were written. I ask, in part, because a lot of those plays still stand up so well.

SHEPARD: Well, hopefully they do, but I don't know. It's hard to say. They were very much of the time, they were very much written out of that chaotic atmosphere that was happening, and for that reason I guess I've always associated *The Unseen Hand* and those earlier plays with the sixties. There are still quite a few of the early plays being done now.

ROUDANÉ: Do you have ambivalent feelings about the sixties?

SHEPARD: You know, man, I'll tell you what: I feel like it's been romanticized, of course, like every era that goes by that tends to get romanticized, except that I've never heard anybody say anything good about the seventies! But the sixties, to me, felt extremely chaotic. It did *not* feel like some heroic effort toward a new world, like many people make it out to be. There was an idealism on the one hand that was so out to lunch in the face of the realities. Vietnam of course shaped everything. Vietnam was the fulcrum behind it all, and there couldn't have been a more serious, a more deadly serious anger. And I suppose you could say that it was morally correct to be against the war. But people got swept up in idealisms – the Jane Fonda thing of going with the North and getting buddy-buddy with Ho Chi Minh – and it was very confusing, and at the same time full of a kind of despair *and* hope. And then when the whole Civil Rights Movement kicked in, everything just doubled and doubled and doubled, until all the barrels were wide open and everybody was shooting and it felt very awesomely chaotic to me. Still, even after the Kennedy and King assassinations and all the killing in the war, it was the idealism that continued to astound, and it just seemed so naive. The reality of it to me was chaos, and the idealism didn't mean anything. I was up against the war in Vietnam myself and was very much against it. But I wasn't ready to become a Marxist; I didn't think Marx was the answer to Vietnam any more than "flower power." There was a crazy kind of ethos – and the Berkeley thing turned me off completely. I never went to college. You know that great Creedence Clearwater song, "I Ain't No Fortunate Son"? I always identified exactly with that tune: I mean this was my anthem. "It ain't me!" And that's the way I kind of felt throughout the sixties: I was on the tail of this tiger that was wagging itself all over the place and was spitting blood in all directions. It was weird, very weird. And then to make it even more weird was acid. When acid hit the streets, then it became a circus. Then it became totally unfathomable because nobody had a *clue*. And there were all these Gurus coming along – Timothy Leary – and then you had the Black Panthers and then you had . . . it was really beyond belief. It was like somebody threw a lighted stick in an ammunition camp. Unbelievable.

ROUDANÉ: And this prompted you to go to London in 1971?

SHEPARD: Oh yeah, very much. I mean I wanted out. I wanted to get out of the insanity. Of course I was also running away from myself! But I figured you can't do that. London was a good respite because there was a really fantastic fringe theatre scene going on there with a lot of good actors. I worked with people like Bobby Hoskins, Stephen Rea, and all those guys before they were known and they were just doing theatre for nothing. London was the first place where I ever directed my own work – at the Royal Court – *Geography of a Horse Dreamer*, with Stephen Rea and Bobby Hoskins and Ken Cranham in 1974.

ROUDANÉ: Music has played an important role in many of your plays, and I understand you're a fairly accomplished drummer yourself.

SHEPARD: Naw, I wouldn't go that far. I can drum a little bit, yeah. I still play music a little bit.

ROUDANÉ: But hasn't that sense of music, from rock-and-roll to jazz and to country, that you've enjoyed, helped you as a playwright?

SHEPARD: Yeah. My dad was a drummer – he was a New Orleans jazz fanatic – and so I grew up listening to that music and he was always playing the drums in the house and stuff. So I've always felt that music is very important. Writing is very rhythmic, there's a rhythmical flow to it – if it's working. I've always been fascinated by the rhythm of language, and language is musical, there's no way of getting around it, particularly written language when it's spoken. The language becomes musical, or at least it should in one way or another. I still play music a little bit. In fact, we've got a band now with a friend of mine, T-Bone Burnett, called *Void*, and we're trying to put something together. But I haven't played for a long time. I used to play with a band called the Holy Modal Rounders in the sixties, which was fun and chaotic because everybody was on dope, everybody was pretty nuts, but it was fun! Music gives you a great insight into the world. When you go to places like Ireland or Mexico, where music is a deep part of the culture, you can get together and sing. Everybody knows the music. People come from very different villages but they know the same songs and sit down and sing them. And it's really great, and primitive. It used to be that way in this country, the Mountain music and all the fiddle players from Kentucky and Tennessee. That's why in part I like the Red Clay Ramblers, another band I worked with out of North Carolina. So, yeah, music is an important part of some of my plays. I use music a lot in *A Lie of the Mind*. They are a great band, the Red Clay Ramblers, who played in *A Lie of the Mind*. They did a great thing on Broadway called *Fool Moon*. That was a good show.

ROUDANÉ: Of the many compelling aspects of your theatre that spark public interest and a private nerve, it's your exploration of the American family that, for many, stands out. Especially in such plays as *The Rock Garden*, *Curse of the Starving Class*, *Buried Child*, *True West*, *Fool for Love*, and *A Lie of the Mind*, strange or absent fathers, distant mothers, wayward sons, and confused daughters animate the stage. Many of us feel the way Shelly must have when she first enters the normal-seeming home in the second act of *Buried Child* only to find a rather bizarre family. Could you comment on your life-long interest in exploring the American family?

SHEPARD: The one thing that keeps drawing me back to it is this thing that there is no escape from the family. And it almost seems like the whole willfulness of the sixties was to break away from the family: the family was no longer viable, no longer valid somehow in every-body's mind. The "nuclear family" and all these coined phrases sud-denly became meaningless. We were all independent, we were all free of that, we were somehow spinning out there in the world without any connection whatsoever, you know. Which is *ridiculous*. It's absolutely ridiculous to intellectually think that you can sever yourself, I mean even if you didn't know who your mother and father were, if you never met them, you are still intimately, inevitably, and entirely connected to who brought you into the world – through a long, long chain, regardless of whether you knew them face to face or not. You could be the most outcast orphan and yet you are still inevitably connected to this chain. I'm interested in the family's biological connections and how those patterns of behavior are passed on. In a way it's endless, there's no real bottom to it. It started with a little tiny one-act play I wrote way back when called *Rock Garden* [1964], where there was, for the first time in my work, a father, a mother, and a son. It was a very simple one-act little play, but it keyed off into *Curse of the Starving Class* [1977], and that keyed off into *Buried Child* [1979], and that keyed off into *True West* [1980], *Fool for Love* [1983], and all of that. I mean, I look back on all of that now as being sort of seminal. It initiated something that I didn't even see, I didn't even recognize that this was going to be the impulse toward other things, and I certainly didn't see myself spending my whole life on it. I've got this new production of *True West* on Broadway now – and the play's twenty years old – and the amazing thing to me is that, now, in this time, for some reason or another, the disaster inherent in this thing called the American Family is very very resonant now with audiences. I mean it's much more so now than when it was back when the play first started in 1980. When *True West* first came out, it just didn't seem to have the punch that it has now, you know what I mean? I mean it attracts an amazingly young audience; it's like the average age is something like thirty years old going to a Broadway play, and I just can't believe the reaction to it – the standing ovations every night. And, granted these are remarkable actors, they are extraordinary actors doing amazing things, but, still, there is a resonance in the material that somehow catches like wildfire, and then you start to recognize the disaster.

ROUDANÉ: And there is a new generation seeing *True West* for the first time now. How do you feel about this younger generation of audiences seeing your plays?

SHEPARD: Oh, it's unbelievable! I mean there are kids going to see it who weren't even born when the play was written, and then I was standing in front of the theatre one night and there were two or three guys standing over to the side and one of their buddies comes up to meet them to go into the theatre and he's just yelling the lines of the play to these other guys. And they're not more than twenty-five years old – they couldn't be – and he's yelling these lines, you know, about "there aren't any mountains in the Panhandle," "It's flat" and all, and it was astounding. Really amazing to me that young people are directly relating to it. You mentioned you took your teenage son to see one of my plays. One of the great things about kids coming to the theatre is that they are directly involved with the question of identity, of who they are. They are actively involved in that. Now we could still be actively involved with that when we're sixty or seventy or eighty years old, but for kids it's monumental because their lives are just becoming and I think that anything that speaks to that question of identity calls the kids' attention. I think we get fooled into this notion of maturity just because we are getting old. I mean there's maturity and there's maturity. A man could be intellectually extremely mature and emotionally a six-year-old. You see that all the time. No wonder people freak out. Our own culture is absolutely full of this, and there are no channels, there are no openings for discovering where to go. I mean there are these bullshit encounter groups but, that, well, you know.

ROUDANÉ: How do you feel about the current [2000] Broadway run of *True West*?

SHEPARD: Oh, I think it's wonderful. Matthew Warchus had done it like that in England. I don't know if the actors were English or expatriate Americans, but they did it in London, so he already had the experience of having handled the actors that way – with Austin and Lee switching roles. I thought it was a great notion because of the nature, the interchangeability of the characters. And you get two dynamite actors like John Reilly and Philip Hoffman and the play takes on an added resonance. The two actors switching roles on various nights is not an easy trick. It's a huge load, but they did it. I think they went a little nuts doing it, but they got it now.

ROUDANÉ: A number of playwrights address in various ways the whole notion of the "myth of the American Dream," however one chooses to define such a term. Many writers have said that the American Dream myth permeates all of American literature, forming an ironical cultural backdrop to the writer's story. Do you think such a myth informs your theatre?

SHEPARD: Nobody has actually ever succinctly defined "the myth of the American Dream." What is the American Dream? Is it what Thomas Jefferson proposed? Was that the American Dream? Was it what George Washington proposed? Was it what Lincoln proposed? Was it what

Martin Luther King proposed? I don't know what the American Dream is. I do know that it doesn't work. Not only doesn't it work, the myth of the American Dream has created extraordinary havoc, and it's going to be our demise. I mean if you want to – and I'm not an historian – but it's very interesting to trace back this European imperialism, this notion that not only were we given this land by God, somehow, but that we're also entitled to do whatever we wanted to with it, regardless of the consequences, and reap all of the fortunes out of the land, much to the detriment of everybody "below" this rampant, puritanical class of European colonialism. If you read in the journals of Lewis and Clark, it's just amazing how these guys approached the Plains Indians, particularly the Sioux, who were not very welcoming to them, as opposed to some of the other tribes to the North who got along with them better. But the Sioux couldn't care less about these jokers. They'd mess with them, they'd fool with them, they shot arrows at 'em, and Lewis and Clark hated the idea of going back through Lakota country because they knew they'd get the shit kicked out of them by these "crazy" people who they considered many notches below the European standard. Now if *that's* the American Dream, then we were in trouble from the get go; if that's the way the myth of the American Dream was established, we were in deep shit. Granted, Lewis and Clark and these other guys were somewhat heroic, they were vigorous, they had all of this vitality and they had all of this adventure of going into strange territory and all of that stuff, but behind the whole thing is land-hungry Europeans wanting to dominate. That's behind the whole deal. So, again, there are so many definitions of the myth of the American Dream. I mean, now you could actually say the American Dream is the computer. It's presented like that: the computer is the American Dream, the computer is the Answer. The Internet is the Answer. OK? Where does that leave you? I think we've always fallen victim to advertising from the get go. From advertising campaigns. The move westward was promoted by advertising. You know, "Come West!" "Free land!" "Manifest Destiny." So we've always been seduced by advertising, and now we're even more seduced by the computer and the Internet. We've fallen into that thing, you know. So the American Dream is always this fantasy that's promoted through advertising. We always prefer the fantasy over the reality.

ROUDANÉ: That's very interesting in that some of our nation's first literature was, in part, a kind of promotional literature: John Smith's *New England Trails* [1620], *The General History of Virginia* [1624], and – listen to the title – *Advertisements for the Unexperienced Planters of New England* [1631]. Does this have something to do, in your plays, with the "split" within the individual's psyche to which you've sometimes alluded?

SHEPARD: Right. I find it to be a huge dilemma. The friction between who we instinctively feel ourselves to be and anything that's influencing us to become something quite different. The friction there, the tensions there, particularly in this country, are huge. You see, there's always this battle going on between what I am inclined to believe through the influences coming from outside, and what I sort of instinctively feel myself to be, which is quite a different creature. So you can't help but get nuts in that predicament. You can't help it. It's almost like *Dr. Faustus*. It's the same predicament, this temptation for what I am not. I am sorry I am not more eloquent about explaining this. But it seems to be that this "split," which I worked with in *Simpatico*, creates a deep problem that we have very little understanding of. It can be divided in all different kinds of ways: male and female, violent and not so. And I think this "split" is where a lot of the violence comes from in the United States. This frustration between imagery and reality. I guess that's why professional wrestling is popular.

ROUDANÉ: Would this in part explain why so many of your plays have key male figures who have trouble functioning outside of the Mojave Desert?

SHEPARD: Yeah, *well*, I grew up in a condition where the male influences around me were primarily alcoholics and extremely violent and, at the same time, like lost children, not knowing how to deal with it. Instead, they were plunked down on the desert not knowing how they got there. And slowly they began receding further and further and further away – receding from the family, receding from society. You see it with some Vietnam vets. It was the same thing, except these guys – my father's generation – were coming out of World War II. I can't help but think that these wars had something to do with the psychological state that they came back in. I mean imagine coming back into the Eisenhower fifties. It must not have been easy. At all. Where everything was wonderful, the front lawns were all being taken care of, there was a refrigerator in everybody's house. Everybody had a Chevy, and these guys had just been bombing the *shit* out of Germany and Italy and the South Pacific and then they come back; I mean it just must have been unbelievable. I mean nobody ever really talks about that. Back then it was taboo to talk about it. "Nobody's crazy; everybody's in good shape." I mean can you believe it? And this happened across the country of course, but my dad came from an extremely rural farm community – wheat farmers – in Illinois, and next thing he knows he's flying B-24s over the South Pacific, over Rumania, dropping bombs and killing people he couldn't even see. And then from that into trying to raise a family and growing up in white America, you know. I mean it's extraordinary. It's amazing the way all that flip flops, from the fifties to the sixties. This monster appears. The monster everybody was trying to keep at bay suddenly turns over.

ROUDANÉ: Perhaps this is why you have so many baffled father figures in your plays, fathers who in part stand as an emblem for a wayward America.

SHEPARD: Yeah, but I don't think you ever begin a piece of writing with that intention; it comes out, you know what I mean? You begin from "character" and as it moves maybe it takes on some of those kinds of resonances. I don't think you begin from saying, "OK, I'm going to make this father figure an emblem for America," you know what I mean? If it comes out through its own force, then it's fine. That's something I never really realized as a writer until I got into *Curse of the Starving Class*, and with *Curse* I began to realize that these characters were not only who they were in this predicament in this little subculture but they begin to have a bigger implication – there are ripples around them, particularly in the father.

ROUDANÉ: Your remarks remind me of what in part makes your plays so intensely personal and yet at the same time they transcend themselves, and touch a collective nerve the way, say, a Willy Loman in *Death of a Salesman* reaches audiences.

SHEPARD: Is it true that Miller wrote that in three days or something? It was very fast, right?

ROUDANÉ: He took about six weeks to finish *Salesman*, but he wrote the first act in one day.

SHEPARD: Yeah, that's happened to me before, too, and it surprised me when I read that because it is almost as if some plays write themselves, they just appear, and you're obliged to take things down. I mean that's almost the feeling. *True West* and actually *Buried Child* were like that. *Buried Child* wrote itself pretty fast. One of the amazing things about playwriting is that it really is a probe, it is a discovery, and there are many things about a play that you may not understand right in the moment of writing, and you may not really understand it actually until years later. *Buried Child* was like that. You know that Steppenwolf production they took to Broadway in 1996? Gary Sinise directed it.

When I saw it, suddenly I understood aspects about the play I hadn't seen before – because of this production.

ROUDANÉ: Much has been said about your portraits of female characters, including that many of the women in your theatre have been marginalized or exploited by the (often demented) male figures. Might you comment on the evolution of your female characters in your plays?

SHEPARD: Yeah, I've been thinking a lot about that. In fact, I've been working on a new play that has two female characters in it, mainly because I just came out of one that was almost all male. So I just wanted to shift a little bit. I'm not sure about the question of maturity or the evolution of my female characters, but I guess they have become more substantive characters rather than being emblems. I think in my earlier plays they were more emblematic, like Miss Scoons in *Angel City*, and stuff like that. I think that the shift in the development of my female characters began with *Curse of the Starving Class*, you know, with the mother and the daughter. And then the mom in *Buried Child*. Maybe some of the women in *A Lie of the Mind*, but the focus there is really on the men. That is one problem you have in the craft of playwriting: when you zero in, when you target two characters, and then you're obliged to have other characters, it's almost as though they're an intrusion, they're there as trappings around the others, which is kind of a fault in one way. But in another way it's probably better if you just write a two-character male play and forget about the others, and not even indicate them. Beckett had a great thing about why he put Nell and Nagg, the parents in *Endgame*, in trash cans. He said he did it so they wouldn't move around! It wouldn't be messy. But sometimes, unfortunately, you target on your central characters and then these other ones kind of pop up who you don't really have any vested interest in. They're trappings. They're almost like furniture, unfortunately, but that's the way it happens.

ROUDANÉ: When Tennessee Williams once was asked which of his female characters he was most fond of, he said Blanche from *A Streetcar Named Desire*. Looking back over all of your plays, which female characters stand out in your mind?

SHEPARD: Yeah, well Williams invested his entire being in Blanche. Blanche and Williams were inseparable. But I think Mae is a pretty solid character in *Fool for Love*. She's probably the most solid female character I've written. She really holds her own. And the mom in *Curse of the Starving Class*, but I think overall Mae is the strongest, not strong just in the sense of her own willfulness, but as a whole character.

ROUDANÉ: Could you discuss your long and rich collaborative association with Joseph Chaikin?

SHEPARD: We didn't really work together until *Tongues*, that was the first thing, at the Magic Theatre, and that was in the seventies. I had known him since the mid-sixties and he had, of course, the Open Theatre, which was down on Spring Street, and I was going with a girl, Joyce Aaron, who was an actress in the company. And I used to go to rehearsals just to sit there and listen to Joe and watch him. He was so eloquent about what he was looking for in the actor. And what he was looking for was completely different from what was going on at the time, which was naturalistic, Stanislavski, Method School of Acting. Suddenly Joe opened up this whole new territory, and I think he was about the only guy in New York who was working in that way. There were some other splinter groups going on, but he was very specific about where he wanted to go with the actor. He was very inspiring, particularly to actors, because he presented opportunities that really you hadn't encountered before. I think the Method style of acting is very limited, to tell you the truth. It is one means of an actor approaching a character, but it certainly is not the final one. It wasn't just that Joe encouraged the actor to let go, but he asked the actor to consider many other possibilities, that the actor isn't only there to cause the audience to believe in his behavior as being real, as being like real life. That's not the only purpose of the actor. The actor can do many, many things. He can shift, go in many different directions: he can become an animal, he can go into all these different transformations, he can borrow from Japanese theatre. The actor can borrow from all these different avenues. He can "declare" himself, he doesn't have to be just *On the Waterfront*. *On the Waterfront* is great, but there can be many other possibilities.

ROUDANÉ: When I met with Joe Chaikin recently he mentioned that when you two collaborated, what was most important was music and humor.

SHEPARD: One of the beauties of working with Joe early on was I was essentially working with him as an actor. He was *the* actor in the piece. He was an amazing actor, I mean this guy – oh my God! – he could do stuff with his voice and the face and body and nobody else was doing that. So I had the incredible luxury of having him, not only as an actor, but as a collaborator in the writing. As we worked, he performed or experimented. So I was directly working with an actor who was also a writer and a director. You can't get any closer to the source. He had a tremendous impact on my work, and it was a kind of writing that I probably would have never approached on my own as a playwright because it was truly a collaborative thing. Joe very much fed into that. Many, many times when we would work, I've used his language directly, particularly in things like *The War in Heaven*, which is almost all Joe's language that I just shaped. In *When the World Was Green: A Chef's Fable*, there's an emphasis on food at the end. That was Joe. The chef. Joe was obsessed with cooking and food, and he just insisted on this food thing. Every time we'd get together it was always about the food, and I just went along with it. I kind of liked this character, this Chef, this Chef who was a murderer. It was great working on *When the World Was Green*. We started off working on the Devil as a subject, and it moved into this other territory somehow.

ROUDANÉ: Do you think that in some of your more recent plays, especially *When the World Was Green*, that you might be bestowing upon your characters a slight sense of hope, or that there may be some hint of a reconnection?

SHEPARD: I don't know, but I don't think you can make it general like that. Each play is so different that you try to be obliged to the material, what's there in the play, and not put anything on it. I think hope and hopelessness are intimately connected, and I don't believe in one or the other. In a way I prefer hopelessness to hope. I think there's more hope in hopelessness.

ROUDANÉ: A number of American playwrights see themselves, despite the carnage on their stages, as moral optimists. That it's too late for a John Proctor in *The Crucible* or Jessie Cates in *'night, Mother* doesn't mean the audience can't be shocked into some form of better awareness about the self and the other, and the culture at large. Do you ever consider yourself to be a moral optimist?

SHEPARD: I don't see myself in any particular light with that; I don't take any sides in that issue. Look at the violence in Shakespeare and, to me, Shakespeare is beyond morality, if you know what I mean. He's not taking sides, he's not interested in morality. What he is interested in is something eternal. He's interested in the gods. He's interested in the forces, the powers at work that cause all of this stuff, and how it flows through human beings, and how human beings behave in ways that they are not even conscious of, or if they become conscious of them, it's still beyond their control. Look at *King Lear*: "Let it not be madness." It *is* madness! There's no way you're going to get out of it. You can't get out of it. You're going to go *crazy*. And that to me is much much closer to the honesty of it than pretending to be on one side or the other of a morality that you don't even really believe in. As much as you can talk yourself into doing "the right thing" as opposed to "the wrong thing," it doesn't make any difference, because it's going to *happen, it's going to go down*, you know? These forces are going to go down, and for us to believe that we're somehow in the position that we individually can manipulate the forces is insanity. At the very best, I think that all we can hope for is to see that these forces are in action, and that we're being pushed and pulled and turned in one way or another and how we ride these waves. The great thing about the Greeks is that they had a god for everything. If the wind shifted, there was a god; if thunder struck, there was a god. Everything could be explained and annotated in certain kinds of ways. It must have been a fabulous culture. I mean, you could say the gods did this, and Zeus is over here causing this thing, and Athena is pissed off over here and, of course, you never know, right now, whether or not in our own contemporary notions of morality, we look at the Greek gods as being silly and illusionary. We have no idea what the Greeks' relationship was to these different cosmic powers. We as contemporary American human beings have no notion whatsoever what their real relationship was to the forces and the powers that were going on. Simply because they named them for this, that, and the other is not, to the Greeks, superstitious so much, as really having an understanding of the forces in nature, the forces that are driving us. I think they were much better off! That cosmology came in handy. It was a great culture. But all these myths about a yearning to reconnect to some higher ritual where there was some "meaning" never really existed in American culture, except in the American Indian culture, which definitely had something akin to that. But the European culture didn't. Manifest Destiny? Manifest Destiny didn't come close to Athena or Odysseus. As Lee says in *True West*, "Built up? Wiped out is more like it. I don't even hardly recognize it." Maybe this is why I've always had a great interest in Indian culture. From what I understand of it, and I've gotten this from some of the Indians I've gotten to know, there was a real relationship between the forces of nature and the human condition. The Indians didn't see human beings as being separate from these various natural forces. They were also big believers in signs, like if the hawk flew on the left side and crossed that way it's going to be a bad day. Which way is the wind turning and stuff like that was very important. The Indians were listeners and in sympathetic relationship with their rituals, and all of their stories and mythologies, like the Hopi mythologies, are extraordinary. But they were put in that place because of a disaster and their purpose for living was intimately connected to the place where they were to step down at the end of that flood. It's biblical stuff and you begin to wonder how this all relates to us.

ROUDANÉ: You've long been involved with the cinema in various capacities, from *Zabriskie Point* [1970] to *Hamlet* [2000] – over thirty films and counting. Could you comment on your work in film? Has your work in Hollywood and in film helped you at all as a playwright?

SHEPARD: I'll tell you what it did do: it gave me a kind of perspective that was kind of surprising when I first started to do film because I didn't realize – and I don't know how anybody could foresee that before they stepped into doing movies – what a contrived situation it is. Everything's contrived: you're in this trailer out in the middle of a prairie getting make-up on and costumes and people are running around with walkie-talkies and putting lights up. It's a kind of controlled chaos, and everything seems conjured out of somewhere, and really intruding into the atmosphere that's there. It's really this strange kind of little circus world that goes on out in the middle of nowhere. And that part of it fascinates me because it's this contest between total fantasy and very much real life. For instance, with hiring extras from the village who come in; I mean some of them have never ever seen a movie, and you're hiring them with Hollywood casting agents. "Warren, sit over there!" That part of it really fascinates me – these extreme contrasts between the contrivance and the actual. And I think that actually plays an influence in some of my short stories, plays, and stuff like that, because you can't help but be shocked by it. We did this film in Mexico and shooting this film in Mexico reminded me of all this again.

ROUDANÉ: Mexico as place, as metaphor for the mind seems to play an important role in your dramas – I think of *La Turista*, *Seduced*, or *Eyes for Consuela*, for instance. What is it about Mexico – the air, the colors, the land, the culture, the history – that engages you?

SHEPARD: Mexico is what America should have been. Mexico still has heart, it still has extraordinary passion, it still has a sense of family and culture, of deep, deep roots. Some of it is awful – the poverty level, the oppression's awful, and stuff like that – but there are places you go in Mexico that just make you feel like a human being. The Indian culture is what I think does it for me. We just got back from Tulum. It really is paradise.

ROUDANÉ: Speaking of paradise, I recently read *Cruising Paradise*. I've read your earlier prose in *Motel Chronicles* and *Hawk Moon*, which I enjoyed, but I was in no way prepared for the imaginative leap you made in *Cruising Paradise*. Your prose was surprisingly textured in a way you don't always see in the stage language and, in a sense, it was as strong a writing as I've seen from you. How was it for you to write fiction as opposed to writing for the stage?

SHEPARD: Oh, thanks. I enjoyed writing that book. The strange thing about playwriting is that you reach certain points where you need to take a rest, and yet you can't completely rest. But the short story is a wonderful little side trip. You can go into a short story in such a way that it's not like writing a play but you can invest the same kind of force in them. I've always loved the form of the short story. It's very firm. It's such a wonderful form, and I like to keep working at it because I feel like I got such a long way to go. You read Chekhov's stuff and you go, "Goddamn, this guy's got volumes and volumes," and they're all amazing.

ROUDANÉ: This story "A Man's Man" in *Cruising Paradise* about the young man – you – unloading the stacks of hay was not only imagistically so vital, but it resonated for me because it brought me back to the time when I was a teenager unloading semis filled with heavy boxes in the warehouses in Chicago during the summer, and you never forget that heavy load.

SHEPARD: That kind of work never leaves you, does it? I don't do that kind of work anymore because, physically, you have to be fairly young. Those three-wire bales, I mean I'll never forget those suckers. They weighed like 150 pounds a piece, and you miss one of those things and you think, how am I going to do this all day long? Your whole body's scratched, your eyes are swollen, it's about 110 degrees! Yeah, that's in *Cruising Paradise*. Have you ever heard of Juan Rulfo, the Mexican novelist? He wrote a bunch of short stories called *The Burning Plain* that are some of the most extraordinary stories I have ever read. Oh, they're beyond belief. And he wrote a novel called *Pedro Paramo*, and he had a second novel that he didn't finish – he killed himself – that's just incredible. He has influenced me a lot.

ROUDANÉ: Do you see your work in prose helping you when you return to writing for the stage?

SHEPARD: It doesn't help with the language so much but with the material itself, the character's place, and the substance of that place, and what Frank O'Connor – one of my all-time favorite short-story writers – called the "glowing center of action." He said that the short story must have that "burning center or burning core of interest." Particularly in the short story, that "burning" or "glowing" has to be apparent right away, and it has to be substantial, and it has to emanate from this "core." It's a tremendous thing to try to go into that and do something with it. I have written a whole bunch of short stories that haven't gone anywhere, that don't have a "glowing center." But it takes you a while to realize it. In fact, I have another book that's due, and I only have a third of it finished. I kicked out a whole lot of stories that didn't belong.

ROUDANÉ: Do you ever work on more than one play at a time?

SHEPARD: I have, but now I've just got one. I finished that one I worked on for so long, *The Late Henry Moss*, and I do have another one that's now about forty-five pages, but I think it's one of those I'm going to set aside and come back to. One interesting thing with *Henry Moss*, having left it for so long, and then come back to it, it was like a new play. I remember Mark Twain saying that he did that intentionally; he'd write something and then set it aside and wouldn't look at it for a year or more, and then would come back. It is another approach to writing. When you're younger you're too ambitious to do that.

ROUDANÉ: You've mentioned before that you've had difficulties with ending your plays. After nearly four decades of writing, do you feel that you've finally gotten a handle on closing your dramas?

SHEPARD: I still hate endings. Beginnings are great because there's so much tension, mystery, anticipation, and build-up, and you can reveal so much material to draw an audience in. But endings are so weird because suddenly you're forced to cut things off. I mean why end all this great action? Because people in the theatre have to go home? So after all this tremendous emotional build-up, just to cut the action off seems crazy. All the action after all keeps going on.

ROUDANÉ: Speaking of endings, perhaps we could wrap up with a question about your latest work. Joseph Chaikin tells me that you've finished *Henry Moss*, which will open at the Magic Theatre in San Francisco in the fall.

SHEPARD: Yeah, right now it's titled *The Late Henry Moss*, which is actually a take-off of an Irish short story called "The Late Henry Conran" by Frank O'Connor. I've been working on it for the last ten years, off and on. I actually abandoned it at one point and then picked it back up again, a lot due to Joe, who read it again and thought that it would be worthwhile, and Joe actually did a workshop production of it. The play concerns another predicament between brothers and fathers and it's mainly the same material I've been working over for thirty years or something but for me it never gets old, although it may for some audiences. This one in particular deals with the father, who is dead in the play and comes back, who's revisiting the past. He's a ghost – which has always fascinated me. Do you know the work of [John Millington]

Synge, the Irish playwright? He uses corpses a lot in his plays. And the corpse is present in the play and the corpse comes alive. I don't know, I find that fascinating, and this features in *The Late Henry Moss*. We start rehearsals October 3 and probably won't get it running to mid to late November, and then we can only run it up to Christmas, so it's a short run. We may subsequently do it in New York, I don't know.

4

JOSEPH CHAIKIN

A note on Sam Shepard

I met Sam Shepard at dinner in 1964 when he was around 19 years old. There were three of us: Sam, me and the director John Stix, who thought the two of us ought to meet.* Then Sam and I walked from the Upper West Side all the way down to the East Village. For eighty blocks we walked and talked. This was one year after the beginning of the Open Theatre. We both felt right away that we would be friends and colleagues and he sometimes visited the rehearsals of the Open Theatre where his friend Joyce Aaron was a member.

During the period of the Open Theatre he also co-authored the screenplay of Michelangelo Antonioni's *Zabriskie Point*, which featured a number of Open Theatre actors. And earlier he helped with the screenplay of Robert Frank's film of *Me and My Brother*, in which I played a leading role.

I asked him if he would write a small scene for the piece called *Nightwalk*, the last production of the Open Theatre. He sent material to us which became part of *Nightwalk* in 1973.

Then Sam and I corresponded in order to work together on a new play but we didn't know what to work on. Then we found a subject – reincarnation. We thought about the Sufis, Buddha, and others who thought about being reborn. It was a good idea and it became the play *Tongues*. Then later, we worked on *Savage/Love*, a play on the themes of romantic love.

In early 1985, Sam and I began work on a story about an angel. We began the work at the American Repertory Theatre at Harvard and we stopped because of other theatre commitments. Later we returned to it after my stroke and the writing of *The War in Heaven* became part of my recovery. Our most recent collaboration is *When the World Was Green*. We wanted to create a fable or story, which I would direct, about the endless procession of wars over the centuries. We began with several of what we called Vengeance Monologues and as we workshopped them over many months,

---

* Thanks to Bill Coco for his assistance in the preparation of this note.

they developed into a dialogue play about a criminal old man and a young woman journalist who visits him in jail.

Sam is an artist. His mind has extraordinary imagination. Sam is never sure what he will do next. But I know he will write another play, and another and another.

New York City
Fall 2001

5

MARC ROBINSON

Joseph Chaikin and Sam Shepard in collaboration

"I'm all these words, all these strangers ..."
SAMUEL BECKETT, *The Unnamable*

The performer's voice is shallow, unable to save the energy needed to qualify sentences after they have been spoken. Each utterance sounds ultimate, even when the words themselves are tempered by his humor or reasonableness, or by his obvious exhaustion after finishing a line. An egotistical actor would indicate triumph over his condition; a maudlin one, shame. Here, the man's voice may reach the limits of his language and then withdraw, but his face continues speaking – of the desire to speak with more precision, and of the knowledge that even if he succeeds, he won't shake his compulsion for making sentences.

There are in fact few sentences in his text, *The War in Heaven*, an enthralling collaboration between Sam Shepard and its performer, Joseph Chaikin, begun in February 1984 but not completed until after a stroke in May left Chaikin aphasic. By the time they resumed work, Chaikin had recovered some of his ability to speak; but as a writer he was limited by a severely depleted vocabulary, and as an actor by his inability to memorize. His character, an angel who "died/the day [he] was born," crashing to earth and "here/by mistake,"[1] testifies about his condition in abrupt phrases, many of which shatter in performance as Chaikin works to sustain his interpretation. The shivered words mark the turns in a second, shadow narrative that transforms the angel's story of his exile from heaven into a parable of memory and language – Chaikin's own exile from the Eden where everything has its name and speech grants life. Chaikin and Shepard dramatize two interdependent losses of faith – one in what the angel calls "a lawful order ... that was clear to me" (139); the other – more painful – in the survival of a language strong enough to depict and then protest such a loss.

The action of *The War in Heaven* is brief and straightforward, and its style, tailored to Chaikin's abilities, is plain. Sitting alone and motionless, the angel recalls images from a once secure and purposeful life; meditates on love, death, and the fate of the soul; and, in telegraphic bursts of complaint, implores his listeners to relieve his suffering by sending him home. But neither form nor content is as memorable as the sight of Chaikin striving to give them life in performance. As a text, *The War in Heaven* conceals too well a vulnerability and anxiety revealed only in the theatre. The ease with which a reader moves through the play irons out its emotional texture; published phrases retain little of the interesting difficulty that accompanied their composition. The same absence of tension weakens radio broadcasts of the play (the medium for which it was conceived): dead air engulfs each line; audiences can't see Chaikin resisting or speaking through the silence.[2]

But as Chaikin returns to his text to reanimate it on stage, this impression changes. A seemingly banal line, when preceded by a gasp and punctuated by an expectant stare, sounds like a victory for ordinariness over the style his infirmity imposes on him. "Music is great," the angel says at one point (155); and the sentence is unexpectedly convincing, even luminous, simply because it *is* a sentence, arriving after we have seen Chaikin try to assemble others. Passages that are uncomfortably frank on the page – an inventory of the modes and benefits of sexual coupling – refer in performance less to their subject matter than to the futility and unpredictable consequences of any intimate act of speech, even that of less afflicted speakers. Phrase after phrase merely arranges bodies in proximity to one another and charts their fumbling toward communion. Occasionally both actor and character win release: the angel utters an obscenity, and Chaikin's face floods with a look of surprise mixed with child-like defiance, as if in pressing against one obstacle to clear speaking he had burst a valve somewhere else, and now can't control the flow of candor.

Of course candor and spontaneity are relative terms for Chaikin, for whom even a line scripted and rehearsed in advance sounds uncertain when he says it. Throughout *The War in Heaven* Chaikin performs on the brink of error: his script lies before him on a small table – he has never recovered the skill of memorization – and between passages of difficult speaking Chaikin abruptly turns business-like as he looks down, turns the page, and scans the lines to come. The page-turning sets a stately pace underneath Chaikin's performance: it serves as a kind of continuo to his arrhythmic speech. He shifts his attention frequently between the script and his audience – only a few lines are printed on each page – and in each case the change is sharp and complete, like the undisguised transitions that Brecht asked from his actors when they prepared to sing. "I'll perish," the angel says at one point (141), but before his emotion can soften or lose credibility Chaikin switches it off with a look at his script. Suffering aspires to the restraint of rhetoric.

Indeed, sitting at his table he looks like a witness giving a deposition, emerging periodically from the narrative he is reliving to check his accuracy and, perhaps, assess his effectiveness. Once again, Brecht provides a model, here with the "Street Scene," yet unlike that bystander Chaikin doesn't sound confident in his account, nor sure that the means even exist for making a fuller version of it. (He also, in an implicit challenge to Brecht, shows the pain of self-demonstration, of never being spontaneous.) Memory itself is on trial: Chaikin's prepared speech, unlike other testimony, lacks the aura of authority; instead it admits its imperfection at every turn. The moments when Chaikin seems about to make a mistake are among the production's sharpest – not because they are alarming or grotesque, as are, say, moments when a dancer falls, but rather because they recreate Chaikin's original fall into speechlessness. Its suddenness and severity, along with its victim's panic, is for an instant made palpable; just as shocking is the grace with which he recovers. Disaster is averted as Chaikin leaps over silence lasting longer than he may have intended, or respaces syllables which collided the first time he pronounced them, or stops himself from omitting even an insignificant word. On such occasions, the writer appears alongside the actor and his character, guiding these other selves back toward the moment when their anxieties about language were first faced and resolved.

In the combat between Chaikin and a language he no longer fully recognizes – or between Chaikin-the-writer, already released from that battle and with the finished script to show for it, and Chaikin-the-actor, now sent in to claim those words for himself – *The War in Heaven* becomes something more than just a stirring depiction of one man's struggle; more, too, than a play whose value could be seen as primarily therapeutic for its performer and, as such, a mere curiosity on the margins of both Chaikin's and Shepard's careers. Rather, during the twenty minutes it takes Chaikin to perform the text, theatre returns to first things – not simply to language unburdened by plot, nor to the actor undisguised by character, not even to the actor's voice, made prominent by the prohibition on gesture, nor to the silence it ruptures, something given such generous space in *The War in Heaven* that it seems like a substance. Chaikin goes deeper, directing attention to the silence before silence, when the absence of speech hasn't yet settled into a shaped pause or controlled rest. There, the mute actor is revealed in turmoil, despite his outward calm, readying himself to speak or suffering the disappointment at not speaking fully, still in a state of expectation and contending with what Freud, in his study of aphasia, calls "an abundance of speech impulses."[3]

Such empty spaces aren't scheduled to escalate suspense or deepen emotion, nor do they mock Chaikin's difficulty in translating writing into speech. Instead, they are arenas for work, where Chaikin can decode and silently rehearse individual words. They also invite him to shore up gains made toward clarity and to muster strength for the next utterance, as he refuses to allow more definitive silences. We are witness to the mesmerizing spectacle of an actor working to enter, and repeatedly to reenter, his role – to engage his text, then stay its course. The play is busiest in these seemingly idle periods. Here one can sense Chaikin's fear of losing his place, his frustration at knowing that there are words more suited to his purposes than those he can say, and finally his need to resist both fear and frustration if he is to say anything at all. When speech does return, it sounds anticlimactic: words are an always disappointing reduction of the activity that occupies him when language is inaccessible.

A delay that for Chaikin is an unwelcome fact of life can be seen as an exaggeration of the seconds just preceding every actor's speech, alive with potential and as yet undiminished by a choice of style. It also matches the related silences at the scene of writing, in which a writer waits before finally locating an elusive word and rejecting its many attractive synonyms. For the writer, too, choice brings regret: there are always other ways to write a sentence, ideal phrasings forever beyond one's reach. "Fail again. Fail better." Beckett's undaunted speakers (this one from *Worstward Ho*) are an inevitable point of reference for *The War in Heaven*. Like Chaikin, they deflect their own discoveries of language's inadequacy and become eloquent in the only form available to them – "worsening words," as Beckett puts it elsewhere in *Worstward Ho*, "leastening words."[4] Several critics have linked Chaikin's post-stroke performances to the Mouth in *Not I* and to Lucky's "divine aphasia"; in recent years, Chaikin himself has acknowledged the affinity by reviving his stage adaptation of *Texts for Nothing* (first produced in 1981) and by giving public readings of a 1988 poem Beckett dedicated to Chaikin in its English translation, "what is the word," its prosody seeming to follow Chaikin's breathing patterns; its unanswered, unanswerable title-question his own.[5] Yet neither Beckett's language nor the silence whose greater strength it confirms is as pertinent to Chaikin's art as the period between them – after a character is compelled to talk, but before the sound of his voice disappoints him – a place Beckett names in *Texts for Nothing* as "a road . . . between two parting dreams" and again in *The Unnamable*: "Gaps, there have always been gaps, it's the voice stopping, it's the voice failing to carry me."[6]

Aphasia maps such a gap precisely, keeping Chaikin suspended between words and their meanings. In *The War in Heaven*, the angel describes getting lost on a mission and finding himself stuck "in between" his origin and destination – a place to which he is condemned indefinitely and from which he speaks to us now. "Every second I'm here/I'm weakening" (140). This condition, and the intermediate space in which he suffers it, are matched in formal terms whenever Chaikin delivers a key sentence which recurs throughout the text: "Take me back," it reads, but its initial unambiguousness is complicated in performance, as Chaikin sets his jaw, squints, and singles out a spectator to address in a tone heard nowhere else in the production – sharp, impatient, raw. There's nothing generalized about his injunction; unable to get God's attention, the angel buttonholes one of us instead. Yet the emotion powering the first word seems to exhaust the resources needed for the next two. Silence follows "Take" like a syntactical emblem of the gulf separating the angel from heaven and Chaikin from his language. As it widens before he speaks again, both actor and character seem to fear the loss of dignity in such a plea and acknowledge the hopelessness of their condition – a realization Chaikin confirms only in the hoarse tone and faster pace for the rest of the sentence.

The "in between" has long been favored territory for Chaikin and Shepard, in their own work and in collaboration. *Tongues* alludes to a man "born in the middle of a story . . . in the middle of a people"; another voice listens to the dead "between the space I'm leaving and the space I'm joining . . . between the shape I'm leaving and the one I'm becoming."[7] Writing of the Open Theatre, the company he founded in 1963 and ran until it closed in 1973, Chaikin praises the actor who is "between a place he knew and moving to where he doesn't know" and the "mysterious encounter" possible in performance, "caused neither by the actors nor by the audience, but by the silence between them."[8] The Open Theatre's *Serpent* addresses the difficulty of what its chorus calls being "in the middle" after the Fall causes "separation."[9] Shepard's own plays offer concrete images for these abstractions. In *La Turista*, Kent describes his life as a jumping between rooftops. Waco, in *The Mad Dog Blues*, feels caught "between livin' and dyin'." Even Dude, the musician-protagonist in *Melodrama Play*, describes his identity crisis in similar terms: gesturing to their posters, he says he's "stuck in the middle" between Bob Dylan and Robert Goulet. Closest to Chaikin may be a description of Weston's father from *Curse of the Starving Class*. "Right in the midst of things," says his son, "he lived apart."[10]

The War in Heaven is an index to Chaikin's and Shepard's art in other ways as well. On stage, Chaikin, like a palimpsest, shows traces of roles he played earlier in his career – not just the speaker of *Tongues*, hoping to "find [his] voice," and of *Texts for Nothing*, but also Woyzeck in his own struggle toward speech, the blank slate of Galy Gay's character, and of course Hamm, paralyzed and skeptical, his talk marking time. Moreover, Chaikin returns us to the principles underlying both his own and Shepard's theatre, if only to test our faith in them. Shepard's ideal of vaulting speech and self-generating narrative; Chaikin's early beliefs about the actor's presence and voice, his or her obligations to a character, and the role of the audience – these must adjust to boundaries set by aphasia, and in the process become more rigorous.

The same is true for the ideal of collaboration itself. As both subject and method, collaboration has preoccupied Chaikin and Shepard, separately and together, for years. At the Open Theatre, as he experimented with trust and interdependence among the members of the ensemble, Chaikin seemed to promote similar ideal arrangements outside the theatre. Shepard credits Chaikin for teaching him to expand the relationship between the actor and the audience in his own work. He is also preoccupied by threats to more general linkages – the "thread in culture," as he put it in an interview, "the connecting river" of generations.[11] The most personal version of the space "in between" – and least examined until the recent collaborations – is that separating Shepard and Chaikin themselves. *The War in Heaven* bridges that gap, giving Chaikin access to more language, but it also envisions what happens when the bond loosens and Chaikin is left alone to fill the silence.

II

The significant encounters in Chaikin and Shepard's four-decade-long relationship are well known and susceptible to myth-making. Shepard started going to meetings at the Open Theatre in 1964, invited by his then-girlfriend Joyce Aaron, a member of the company. Under Chaikin's guidance, the Theatre was expanding the actor's affective range, dismantling traditional hierarchies in theatrical collaboration, and, in a series of landmark works, posing the most persuasive challenge to the then-dominant representational tradition in American theatre. By his own account, Shepard was more on-looker than participant in these efforts, but he did contribute material to the workshops for two collectively created productions. For *Terminal* (1969), he wrote three speeches, none of which were included in the final text written by Susan Yankowitz. (Shepard's speeches are published in his *Hawk Moon*.) After moving to London in 1971 he sent Chaikin texts for *Nightwalk* (1973), the final Open Theatre production; one passage, about "me on [a] ship . . . staring out to myself in [a] house," anticipates images of self-division in his later work.[12] During these years, the collaborative energies flowed both ways: Open Theatre actors performed in Shepard's own work, most notably in *Icarus's Mother* (1965). One of those actors, Ralph Lee, also designed *The Mad Dog Blues* (1971) at Theatre Genesis. An Open

Theatre director, Sydney Schubert Walter, staged the premiere of *Fourteen Hundred Thousand* (1966). Chaikin himself acted in a later television production of the same play. The Theatre also supported Shepard's earliest work in screenwriting – Chaikin and other company members appeared in Robert Frank's *Me and My Brother* (1968); the entire ensemble appeared together in one scene in Michelangelo Antonioni's *Zabriskie Point* (1970).

After the demise of the Open Theatre in 1973, Shepard wandered the periphery of Chaikin's new group, the Winter Project, but the pair didn't work closely together again until 1978, when they created two works of music-theatre, *Tongues* and *Savage/Love*, both performed by Chaikin, with Shepard accompanying him on percussion in early performances. (A year earlier, Shepard had adapted Chaikin's approach to collective creation and improvisation to his own purposes, producing *Inacoma*, a music-theatre piece inspired by the case of Karen Ann Quinlan.) In 1991, seven years after the original broadcast of *The War in Heaven*, they met to revise the text for a stage production. In 1996, the pair co-wrote *When the World Was Green* (the one collaboration in which Chaikin did not act) for Atlanta's Seven Stages Theatre; it was remounted for the Signature Theatre Company's 1996–97 retrospective of Shepard's work, a season in which Chaikin also staged a new production of Shepard's 1965 play *Chicago*. Most recently, in 2001, Chaikin directed the New York premiere of Shepard's *The Late Henry Moss*.

A second history of the two men's relationship shadows this narrative. It is harder to chronicle, for it lacks the obvious denouements of productions and publications, but it is the context for such work, where Chaikin and Shepard maintain the flexibility of collaboration itself. In this broader view, Chaikin and Shepard win and then direct one another's attention with many unremarkable exchanges – of articles, photographs, recordings ("Did you receive the Bach piano–violin sonatas?" Chaikin writes, "Did you enjoy them?"), and especially books and recommendations of books – de Beauvoir, Kierkegaard, Vallejo, Bettelheim's *The Informed Heart*, a poem by James Dickey, and an unnamed book, probably by Kafka, in which Shepard reads only the parts Chaikin has underlined. (Here even attention is collaborative.) In many of these transactions, the two artists cultivate one another's tastes and enthusiasms without regard for their eventual translation into a play. In turn, the accumulation of offerings, and the shared language they constitute, give stability to a professional intimacy derived as much from error, uncertainty, and misunderstanding as from the pleasures of shared creativity.

Shepard and Chaikin's letters, edited by Barry Daniels, track this hesitant progress.[13] From his earliest visits to the Open Theatre, Shepard worried about his place, fearful that the wayward, unsocialized imagination of the solitary writer would be harnessed by an ensemble seeking a common language. Later, when Shepard mailed in texts for Winter Project productions, he again found himself anxious, this time less about relinquishing control than about his ability to share the obsessions of a group he hadn't joined. Shepard's worries over his place became literal in the months they worked on *Tongues* and *Savage/Love*. The logistics of bringing the two artists together in one city long enough to complete a project is a leitmotif of their correspondence, as Chaikin resists leaving home and Shepard, averse to New York, spends long stretches on the West Coast, out of the country, or in perpetual transit as a film actor. Even when they do meet, they keep changing locations – beach, restaurant, hotel – as if afraid that familiar scenery will cause complacent work.

In these periods of willed nomadism, or unavoidable detachment, letters sustain the relationship. In fact, to a large extent correspondence is the medium of their collaboration. In the making of *Tongues* and *Savage/Love*, letters enabled the exchange of research, initial discussions about structure and substance, and later revision of one another's material. Set against this record, the sporadic and brief face-to-face meetings, while rich in invention themselves, nonetheless seem like the denouement of a much longer, freer, and more various process of discovery. To a pair of artists sensitive to how the environment conditions the imagination (and determined to control that relationship), correspondence itself establishes an ideal zone for work – unpopulated, uncontaminated by uses other than their own, resistant to distraction. This kind of collaboration depends for its success on each partner's solitude.

Even more crucial is the delay before the writer receives a response. Each letter borders a silence filled with second thoughts and anticipated reactions. Such purposeful waiting rarely occurred in the collaborative theatre-making Chaikin supervised at the Open Theatre, where the actors reacted to one another's suggestions quickly, nimbly, before reason could inhibit or prettify their actions. But Chaikin and Shepard may welcome delay – for in the time between when a letter is sent and answered they experience a version of the same condition they dramatize: it is another "in between" space, where they, like the characters in all four of their pieces, are severed from a listener, uncertain of their verbal reach, and acutely aware of the gulf they hope to cross.

Long before he had adapted his language to the aphasic delays in *The War in Heaven*, Shepard had paid tribute to this kind of segmented collaboration, or collaboration-in-separation, in his own work.

> KOSMO I've had a vision! . . .
> YAHOODI Sing it.
> KOSMO I can't. I can't get my head straight. I have to take a trip. I have to go somewhere else.

YAHOODI Me too.

KOSMO The city's gettin' me down. Too many tangents. It's no place to collaborate.

YAHOODI Maybe we could do it by mail. I'll go to the jungle and write you.

KOSMO Good idea. I'll go to San Francisco and do the same.[14]

More than geography frustrates the relationship between these two visionaries from *The Mad Dog Blues*. They are also unsteadied by their chronic loss of confidence in their imaginations. Even as they summon and set in motion various larger-than-life figures – Captain Kidd, Paul Bunyan, Jesse James – they doubt they can sustain the same high level of invention throughout the play. Moreover, they fear they lack the self-discipline to sort out and see to completion all the picaresque narratives they have initiated. Finally, as the play ends and the cast of characters under their direction wanders the stage, no longer supported by plot or even their inventors' interest, Kosmo and Yahoodi discover the depth of their incompatibility, something hitherto obscured by the exuberance of their playing.

Shepard's candor about the flaws in their pact, and more generally about the weakness of inspiration when faced with the demands of craft, derives from a broad distrust of all forms of romanticism: it's a commonplace of Shepard criticism that his theatre exalts only to explode American symbols, shared narratives, and, especially, the articles of faith that bind together families, couples, and even the many personae latent within a single character. The anti-idealism Shepard shines on public and private stages is especially unforgiving when directed at theatre itself. Not just at any theatre: to a spectator schooled by the Open Theatre or fresh from *The Presence of the Actor*, Chaikin's eloquent 1972 catechism, Shepard's plays may seem private commentaries on their lessons.

One such response, his adapting of Chaikin's so-called transformation exercises, is well documented. As several critics have argued, the playwright's shapeshifting characters may owe their freedom from transitions (and the over-explicit psychology such transitions indulge) to the director's technique, illustrated by Open Theatre actors changing personae in performance without regard for credibility.[15] But Shepard also engages Chaikin in other, less acknowledged ways. *The Mad Dog Blues* is only one of many early plays in which he seems to be cross-examining his collaborator, testing workshop hypotheses about ensemble loyalty, improvisation, and the freedom of the imagination in the rougher arena of his characters' lives, then forcing a closer look at the consequences. These early plays seem even more skeptical after one sees *The War in Heaven*. Admirers of Chaikin's performance may find that the impasse he reaches had been anticipated by Shepard in many plays where vibrant language and surprising action conceal a deeper uncertainty.

Readers of Shepard tend to remember best a protagonist's "arias" (as Patti Smith was the first to call them) and the lyrical ambitions they inspire in the other characters, but equally important are the sinkholes that open up between them when inspiration flags. Time and again, Shepard's characters will launch an improvisation only to see it collapse before it lifts them beyond their circumstances. Many of their verbal games, structured like Open Theatre exercises, promise to tighten relationships among the speakers. They do so, but inevitably they end, and then the security they conferred turns doubtful. Characters are alone once more, even when together, as the promise of collaboration vanishes. Shepard lingers in the aftermath, making his characters wait before they start a new conversation, for as the later plays with Chaikin make explicit, his brand of speech is meant to be heard in counterpoint to his silences. These reassert the power of a character's self-consciousness, unrelieved by any act of impersonation, and of the reality from which they hoped their talk would free them.

Assuming that *Cowboys #2* is a fair facsimile of the lost *Cowboys*, Shepard's first play, the young writer was wise to the frustrations of artistic exchange long before he had initiated his own collaborations, and critical of the deceptions of his style even as he was learning its range. The youthful high spirits of the play's two protagonists conceal the awkwardness and ultimate failure of their attempt to synchronize their separate fantasies of the Old West. Stu and Chet become "Mel" and "Clem," bowlegged old-timers dropping the ends of gerunds as they hobble around the stage complaining about the weather and fearing an Apache ambush. At the start, they pick up one another's cues easily, without needing to confer first on the direction of their impersonations. But after only a few moments they diverge. "Hey! Come back!" says Stu, in his own voice, as Chet gets carried away dancing and whistling. Stu falls behind again when Chet, as Clem, nags him to come up with a poetic simile for the clouds. "Would you give me a chance," Stu says, dropping his role again. "I haven't even thought of it yet."[16]

As they tinker with their partnership, they offer a useful corrective to the mythology of collaboration. Their private theatre succeeds only if they check one another's impulses as often as they cue them, and keep in mind the larger premises of their improvisation even as they respond to immediate stimuli. Moreover, the work of readjustment is ongoing. *Cowboys #2* is a work of stops and starts, as one character must be persuaded to move on after his partner had changed the subject, or both characters exhaust the possibilities of one "scene" and, after pausing to stare at one another expectantly, reorient themselves. At the end, after Stu is "shot" by the "Indians," he remains unresponsive long after this particular plot has run its course. A play that, at its opening, seemed designed to celebrate imaginative kinship and showcase the range of its inventions, ends by confirming each player's alienation – from an imagined world, whose falseness grows undeniable as the lights brighten and the real-world noise of car horns fills the barren stage, and finally from each other.

Shepard deepened his critique in the years ahead. In *Icarus's Mother*, as Pat struggles to disengage from her overattentive friends, fellowship is always coerced; independent thinking is always a threat. To the musician at the center of *Melodrama Play*, other characters appear less as sympathetic colleagues than as potential threats to his originality. Along with those in *Suicide in B-Flat* and *The Tooth of Crime*, Shepard's artist-protagonists resist influence even as they acknowledge, reluctantly, their dependence on it. At no moment in their playing are they able to forget the principles they compromise when they agree to work with others. As if sobered by the fate of these characters, Shepard offered a more modest and thus more viable image for collaboration in *La Turista*. The Boy tells of a father and son who walk toward each other on a long road, stop to share stories and sing a song, and then separate, each returning the way the other came. The meeting's success depends on the partners' willingness to forgo intimacy.

Cowboy Mouth (1971) and *Action* (1975) dissect intimacy with ruthless precision. Like the later works with Chaikin, *Cowboy Mouth* reflects the circumstances of its creation. According to legend, Shepard and Patti Smith, with whom he both wrote and, on one occasion, performed the play, began work by sitting across from each other, pushing a portable typewriter back and forth on the table between them, as each writer's inspiration struck and faltered. (This ritualized, even erotic mode of writing together, would be cited in a more vicious context in *True West*, as Austin and Lee negotiate a relationship using their own typewriter.) The rhythm of Shepard and Smith's collaboration, controlled by the exchange of the typewriter, is picked up in their play, as each character runs up against the limits of his or her own imagination and seeks a partner's help. In one sequence, they tell each other stories from their childhood – about Slim damming a river, Cavale acting in a grade-school *Ugly Duckling* – then, exhausting that vein, transform into a coyote and a crow, hungry predator chasing his prey, until that game also peters out. "Now what'll we do?" asks Slim, to which Cavale can only say, "I don't know."[17]

Her confession unseals their utopia, opening it to a sudden blast of real-world anxieties, before Slim manages to resecure the stage with another game: "We could call back the lobster man just for laughs" (159). Variations on this rupture recur throughout *Cowboy Mouth*. In fact, the play opens on a note of defeat: Slim sings a few lines of Patti Smith's "You Cheated, You Lied," only to break off abruptly into self-ridicule: "Fuck it," he says, less to dismiss his efforts than to mock the hope of transcendence motivating them (148). Later, when Slim and Cavale imagine themselves out stealing Cavale's dream pair of shoes – fancy tap-dance shoes, "red, with pretty ribbons" – they play easily, successfully, but nonetheless reach the same end. At the peak of their fantasy, Slim produces a "beat-to-shit pair of high-topped sneakers" (151). Reality has trumped invention.

It does so again, definitively, in *Action*, a play whose conclusions prepare the way for the portraits of solitude in the Chaikin collaborations. Its characters surrender to centrifugal force, scattering to the margins of their stage-world, where they are marooned on their own self-interest. The action, such as it is, is occasioned by a communal ritual – a Christmas dinner – and the four characters gesture toward various other allegiances throughout the play. The women pair off to hang laundry; the men tap-dance together and pretend to be bears; all four gather around a mysterious book, taking turns reading aloud as if it were a Bible. But none of these relationships survives the characters' eventual indifference or the appeal of other activities. The ensemble rearranges itself in numerous combinations but changes neither the overall composition of its world, nor the low-grade emotional temperature limiting their activity. In this world of false starts and dashed expectations, *Action* shifts attention to the self-doubt preceding an attempt at kinship, and to the helplessness following its inevitable refusal or severance. Shepard paces his play according to this awkward advance and retreat, and, as in other works, leaves intact the empty, introspective spaces between the movements, in which we may imagine the need which compels the characters to pledge themselves to one another, experiment with personalities they hope will win them a place in the group, and tell stories to manufacture intimacy with a listener.

The benefits of such companionship have always been assumed rather than argued, as Jeep discovers when he asks "What's a community?" and no one can answer him. "A sense of – ," Lupe says. "A sense um – ." Shooter tries next: "Oh uh – ." Lupe concludes: "It doesn't need words."[18] But it does, for it's only with language that these individuals evolve into citizens of a kind, supported by something larger than themselves by virtue of their ability to describe it. Speech alone establishes kinship: "We hear each other ... We know each other's voice," says Jeep, "We're not completely stranded ..." (184). Such is the ideal, but Shepard doubts its viability throughout *Action*. When Shooter launches into his own description of this community – "I can picture it ... a whole house is being built!" – his listeners don't join in the fantasy, as characters do elsewhere in Shepard, but instead cut him off. "Keep it to yourself," says Lupe (184). And so he must, locked within his own language, imagination, and even stage space. He anticipates

Jeep's own isolation, acknowledged obliquely when he speaks of feeling "dismissed" – from the group, perhaps, but also from his own history and even from consciousness, the means by which he engages the present. "Gone," he says, nostalgic for a world he was never allowed to join in the first place (188).

Once more, Shooter, the play's ignored visionary, finds the appropriate image for a condition he shares with all four characters. He speaks of standing in the snow at night, his face pressed up against the windows of a cozy, candlelit house, expecting a warm welcome when he finally comes inside, only to discover that "it's not like how you expected" and that he must "hunt for a way of being with everyone." As David Savran stresses, this shift isn't just territorial: it's also from exterior silence to an interior where (as Shooter puts it) "everyone [is] using a language."[19] "It's a shock," Shooter continues, for his own language, surfacing with difficulty, can't compete. It seems incurably private, derived from some other, unshared lexicon, or keyed to a context unknown to his listeners. His only recourse: "You act yourself out" (178).

Earlier in the play, and in response to a different subject, Jeep had said to Shooter, "Don't act it out!" (171). He was irritated by Shooter's need for attention, of course, but he also sounded like someone unable, or by now unwilling, to believe in art's consolations. Yet where would he and the others be without their stories, impersonations, dances, and recitations? After commands such as Jeep's, Shepard's theatre stops short, as it does in his other plays whenever a character can't keep the dialogue going. In these ellipses, their theatrical landscape no longer transforms as it does when the four characters speculate about the future, reminisce about an equally uncertain past, or imagine alternate worlds in which they might flourish. Instead, the stage hems them into the present tense, where they are reconciled to and reduced by their own dull presence. The ideal which Chaikin envisioned in *The Presence of the Actor* has become a burden.

III

The art derived from Chaikin's aphasia pushes forward from what Shepard, in *Action*, had treated as a dead-end. Like Jeep, the Chaikin who performs *The War in Heaven* scorns the pretense of "acting it out." Like Shooter, he speaks from under the weight of silence, his words showing the strain to be heard, as well as his fear that even if they are, they won't be understood. Along with both characters, Chaikin feels "dismissed" – an exile from communities convened and maintained by speech, and from his own earlier self, once whole, with a history that fell away when he lost the language to think about it. He, too, could be "spying on his body," as Shooter describes the sensation of not recognizing oneself in the bathtub, a body that eventually "killed him" (182). Indeed, Chaikin's angel echoes this when he says "I'm hovering / above myself / looking / for a way / back in" (144). Finally, he heeds Lupe's command to "keep it to yourself" with a thoroughness and pathos beyond anything seen in *Action*.

Alongside Shepard's characters, Chaikin may seem literal-minded – presenting a neurological version of a condition Shepard envisioned as metaphysical – but he doesn't make it any less allusive. Far from it: unable to step outside his condition by speaking of it, as the characters in *Action* do, Chaikin conducts a self-exposure more primitive and thus more punishing than conventions of acting (and character-drawing) usually allow. He doesn't present a mere portrait of aphasia but something changeable and thus harder to reproduce – an endless cycle of loss and retrieval and loss again. Like any play, *The War in Heaven* dissolves as we hear it; yet here its passage becomes a narrative superseding all others, made suspenseful by the steadiness with which Chaikin resists it. Unlike most actors, who draw energy from the momentum of their performance, Chaikin seems to push back against his own. The end of each minute leaves him wishing for more time to find and perfect his words, and confirms how much more remains to be said. Here is a vision of presence and the present-tense even more stringent than in *Action*: Chaikin is trapped in the present, denied access to the language needed to summon his past, unable to retain most of the words he does learn. But he also wishes the present to last indefinitely, or at least until he's finished the long process of recognizing and naming everything he experiences. The future, with its promise of further loss, always arrives before he's ready.

The neurologist most associated with aphasia, A. R. Luria, elaborates on this antagonistic relationship with time in his extraordinary book, *The Man with a Shattered World* (1972). Or rather, his subject does, for much of the text is given over to the writings of Lev Zasetsky, who describes with excruciating precision his own case, including the challenge of writing about it – a continuous twenty-five-year struggle with a memory conspiring to erase what it records. Zasetsky's brain suffered an "insult" far more grievous than Chaikin's – during World War II, he was shot in the head; aphasia was only one of his many forms of brain damage – yet the very extremity of his experience with language illuminates Chaikin's own frustration, something easily minimized by the fact of Chaikin's improvement (if not full recovery) and the poise of the art it made possible. Like Chaikin, Zasetsky was always having to reset his curiosity to the slower pace of his comprehension, his mind inventing strategies to outwit his brain. In another variation on a life spent "in between," Zasetsky writes of learning to "detour around the gaps in my memory . . . the gaps between a word and its meaning."[20] In one section, he describes how he regained the ability to read after the injury:

> I read printed matter letter by letter. When I first started to read again, I often couldn't recognize a letter at first and had to run through the alphabet until I found it . . . Often after I've figured out the letters in a word, I forget the word itself and have to read every letter over again in order to understand it . . . Only after I read a word and understand it can I go on to the next word, and then the third. By the time I get to the third word I often forget what the first or sometimes even the second word meant. (69)

Writing meant a different kind of exertion. As an act requiring movement as well as thought, writing came easier than reading: there seemed to be a bodily memory of language that survived the damage to his brain. Yet he still had to trigger the act – only when he remembered the words could he write them – and when it came time to read in order to develop or simply enjoy his ideas, he suffered as much as he did reading someone else's prose. Moreover, he sometimes would forget a word before he reached his desk, so he began writing on scraps of paper – "clamp[ing] the words to the idea as much as I could" – and then later transferring them to a notebook, "regrouping the words and sentences, comparing them with others I'd seen in books" (79–80). Zasetsky divides himself in two, treating his own writing as found texts. No longer abstractions or mere signs, words become things, notes to be mastered by the body in lieu of the mind, arranged and rearranged like parts of a collage, in this form alone capable of withstanding the passage of time. It's as if he hopes that each piece of paper will seal a gap in his perforated memory.

This sensitivity to a word's material life is an extreme form of a trait shared with many other aphasics, including Chaikin, and has important consequences for the theatre he makes with Shepard. While aphasia comes in many forms – Roman Jakobson provided one useful taxonomy when he distinguished between "similarity" and "contiguity" disorders, the former affecting one's understanding of metaphor, the latter, one's understanding of metonymy – in most cases the aphasic resists abstractions.[21] Seen as a liability, this symptom is what one neurologist has called the aphasic's inability to "propositionize."[22] But seen as a virtue, it causes the aphasic to develop a passionate attachment to empirical reality. The aphasic unable to think metaphorically confines language to its context; words can't be understood apart from their specific uses. A well-known case-study describes a patient who couldn't say "no," despite repeated prodding, until finally he blurted out "No, no, I told you I can't say 'no!'"[23]

The opposite type of aphasic lacks the language to perceive any form of relationship: his or her vocabulary is stripped of conjunctions, prepositions, pronouns, and other connective tissue. Zasetsky writes of how he knows the words for "mother" and "daughter" but can neither understand the phrase "mother's daughter," nor distinguish it from "daughter's mother." Another aphasic is able to say the word for "oar" but not its intangible conjunctive homonym, "or." Chaikin's colleagues have described how the director himself is most challenged by such simple abstract terms as numbers.[24]

Chaikin's theatre with Shepard reflects this courtesy toward the concrete. Even before aphasia enforced it, their collaborations guided one's attention away from metaphysics, toward bodies and their unambiguous, secular reality. In *Tongues*, *Savage / Love*, *The War in Heaven*, and *When the World Was Green*, the carnal wins out over the spiritual before an actor says a word. Despite Shepard's description of *Tongues* as "a piece to do with the voice,"[25] it and the other collaborations are also about physical confinement, often Chaikin's own, as the actor is wedged in a narrow alcove in *Savage/Love*, kept in a chair and covered in a Mexican blanket in *Tongues* (a concession to Chaikin's weak heart), sitting at the table and, in some performances, strapped into a heavy white robe in *The War in Heaven*, pacing around a cell in *When the World Was Green*. The texts keep returning to the immobilized actor, especially at moments when his language threatens to turn vaporous. The discussion of sex in *The War in Heaven* is only the most explicit instance of the collaborators' ongoing examination of lives stripped of lyricism, unable to hide in allegory or even narrative, reduced in some cases to pure biological function. In *Tongues*, the speaker describes a hunger "that knows no bounds ... hunger eating the hunger" (309) – an extreme version of his continuous surrender to sensory and sensual appeals. A beautiful long passage earlier in the play, bearing Shepard's signature, lists the colors and textures of a room inhabited by a blind man: "the walls around you are green ... the night is absolutely black ... the light of [a] plane keeps passing slowly, blinking. Red and blue. Yellow and blue ... Your shirt is blue ... " (307–8). As the details accumulate, a character's psychology, even history, are edged aside, rendered ephemeral by the testimony of the senses. "The whole of my self. / Vanished," the speaker says in another section. "The whole of my body was left" (312).

The ignoble conclusion (and its flat tone) echo throughout *The War in Heaven* – "one day / dead / dead / and nothing else / just dead" (149); "sometimes God ... / sometimes nothing" (142) – and again, by implication, in *When the World Was Green*. In the latter play, hunger also rules its protagonist, a celebrated chef who describes in detail his favorite dishes, yet his nostalgia is hindered by his environment. As the all-too-present prison cell disciplines his memory, our way of seeing changes accordingly, as it does in all these collaborations. Theatre that forces recognition of an actor's presence ends by making us unusually aware of our own. Not just when Chaikin's angel asks us to "turn me loose" or "take me back": This theatre's attentions are both more general – during *The War in Heaven*, Chaikin makes us feel that we are summoning his language merely by being there to hear it – and more intimate, as in *Savage/Love*, which ends with Chaikin looking at his audience, now merged with his character's absent lover, and saying "You You You You."[26] The stage directions allow for an indefinite number of repeats: Chaikin won't sever his link to us – the only reliable one in a work which, like the other collaborations, is suffused with loneliness – and thus the play can't end.

Repetition becomes echolalia for the aphasic speaker – a deliberate, sometimes desperate attempt not to sink back into incomprehension the moment the voice rests. *The War in Heaven* seems to idle whenever Chaikin lingers over a phrase – "and more / and more / and more"; "so much / so much more / so much" ; "open / open" – but in fact these passages are among his most engaged. The words themselves express the desire to expand and deepen perception, as Chaikin dwells on – and in – each word, deeming it a complete statement in itself, varying its timbre as if to keep before him an insight and the world it clarifies longer than his memory allows. The repeated words are placeholders in his thinking, as well as spurs to a useful form of self-consciousness. The director who once encouraged "transformation" in the theatre now, as an actor, wants only to maintain his identity. Likewise, the playwright who once insisted that "the real quest of a writer is to penetrate into another world. A world behind the form" (as Shepard put it in a 1977 essay) returns to the here-and-now.[27] It is as if both were afraid of the answer to the question haunting *The Unnamable*: "Can that be called a life which vanishes when the subject is changed?"[28]

In these recurrent one- and two-word phrases Chaikin gives the lie to those who pity him as a "disintegrating actor" (in the words of one critic) and, no less forcefully, to those who praise him as heroic.[29] He is, rather, engaged in the work of reassembly, contending with the uncertainty of success. The note of humility on which his character ends *Tongues* captures his own attitude: "Today the tree bloomed without a word. / Tonight I'm learning its language" (318). Forced to postpone mastery, he rejuvenates all aspects of theatrical form, not just the simplest act of speaking but also the words themselves, along with narrative structure, rehearsal, and memorization, and even conventions of spectatorship. He also forces one to reexamine others' attempts at rejuvenation. Jonathan Kalb has suggested that Chaikin's performance – an extreme version of the actor's ideal of "as-if-for-the-first-time" – recalls, and realizes, Artaud's vision of the theatre. Indeed, one might point to a famous passage from "No More Masterpieces" – "Any word, once spoken, is dead and functions only at the moment of utterance" – as a summary of Chaikin's own supercharged relationship to language.[30] Yet it would be a mistake to ascribe to Chaikin Artaud's motives. Artaud envisions a "rhythmic repetition of syllables which [will] veil the precise sense of words [and thus] evoke multiple images in the brain."[31] While Chaikin can't help but share Artaud's experience of words as "spasms" or "movements,"[32] he moves toward, not away from, that "precise sense," burrowing into a word's meaning as he repeats it. In 1977, Chaikin implied such an approach in terms that now, after his stroke, have added urgency:

> Many mystical people I come across are rejecting language and saying, "We can't speak, we meditate the silence, we can make sounds together, we can do different kinds of trips together, but when it comes to speaking it destroys meaning." I don't think that way. I think it is for people ... who are agitated by the erosion of language to reconstruct it.[33]

He might have been reevaluating, or at least sharpening, his own, earlier beliefs: in *The Presence of the Actor* he borrows T. S. Eliot's image of a "raid on the inarticulate" as he urges actors to get beyond "the reporting of sounds we use for conversation" – in them "there is the same potential for articulation as there is over coffee and a danish" – and instead "use the voice, not to refer to a condition, but to enter it."[34] What Eileen Blumenthal calls Chaikin's "somatic" approach to acting is visible, or audible, in the keening laments in *The Serpent* and *Terminal*. The ideas motivating these sections are made explicit in the Open Theatre's *The Mutation Show* (1971), in which two wild, speechless figures – one based on Kaspar Hauser – lose their identity once they are named, and narrow their vision once they are taught to speak. "The noise," says the Kaspar in protest, "was me."[35]

But now that Chaikin himself has arrived at a Kaspar-like state (a comparison he himself made in a 1987 speech), a more nuanced view of the value of language is required.[36] Despite its simplifications and distortions, language nonetheless offers the means to engage what might otherwise be overwhelming, keeping at bay the fear of helplessness. Even mechanical speech recovers its value: in minds such as Chaikin's, the only words that don't drain away are those secured by habit, a force miraculously stronger than aphasia. Freud cites the case of an aphasic navy captain who could only remember the words connected to his profession: every experience or object now required a sailing analogy if it was to be acknowledged. Other patients whom Freud observed could sing a popular song or recite the days of the week – sequences of words drilled into them long ago and hard to dislodge – but fell silent when asked to repeat a single word of the lyrics or list the days in reverse order.[37] Chaikin's own history confirms this trend. Just before his stroke, he was memorizing lines from *King Lear* – he was to play the king (a character reduced to syllables himself) for the New York Shakespeare Festival; a friend remembers Chaikin reciting one of Lear's speeches as he was wheeled into the operating room – and he could still recite some of his lines in the early weeks of his recovery, when few other words were available to him.[38] The director who once lampooned automatic behavior – the superficial dinner-party scene in *The Mutation Show* is typical – is now grateful for his frozen script and for rehearsal. Habit isn't the "great deadener" Vladimir said it was; rather it's the only thing that restores his humanity – the feeling that the language is once again his own – and rescues him from the humiliation experienced in the presence of the unspeakable.

As it did with habit, aphasia may force Chaikin to revise his opinion of narrative as well. Much of his work with the Open Theatre welcomed interruptions, elisions, and reversals in narrative, or eschewed narrative altogether in favor of juxtaposed responses to a given theme. *The Serpent* dissects the Kennedy assassination and Adam and Eve's expulsion from Eden – isolating, reversing, and re-pacing the frames of the Zapruder footage; arresting the Fall at key moments to gauge the intensity of temptation. *Terminal* is even more episodic, presenting discrete portraits of dying with a minimum of explanatory comment. (Anything more linear would suggest a logic that the subject doesn't allow.) Yet this fractured vision, so desirable when the Open Theatre worked to break apart preconceptions and create more immediacy in performance, is redundant to the aphasic, contending with so many other severed connections. Even if Chaikin remains skeptical of narrative's assumptions about order, he nonetheless now hopes to follow and create other linear forms – a train of thought, a conversation, a sentence. Oliver Sacks, in his own discussion of Lev Zasetsky's brain damage, points out that the patient's all-consuming, identity-giving ambition was to recover the means of forming a story; only then could he hope to gain mastery over his discrete sensations and perceptions, assigning them degrees of importance, then storing them in the past.[39] This narrative thread is a lifeline, no less necessary for being forever out of reach, its existence Platonic. As Peter Brooks argues in *Reading for the Plot*, this dependency claims us all, even those who resent it: we keep our lives going by telling ourselves our story.[40]

The post-1984 Chaikin–Shepard collaborations render precisely this ambivalent relationship to narrative. From one perspective, the two artists resist it as surely as they did in any of their earlier collaborations. *The War in Heaven* depicts a suspended life, the fallen angel barred from participating in any story other than that of his own suffering. *When the World Was Green* is static for more realistic reasons – the hopelessness of the prisoner's state – although Chaikin and Shepard also argue the more general point that little is revealed about trauma in the mere recounting of it. Yet for all this caution about narrative, both plays are also tributes to its power – or at least to the power of its promise. Over and over, the angel grasps at conventions of storytelling – "once before," "there was a time when," "since then," "I remember" – even though he has to drop them when they neither grant historical perspective on his condition, nor restore him to the world he has lost. He does finish one story – about waiting, in vain, at a dead man's casket to see the soul depart from the body – only to be left with the irony that in the play's only complete narrative, nothing actually happens.

Something does happen in *When the World Was Green*: a journalist interviews the prisoner on several occasions, until at the end she thinks she has learned his motive and reveals herself to be his victim's daughter. Yet this denouement, predictable almost from the start, is far less interesting than the preceding search. Direct questions elicit evasive answers, which in turn prompt veiled questions and sudden confessions, until piece by piece their shared history emerges. The interrogation structure had been attractive to Chaikin as early as his 1966 production of Jean-Claude van Itallie's *Interview* – Eileen Blumenthal describes workshop exercises that seem derived from it, and notes its recurrence in Winter Project productions.[41] An invisible questioner goads the speaker in parts of *Tongues* and *Savage/Love*. Early, pre-aphasia drafts of *The War in Heaven* include an interlocutor character, but only since Chaikin's stroke has the form had such far-reaching significance. It mimics his own ritual hunt for lost words, linkages, and histories: whenever he needs to speak, he seems to ask an earlier, now recalcitrant self to disclose the words he once knew. Beyond that, the interview form suggests that any story's claim on us depends on its incompleteness. In *The War in Heaven* and *When the World Was Green*, Chaikin and Shepard create the only narrative that a skeptic about narrative could accept: the story of its assembly upstages the story it tells. Every destination in the plot recedes as the teller approaches. Its answers solve nothing. Its pattern is full of lacunae shaped to the things which memory continues to withhold.

A trend is emerging. In Chaikin and Shepard's aphasic art, narrative seems less facile when it acknowledges the turmoil of narrating. The teller's language, once taken for granted, recovers depth and texture in the hardship of speaking. Finally, the same shift to openendedness – from noun to gerund – occurs in memory itself, its surface disturbed by the work of re-membering. It's for this reason that Chaikin and Shepard eliminate catharsis in *The War in Heaven* (despite the angel's certainty that "music delivers") and treat the prisoner's confession in *When the World Was Green* as anti-climactic. Any single memory is less significant than its pursuit. Once more, Beckett anticipates Chaikin and Shepard. In *Proust*, he shows that a "good memory" usually means a dead mind:

> The man with a good memory does not remember anything because he does not forget anything. His memory is uniform, a creature of routine, at once a condition and function of his impeccable habit, an instrument of reference instead of an instrument of discovery . . . [His] memory is a clothes-line and the images of his past dirty linen redeemed . . . [42]

This personal complacency about the past has a cultural equivalent: the obsession with the documents, monuments, hallowed territories, and other records of lived experience which Joseph Roach in *Cities of the Dead* sets against a second, more suggestive repository of memory. This latter form is in fact formless, or at least variable – the "patterned movements made and remembered by bodies," as Roach calls them, and the parallel histories recovered in oral culture, responsive to the needs, expectations, and biases of the present even as they summon the past.[43] (One could see them as the figures to whom Beckett's "dirty linen" belongs.) As constituted by bodies and voices, this memory is vulnerable to their afflictions and thus in need of the kind of ongoing renewal of attention Beckett envisions. Roach gives actors the job. They are "caretakers of memory," he writes elsewhere.[44] In their own resurrection of characters and of the culture surrounding their plays, actors define history as a force forever in circulation and subject to revision or redirection – something never past. For the actor, the past can only be recovered by rehearsal, improvisation, the trial and error of mem-orization, and the dying-in-life of performance. Roach cites Pierre Nora's terms: "Moments of history" are never "torn away from the movement of history."[45]

But what if the actor himself is "torn away from the movement of his-tory"? Imprisoned in the present tense, the aphasic Chaikin challenges one's faith in oral and kinesthetic memory (and complicates the theory de-rived from it) by showing that orality itself can be just a "moment" – lost along with the events, places, and people one used to talk about. (Moreover, in his work with the Open Theatre, Chaikin took aim at conventions of speech as emptied out of meaning as are certain sites and artifacts.) In his attempt to recover language, Chaikin by necessity goes deeper into the past than do most actors. He's not merely embodying or referring us to memory. Each time he seeks an individual word, he also, implicitly, revisits the distant moment when, by the act of naming, a speaker first ushered into consciousness a strange new phenomenon. Enunciating a word as if it had just been coined, Chaikin recreates the larger industry involved in forming a world. Forgetting that word soon afterwards and seeking it anew, he offers himself as a model of sustained historical awareness and engagement.

IV

At the intersection of these revisions to language, habit, narrative, and memory, Chaikin is nonetheless still Chaikin. On stage in *The War in Heaven*, he twists his head up and back, furrowing his brow before he delivers a line, then recovers his poise in the motionless aftermath, inhabiting a thicker stillness from which to enjoy saying unusual and presumably hard-won words: "throngs," "turtle," "extraordinary." Often he looks at us with an expression that moves between guilelessness and disappointment, reflecting but never retaining our interpretations of his exposed state. Perhaps he is *too* exposed. As Jonathan Kalb and others have asked (if only as devil's advocates), what distinguishes this art from Barnum's, beckoning audiences to gawk at what the impresario called "anomalies?"[46] (The question will be familiar to those troubled by their enjoyment of Robert Wilson's early work with the deaf and mute Raymond Andrews and the brain-damaged Christopher Knowles.)

In response, one might point to the many modes of resistance in *The War in Heaven*. As he turns the pages of his script, Chaikin seems to control the pace of his exposure. When he waits onstage after the performance, in the still-roiling wake of his speech, he faces down and outlasts our own watching. At those moments when Chaikin selects an individual spectator to hear him say "turn me loose," he could be referring to the confining stage as much as to his condition. But the notion of mere resistance is too flat to suggest all the ways Chaikin and Shepard keep us from being complacent about what we see. In fact, in performance Chaikin seems to confide in us so totally that he moves us past voyeurism – and beyond mere sympathy and even identification – until we are enveloped by his wordless world. It becomes the standard alongside which the memory of our own begins to seem the "anomaly."[47]

Moreover, despite the candor of his testimony, Chaikin manages to keep his distance, withdrawing even as he makes himself available for scrutiny. This kind of presence is proprietary: he is there, but not there for *us*. In this respect, Chaikin (and Shepard) recall a much earlier, little-discussed project,

Robert Frank's quasi-documentary *Me and My Brother*, for which Chaikin acted the "brother," Julius Orlovsky (the real Julius also appeared in the film), and Shepard collaborated with Frank on the screenplay. Although it was made only a few years after Chaikin and Shepard met, the film can stand as a kind of coda to the history of their collaboration – uncannily anticipating ideas about representation that only now are being addressed with the same depth in their theatre. Frank's own one-line synopsis guides viewers returning to the film from the recent collaborations: "A film about a silent man and an actor who became silent."[48] Like *Tongues*, it is mindful of the explosiveness of even the simplest utterance. Like *When the World Was Green*, it features a protagonist defending himself against scrutiny, refusing to disclose his secrets. Like *The War in Heaven*, its closest kin, it points the significance of the protagonist's struggle by chronicling its own struggle toward completion.

Orlovsky is schizophrenic, and an ambivalent participant in the documentary he shares with his brother Peter and Peter's companion, Allen Ginsberg. Mid-way through the shooting, Julius withdraws: never reliably communicative, he responds even less to Frank's direction, and becomes a taciturn, mildly reproachful presence on the film's margins. Frank hires Chaikin to speak for Julius – Chaikin plays him in scenes Julius himself won't do – but the actor acquires his character's attitude and most prominent symptom. In one scene, Chaikin, as himself, says, "My speech is all used up. I have nothing else to say. Nothing else to read from. I don't know what to play. Who should I be? Who shall I play?"[49]

Stronger than Chaikin's desire to act (and more pertinent to the challenges Chaikin faces now), though, is Julius's desire not to be acted. *Me and My Brother* is a compendium of dodges and feints, its protagonist (or is he its antagonist?) a master of elusiveness, for whom silence and other forms of absence are essential to his claim of presence on his own terms. The film's opening sequence sets the tone – the camera lingers over a sign reading "Stop. Do Not Enter" – and for the next eighty minutes Julius deflects the approach of Frank's camera, won't follow Shepard and Frank's script, undermines Chaikin's impersonation, and ignores the attentions of other "characters" and finally ourselves. He doesn't resist so much as avoid encounters in which resistance would be required. At a poetry reading, Ginsberg and Peter Orlovsky try to get Julius to take the microphone; instead, he sits on the floor behind them, impassive, onstage but not on display. In another scene, a psychiatrist questions Julius, but Julius dispenses only that information about the self that doesn't give the self away – his and his brother's names, their shared address. He foils a second interview soon afterward, shaking his head almost imperceptibly as the questioner tries to compare their eyes.

He changes his appearance over the years of filming – a beard, a different haircut, and so forth – and at one point disappears entirely.

Finally, in the film's beautiful last scene, Julius speaks freely. Frank's camera is distanced, kept behind a window through which it frames Julius sitting on a porch. Yet even now Julius won't meet its gaze. As he keeps his head in profile, Frank, off-camera, asks, "What do you think about acting?"

> – Acting is something beyond my collaboration.
> – Say something to the camera.
> – The camera is a reflection of disapproval or disgust or disappointment or unhelpfulness or unexplainability to disclose any real truth that might possibly exist.
> – Look into the camera and say your name.

"My name is Julius Orlovsky," he says, and then he does look at us, leaning in with mild defiance and curiosity. Here, Julius sets his real presence against the memory of Chaikin's actorliness, just as, in *The War in Heaven*, Chaikin himself sets his own history against his scripted parable. The film ends with small talk, crucial for being scaled to Julius's specifications. He begins:

> – It's chilly, chilly.
> – It's cold [says Frank].
> – Well, whether it's cold, I don't know.

After finally emerging from his silence, Julius has the last word.

NOTES

1 Joseph Chaikin and Sam Shepard, *The War in Heaven: Angel's Monologue*, in Shepard, *A Lie of the Mind* (New York: New American Library, 1987), 137. Page references in parentheses within the text are to this edition.

2 Hugh Kenner acknowledged the tyranny of radio in his discussion of Beckett's own radio plays: "A purely aural landscape capitaliz[es] eerily on the fact that whatever falls silent disappears" – a fact, Kenner notes, that Mrs. Rooney objects to in *All That Fall*: "Do not imagine, because I am silent, that I am not present, and alive, to all that is going on" (Kenner, *Samuel Beckett: A Critical Study* [Berkeley: University of California Press, 1968], 167–68).

The original radio broadcast of *The War in Heaven* was taped and distributed by Raven Recording (New York, NY) under the title *Joseph Chaikin Performs Struck Dumb and The War in Heaven* (1984). The 1991 stage production of the play, directed by Nancy Gabor and produced by the American Place Theatre, was videotaped and is housed in the Theatre on Film and Tape Collection of the New York Public Library for the Performing Arts. My discussion of Chaikin's performance refers to a 1999 presentation I saw at the Yale School of Drama and to this videotape. Both productions use a slightly revised version of the text, as yet unpublished.

3 Sigmund Freud, *On Aphasia: A Critical Study* (New York: International Universities Press, 1953), 23.

4 Samuel Beckett, *Worstward Ho*, in *Nohow On* (London: John Calder, 1989), 116, 118.

5 Gerry McCarthy, "'Codes from a Mixed-up Machine': the Disintegrating Actor in Beckett, Shepard, and, Surprisingly, Shakespeare," in Enoch Brater (ed.), *The Theatrical Gamut: Notes for a Post-Beckettian Stage* (Ann Arbor: University of Michigan Press, 1995), 181–87. Stanton B. Garner, Jr., *Bodied Spaces: Phenomenology and Performance in Contemporary Drama* (Ithaca: Cornell University Press, 1994), 120–24. Also see Enoch Brater, *The Drama in the Text: Beckett's Late Fiction* (New York: Oxford University Press, 1994).

6 Samuel Beckett, *Stories and Texts for Nothing* (New York: Grove Weidenfeld, 1967), 131. Beckett, *Three Novels* (New York: Grove Press, 1977), 369.

7 Sam Shepard and Joseph Chaikin, *Tongues*, in *Sam Shepard: Seven Plays* (New York: Bantam Books, 1981), 302, 311. Page references in parenthesis within the text are to this edition.

8 Joseph Chaikin, *The Presence of the Actor* (New York: Theatre Communications Group, 1991), 152, 97.

9 Jean-Claude van Itallie and the Open Theatre, *The Serpent* (New York: Dramatists Play Service, 1969), 21, 33.

10 Shepard, *La Turista*, in *Sam Shepard: Seven Plays*, 293; *The Mad Dog Blues*, in Shepard, *The Unseen Hand and Other Plays* (New York: Bantam Books, 1986), 290; *Melodrama Play*, in Shepard, *Fool for Love and Other Plays* (New York: Bantam Books, 1984), 134; *Curse of the Starving Class*, in *Sam Shepard: Seven Plays*, 168. Also see Shepard's explicit portraits of aphasia – the untitled prose description of his mother-in-law's stroke in *Motel Chronicles* (San Francisco: City Lights Books, 1982), 126–42, and the character of Beth in *A Lie of the Mind* (1985).

11 Carol Rosen, "Silent Tongues: Sam Shepard's Explorations of Emotional Territory," *Village Voice*, 4 August 1992, 35–36.

12 Karen Malpede (ed.), *Three Works by the Open Theatre* (New York: Drama Book Specialists, 1974), 142.

13 Barry Daniels (ed.), *Joseph Chaikin and Sam Shepard: Letters and Texts, 1972–1984* (New York: Theatre Communications Group, 1994).

14 Shepard, *The Mad Dog Blues*, in *The Unseen Hand and Other Plays*, 258–59.

15 See, among others, Stephen J. Bottoms, *The Theatre of Sam Shepard: States of Crisis* (Cambridge University Press, 1998), 32–33; Michael Vanden Heuvel, *Performing Drama/Dramatizing Performance: Alternative Theatre and the Dramatic Text* (Ann Arbor: University of Michigan Press, 1991), 193–229; Bonnie Marranca, *Theatrewritings* (New York: Performing Arts Journal Publications, 1984), 24; Richard Gilman, "Introduction" to *Sam Shepard: Seven Plays*, xvii. Shepard disputes such influence in Carol Rosen, "Emotional Territory: an Interview with Sam Shepard," *Modern Drama*, 36.1 (1993): 7–8.

16 *Cowboys #2*, in Shepard, *The Unseen Hand and Other Plays*, 142.

17 *Cowboy Mouth*, in Shepard, *Fool for Love and Other Plays*, 159. Page references in parenthesis in the text are to this edition. In his Introduction to this collection, Ross Wetzsteon links these lines to *Waiting for Godot*.

18 *Action*, in Shepard, *Fool for Love and Other Plays*, 183. Page references in parenthesis in the text are to this edition.

19 David Savran, "Sam Shepard's Conceptual Prison: *Action* and *The Unseen Hand*," *Theatre Journal*, 36 (March 1984): 57–73, 65. For a more general discussion of Shepard and memory – what its author calls "the anxiety of erasure" – see Jeanette R. Malkin, *Memory-Theatre and Postmodern Drama* (Ann Arbor: University of Michigan Press, 1999), 115–54.

20 A. R. Luria, *The Man with a Shattered World: The History of a Brain Wound* (Cambridge, MA: Harvard University Press, 1972), 106, 108. Page references in parenthesis within the text are to this edition.

21 Roman Jakobson, "Two Aspects of Language and Two Types of Aphasic Disturbances," in Jakobson and Morris Halle, *Fundamentals of Language* (The Hague: Mouton, 1971), 67–96.

22 John Hughlings-Jackson, quoted in Oliver Sacks, *Seeing Voices: A Journey Into the World of the Deaf* (Berkeley: University of California Press, 1989), 19.

23 Howard Gardner, *The Shattered Mind: The Person After Brain Damage* (New York: Alfred A. Knopf, 1975), 78.

24 These and other cases are mentioned in Jakobson, "Two Aspects of Language," 86; Gardner, *Shattered Mind*, 65; Luria, *Man with a Shattered World*, 132. Chaikin's situation is described in Jonathan Kalb, "Chaikin Through the Flames," in *Free Admissions: Collected Theatre Writings* (New York: Limelight Editions, 1993), 181, and in a short film, *Joseph Chaikin: Working Director*, by Aviva Slesin (1996).

25 Shepard, "Note" to *Tongues*, in *Sam Shepard: Seven Plays*, 300. See also his letter to Chaikin in Daniels, *Joseph Chaikin and Sam Shepard*, 36.

26 Shepard, *Savage/Love*, in *Sam Shepard: Seven Plays*, 336.

27 Sam Shepard, "Language, Visualization, and the Inner Library" (1977), reprinted in Bonnie Marranca (ed.), *American Dreams: The Imagination of Sam Shepard* (New York: Performing Arts Journal Publications, 1981), 217.

28 Beckett, *Three Novels*, 353.

29 McCarthy, "'Codes of a Mixed-up Machine.'"

30 Quoted in Naomi Greene, *Antonin Artaud: Poet Without Words* (New York: Simon and Schuster, 1970), 151. Beckett anticipates this image in *Murphy*, when he describes a character feeling "spattered with words that went dead as soon as they sounded" (quoted in Christopher Ricks, *Beckett's Dying Words* [Oxford University Press, 1993], 60). The original definition of aphasia further suggests how the condition may actually preserve a word's life: the first recorded use of the term (by Sextus Empiricus) referred to "a condition of mind according to which we neither affirm nor deny anything" (quoted in Gardner, *Shattered Mind*, 89.) Kalb's own reference to Artaud appears in "Chaikin Through the Flames."

31 Quoted in Greene, *Antonin Artaud*, 149.

32 Antonin Artaud, *The Theatre and its Double* (New York: Grove Press, 1958), 113, 119.

33 Joseph Chaikin, "The Search for a Universal Grammar" (interview with Andrzej Bonarski), in Bonnie Marranca and Gautam Dasgupta (eds.), *Conversations on Art and Performance* (Baltimore: Johns Hopkins University Press, 1999), 443–44.

34 Chaikin, *The Presence of the Actor*, 129, 85, 132. A "raid on the inarticulate" is from Eliot's "East Coker," much of which is pertinent to Chaikin's current condition: "And so each venture / Is a new beginning, a raid on the inarticulate / With shabby equipment always deteriorating . . . " Thanks to April Bernard for drawing this to my attention. In a different context, and with different motives, Richard Foreman also envisions using the voice to enter a condition when he writes of being "in speaking" in his play *Permanent Brain Damage* (1996).

35 Malpede, *Three Works by the Open Theatre*, 98. Eileen Blumenthal discusses "somatic" acting in *Joseph Chaikin: Exploring at the Boundaries of Theatre* (New York: Cambridge University Press, 1984), 54ff. and elsewhere. In a videotape of workshops for *Terminal*, appended to the public television version of *The Serpent*, Shami Chaikin demonstrates this approach particularly well: she begins an improvisation with the line "I thought he was dead," and says it over and over until it loses its word-sense and becomes a wail.

36 Chaikin made his comparison to Kaspar Hauser in an address at City University of New York Graduate Center, where he was awarded the 1987 Edwin Booth Award. The speech is on videotape; thank you to Joseph Chaikin for loaning me his copy. Shepard acknowledged his own interest in the Kaspar theme as early as 1978; see his letter to Chaikin in Daniels, *Joseph Chaikin and Sam Shepard*, 46.

37 Freud, *On Aphasia*, 88. Also see Luria, *Man with a Shattered World*, 19–20.

38 Alex Gildzen and Dimitris Karageorgiou, *Joseph Chaikin: A Bio-Bibliography* (Westport, CT: Greenwood Press, 1992), 19.

39 Oliver Sacks, "Foreword" (appears only in the 1987 edition) to Luria, *Man with a Shattered World*, xvii. Luria's book *The Mind of a Mnemonist* (New York: Basic Books, 1968) describes a patient with the opposite and no less agonizing condition: he could never forget anything.

40 Peter Brooks, *Reading for the Plot: Design and Intention in Narrative* (New York: Vintage Books, 1985).

41 Blumenthal, *Joseph Chaikin*, 81–83. Also see Daniels, *Joseph Chaikin and Sam Shepard*, 111, 122, and the workshop drafts of *The War in Heaven* included in that volume.

42 Samuel Beckett, *Proust* (New York: Grove Press, 1970), 17.

43 Joseph Roach, *Cities of the Dead: Circum-Atlantic Performance* (New York: Columbia University Press, 1996), 26.

44 Joseph Roach, "The Emergence of the American Actor," in Don B. Wilmeth and Christopher Bigsby (eds.), *The Cambridge History of American Theatre*, vol. I: *Beginnings to 1870* (Cambridge University Press, 1998), 338.

45 Roach, *Cities of the Dead*, 26.

46 Kalb, "Chaikin Through the Flames," 183. Kalb defends Chaikin against such criticism – here, in reference to his performance in Susan Yankowitz's own play inspired by Chaikin's aphasia, *Night Sky* – by writing that he "conveys something of [the] dignity . . . of the actor in extremis."

47 A similar change happens during performances of Robert Wilson's *Deafman Glance*. The production is virtually silent – to replicate the aural world of the deaf actor at its center, Raymond Andrews – and before long spectators are seeing more than they ever did when sounds competed for their attention.

48 Robert Frank, *The Lines of My Hand* (New York: Pantheon Books, 1989), unpaginated.

49 Quoted in Frank, *Lines of My Hand*.

6

THOMAS P. ADLER

Repetition and regression in *Curse of the Starving Class* and *Buried Child*

In a 1988 interview, Sam Shepard commented on the centrality of the notion of family and heredity to his thought: "What doesn't have to do with family? There isn't anything, you know what I mean? Even a love story has to do with family. Crime has to do with family. We all come out of each other – everyone is born out of a mother and a father, and you go on to be a father. It's an endless cycle."[1] Whether critics consider *Curse of the Starving Class* (1977) and *Buried Child* (1978) the first two parts of a "family trilogy" completed by *True West* (1980), or the first two movements in a quintet – those three works plus *Fool for Love* (1983) and *A Lie of the Mind* (1985) – they all agree that these two plays mark a turning point to a more realistic, perhaps somewhat O'Neillian dramaturgy. Yet, as Charles R. Lyons insists, it is a realism to which Shepard attaches his own original signature by ironically undercutting it: "Shepard took up another highly conventionalized aesthetic form – dramatic realism – and reconfigured its typical structure to accommodate the more open, fluid conventions of his writing ... this shift forms another 'appropriation': Shepard's borrowing of the conventions of dramatic realism, theatrical schemes which, by this point, were also 'popular' although decidedly not ideologically radical."[2]

Shepard's realism, however, because it is so intent on bringing to light the subversive and transgressive elements that more traditional examples of the genre often keep buried or repressed, approaches to a kind of American neo-Gothic.[3] The way in which Margot Gayle Backus delineates between realism and Gothicism in Irish literature in her recent study of *The Gothic Family Romance* is applicable to Shepard's plays as well: "Whereas realism characteristically disavows all knowledge of 'unauthorized versions' of the family, in the gothic such patterns of familial transgression are inescapable. These opposing stances self-evidently serve complementary ends, however: both assert an absolute disjunction between all forms of deviance and bourgeois reality. Such deviations may occur in geographically and cultural [sic] remote fantasies, but never in real life."[4] But in Shepard's family plays just such deviations do occur within the context of "real life," and what is ordinarily "unauthorized" suddenly becomes "authorized" and uncovered for all to see through patterns of ritual action and sociopolitical analysis of a collective guilt in which the audience is implicated if not complicitous.

I

Shepard displays a peculiar power in his highly symbolic family problem plays of allegorizing the American experience, of deflating the myth of America as the New Eden – whether the proverbial "garden" be an orchard in California or a farm in the midwest – and of showing the new American Adam as the cause of a new fall from grace. *Curse of the Starving Class*, which premiered on 21 April 1977 at London's Royal Court Theatre (where almost exactly two decades earlier John Osborne's legendary "kitchen sink" drama *Look Back in Anger* had played) before enjoying its American opening a year later at Joseph Papp's New York Shakespeare Festival on 2 March 1978, focuses on the severely dysfunctional Tate family to explore issues of home and heredity, of rootedness and escape, of determinism and change. The "curse" of the play's title is biological and familial, as well as a result of social and economic forces. The starvation is multilayered, not only physical and emotional, but spiritual as well; a prominent part of the stage set is a refrigerator into which one or other of the characters is often found staring, and the defeated observation of "Nothing"[5] when it is found to be empty of food conveys an almost metaphysical feeling of anguish and desperation. Bert Cardullo even tellingly connects "the spiritual starvation amidst plenty" to Shepard's dramaturgic device of the narcissistic monologue that isolates characters from one another.[6]

Already in the play's opening image of the son Wesley carting off the wood from a broken-down door, the home as a place of shelter and security has been violated. The proximate cause was the father Weston's drunken arrival the night before, yet both Taylor, lawyer friend and probably lover of the mother Ella, and Ellis, a local club-owner to whom Weston owes money for some desert property, have also laid siege to the house and avocado farm on which it sits. So the question becomes who and what will nurture this family, and who and what will destroy it. Ella is intent on selling the house and property in order to effect "change" and "bring a little adventure into [their] lives" (148): she will use the money to free herself, to travel – in a kind of Jamesian echo – to old-world Europe and become cultured, even though it is difficult to imagine her having the interest that she professes in "High art. Paintings. Castles. Fancy food" (144). But she seems to believe that by changing places she can somehow remake herself. Although Weston and Ella's daughter, Emma, feels certain they would "all be the same people" (148) anywhere else as they are in California, she, too, dearly wants "escape" and is the one who most obviously reinvents or refashions herself: a "fireball" who has refused to be held to socially constructed gender roles in the various jobs she has worked at, she dons Western garb and rides her horse through the town, shooting things up. Sensing that ownership goes finally to the one who controls the money, she determines to enter upon a life of crime, "the perfect self-employment" with its promise of "Just straight profit. Right off the top" (197–98).

Weston has left Ella because of an inability to countenance the notion "that everything would stay the same" (195), and so has looked outside the home for what he thought he could not find there. At various points, he muses about going down to Mexico, though he appears tentative about the possibility of "start[ing] a whole new life" (195); while Wesley talks about desiring to set out for "Alaska, maybe . . . The frontier . . . It's full of possibilities. It's undiscovered" (164) If initially Weston brings only artichokes home to feed the family, later he sobers up and assumes the role of nurturer, cooking full breakfasts and doing everyone's laundry, through which he once again establishes a connection to the family. Wesley, who displays his own nurturing side by bringing the lamb into the kitchen for warmth, is, however, the only one committed to trying to keep the orchard in the family, even to fighting physically for it, since he sees it as a part of what he belongs to and what belongs to him as "offspring" of his father.

Weston's sense that "It was good to be connected by blood like that. That a family wasn't just a social thing. It was an animal thing" (187) when he washes the family's clothes, and Wesley's shedding of his own blood in trying to reclaim the father's money from Ellis, are only two among several images of blood in the play, including the blood of the butchered lamb. The earliest mention of blood, in fact, is to the "curse" of Emma's first menstrual period; Ella greets the occasion with all kinds of crazily comic misinformation, while Emma inappropriately questions Taylor whether her mother still "has blood coming out of her" (153). Ironically, however, Emma's coming to fertility barely precedes her death in what can be assumed to be a bloody car bombing meant to kill her father. So the bloodline itself becomes a curse: the past catches up with one, the child paying for the sins of the father. The family curse extends both backward to the past and forward into the future: "It goes back and back to tiny little cells and genes. To atoms. To tiny little swimming things making up their minds without us. Plotting in the womb. Before that even. In the air. We're surrounded with it . . . It goes forward too. We spread it. We pass it on. We inherit it and pass it down and then pass it down again" (174–75). Likening the curse to original sin, Lynda Hart explains that it "controls from within and from without; it is both an internal biological and psychological structure and an insidious invader that penetrates the family's enclosure."[7]

When Wesley urinates in full view of the audience on the poster for his sister's 4-H project, his mother can see the circumcised penis that, in her eyes, marks him as somehow identified more closely to her own father, his grandfather who was "sensitive," rather than to Weston and the paternal grandfather known for their "short fuse" (152). Yet Wesley, first by drinking so that he feels himself, whether he likes it or not, "infected" by his father's and grandfather's "poison," and then later by dressing himself in his father's dirty clothes, seems destined – despite his inklings and intentions to the contrary – to choose to inhabit or repeat his father's ways rather than break free and emulate his maternal grandfather. And so the curse on this family that has now lost its land – its claim on America and its future – is poised to continue unabated.

A similar strongly deterministic aura – what David J. DeRose calls "the crippling disease of heredity"[8] – infects *Buried Child*, which was first produced at San Francisco's Magic Theatre on 27 June 1978 and went on to win Shepard the Pulitzer Prize for Drama in 1979. This tale of the return of the prodigal sons and grandson to the ancestral farmstead in Illinois is an even more insistent castigation of the failure of the father to hand on a potentially fruitful, life-giving legacy than *Curse of the Starving Class* had been. As Dodge the father sits corpse-like and immobile before a staticky, blinking television screen, his wife Halie descends from upstairs dressed completely in black, a mother in mourning at a wake not only for the family, but metaphorically for something much larger. When their grandson Vince returns after six years away, he brings with him his girlfriend, Shelly, the outsider who thinks she is about to enter a world like "a Norman Rockwell cover" (83) of "turkey dinners and apple pie and all that kinda stuff" (91); but Shepard steadily undercuts such mythicizations of the American nuclear family as it appears in popular culture by showing the disparity between the real and the imagined. For this is a family in denial, inhabiting a fetid atmosphere.

Only two of Dodge and Halie's three sons appear on stage. Tilden, the all-American fullback and Vince's father, has been gone for twenty years out West, serving time for an unnamed crime in New Mexico, and now roams the property half-crazed. Bradley, who lost a leg in a chain-saw accident and harbors enormous resentment against his father, is vicious and violence-prone, placing his fingers in the traumatized Shelly's mouth in a simulated act of sexual aggression – only to have his wooden leg later used against himself as a grimly comic weapon. Their third son, the basketball star Ansell, who was Halie's special pride and joy and evidently the one demonstrating most promise to achieve greatness, died ignominiously in a hotel bedroom rather than as a vaunted war hero. As a drunken Vince – in a visual echo of Weston from *Curse* – plunges through the screen door, "tearing it off its hinges," Halie pointedly asks, "What's happened to the men in this family! Where are the men!" (124). Halie herself has evidently long ago given up on Dodge, and now appears to be having an affair with the effete Father Dewis; if repeated rituals fail to revivify in *Curse of the Starving Class*, in *Buried Child* organized religion seems equally moribund and ineffectual.

Dodge denies any affective bond with his family, claiming that "just because people propagate [does not mean] they have to love their offspring[.] You never seen a bitch eat her puppies?" (112). And the details of one particular act of propagation, a child born most likely – though there remains a degree of indeterminacy and unverifiability about the biological father – of an incestuous relation between Halie and Tilden, Dodge attempts to keep hidden, since "It made everything we'd accomplished look like it was nothing. Everything was cancelled out by this one mistake. This one weakness" (124). The existence of the child and its fate are the secrets upon which the play pivots. The play becomes, in part, a commentary about silencing, about limiting discourse, as Dodge attempts to prevent the subversive narrative from coming to speech. Ultimately, however, under persistent questioning from Shelly, the audience discovers not only the secret of the incest at the heart of this family, but that Dodge himself drowned the child, "Just like the runt of the litter," and buried its remains out back, since "We couldn't allow that to grow up right in the middle of our lives" (124). After Dodge confesses and wills his inheritance to Vince, he significantly falls into stammering and then silence.

The act of incest, sexuality turned in on itself, not only is replicated in the circular rather than linear movement of the play, which opens with Halie addressing Dodge and ends with her talking to him again, though now in the person of Vince, about the rain; but it images as well the (grand)son's inability to break free and change – a determinism linked to heredity. The unseen pictures that adorn the upstairs walls are traces of the family "heritage" with which Vince wishes to reconnect. That his reflected image later "became his father's face. Same bones. Same eyes. Same nose. Same breath. And his father's face changed to his grandfather's face. And it went on like that...Clear on back to faces I'd never seen before but still recognized" (130) suggests a tale about the hold of the past upon the present, of sin and guilt and retribution as inexorable as any in Greek drama.

II

When, near the end of *Buried Child*, Shelly reveals that she knows the family has a secret, Dodge remarks, "She thinks she's going to get it out of us. She thinks she's going to uncover the truth of the matter. Like a detective or something" (122). For the audience, his response becomes self-referential, acting as a metacritical commentary since it undercuts their own expectations of being provided with an unambiguous answer, and in that sense helps deconstruct the realistic form with all its built-in contrivances and artificialities as it moves toward a tidy resolution.[9] Partly because Shepard's plays refuse to provide the definitive sense of closure that audiences traditionally experience from dramatic realism, they invite multilayered readings – as allegorizations of experience, as symbolic structures, as mythic constructs. Built into both *Curse of the Starving Class* and *Buried Child* are extensive and highly visual patterns of ritual action; the similarity of these movements in the two plays is brought into focus when, at the end of each, the mother (Ella, Halie) identifies the son or grandson (Wesley, Vince) with the absent or dead father or grandfather (Weston, Dodge).

The ritual actions – the first drawn from biblical theology, the second from anthropology – in each case might be termed "religious" in nature, in at least a loose sense of that term, since they center on death and rebirth. In *Curse*, the ritual in question is first narrated by the father and then later acted out by the son. In Act 3, Weston, who earlier has been unkempt, drunk, and violent, appears clean shaven, sober, and otherwise chastened. In a lengthy monologue spoken to Wesley, he recounts taking a peaceful walk at dawn around the avocado orchard during which he experienced a kind of epiphany, suddenly being struck that he "actually was the owner. That somehow it was me and I was actually the one walking on my own piece of land. And that gave me a great feeling" (186). He then discarded his old dirty clothes and "Just walked through the whole damn house in [his] birthday suit . . . It was like peeling off a whole person." He followed this with a hot bath, and then a cold bath, and then a hearty farm breakfast cooked from the unexpected profusion of groceries in the refrigerator that came as a surprise, "Just like somebody knew I was going to be reborn this morning or something . . . Like I was coming back to my life after a long time a' being away" (186–87). He then, as was mentioned earlier, washes everyone's clothes, which engenders a feeling of closeness and interconnectedness.

Several pages later, however, we discover why this apparently cleansing and redemptive ritual does not have the desired effect of restoring a renewed patriarch to his family or bringing a "paradise" regained "for a young person" like Wesley to the farm. For Weston believes that simply by declaring himself "REBORN! I'M A WHOLE NEW PERSON NOW!" he has achieved his salvation; he no longer needs to "feel guilty . . . because I don't have to pay for my past now!" (193). Yet Shepard apparently rejects Weston's brand of painless atonement theology as a too easy escape from the ramifications of one's actions: Weston must still "pay" for his past frailties and "sins," not only by the loss of the land but also by the death of his daughter who perishes as his substitute in the car bombing intended for him.

Throughout the play, the son Wesley has always been closely connected with the lamb that he first brings onto the stage in Act 1. After hearing of his father's ritual purification, he literally acts it out, and then expands upon or embellishes it in an almost liturgical manner. Following his father's request that he bathe and wash the blood off his face from trying to retrieve Weston's money, Wesley goes off and later returns to the kitchen looking "dazed," "completely naked, his hair wet" (190). He then takes the lamb from its pen and exits. When he enters again moments later wearing Weston's castoff "baseball cap, overcoat, and tennis shoes," he reports that he has "butchered" the lamb for "some food," and then "crosses quickly to the refrigerator, opens it, and starts pulling out all kinds of food and eating it ravenously" (192). The biblical echoes are many. In the Old Testament, the obedient Abraham is willing to sacrifice his son Isaac but, at the behest of an angel, slaughters the lamb instead; also, the blood of the lamb is smeared on the doors of the faithful Jews going out of Egypt as a protection against the angel taking their firstborn sons. In the New Testament, Christ, prefigured by Isaac, is the submissive lamb who sheds his blood on the cross for the sins of mankind, after giving himself under the auspices of bread and wine to his disciples to be eaten in communion; also, Christ becomes the Good Shepherd tending and watching over his flock of lambs, who are the new faithful ones.[10]

Yet even though Wesley imitates his father's ritual cleansing in hot and cold baths and dons his clothing, and is, in a manner of speaking, washed in the blood of the lamb as the gospel hymn triumphantly proclaims, the ritual proves ineffectual: "it didn't work. Nothing happened" (196). Wesley thought of himself as the lamb being sacrificed to bring salvation – not only did he have "the lamb's blood dripping down [his] arms," but "for a second [he] thought it was [himself] bleeding" as well; yet simultaneously he felt that "a part of [Weston] was growing on [him] . . . taking over," so that he sensed he was "going backwards" (196, 198). The sacrifice was not efficacious; and what should have been a sacrament of communion became instead a grotesque gorging that did not satisfy the spiritual hunger. The last image we see of the lamb is of its skinned carcass when the henchmen Slater and Emerson enter, commenting that it "Looks like somebody's afterbirth" (199).

And Ella addresses Wesley as if she were speaking to Weston the husband and father rather than to the son, signaling that Wesley's regression, as Phyllis Randall also argues, is now complete – although Bert Cardullo proposes that "the play is open-ended" in its "judgment" of whether Wesley "has truly learned anything and will succeed where his father failed."[11]

If, at first glance, the rituals in *Curse of the Starving Class* might seem potentially salvific – although perhaps none too subtle – those in *Buried Child* are distinctly rites of burial or entail a robbing of potency. In his article entitled "Sam Shepard's *Buried Child*: the Ironic Use of Folklore," Thomas Nash locates the play within what Northrop Frye terms the ironic mode, since it begins in realism but turns increasingly toward ritual, reenacting in modern dress the sacrificial death of the Corn King, here represented by Dodge, and the rebirth of the new King in the person of Vince, Tilden's surviving son. And yet Nash neglects to point out the most basic irony of all: the new god is as impotent and as unable to bring renewal as the old.[12] Shepard punctuates the action visually with well over half a dozen ritual burials of Dodge, whose body Halie describes as "decomposing" and "putrid": Tilden puts the corn in Dodge's lap, later he covers his father with a blanket, and finally he places the corn husks on him; Bradley tosses Shelly's rabbit-fur coat over Dodge; both Halie and Vince place a rose or roses on him; and Vince, too, covers him with a blanket. And in an image that suggests removal of potency, Bradley clips off his father's hair, cutting his scalp in the process. Like Weston in *Curse*, Dodge resists seeing any moral connection between past actions and present consequences. Denying any resemblance between himself and "Somebody who looks just like [he] used to look" in the gallery of family photographs displayed on the upstairs wall, Dodge claims, "That isn't me! That never was me!" (111); furthermore, he professes an inability to "know about the past" and the desirability of making believe it "never happened."

After Vince returns from his night-long drive across Illinois, during which he saw reflected in the windshield not only his own face but perceived it changing into that of his father and of his grandfather and of all his ancestors "Clear on back to faces I'd never seen before but still recognized. Still recognized the bones underneath" (130), he lies down and assumes exactly the same posture of his grandfather who is now dead. Rejecting change, he either cannot or will not flee from the pattern of the past which he has beheld so clearly. And when Tilden enters bearing the remains of the dead baby wrapped in muddied cloth that he has exhumed from the garden, that skeleton of the half-brother becomes linked with the "mummy's face" Vince glimpsed in the windshield. As Halie speaks from upstairs, she talks as if to Dodge, though she is heard now only by Vince, remarking that what is sown and washed in by the rain will be reaped, and assigning a cause to the growth of the crop: "Maybe it's the sun" (132).

The pun in the curtain line on "sun/son" alludes directly to Ibsen's *Ghosts*, reminding audiences not only of a source for the realistic modern family drama structured around a secret that is only gradually revealed, but also of the earlier playwright's delineation of the sins of the fathers being visited upon the children.[13] The remains of the buried son have literally fertilized the earth in a grimly Gothic manner (perhaps appropriately calling to mind the line from T. S. Eliot's *Waste Land* asking whether "that corpse you planted in your garden has begun...to sprout").[14] The other "son" Vince returns and the sun breaks through, yet neither his homecoming nor the sunrise, nor Halie's bright yellow dress that has replaced her earlier black of mourning, betokens resurrection or augurs renewal. What Bradley has called a "paradise" remains firmly a postlapsarian, fallen world, just as the play's ending, whatever signs there may be to the contrary, remains heavily ironic, dark rather than bright.

III

While Shepard asserts that his primary focus rests on the family unit and has been known to disclaim any interest in social concerns, stating that "the American social scene...totally bores me,"[15] the families in *Curse of the Starving Class* and *Buried Child* are so rooted in a particular time and place that it is difficult to see them as divorced from a larger political canvas. And the plays are filled with verbal and visual imagery to support this view. The New West of the California avocado farm in *Curse* is fast becoming a kind of concrete frontier. After Emma puts on her Western outfit, she mounts her horse and rides it down the freeway, and eventually is arrested for shooting up the Alibi Club. Both Weston and Ella are engaged in making separate deals that would sell out the orchard land and the desert plot to speculators and developers, who will turn them into vast suburbias, replicating those anonymous tracts back east characterized by their egalitarian sameness. Weston calls this "a zombie invasion" (163), and later Wesley rails against the money men who "moved in on us like a creeping disease. We didn't even notice" (194). The father here, like Willy Loman in Miller's *Death of a Salesman*, has bought unquestioningly into the ethic of consumerism that sees buying and owning things as a guarantee of future success; but living a generation later, he not only borrows to buy, but uses "invisible money...plastic shuffling back and forth" (195) to pay for his purchases.

This decidedly anti-capitalistic strain, with its implied criticism of a warped myth of masculinity that puts the attainment of money and power over providing emotional sustenance for one's family, links up in *Curse* with an exposure of a myth of nationhood that pits the militarily strong against the weak and prides itself on dominance and conquest and oftentimes false heroics. When Weston drives back to the farm in his Packard the night before the action begins and drunkenly breaks down the front door, his son is lying in bed staring up at his model airplane collection ("My P-39. My Messerschmitt. My Jap Zero" [137]) and connects the automobile with foreign reconnaissance planes ready to invade. Later, Weston himself likens the sensation of macho power and destructiveness – the feeling of explosiveness in his blood – with the heady thrill of his days in the war when he "flew giant machines in the air. Giants! Bombers. What a sight" (172). And as he contemplates various acts of gruesome violence against the wheeler-dealers from whom he bought worthless desert land, he blames the military for giving him practice in and the dulled conscience needed for killing: "I was in the war. I know how to kill . . . I've done it before. It's no big deal. You just make an adjustment. You convince yourself it's all right . . . It's easy. You just slaughter them" (171). He repeats the image of the American B-49 bombers at the beginning of Act 3, when, talking to the penned lamb, he tells the story about cheering on the giant eagle (traditional symbol of America) that swoops down out of the sky, demonstrating some kind of "downright suicidal antics" (184) like a flyer's crazy exploits, to gobble up the ram testicles that Weston has thrown up on the roof after castrating the lambs. Since the testicles are "remnants of manlihood," might this not be seen as America destroying not only its supposed enemies but sacrificing its young manhood in the process as well? When Ella, addressing Wesley whom she misidentifies as Weston, narrates the story's conclusion at the end of the play, she tells of the eagle with a cat in its mouth engaged in a mutually destructive battle that devours both predator and victim alike. And when Emerson and Slater blow up the Packard, already equated with American hegemony and its imperialist agenda, they use explosives developed by the Irish, bringing to mind still another instance of colonial oppression.

A similar quite explicit echo of America's Manifest Destiny occurs in *Buried Child* when Vince returns to the farm in Act 3 to claim his patrimony, drunkenly breaking bottles while singing the Marine hymn ("From the Halls of Montezuma to the Shores of Tripoli. We will fight our country's battles on the land and on the sea" [125]), shouting out to an "imaginary army" as if across a battlefield and making a "whistling sound" like bombs falling. The other central image of America at war comes through discussion of Ansell – to hear his mother talk, the youngest and smartest and most promising of Dodge and Halie's three sons – who became a soldier, not to die on a battlefield but in a motel room instead. If we are to believe

Halie's bigoted ravings, he fell victim of the Mafia after marrying a Catholic. Now, Halie talks with Father Dewis about raising a memorial to him in the town that would pay homage to him as high school athlete and untested and therefore unproven soldier, "A big, tall statue with a basketball in one hand and a rifle in the other" (73). Prowess at athletics and war become, then, the two ways that manliness is measured in America, yet in *Buried Child* both emerge as more hollow than heroic. For, as Halie bemoans, athletic exploits that at one time promoted moral authority and maturity have become "More vicious," bloodier and debased, with sports figures regularly "allow[ing] themselves to run amuck. Drugs and women" (117).

If, on the level of familial guilt, *Buried Child* exposes the way in which the patriarchy tries to impose order by silencing transgressive sexuality, on the level of national guilt the play, as Stephen Bottoms hints,[16] may well be suggestive of a kind of historical amnesia, through which an unresolved historical event has been repressed. Halie makes this connection explicit when she remarks that "the smell" from "the stench of sin in [the] house" (116) arises not only from personal sin (the incest) but from public actions (military engagements) as well. Though assuredly not as concretely and tactilely presented as the skeleton, the nation's guilty past – be it racism, or religious and ethnic prejudice, or, as appears most likely given the time frame of the play and Ansell's involvement in the military, the Vietnam War – comes back to haunt the present. What might be seen as its neo-Gothic elements – such things as exhumed skeletons of dead babies – do not necessarily sit easily upon the traditional structure of dramatic realism; they might even, in fact, be seen as an attempt to subvert it by making it less shackled and more inclusive. But the narrative that Shepard contains within his now expanded form might itself also be equally subversive, giving voice through resonant use of ritual and symbol to destructive and frightening aspects of American society that have long been silenced. The unspeakable act that Dodge fights to keep unspoken can, finally, no longer be suppressed. Through plays such as *Curse of the Starving Class* and *Buried Child*, Shepard might ultimately be signaling the way in which contemporary American drama itself refuses to be bounded any longer in either content or style. It is a project in which he has helped lead the way, by wedding radical ambitions to traditional form.

NOTES

1 Henry I. Schvey, "A Worm in the Wood: the Father–Son Relationship in the Plays of Sam Shepard," *Modern Drama*, 36.1 (March 1993): 12–26.
2 Charles R. Lyons, "Shepard's Family Trilogy and the Conventions of Modern Realism," in Leonard Wilcox (ed.), *Rereading Shepard: Contemporary Critical Essays on the Plays of Sam Shepard* (New York: St. Martin's Press, 1993), 115–30.

3 For a discussion of Shepard's appropriation of Gothic elements, see Stephen J. Bottoms, *The Theatre of Sam Shepard: States of Crisis* (Cambridge University Press, 1998), 159–60.

4 Margot Gayle Backus, *The Gothic Family Romance: Heterosexuality, Child Sacrifice, and the Anglo-Irish Colonial Order* (Durham: Duke University Press, 1999), 242.

5 All references to *Curse of the Starving Class* and *Buried Child* are from *Sam Shepard: Seven Plays* (New York: Bantam Books, 1981). Page references in parentheses within the text are to this edition.

6 Bert Cardullo, "Sam Shepard's Use of the Monologue in *Curse of the Starving Class*," *Notes on Modern American Literature*, 9.2 (Fall 1995): item 11.

7 Lynda Hart, *Sam Shepard's Metaphorical Stages* (Westport, CT: Greenwood Press, 1987), 71.

8 David J. DeRose, *Sam Shepard* (New York: Twayne, 1992), 108.

9 For a subtle treatment of Shepard's deconstruction of realism, see Charles Lyons's "Text as Agent in Sam Shepard's *Curse of the Starving Class*," *Comparative Drama*, 24.1 (Spring 1990): 24–33; and for a consideration of Shepard's realism as postmodern pastiche, see Rodney Simard's *Postmodern Drama: Contemporary Playwrights in America and Britain* (Lanham, MD: University Press of America, 1984), 78–79.

10 Lyons points out many of these biblical patterns, but with a somewhat different emphasis: "Shepard's Family Trilogy," 127.

11 Phyllis Randall, "Adapting to Reality: Language in Shepard's *Curse of the Starving Class*," in Kimball King (ed.), *Sam Shepard: A Casebook* (New York: Garland Press, 1988), 132; Bert Cardullo, "Wesley's Role in Sam Shepard's *Curse of the Starving Class*," *Notes on Modern American Literature*, 8.1 (Spring–Summer 1984): item 6.

12 Both Hart (*Sam Shepard's Metaphorical Stages*, 86) and Simard (*Postmodern Drama*, 90) arrive at a conclusion similar to that of Thomas Nash, "Sam Shepard's *Buried Child*: the Ironic Use of Folklore," *Modern Drama*, 26.4 (1983): 486–91.

13 For a fuller discussion of these parallels, see my "Ghosts of Ibsen in Shepard's *Buried Child*," *Notes on Modern American Literature*, 10.1 (1986): item 3 (unpaginated). Several later critics, including David DeRose (*Sam Shepard*, 108), also explore this connection.

14 Simard considers *Buried Child* "a postmodern dramatization of *The Wasteland*" (*Postmodern Drama*, 87), while Stephen J. Bottoms examines it for its allusions to the myth of the Fisher King in *The Theatre of Sam Shepard: States of Crisis* (Cambridge University Press, 1998), 178.

15 Quoted in DeRose, *Sam Shepard*, 94.

16 Bottoms, *Theatre of Sam Shepard*, 176.

7

BRENDA MURPHY

Shepard writes about writing

Because he uses theatrical techniques that have been identified with postmodern theatre, Sam Shepard is often written of as a postmodern playwright.[1] Certainly his theatrical techniques have much in common with those of the postmodern theatre. His stage reality is layered and fragmented, his characters sometimes intersubjective and transformational. He juxtaposes borrowings from and allusions to popular culture with those of history and high culture in an often free-form, playful way. He often uses sets that call attention to the theatre's existence as theatre, and invites acting techniques that call attention to the actor as performer and the play as performance. All of this Shepard shares with his postmodern contemporaries. His conception of the playwright's art, however, is far from the distant, ironic stance of the postmodern artist. In fact, as Michael Early has pointed out, Shepard has a great affinity with the American Romanticism of nineteenth-century Transcendentalists like Emerson and Whitman. Unlike theirs, however, Shepard's is a dark Romanticism, closer to the Gothic imagination of Poe or the cosmic despair of Melville than to the Transcendental optimism of Emerson or Whitman. What he chiefly has in common with the Romantics is his sense of the artistic imagination, his awe for his own gift and his compulsion to understand it.

Shepard began his career writing plays that featured what he has called "arias," long speeches with startlingly original imagery that went on for two or three pages. Like nineteenth-century Romantics such as Coleridge and Poe, he wrote from an often drug-induced inspiration. In a 1997 interview, he told the *Paris Review*: "I felt kind of like a weird stenographer. I don't mean to make it sound like hallucination, but there were definitely things there, and I was just putting them down. I was fascinated by how they structured themselves, and it seemed like the natural place to do it was on a stage."[2] Shepard's conception of artistic creation has a great deal in common with Coleridge's seminal description of the artist's imagination, as a "secondary" reflection of the "primary imagination" that is "the living Power and prime Agent of all human Perception . . . a repetition in the finite mind of the eternal act of creation in the infinite I AM."[3] In Coleridge's system, the artist must combine the power of the imagination with the conscious will of the craftsman to create art. A similar division between unfathomable imagination or inspiration and conscious, rational craft and control can be seen in many Romantic and post-Romantic formulations of the artistic process, such as Nietzsche's division between the Dionysian and the Apollonian creative forces. In his early years, Shepard eschewed revision, as though unwilling to tamper with the unalloyed products of the imagination, but as he has matured, and left mind-altering substances behind, the many drafts of plays like *Fool for Love* and *A Lie of the Mind* attest to his bringing the craftsman in him to operate extensively on the pure products of the imagination.

That the imagination and the act of writing have continued to preoccupy Shepard is evident from the appearance of the artist as character in so many of his plays from the seventies and eighties. Along with the plays that depict the artist as musician, such as *The Mad Dog Blues* (1971) and *The Tooth of Crime* (1972), is a group of plays that address the subject of the writer, and more particularly the writer's relationship to the overwhelming power of the imagination in the writing process. While there are allusions to the subject in many of Shepard's plays, the most substantial treatment of this subject occurs in *Geography of a Horse Dreamer* (1974), *Angel City* (1976), *True West* (1980), and *Fool for Love* (1983).

Horse Dreamer and *Angel City* are directly related to Shepard's experience when, as a young Off-Off-Broadway playwright of 24, he was chosen by Michelangelo Antonioni to write the screenplay for his film about the new generation of American youth, *Zabriskie Point* (1970). Shepard worked with Antonioni for two months in Europe, and then returned with him to Los Angeles, but he did not stay with the film, which has three other screenwriting credits besides Shepard's and Antonioni's, to its completion. Shepard has said that his leaving the project was simply a matter of not being able to do the kind of writing Antonioni wanted at that point: "He wanted political repartee and I just didn't know how."[4] Although Shepard left *Zabriskie Point*, he did not immediately leave the film industry. As he described his experience to the *Village Voice* in 1975: "As soon as you start writing a movie you get these scripts showing up in the mail . . . Twenty thousand for this one and 30 thousand for that one. It's like an open auction – suddenly you're in the screenwriters' market. I find it exhausting, not only exhausting – debilitating."[5] Working in several capacities as a writer and script doctor, Shepard was appalled by the position of the screenwriter in the movie industry. "Here's a guy who's an artist in the traditional sense, and then all the accouterments – the life – everything that surrounds him just brings the whole thing down."[6] In 1980 he said that "screenwriting's been amputated by a bunch of corporate businessmen figuring they're artists... it's too bad, too. That's a legit form, screenwriting."[7]

Shepard's early experience with the movie industry was disillusioning and deeply disturbing. After the heady experience of being able to have his plays produced Off-Off Broadway, almost at his will, uncut and with the playwright as final arbiter on aesthetic decisions, it was shocking to encounter art as business, with the writer simply one of the instruments by which a salable product, the movie, was to be produced. In 1975 he said he hated working on films: "Because it's never just that. It's never just working on a film. It has to do with studios, with pleasing certain people, cutting things down, and rewriting. It's not a writer's medium – the writer is just superfluous... to submerge yourself in that world of limousines and hotels and rehashing and pleasing Carlo Ponti is just... forget it."[8] It was immediately following his experience with Hollywood, in 1971, that Shepard moved his family to London for three years and began writing deeply introspective plays about the artistic process and the position of the artist in contemporary society. Being Sam Shepard, he did not address these issues head on, but they emerged from deep inside the creative ferment of his imagination.

Crucial to the plays about writing is the concept of character that Shepard was developing in the seventies and eighties. Because his characters are not "integrated subjects" – because they fragment and transform during the play – Shepard's conception of character is often considered to be postmodern – that his characters have no essential self but are sites of continually shifting subjectivity.[9] Shepard's view of character belies this notion, however, as when he says: "I think character is something that can't be helped, it's like destiny. It's something that's essential... I think character is an essential tendency that can't be – it can be covered up, it can be messed with, it can be screwed around with, but it can't be ultimately changed. It's like the structure of our bones, the blood that runs through our veins."[10] This description, with its concept of character as an immutable essence, is much closer to Aristotle's than to the shifting, unstable subjectivity or intersubjectivity of the postmodern conception. What lends Shepard's characters to postmodern analysis is his ability to make use of postmodern techniques in dramatizing his characters. Perhaps his clearest formulation of what he is after is in his "Note to the Actors" in *Angel City*, where he speaks of character as "a fractured whole with bits and pieces of character flying off the central theme. In other words, more in terms of collage construction or jazz improvisation." The actor should be "mixing many different underlying elements and connecting them through his intuition and senses to make a kind of music or painting in space." The "abrupt changes" in the characters "can be taken as full-blown manifestations of a passing thought or fantasy, having as much significance or 'meaning' as they do in our ordinary lives. The only difference is that here the actor makes note of it and brings it to life in three dimensions."[11] The allusion to jazz improvisation is telling. For Shepard, who is a musician, the notion of character as playing many variations around a single theme comes naturally, and it is crucial to the startling originality of his work. What divides his work in the seventies from that of the postmodernist is that the central theme is there in the character. It has an essence.

In *Geography of a Horse Dreamer* and *Angel City*, Shepard's subject is the artist's imagination, and the danger of "messing with it" by selling it to a capitalist enterprise, like the movie industry, that simply seeks to commodify the artist by turning him into an instrument for producing a product that will generate profit for its owners. The play's *imaginaire* grows out of Shepard's most immediate experience in the movie industry and in moving his family to England. When Shepard first moved to London, he lived in Shepherd's Bush, then a working-class neighborhood, where there was a greyhound track. Shepard had had a deep affection for horse-racing since his teenage years, when he worked at the Santa Anita racetrack in California. He formed a similar attachment to greyhound racing in England, even buying and racing his own dog, Keywall Spectre.

Geography of a Horse Dreamer gestures strongly toward Harold Pinter's absurdist classic, *The Dumb Waiter*, in which two hit men wait in a room to get their orders for the next job. *Horse Dreamer* opens in *"an old sleazy hotel room. Semirealistic with a beat-up brass bed, cracked mirror, broken-down chairs, small desk, etc."*[12] The protagonist Cody (who shares his name with Buffalo Bill), a young man from Wyoming wearing jeans and a cowboy shirt, lies spread-eagled on his back on the bed, his arms and legs handcuffed to the bedposts, asleep with dark glasses on. He is watched over by two forties-style gangsters, Santee and Beaujo. As the situation emerges in the first act, it becomes clear that Cody is a "horse dreamer," someone with the power to dream the winners of horse-races, and he has been, as he says, "kidnapped," or "wined and dined" (287), by a sinister organization headed by a character named Fingers, who exploits his dreams to win at the races. The situation in Act 1, "The Slump," is that Cody, "Mr. Artistic Cowboy," as Santee calls him, has lost the ability to dream winners, and the team has been demoted from the luxury of the Beverly Wiltshire Hotel to this sleazy dump. Fingers has imprisoned Cody in the room, feeding him barbiturates so he'll sleep and dream, but Cody says he will never recover his ability to dream horses there: "He don't understand the area I have to dream in . . . the inside one. The space inside where the dream comes. It's gotta be created" (283).

Cody complains that, by locking him in a room, Fingers has "blocked up my senses. Everything forces itself on the space I need. There's too much chaos now" (283–84). Tellingly for Shepard at this stage in his career, Cody tries to answer Beaujo's question, "how did it happen before? It used to be a snap for you." "I don't know," he says, "It was accidental. It just sort of came to me outa' the blue ... At first it's all instinct. Now it's work" (285). Cody wants to go back to the Great Plains, to Wyoming, where his real horse dreams are inspired, complaining that Fingers has "poisoned my dreams with these cities" (287), but instead Fingers assigns him to "start dreamin' dogs," despite Beaujo's objection that "he can't suddenly change his whole style a' dreaming like that. It might kill him" (288). Santee explains that he has no say in the matter: "The pressure's there. It comes from the outside. Somewhere out there ... That's how it is. You got the genius, somebody else got the power. That's how it always is, Beethoven. The most we can hope for is a little room service and a color TV" (291).

In Act 2, "The Hump," the team has been moved to a fancy hotel room, and all the characters have new clothes. Cody has acquired an Irish accent and now dreams and talks of nothing but dogs. Beaujo suggests that he has "some kind a' weird mental disorder. I told ya' he was a genius. There's a very fine line between madness and genius ya' know" (295). Santee is unimpressed, answering, "He's gone bananas and that's all there is to it. It just happens to coincide with our needs" (295). As the act goes on, Cody literally turns into a dog, at first dreaming and talking from the dog's point of view, and then behaving like a dog, leaping around the room and crashing into things, squealing and squirming when Santee catches hold of him. Fingers appears with an ominous figure called "the Doctor" who looks like Sydney Greenstreet. The Doctor prepares to cut the "dreamer's bone" out of Cody's neck, in hopes of making use of his power for a while longer. Cody begins to speak of the power of the white buffalo: "This day has sent a spirit gift. You must take it. Clean your heart of evil thoughts. Take him in a sacred way. If one bad thought is creeping in you it will mean your death" (306). As the Doctor cuts into the back of Cody's neck with a scalpel, Cody's two brothers, huge cowboys named Jasper and Jason, come through the door with a shotgun blast. After killing the Doctor and Santee, they take Cody back home to Wyoming, telling him, "come on, now. You gather yerself together. A little beef stew in yer gullet, you'll be good as new" (306).

Ross Wetzsteon has called the play "an extended metaphor for the personal dilemma of the artist himself," noting that it was written while Shepard was in England, "when, hardly coincidentally to the plot, his new fascination with dog racing paralleled a resurgence of interest in his work by a new audience. (Suddenly, as in the play, he dreamed 'winners' again.)" Wetzsteon suggests the play's import is that "Shepard was clearly ill at ease in England"[13] citing Cody's Irish ("outsider's") accent and the fact that Fingers is depicted as an effete Englishman in a bowler hat. This sense of dislocation is certainly there in the play, but it goes deeper than the geographic dislocation from the US to the UK. Shepard is also writing out of the more fundamental dislocation he had recently felt as a writer for the movies, where he and his creative power had been treated as salable commodities. Like Cody, he had been expected to produce "winners" on demand, whether he had any affinity for or knowledge of the subject or not, as with the "political repartee" of *Zabriskie Point*. And, like Cody, he had been "wined and dined" and removed from the environment that inspired him, placed in what was to him a luxurious and hermetically sealed prison, and expected to be creative. The heart of the play is the artist's fear of losing his creative power, or more specifically, of having it stolen from him by businessmen who place no value on it except as a profit-making instrument. The danger of violating the artist's imagination is set out in its most primal terms, which are also major themes of the dark Romantics – the destruction of the artist through madness and death. Through the image of the sacred white buffalo at the end of the play, Shepard conveys the reverential spirit with which the artistic imagination must be approached: "Take him in a sacred way. If one bad thought is creeping in you it will mean your death. You will crumble to the earth. You will vanish from this time" (306).

Martin Tucker writes that *Horse Dreamer* presents a very dark representation of the suffering of artists in contemporary America, suggesting that perhaps "the only way out for the contemporary artist, once he has entered the world of public attention/performance, is a lobotomy of his dreams."[14] This play certainly is dark, but how dark it is depends on how the imagery of its ending is dramatized on stage, and how the particular spectator reads that imagery. Shepard's stage directions say that "*Cody sits on the bed with the back of his neck bleeding. He doesn't know where he is*" (306), which might suggest that the "dreamer's bone" has been removed from his neck. But he is being taken back to Wyoming, the original geography of his horse dreaming, and the play ends with the zydeco music that he has called his "source of inspiration" (285). Shepard opens up the suggestion that there is hope for the artist who breaks free of the profit-making machine and goes back to the sources of his creativity.

Angel City has a similar aesthetic to that of *Horse Dreamer*, and it might be seen as a development and intensification of its theme of the commodification of the artist. Unlike *Horse Dreamer*, it is a direct treatment of the Hollywood movie industry. As Leonard Wilcox has shown, *Angel City* is in the tradition of "L.A. *noir*," and it alludes powerfully to such classic texts about Los Angeles and the movie industry as Nathanael West's *The Day of the Locust* and the works of Raymond Chandler. Its situation is that Rabbit Brown, an artist who has been living on the desert, is summoned by two movie producers named Lanx (read LAX) and Wheeler (wheeler-dealer) to come and serve as a script doctor on a failing movie project. They have called Rabbit in because he is "supposed to be an artist, right?... a kind of magician or something... You dream things up" (67). The parallel with Shepard's experience is plain here, and, as in *Horse Dreamer*, he identifies Rabbit as a specifically Western writer who has drawn his inspiration from the land and the old traditions. Rabbit (like Shepard) doesn't fly, and he has come to L.A. in a buckboard, stopping at all the old Spanish missions along the way to pray. He has *"bundles of various sizes attached to him by long leather thongs and dragging on the floor behind him"* (64), Indian medicine bundles that are to be laid out on a wheel representing the universe. The West is the "Looks-Within place," and its bundle is "very dangerous" (97). The East, on the other hand, is "the place of illumination, where we can see things clearly far and wide" (98).

The plan of Lanx and Wheeler is to exploit Rabbit's "magic" to save their movie. Believing that they can save themselves from "total annihilation" (71) only by injecting a major disaster in the picture, they assign him to come up with "something which will in fact drive people right off the deep end... something which not only mirrors their own sense of doom but actually creates the possibility of it right there in front of them... we must help them devour themselves or be devoured by them" (71). Rabbit at first demurs, suggesting that this is something "totally out of my ball park... I've conjured a little bit. I collect a few myths, but this sounds like you need a chemical expert or something" (71). Again, the reflection of Shepard's experience on *Zabriskie Point*, which ends with an apocalyptic conflagration, is obvious. Rabbit's gift is completely inappropriate to the job. Nevertheless, Rabbit succumbs to the temptation. Addressing the audience, he says, "I'm ravenous for power but I have to conceal it" (69). The will-to-power is only one part of Rabbit's motivation for succumbing to the siren lure of L.A. Another is revealed by Tympani (like Shepard, a drummer), a studio musician whose goal is to discover a rhythm structure that is "guaranteed to produce certain trance states in masses of people" (72). He says the force that drew Rabbit is simple, "money." And Rabbit confesses, "That's right. So what?" (88). Lanx makes it clear that Rabbit has lost any special claims for his creative gift by turning it into a commodity: "So don't go pulling rank on me with that 'Artist' crap! You're no better than any of us" (88). The third part of

Rabbit's motivation is revealed by Miss Scoons, a secretary: "The ambition behind the urge to create is no different from any other ambition. To kill. To win. To get on top" (88). In agreeing to work for Lanx and Wheeler on creating a new level of disaster, Rabbit acknowledges that the values of power, money, and ambition have replaced the purer, more spiritual inspirations for creation that he had experienced on the desert, the Spanish missions, and Indian mythology.

In Act 2, the characters are, as Tympani says, "locked into the narrowest part of our dream machine" (97), and restricted to enacting the central "themes" of their particular essences. Lanx spends the act shadow boxing and Rabbit is preoccupied with his medicine bundles, trying to manipulate their spiritual power for his new ends. Wheeler has turned into a monster with slimy green skin, fangs, and extra-long fingernails that turn into claws as the act proceeds. Rabbit discovers in the course of the act that he has become Wheeler. Wheeler shows him a kind of Ur-movie, an epic battle between a man and a woman that ends with the woman stabbing the man and then embracing him. As Wheeler describes the ending: "They were one being with two opposing parts. Everything was clear to them. At last they were connected. In that split second they gained and lost their entire lives" (108). This myth of gender is rejected by Rabbit, who is now a monstrous reflection of Wheeler. He complains that this was not a disaster, and says, "We're not interested in hanky-panky love stories, romantically depicting the end of the world" (108), a fair description of *Zabriskie Point*. Rabbit tells Wheeler he's finished in the movie business, "dead and gone" (110). Wheeler picks up the medicine bundle that represents the West and self-knowledge, and they stand watching as out of it *"a slow, steady stream of green liquid, the color of their faces, oozes from it onto the stage"* (111). The play ends with Lanx and Miss Scoons, who have transformed into teenager spectators, arguing about whether they will stay for the next movie or not.

The darkness of this representation of the movie industry certainly rivals that of *Day of the Locust*. It is telling, however, that the imagery Shepard uses is not the purifying fire of Armageddon with which West ends his novel, but the green slime of disgust, undoubtedly self-disgust. The target of *Angel City* is not so much Los Angeles or the movie business as it is the writer who sells out, the artist who succumbs to ambition and the desire for power and money, turning his creative imagination into a commodity that is for sale to the highest bidder. As in *Horse Dreamer*, the danger here is that this violation of the artist's mysterious creative power will destroy the imagination, and therefore the artist. The disaster for Rabbit is that he achieves his ambition in becoming Wheeler. As Wheeler says: "I'm in the business. I'm in pictures. I plant pictures in people's heads . . . I spread their disease. I'm that powerful" (109). Rabbit, whose hope as an artist was to use the spiritual "medicine" with which he was in tune to create, has become a spreader of the disease he was fighting, a promoter of fear through fake disaster.

True West is built on much starker aesthetic lines than *Horse Dreamer* or *Angel City*, but it is a further development of Shepard's treatment of the bifurcation of the artist into imagination and craft, and the danger of commodifying the imagination. In a well-known statement about the play, Shepard has laid out its general schema:

> I wanted to write a play about double nature, one that wouldn't be symbolic or metaphorical or any of that stuff. I just wanted to give a taste of what it feels like to be two-sided. It's a real thing, double nature. I think we're split in a much more devastating way than psychology can ever reveal. It's not so cute. Not some little thing we can get over. It's something we've got to live with.[15]

Early reviewers referred to *True West* as a Cain-and-Abel or Jekyll-and-Hyde play, and several critics have examined the issue of bifurcation in detail, placing it in a variety of interpretive contexts.[16] In the context of Shepard's earlier plays about the artist's relation to the movie industry, Lee and Austin emerge as representations of imagination and craft, and the play as the drama of their interrelation in the context of the movie business.

As *True West* opens, Austin is seated at the table in his mother's kitchen, trying to concentrate on writing what he later identifies as "research" for a movie "project" he is developing with a producer, Saul Kimmer. Austin refers to his movie as a "period piece,"[17] a "simple love story." Austin inhabits the domestic sphere in the play. He has been entrusted by his mother with watching her house and nurturing her plants, and he is working at his job as a screenwriter to support his family, who live somewhere "up North." For Austin, screenwriting is clearly a craft. He refers to it at one point as "doing business" (14). Austin's brother Lee has been living out on the desert, where their father, a penniless alcoholic, has been living since he left the family. Lee has not been "anywhere near" Austin for five years and claims to be a "free agent." When Austin offers Lee some money, Lee accuses him of trying to buy him off as he has the Old Man, with "Hollywood blood money," saying "I can git my own money my own way. Big money!" (9). Lee claims to have done "a little art myself once" that was "ahead of its time" (6), but now he lives by his wits. Lee does not sleep.

Viewed as a monodrama that dramatizes the conflicting pulls of the imagination and the craftsman within the writer, the play's opening scene presents the artist who is functioning completely at the level of craft (Austin) within the movie business. His aim is to produce an outline that Saul Kimmer will like well enough to pay him an advance, which will in turn allow him to turn it into a salable script that appeals to "bankable" stars. He is visited by Lee, the imagination, completely out of the blue after a long absence. While Austin has been domesticated in the mother's kitchen, under the "female" influence of middle-brow culture, Lee has been roaming the desert, Shepard's "true West," the domain of the father and the masculine. In the course of the play, the imagination, in the form of Lee, forces itself upon the writer, drawing him into working on his "true-to-life" "Contemporary Western" (18) instead of the love story. Austin refers to Lee's story as "two lame-brains chasing each other across Texas" (30), which it is (like Shepard's movie *Paris, Texas*). But Lee's narration suggests the power of the imagination in evoking some primal human feelings:

> So they take off after each other straight into an endless black prairie. The sun is just comin' down and they can feel the night on their backs. What they don't know is that each one of 'em is afraid, see. Each one separately thinks that he's the only one that's afraid. And they keep ridin' like that straight in to the night. Not knowing. And the one who's chasin' doesn't know where the other one is taking him. And the one who's being chased doesn't know where he's going. (27)

The power of the imagination is mixed up with the venality of Hollywood when Lee wins an advance for his story from Saul on the golf course, but Saul tries to convince Austin to help Lee write the screenplay because "it has the ring of truth . . . something about the real West . . . Something about the land" (35). Besides, as Saul tells Austin, "nobody's interested in love these days" (35).

The brothers switch places as Lee tries to write without the aid of Austin, and Austin lies drunk on the floor (the writer's imagination takes hold of him, driving out the craftsman). Austin says that Saul "thinks we're the same person . . . he's lost his mind" (37). Lee at first claims that he can write the whole script on his own, but he is soon begging Austin for help. The imagination may "never sleep," and may force whole stories into the artist's consciousness, but it cannot create art without the aid of conscious craftsmanship. Austin taunts Lee with the precarious position of the imagination in the context of the business of Hollywood: "Oh, now you're having a little doubt huh? What happened? The pressure's on, boy. This is it. You gotta' come up with it now. You don't come up with a winner on your first time out they just cut your head off. They don't give you a second chance ya' know" (40).

The relationship of the brothers turns into a symbiotic one as both see the inadequacies of their own positions. Austin wants Lee to teach him to live on the desert because he has come to see that "there is nothin' down here for me. There never was . . . there's nothin' real down here, Lee! Least of all me!" (49).

For his part, Lee says that he can't "save" Austin: "Ya' think it's some kinda' philosophical decision I took or somethin'? I'm livin' out there 'cause I can't make it here! And yer bitchin' to me about all yer success!" (49). When Austin agrees to help Lee write the screenplay in exchange for Lee's taking him to the desert, some integration of craft and imagination begins to seem possible, and they do manage to work together, despite their drunken, quarrelsome state, and the chaos that now surrounds them in the kitchen, as Austin takes Lee's dictation and agrees to his dictum, "You hear a stupid line you change it. That's yer job" (51), and Lee sees the imaginative implications of Austin's line, "I'm on intimate terms with this prairie": "sounds real mysterious and kinda' threatening at the same time" (52).

This short-lived integration falls apart when Mom appears, however, with her desire for order, her contention that high culture, in the person of Picasso, lives, and her contempt for the Old Man and the boys, who, she says, will "probably wind up on the same desert sooner or later" (53). Mom has to leave the house despite Austin's plea that "this is where you live," because she doesn't "recognize it at all" (59). Lee's visitation to the domestic sphere that Austin had previously inhabited ruptures Austin's relationship to the culture that Shepard identifies with the female. Before she leaves, Mom tells Austin that he cannot kill Lee because "it's a savage thing to do," and he responds, "yeah well don't tell me I can't kill him because I can" (58). The status of the imagination remains in doubt as the brothers stand facing each other at the end of the play, but their interaction has wreaked havoc on the realistic set, a visual representation of the impossibility of containing the writer's imagination within its limits and conventions. This is, of course, a metatheatrical reference to *True West* itself, which begins on a set that, Shepard notes, "*should be constructed realistically with no attempt to distort its dimensions, shapes, objects, or colors*" (3), and ends with the two brothers facing each other in the night: "*a single coyote heard in distance, lights fade softly into moonlight, the figures of the brothers now appear to be caught in a vast desert-like landscape*" (59). Whatever the outcome of the struggle between Lee and Austin, it appears that the Old Man has won.

Shepard's exploration of the writer's attempt to negotiate his bifurcation between what he has come to define more and more clearly as the male and female principles – the cowboy and the lady, the Old Man and Mom, the desert of the West and domesticated culture – reaches its full development in *Fool for Love*. In 1993, Shepard told Carol Rosen that his work in the mid-eighties was influenced by feminism, to the extent that

> there was a period of time when there was a kind of awareness happening about the female side of things. Not necessarily women but just the female

force in nature becoming interesting to people. And it became more and more interesting to me because of how that female thing relates to being a man ... as a man what is it like to embrace the female part of yourself that you historically damaged for one reason or another.[18]

The most obvious reference for this comment is to *A Lie of the Mind* (1985), but it is equally important to understanding *Fool for Love*. Shepard said in 1997 that "the play came out of falling in love. It's such a dumb-founding experience. In one way you wouldn't trade it for the world. In another way it's absolute hell. More than anything, falling in love causes a certain female thing in a man to manifest."[19]

Like *True West*, *Fool for Love* is at one level a monodrama about the writer's bifurcation. In this case, the important split is between the aspects of his creativity that Shepard identifies as male and female forces. What is at stake is whether Eddie will succumb to the influence of the male principle, the Old Man, or the female principle, his lover/sister May, and by extension her mother and some version of the Eternal Feminine. Eddie is described by the Old Man as "A fantasist ... You dream things up."[20] The primal relation of truth to stories, or lying, is raised in one of the play's most memorable images, the empty picture frame that the Old Man tells Eddie is "somethin' real ... Somethin' actual" (27), a picture of Barbara Mandrell. Since the Old Man is "actually married to Barbara Mandrell in [his] mind," the picture, he tells Eddie, is "realism." Because the Old Man considers his own subjective experience to be the only reality, it is easy for him to claim that his love for Eddie's and May's mothers was "the same love. Just got split in two, that's all" (48). In his solipsistic view, his love remains unchanged even though he has deserted both of the women: "I wasn't disconnected. There was nothing cut off in me. Everything went on just the same as though I'd never left" (55).

In realizing that he still loves May but feels compelled to pursue his new passion for the Countess, Eddie is confronting his "male" heritage from the Old Man: "He had two separate lives ... two completely separate lives. He'd live with me and my mother for a while and then he'd disappear and go live with her and her mother for a while" (48). Eddie faces three alternatives: he can win May back and remain with her; he can leave her and continue his relationship with the Countess; or he can do what the Old Man did, and split himself in two by trying to fulfill his desire for both of them.

The second half of *Fool for Love* stages an agon in the form of a story-telling contest, with May's suitor Martin standing in for the spectators as the judge of what is most believable, and therefore "real." Eddie's is a coming-of-age story in which he undergoes a kind of initiation into love by his father. He tells of his father's disappearances and reappearances, and then the period when the Old Man says he was "making a decision" (49), taking long walks across the fields. In Eddie's story, he asks if he can go with his father one night, and they walk off across the fields together, silent the whole time. The Old Man buys a bottle, and the two pass it back and forth wordlessly as they walk, finally reaching the "little white house with a red awning" where May and her mother live. As May's mother and the Old Man fall into each other's arms, May appears, "just standing there, staring at me and I'm staring back at her and we can't take our eyes off each other. It was like we knew each other from somewhere but we couldn't place where. But the second we saw each other, that very second, we knew we'd never stop being in love" (50).

Eddie's is a "male" story of inarticulate father–son bonding and imitation – of the son becoming the father – and a dark romantic tale of succumbing wordlessly to illicit, passionate love as to a star-crossed destiny. May responds by telling Martin that "none of it's true": "He's had this weird, sick idea for years now and it's totally made up. He's nuts" (51). She says that Eddie's told her the story a thousand times and "it always changes" (51). When Eddie retorts, "I never repeat myself," May responds, "You do nothing but repeat yourself" (51). The spectator's response to the story is signaled by Martin's. When Eddie asks if he thinks he made the whole thing up, Martin replies, "No. I mean at the time you were telling it, it seemed real" (51). Eddie suggests that he is doubting it now because May said it was a lie: "She suggests it's a lie to you and all of a sudden you change your mind? Is that it? You go from true to false like that, in a second?" (51). Of course he does, as the play's audience has, and as it was set up by Shepard to do. One of the major issues the scene raises is the relation of reality, and of truth, to art. The reliability of the narrative is made even more questionable in the Robert Altman film of *Fool for Love*, in which Shepard played Eddie, and for which he wrote the screenplay. There the stories are told in voiceover as sequences of "the past" appear on screen. Many details of the action the spectators are watching contradict those in the story they are hearing.

The men's responses are telling when May proposes to tell "the whole rest of the story ... just exactly the way it happened. Without any little tricks added onto it" (52). "What does she know?" says the Old Man, and Eddie responds, "She's lying" (52). May's story is a classic tale of woman scorned. May's mother is "obsessed with [the Old Man] to the point where she couldn't stand being without him for even a second" (53). She follows him from town to town, until finally she "dogs him down." She is "on fire" and her body is "trembling" as she searches the town for him, yet she is "terrified" because she knows she is "trespassing ... crossing this forbidden zone but she couldn't help herself" (53). As Eddie imitated his father, May imitated her mother, becoming obsessed with Eddie to the extent that she didn't even feel sorry for her mother, who was again deserted by the Old Man, because "all [she] could think of was him" (54). The Old Man interrupts May's story with pleas to Eddie: "Boy, is she ever off the wall with this one. You gotta' do somethin' about this . . . she's gettin' way outa line, here" (53–54). When May says that Eddie's mother "blew her brains out" when she heard about May and Eddie, the Old Man makes a direct appeal to Eddie:

> This story doesn't hold water. (*To Eddie, who stays seated*) You're not gonna' let her off the hook with that one are ya'? That's the dumbest version I ever heard in my whole life. She never blew her brains out. Nobody ever told me that. Where the hell did that come from? . . . Stand up! Get on yer feet now goddammit! I wanna' hear the male side a' this thing. You gotta' represent me now. Speak on my behalf. There's no one to speak for me now! Stand up! . . . We've got a pact. Don't forget that. (54)

This is an explicit challenge to Eddie to join in solidarity with the "male side," eschewing the female point of view as his father has, and living completely within his own solipsistic reality. Eddie refuses the Old Man, affirming May's story instead. As Eddie's and May's eyes meet, and they begin to draw together, the Old Man pleads with Eddie: "You two can't come together! You gotta' hold up my end a' this deal. I got nobody now! Nobody! You can't betray me! You gotta' represent me now! You're my son!" (55).

Although Eddie and May do come together momentarily, signifying their union with an embrace and kiss, this fusion of male and female is unstable in Sam Shepard's world. Sexuality intrudes, in the form of the Countess, who sets off an explosion and a consuming fire. Eddie goes out to "take a look," and May knows that "he's gone" (56). After May leaves with her suitcase, it is the Old Man who has the last word, pointing to the empty picture frame, and saying "that's the woman of my dreams. That's who that is. And she's mine. She's all mine. Forever" (57). Which of course she is, since she exists completely within the Old Man's consciousness anyway.

In the context of Shepard's writing about the writer and his imagination, the import of this exploration of the male and female principles is not particularly hopeful. Although he consciously rejects the Old Man's demand for blind affiliation with the "male side" of things, Eddie cannot escape his influence, and he seems destined to act out the story if not to endorse it. On the other hand, although it is not clear where May is going at the end of the play, unlike her mother she accepts the fact that her lover is "gone," and moves on with her life. This is made even clearer in the film, as May walks determinedly out onto the road while Eddie chases after the Countess on horseback, ridiculously trying to lasso her Mercedes.

Shepard would seem to recognize the need to see the "female side" of things as he recognizes the need to fight such assaults on the writer's imagination as Hollywood's attempt to commodify it and the attempts by middle-brow cultural forces to domesticate it. He also realizes that these are ongoing conflicts the artist must face, not issues that can be "solved" by writing plays about them. Speaking about the power of family influences, Shepard has said, "I think that there is no escape, that the wholehearted acceptance of it leads to another possibility. But the possibility of somehow miraculously making myself into a different person is a hoax, a futile game. And it leads to insanity, actually . . . People go insane trying to deny what they really are."[21]

NOTES

1 Sheila Rabillard, "Shepard's Challenge to the Modernist Myths of Origin and Originality: *Angel City* and *True West*," in Leonard Wilcox (ed.), *Rereading Shepard: Contemporary Critical Essays on the Plays of Sam Shepard* (New York: St. Martin's Press, 1993), 77–96 and Leonard Wilcox, "West's *The Day of the Locust* and Shepard's *Angel City*," *Modern Drama*, 36 (1993): 61–75.

2 Mona Simpson, Jeanne McCulloch, and Benjamin Howe, "Sam Shepard: the Art of Theatre XII," *The Paris Review*, 142 (Spring 1997): 204–25.

3 Samuel Taylor Coleridge, *Biographia Literaria*, ed. James Engell and W. Jackson Bate, 2 vols., *The Collected Works of Samuel Taylor Coleridge*, vol. 1 (Princeton University Press, 1983), 304.

4 Irene Oppenheim and Victor Fascio, "The Most Promising Playwright in American Today is Sam Shepard," *Village Voice*, 27 October 1975, 81.

5 Ibid.

6 Ibid.

7 Robert Coe, "The Saga of Sam Shepard," *New York Times Magazine*, 23 November 1980, 124.

8 Oppenheim and Fascio, "Most Promising Playwright," 81.

9 Rabillard, "Shepard's Challenge to the Modernist Myths."

10 Carol Rosen, "Emotional Territory: an Interview with Sam Shepard," *Modern Drama*, 36.1 (1993): 8.

11 Sam Shepard, *Angel City* in *Fool for Love and Other Plays* (New York: Bantam Books, 1984), 61–62. Page references in parentheses within the text are to this edition.

12 Shepard, *Geography of a Horse Dreamer* in *Fool for Love and Other Plays*, 279. Page references in parentheses within the text are to this edition.

13 Ross Wetzsteon, "Looking a Gift Horse Dreamer in the Mouth," in Bonnie Marranca (ed.), *American Dreams: The Imagination of Sam Shepard* (New York: Performing Arts Journal Publications, 1981), 133–34.

14 Martin Tucker, *Sam Shepard* (New York: Continuum, 1992), 98.

15 Coe, "Saga of Sam Shepard," 122.
16 William Kleb suggests that "Austin represents objectivity, self-control and self-discipline, form and order, the intellect, reason. Lee stands for subjectivity, anarchy, adventure, excess and exaggeration, intuition and imagination." See William Kleb, "Worse than Being Homeless: *True West* and the Divided Self," in Marranca, *American Dreams*, 121. Tucker Orbison has suggested that "Lee and Austin form dual opposed elements in a single self," with Lee functioning as a Jungian "shadow figure" for Austin. See Tucker Orbison, "Mythic Levels in Sam Shepard's *True West*," *Modern Drama*, 27.4 (1984): 513, 515. See also, David Wyatt, "Shepard's Split," *South Atlantic Quarterly*, 91.2 (Spring 1992): 333–60.
17 Sam Shepard, *True West* in *Sam Shepard: Seven Plays* (New York: Bantam Books, 1981), 13. Page references in parentheses within the text are to this edition.
18 Rosen, "Emotional Territory," 6–7.
19 Simpson et al., "Sam Shepard: the Art of Theatre XII," 221.
20 Sam Shepard, *Fool for Love* in *Fool for Love and Other Plays* (New York: Bantam Books, 1984), 27. Page references in parentheses within the text are to this edition.
21 Rosen, "Emotional Territory," 9.

8

LESLIE KANE

Reflections of the past in *True West* and *A Lie of the Mind*

> We are not merely more weary
> because of yesterday, we are other, no
> longer what were we before the calamity of yesterday.
> SAMUEL BECKETT, *Proust*

As James Knowlson and John Pilling observe in *Frescoes of the Skull,* "the past will not be treated as if it were a butterfly to be caught in a net... For once the attempt has been made to capture it in words, the memory of 'that time' simply melts away, or changes its shape and its nature, or again is transformed by another and rather different 'that time.' "[1] Two Sam Shepard family-themed plays written in the 1980s, *True West* (1980) and *A Lie of the Mind* (1985), in particular, are flooded with references to the past which characters attempt to capture but which "changes its shape and its nature," eluding individual or collaborative efforts to recall and fix familial and cultural history.

Shepard's recent fascination with the past reflects not only the influence of Samuel Beckett, whose work is similarly colored by memory, but also the impact of the playwright's personal experience, loss, and middle age. Speaking with Stephanie Coen he remarked, "The past is a memory. I mean, what is the past? Of course, as you grow older, the past looms a lot larger... [N]ow it becomes important to me to understand the way my stuff is interconnected, the way it's the result of the past. I'm beginning to understand that I'm the direct product of something that's wild and woolly."[2] And to Jonathan Cott Shepard suggested,

> It's interesting how you can be lost in an area like memory – memory is very easy to get lost in. Some things can't get lost, though, because they're based on *emotional* memory, which is a different thing from just trying to remember the name of a person or some fact. But to remember where you were touched has more of a reverberation. It remembers itself to you.[3]

The tension between memory and forgetting largely informs Shepard's "time-plays" about the American family,[4] although, as Jeanette Malkin has noticed, "the obsession with marking memory may in fact portend an awareness of its erosion, perhaps even a desire to forget."[5] Hence, in Shepard's late plays, characters are as likely to seize upon scraps of personal and national history as they are to attempt to elude what Lawrence Langer terms "the burden of a vexatious past."[6] For those intent on the latter, numerous strategies abound. In fact, Langer suggests that they may "forget, repress, ignore, deny, or simply falsify the facts" (96). Shepard's characters make full use of all these methodologies or, as in the case of Dodge in *Buried Child* and Lorraine in *A Lie of the Mind*, they attempt to obliterate the past by setting it ablaze in a pyre of personal possessions.[7]

The scene in *A Lie of the Mind* in which Lorraine and her daughter Sally prepare to leave the family homestead is illustrative. Intent on traveling light, Lorraine, who has instructed Sally to destroy everything, is seen amassing a *"large pile of junk"* that contains her brother Jake's model airplanes, old letters, and photographs.[8] At first discarded and then retrieved, one picture of her mother catches Sally's eye. After initial bewilderment, Lorraine places the time and event with sudden clarity. "Oh – I know," she says. "This was down in Victorville. Had a big 'Frontier Days' blowout ... Musta been 'forty-five, 'forty-six" (116). Immediately, memories of a young, spirited Lorraine in love with Sally's father flood the scene implicitly underscoring Shepard's observation that "It must be true that we're continuously taking in images of experience from the outside world through our senses, even when we're not aware of it. How else could whole scenes from our past which we'd long forgotten suddenly spring up in living technicolor?"[9] Given the vitality of the memory that recalls a time when husband and wife were living well and happily, Sally thus infers, "You wanna save this one, then?":

LORRAINE (*Hands photo back to* SALLY) Naw, burn it.
SALLY (*Taking photo*) You sure?
LORRAINE What do you wanna save it for? It's all in the past. Dead and gone.
   Just a picture. (117)

However, in Shepard's work, nothing could be further from the truth. One of the more striking ways that the playwright employs to portray the manner in which the past "remembers itself" in a quintet of family plays – *Buried Child*, *Curse of the Starving Class*, *True West*, *Fool for Love*, and *A Lie of the Mind* – is through photographs. Literal and figurative snapshots abound in his work, some prominently displayed, such as those that prompt Shelly in *Buried Child* to correctly presume of a display of family photographs that "Your whole life's up there hanging on the wall," and Sally to spot pictures of her siblings and herself plastered to the walls of her father's fetid trailer among photographs of his favorite pop culture heroes of the 1930s and 1940s.[10] Others are buried deep in the unconscious. As timeless icons of identity, photographs, which prompt memories of another time and place, are inextricably bound to the notion of continuity and discontinuity. And, suggests Una Chaudhuri, they prove "the ideal figure" for the "unraveling of the old discourse of home and family ... enter[ing a play] as carriers of an undeniable dissemination, of which the first casualty is the mythic family of tradition."[11] If in *True West* and *A Lie of the Mind* images of the past are not always tangible – or especially welcome – they are no less discernible, providing a critical dramatic and cinematic framework in family-themed plays that share the locus of the home.

Although Malkin suggests that Shepard is not "seriously concerned with the past as history" in his earlier work, the late plays, she rightly observes, "turn *back* toward the root-themes of more traditional American realist drama: homecoming, heritage, dynastic curse, and the intertwined fate of the clan."[12] *True West* and *A Lie of the Mind* share at-home settings (or in the case of the latter, two homes), paradigmatic homecoming, and the "vicissitudes of returning to the place marked as home..."[13] But in as much as these are Shepard plays, the terms "homecoming" and "heritage" are grenades capable of shattering any preconceived notion of either. Upon closer inspection, legacy largely takes the form of addiction, disconnection, and displacement whereas homecomings, both literal and figurative, paradoxically provide shelter *and* entrapment, offering myriad opportunities to recover, rake up, or scatter the ashes of the past. Enoch Brater observes of Shepard's "time plays" that "There is no stable 'past,' only ... compelling versions of it."[14] Not merely compelling, but also competing versions of the past inform *True West* and *A Lie of the Mind*, riveting our attention to the shifting ground of memory, the ways in which fact and fiction blur, and the manner in which siblings, parents, and children (and immediate or extended family members) remember (or forget) the past, frequently as it suits them.

I

The obsession with the "memoried world," to use Malkin's phrase, is evident from the opening beat of *True West*. Shepard's predominantly two-character play about two brothers, Austin, a Hollywood screenwriter who leaves his home and family in northern California to develop a synopsis for a film in the privacy and quiet of his mother's home, and Lee, a loner and thief who spends his time in the desert, chronicles their recollections of family and childhood and reveals the resentments and frustrations each harbors. Beginning at night and concluding with dusk four days later, the passage of time in this play is reflected in the sunrises and sunsets, the accumulating junk, the death of the house-plants, and the growing pile of empty alcohol bottles. Lee, the older brother by a decade, is the principal historian of the family who intrudes on Austin at work on "a 'period piece.' " [15] Although his monosyllabic responses to Lee's insistent questions and incessant commentary signal his reluctance to engage in conversation and encourage Lee's continued presence in their mother's home, Lee immediately bridges the gap between past and present by drawing attention to their mother's habitual obsession with cleanliness – a fact obviously well known to both – to her antiques, which he disparages as "the same crap we always had around" (10), and to the candlelight by which Austin has been writing. "Isn't that what the old guys did?...The Forefathers. You know...Candlelight burning into the night? Cabins in the wilderness?" (6), he asks. To stop Lee's badgering, Austin makes a deal to buy his brother's silence by agreeing to give him the keys to his car, inspiring Lee to recall nostalgically in an ensuing scene an occasion when he lent Austin his "Forty Ford" (14) and to remember time spent in the nearby foothills, where, as children, Lee caught snakes and Austin pretended to be "Geronimo or some damn thing" (12).

Lee's seemingly innocuous comment about "The Forefathers" immediately introduces what Christopher Bigsby terms "a radically foreshortened moment" in which past and present dissolve. [16] It conjures up images of a mythical West, anticipates Lee's narration of an idea for "a Western that'd knock yer lights out...Contemporary Western. Based on a true story..." (18), and raises the issue of their dissolute progenitor. Moreover, it foreshadows Lee's rivalry for the approval of father-surrogate Saul Kimmer, a producer who Austin expects will option his screenplay, but who favors Lee's story, believing it has the "ring of truth...[of] the real West" (35). The playwright confirms that "there's a current in the play about what's true and what isn't, what is reality and what's fantasy." Yet, "the scripts being concocted are the fantasy...[I]n the course of it all, the two guys come up with stories about their father, simple, defined stories about him losing his teeth, going to Mexico, that are the real stories." [17] Similarly, Lee's remark provides an apt opening for Shepard's exploration of what is bona fide and baseless in collective memory – both familial and cultural – so that in effect "the past becomes the present reality, a memory, a three-dimensional fact." [18]

Thus, the disparity between Austin's concept for a film, which by its very nature is time-driven, and Lee's is especially notable. Buying into the Hollywood formula of the new West, Austin makes no pretense that his story is real. Relying on a time-honored, romanticized notion of movie-making, he has fashioned "a simple love story" (31) intended to be as familiar and comforting as the warm, buttered toast with which he welcomes the dawn of a subsequent morning when he forgoes temporarily the world of dreams for one of action by stealing an armful of toasters. Although we learn little else about Austin's idea for a screenplay, Lee's story, which he narrates (but can neither develop nor type) is given ample exposure, although in Austin's professional – and prejudicial – view, it is "idiotic." "It's a bullshit story . . . Two lamebrains chasing each other across Texas" (30). Nonetheless, Lee has "recognize[d] and manipulate[d] the fiction that is America's past." [19] And, importantly in this competitive environment and culture, he has capitalized on its worth, much as he has stolen a television from a neighborhood home far more valuable on the black market than all the toasters Austin swipes in his nighttime raid.

Likewise, their tactics in winning Kimmer's support differ markedly. Whereas Austin has endeavored to establish a relationship over time with Kimmer based on trust and Austin's talent, the feckless producer, much like their alcoholic father, loses all memory of their ostensibly negotiated deal when Lee goes into action. Challenging Kimmer to a game of golf, Lee raises the stakes to induce Kimmer to gamble Austin's future. Moreover, he uses his financial support of their "destitute" (33) father, though fictional, as leverage to win Kimmer's approval, painting a picture of this patriarchal figure as bogus as the West he portrays. Not only is Austin furious about the double betrayal, he is enraged by Lee's revelation and distortion of family history and fact: "I gave him money! I *already* gave him money. *You* know that. He drank it all up!" (my emphasis, 33). Despite his protest that his brother is out of touch with "what people wanna' see on the screen . . . " and that "[t]here's no such thing as the West anymore!" (35), Kimmer buys and sells Lee's "images of an unattainable past," which, as Megan Williams contends, "testifies to the present's inability to construct a living image of an American past." [20]

At issue from the first is the nature of Austin and Lee's past and present relationship with their alcoholic father, who, like Lee, resides in the desert. Paralleling Godot in *Waiting for Godot*, the father, a central figure in Shepard's drama, is absent, but made dramatically present by their continual reference to him. Despite their forced pleasantries, animosity bubbles up and old – and current – resentments surface. Sparring with his brother, Lee takes shots at Austin's eastern education, his ability to finesse a living with words, the "guilt" money that he gives their father. Critics generally regard this third play of Shepard's family quintet as a "civil war" of family life, a showdown between brothers. William Demastes maintains that *True West* may be more accurately viewed as a struggle between two halves of the self. [21] Stephen J. Bottoms concurs, arguing that dualistic, complementary pairings in Shepard's late plays, which date back to *The Tooth of Crime* (1972) (and Bottoms also traces to numerous "two guys" manuscripts in the 1970s), "are both interdependent and self-destructive."[22] This reading, of course, is consistent with Shepard's contention that "I wanted to write a play about double nature, one that wouldn't be symbolic or metaphorical...I think we're split in a much more devastating way than psychology can ever reveal."[23]

However, an interpretation of sibling rivalry and split personality that neglects the crucial factor that Lee is at home in the desert (Shepard's characteristic refuge for fathers as far back as *Holy Ghostly*) fails to recognize the older brother as rival *and* extension of the father. Crashing into Austin's successful, independent and carefully controlled world, Lee destroys Austin's autonomy, shatters his pride, and steals his identity and mobility. His demand for and receipt of Austin's car keys is an act of emasculation and aggression not lost on his younger brother nor forgotten by him and the audience in the closing moments of the play. And, increasingly, the effect of Lee's will and booze is observed in Austin's behavior and drunken singing. After he usurps Austin's position with Kimmer, nightfall of day three finds Lee at Austin's typewriter, attempting to write a draft of his screenplay by candlelight, having reversed positions, if not skills, with his brother while Austin drowns his sorrows in a bottle. Incapable of writing the screenplay, Lee posits a collaborative effort, offering Austin half the money from its sale; yet, the next morning he rescinds the terms of this deal, denying Austin both credit and cash for his "artistic hocus pocus" (50) but agreeing, at Austin's insistence, to compensation in the form of Lee's accompanying him to the desert, much as his older brother took him to play in the foothills in the past. The level of intoxication and its potential for disorientation, intimidation, and destruction are obvious, however, in the domestic debris of this battle to prove virility and superiority: a twisted typewriter, demolished toast, bent golf clubs, murdered plants, and a ripped-out telephone. Hence when their mother returns from her trip to Alaska, she does not even recognize her own home as a home.

Lee's catalytic presence, as Bottoms also notes, "inevitably brings the buried past back to the surface...," a device by which Shepard calls direct attention to the connection between the alcoholic father and his sons.[24] Thus, when Lee remarks that Austin sounds like the old man, Austin snipes, "Yeah, well we all sound alike when we're sloshed" (39), a far cry from his earlier defensive stance that he bears no resemblance to his father. In fact, Austin's narration of what he characterizes as "a true story. True to life" (42), one he contrasts with Lee's film which in his view is "not enough like real life" (21), further links son and father in an itinerant quest. According to his tale, Austin traveled from bar to bar in an unsuccessful search for his father's false teeth which the inebriated patriarch put in a doggie bag of Chop Suey and forgot in one of many bars. In so doing, Williams suggests, "he becomes embroiled in the same unsatisfied quest that defines Lee's cowboys and most of Shepard's characters" in his search "for the object that will piece the image of the family back together again..."[25] Yet in each listening to the other's narrative of past events Austin and Lee concretize both the implied unity of narration and the dramatic tension inherent in the act of listening that Shepard, after Beckett, employs to perfection. Moreover, the confessional nature of Austin's story draws these brothers back into the past, which, resembling the home they trash, has been transformed into something unrecognizable. Recalling the 1950s Austin admits, "When we were kids here it was different... that don't even exist anymore" (49).

Considering the circumstances of Shepard's life noted in numerous interviews before and after the death of his father, a World War II flyer and an alcohol-addicted intellectual who frequently fought with his son and periodically vanished into the desert, it seems hardly surprising that Shepard's plays are haunted by ghostly fathers plagued by alcoholism. Gcringer Woititz's landmark study, *Adult Children of Alcoholics*, posits a working model of an alcoholic home typified by violence and role reversal in which an alcoholic parent demonstrates psychopathic shifts in personality (from super-irresponsible to super-responsible), while the child assumes adult responsibilities.[26] A child raised in these circumstances survives by coping behavior. Such an individual may become a renegade like Lee or a "control freak" like Austin, whose neurotic behavior imposes order on a disordered world. Additionally, the child's desperate need for approval compels him to be extremely loyal, even though that loyalty is undeserved. Shepard recounts his own efforts at reconciliation with his father, sometimes taking the form of father and son going out drinking together. "[I]t would always veer on that thing of accusation," recalls the playwright. "[I]t would always turn, inevitably, on this accusation that there was something wrong and it had to do with me."[27] As metaphor the abuse of alcohol in Shepard's plays informs the denial of responsibility, the conflicted loyalty, the brutal bullies that people his world, and the unconsciousness "locking families in deceit and unknowingness" in the present moment and the past.[28]

Determined to fight for a "paradise" without his father in it, Austin demonstrates typically ambivalent behavior, at once fiercely protective of his world apart even as he imagines living in the desert with Lee. Once challenged, however, Austin trades his "woman-man" image (a term coined by Beth in *A Lie of the Mind* to describe the gentle brother of her violent husband) for that of the macho-man capable of hard drinking, stealing, and murder. When Lee disappoints Austin by refusing to take him to the desert, an act

symbolizing a lifetime of betrayal and duplicity, his rejection of familial connection and refusal to teach Austin desert survival skills open the floodgates
of Austin's rage. Threatened by Lee's now predatory behavior, Austin lunges
at his brother while his back is turned, choking him with the telephone wire
as he endeavors to cut off all communication and create an opportunity to
"get outa' here" (59).

In a final tableau we see Austin drop the cord in what may be interpreted as
a moment of guilt, grief, weakness, or daring escape, but despite his efforts to
dodge Lee and the past that he both personifies and shares, Austin is thwarted
in his attempt to break free when Lee springs to his feet, blocking Austin's
escape, much as he did earlier in the play with Kimmer. The playwright's stage
instructions are powerfully dramatic and symbolic: "*They square off to each
other, keeping a distance between them*" (59). Recalling the story of the cat
and the eagle in *Curse of the Starving Class*, these siblings are "caught in an
impossible bind of mutual incompatibility" with deep roots in the past.[29]
This "impossible bind" is reflected in the closing moments of the play, where
mythic memory is "inscribed as a filmscript."[30] Thus, Shepard's time-driven
picture of the history of this family – and America – conveys an enduring
"truth," namely, that we are largely unsuccessful in affixing meaning to the
past, in understanding its connection to the present, in breaking free of its
vise-like grip.

II

Similarly, in *A Lie of the Mind*, Shepard's epic drama of two families bound
by the marriage of their children, one fatherless and matriarchal and the
other patriarchal, the past casts a long shadow over present events. The
first scene depicting a conversation between two brothers is compelling and
prophetic: Jake's most recent beating of his wife Beth establishes an immediate bond with his brother Frankie and his physically and psychologically
abusive father, who, like him, drank too much and too often. The opening
moments of *A Lie of the Mind* immediately introduce a history of Jake's
trouble-making, his child-like refusal to accept responsibility for his actions,
and his abusive behavior. "Name a day he wasn't in trouble? He was trouble
from day one," exclaims his mother Lorraine (22). Hence when Jake tells
Frankie, "She got me in trouble more'n once," his brother has a firm pulse
on the truth and the past: "You lost your temper ... You've always lost your
temper" (12).

Although "The action of the play," as Leslie Wade rightly recognizes,
"has as its axis the turbulent marital relations of Jake and Beth," *A Lie of
the Mind*, like *True West*, is predominantly focused on the swirling vortex

of remembrance and forgetfulness.[31] As each spouse seeks refuge, Jake in California and Beth in Montana, where he is fed broccoli soup and she convalesces under the watchful care of her family – or what her father Baylor thinks of as "play[ing] nursemaid to a bunch a' feeble-minded women..." (106) – Jake and Beth "replay their childhoods at the foundation of subjectivity, the family home."[32] Selective memory prevails in both locales. Lorraine, for example, who has no recollection of her daughter-in-law Beth, asks Jake's sister Sally, "Who's Beth?...Never hear a' her" (22). Yet she remembers that Jake was "Just a spit of a thing" when she and his father "were in love...back before things went to pieces" (37), the pain of her husband's drinking and abandonment, her ancestors in Ireland.

In *A Lie of the Mind* structural pairings of siblings, fathers and sons, and husbands and wives are duplicated and intertwined as is time and place, a point underscored by Shepard's adapting filmic techniques to the dramatic stage to simulate "parallel time." Enoch Brater has noticed, moreover, that this play "features two cosmically (and sometimes comically) dysfunctional families in three playing times," which, coupled with the set, provide for "several stunning intersections of subjective, objective, linear, and imaginary time."[33] As if beaten unconscious or in a drunken stupor, Jake, for example, has difficulty in connecting the present time to "that" time – before he beat Beth, before his father died, before he lived in this childhood home. Although Lorraine endeavors to fill in the blanks of family history by recounting events "before," Jake's connection to his father and to the past is further underlined by his inheritance of his father's ashes and funeral flag, both dusty with neglect. In a startling image of undress Jake, in boxer shorts and shirt-sleeves, dons his father's World War II leather flight-jacket, an act blending present time with historical events. Implicitly assuming his elder's mantle, medals, and masculinity as he has his behavior, Jake admits to his surprise that the presence and pressure of his father weighs heavily: "'He's kinda' heavy'" (39).

Surrounded by images of his youth – his toy airplanes, his childhood bed, his mother's broccoli soup, which he petulantly overturns – Jake refuses adamantly to remember the drinking competition with his father that led to his father's death:

> JAKE How was it he died?
> (*Pause. They stare at each other.*)
> LORRAINE Jake, you remember all that...Truck blew up and he went with it. You already know that. (40)

Jake, however, has blocked memory or feigns amnesia about that night. Yet, when he slips away from Lorraine's home to go to Beth in Montana, torn between "the father he can't escape and the woman he can't stop loving," we see him, dressed only in underpants and the American flag, carrying his father's ashes.[34] Hoping his mother will mistake his sister, who conspires with him and has assumed his place in the bed, Jake escapes under cover of night, leaving Sally to shoulder the weight of his past deeds.

In *A Lie of the Mind* the role of historian is splintered so that each member of each family remembers some aspect of family behavior and history, though some can't remember whether events happened to them or others. In the California family, for example, Sally's memory stands as the only record of the events leading up to her father's death. In compelling testimony, which as Langer reminds us "presumes a chronology or sequence and the act of retreating in time and space to a period and place preceding and different from the present,"[35] Sally recalls what she perceives to be the truth to maintain her "lie of the mind" that she was not responsible for her father's death, although the facts of her narrative are neither validated nor refuted by Frankie, who apparently did not join her and Jake in their journey to Mexico. Her story, nonetheless, is a confession of a secret, "produc[ing] a reckoning of both facts and persons."[36] While she would like to recall a vulnerable old man, what she does remember began as a drinking competition between father and son of double shots of tequila, a kind of "brotherhood they'd just remembered" that escalated to who could throw a ball harder, who could run fastest and longest. The challenge began to harden into a hatred fueled by more double shots when "Jake came up with a brilliant idea" (92, 94), a footrace to the American border, although her father was already so drunk "He didn't even know what country he was in anymore!" (95). Like Lee's story of the Old West in *True West*, Sally's has the ring of truth, her recollection overflowing with a plethora of minutiae and searing images triggered by what Saul Friedlander terms "the curious preciseness of memory."[37] Even as Lorraine characterizes Sally's story as pure fiction and her motives as unadulterated malice, Lorraine's actions belie her words when she struggles to stand, steadying herself by leaning against the bed. Remembering little else but the pain left behind by her weak husband, Lorraine, typically American in upping stakes and starting anew, resolves to make a clean sweep, ironically hoping she will find release from the past and from the reality of her son's brutality by retracing her ancestral roots in Ireland.

The treatment of memory is no less fascinating in the Montana family, where Beth's brother Mike is both her protector and the family's principal historian, the custodian of memories of the abuse done to his sister during the years that span her marriage to Jake. Committed to helping her forget Jake, Mike repeatedly tells her, "You gotta forget about him for now! You gotta just forget about him!" (19). But Jake neither forgets him nor the final beating that irrevocably changed his sister's life. Hence, in Act 3, Scene 3, when Jake finally closes the gulf between his home and hers, Mike not only takes Jake prisoner, he brings him to his knees, beats him down, scripts his apology, and acts as a prompt coach to prepare Jake for his encounter with Beth. " . . . You remember her, don't ya? (JAKE *nods.*) You remember what you're going to say to her? (JAKE *nods.*) You're not going to forget?" (121).

Beth's mother, Meg, a passive woman who at first glance bears little resemblance to the forceful, domineering Lorraine, is, nonetheless, as confused in her recollections of Jake as Lorraine is of Beth. Informed by Mike that Jake inflicted the brain damage that Beth has sustained, his name seems to mean nothing to her:

> MEG Who's Jake?
> MIKE Her husband, Mom. Jake . . . You remember Jake, don't ya? (28–29)

Meg's recall of her own family history is shaky, as well, a fact revealed when Beth's hospitalization prompts Meg's mistaken memory. "They locked me up once, didn't they, Dad?" she asks husband Baylor who, correcting her, responds, "That wasn't *you.* That was your mother . . . That was a long time ago, anyhow" (my emphasis, 30). And when Beth proposes marrying Frankie, who travels to Montana at Jake's insistence to inquire about Beth's condition and is shot by Baylor for his trouble when he trespasses on Baylor's land, Meg gets so caught up in planning a romantic wedding in "the high meadow . . . Just like the old times" that she prattles on oblivious to Beth's prior marriage to Jake (112).

For his part, Baylor is keenly aware of time – the time to have his feet oiled, to hunt antelope, to get his mules to market, to have his injured daughter commence recovery and assume responsibility. He remembers his rights as a land-owner, the time Meg's crazy mother lived with them, that he went fishing when Beth married Jake instead of attending the wedding, that the flag of this nation must be respected, and to Meg's surprise, even how to kiss his wife after twenty years. And although it is eons since Baylor was in the armed service, he remembers how to fold the American flag in traditional military style, "like right outa the manual" (130). What he doesn't seem to remember or care about is Jake, the perpetrator of Beth's beating, his attention drawn to what David Savran terms "reinforc[ing] and even glorif[ying] the American past."[38]

Memory – or the absence of it – is most striking in brain-damaged Beth, who, when we first encounter her in the hospital, is terrified, disoriented, and in pain. Confused about her surroundings and about who hurt her, she repeatedly demands of Mike, "WHO FELL ME!!!" (5). Barely able to walk or speak, Beth believes she is dead – "mummified" in bandages – and buried in a tree. She has difficulty remembering her home, though once coached by Meg, she stares at her surroundings trying to place them in memory. Her inverted syntax, disconnection between word and meaning, simplicity of sentence construction, guilelessness, and slippage of tenses are child-like. Abstract concepts elude her completely. When Mike assures her that she is "safe" as long as she remains within the protective bosom of her birth family, she exhibits no more understanding of the phrase "safe" than she does the premise of her brain healing: "What brain?... Where? In me... Iz in there like a turtle? Like a shell?" (49). Lacking connection between cause and effect, Beth is thus convinced of a nonexistent surgery to remove her brain – even showing Frankie a mythical scar to illustrate the cataclysmic change wrought in one moment in time. As she explains it to Frankie, "Your whole life can turn around. Upside down. In a flash... Everything you know can go... " (81), yet, like a child, she has little comprehension of what it is that she has lost.

Unlike Jake, whose immaturity, irrational rages, and sniveling demeanor mimic that of a child, Beth regresses into childhood. Her amnesia is protective, a lie of the mind that like the "deceitful tricks that the mind can play" permits her to be cognizant of the pain of the beating but not remember the beating itself. [39] She lacks memory of the play she was rehearsing at that time, the event(s) and jealousy that drove Jake to violence this time, even that she was married to an alcoholic wife-beater. And she lacks inhibitions, removing her shirt because she thinks Frankie needs it to bind his wound, proposes marriage forgetting previous bonds, remembers love but forgets its price.

When Jake longingly remembers Beth's physicality, she appears in his vision as a beautiful woman, naked from the waist up, seductively oiling her body. Yet, in Act 3 Beth descends the staircase from her bedroom dressed in what Shepard characterizes as "*a bizarre combination of clothing... straight out of the fifties*" and Baylor describes as the outfit of "a roadhouse chippie" (111). Blending her past and present identities, the young woman we see now is both actress and adolescent; she looks as if she is playing dress-up with her mother's clothes and make-up. Her garish appearance and announcement that she intends to marry, as if her marriage to Jake did not exist, provoke Baylor's rebuke on both counts. Apparently Beth has little or no memory of the past and little grasp of chronology. Her world is neatly divided into "before" and "now." Some shards from "before" remain, but she lacks the ability to recall memories with complexity or subtlety.

Finding refuge in a romanticized version of love, Beth's emotional memory of Jake, for example, is disconnected from him. He is a name, a voice, an elusive past. In fact, when Jake appears on her doorstep she does not recognize him, believing him to be a stranger. And when she remembers his face in a slow-motion rendition of Lorraine's recollection of the events captured in the photograph that Sally retrieves from the garbage, time has turned back to the first time Beth ever saw him – not the last. Yet, she has recognized the timbre of Jake's voice in Frankie's, concluding, "That's a voice of someone. Before. Someone with a voice before..." (43). On the contrary, she introduces herself as she is "now":

> This is me. This is me now. The way I am. Now. This. All. Different. I-I live inside. Remember. Remembering. You. You – were one. I know you. I know-love. I know what love is. I can never forget. That. Never. (57)

Shepard has characterized *A Lie of the Mind* as a legend about love. It is, moreover, a stunning reflection on the past, on the elusiveness of memory, on the proclivity to forgetfulness that has broad implications for the audience personally and culturally.

"I don't think it's worth doing anything unless it's personal... unless you're dealing with most deeply personal experiences," the playwright told Freedman. Referring specifically to the difficult relationship with his own father, he remarked, "You spend a lot of time trying to piece these things together and it still doesn't make sense." Yet despite the fact that Shepard understands resolution is unattainable, "at the same time," he admits, "it was well worth the journey, trying to reestablish things."[40] Likewise, the closing moments of *A Lie of the Mind* – the flickering flame and the perfectly folded flag – reflect our craving for order and reconciliation in our own lives. In fact, in looking back in *True West* and *A Lie of the Mind*, Shepard has fashioned family plays of the most deeply personal experiences that nonetheless widen to encompass a psychic journey we all share in our private and collective journeys to link memory with meaning and ourselves with history.

NOTES

1 James Knowlson and John Pilling, *Frescoes of the Skull: The Later Prose and Drama of Samuel Beckett* (New York: Grove Press, 1981), 211–12.
2 Interviewed by Stephanie Coen, "Things at Stake Here," *American Theatre*, 13 (September 1996): 28.
3 Interviewed by Jonathan Cott, "The *Rolling Stone* Interview: Sam Shepard," *Rolling Stone*, 18 December 1986–1 January 1987, 170.
4 See, in particular, Enoch Brater, "American Clocks: Sam Shepard's Time Plays," *Modern Drama*, 37.1 (1994) 607.

5 Jeanette R. Malkin, *Memory-Theatre and Postmodern Drama* (Ann Arbor: University of Michigan Press, 1999), 11.

6 Lawrence L. Langer, *Holocaust Testimonies: The Ruins of Memory* (New Haven and London: Yale University Press, 1991), 96.

7 Notably, in *Buried Child* fire is one of many methodologies employed to obscure or eradicate the past.

8 Sam Shepard, *A Lie of the Mind*, in *A Lie of the Mind and The War in Heaven* (New York: New American Library, 1987), 115. Page references in parentheses within the text are to this edition.

9 Shepard, "Language, Visualization and the Inner Library" (1977), reprinted in Bonnie Marranca (ed.), *American Dreams: The Imagination of Sam Shepard* (New York: Performing Arts Journal Publications, 1981), 215.

10 Shepard, *Buried Child*, in *Sam Shepard: Seven Plays* (New York: Bantam Books, 1981), 111.

11 Una Chaudhuri, *Staging Place: The Geography of Modern Drama* (Ann Arbor: University of Michigan Press, 1995), 108.

12 Malkin, *Memory-Theatre*, 129, 152.

13 Chaudhuri, *Staging Place*, 92.

14 Brater, "American Clocks," 609.

15 Shepard, *True West*, in *Sam Shepard: Seven Plays*. Page references in parentheses within the text are to this edition.

16 Christopher Bigsby, *Modern American Drama, 1945–1990* (Cambridge University Press, 1992), 165.

17 Quoted by Bruce Weber, "Spring Theatre/Visions of America: an Unusual Case of Role Reversals," *New York Times*, 27 February 2000, Section 2: 10, 37.

18 Bigsby, *Modern American Drama*, 169.

19 Megan Williams, "Nowhere Man and the Twentieth-Century Cowboy: Images of Identity and American History in Sam Shepard's *True West*," *Modern Drama*, 40 (Spring 1997): 66.

20 Ibid., 62–63.

21 William Demastes, "Understanding Sam Shepard's Realism," *Comparative Drama*, 21.3 (1987).

22 Stephen J. Bottoms, *The Theatre of Sam Shepard* (Cambridge University Press, 1998), 191.

23 Quoted in Weber "Spring Theatre," 10.

24 Bottoms, *Theatre of Sam Shepard*, 124.

25 Williams, "Nowhere Man," 66.

26 Geringer Woititz, *Adult Children of Alcoholics* (Hollywood, FL: Health Communications, 1983).

27 Quoted in Samuel G. Freedman, "Sam Shepard's Mythic Vision," *New York Times*, 1 December 1985, Section 2:1, 20.

28 Rodney Simard, *Postmodern Drama: Contemporary Playwrights in America and Britain* (Lanham, MD: University Press of America, 1984), 85.

29 Bottoms, *Theatre of Sam Shepard*, 191.

30 Malkin, *Memory-Theatre*, 128.
31 Leslie A. Wade, *Sam Shepard and the American Theatre* (Westport, CT: Praeger, 1997), 123.
32 Janet V. Haedicke, "A Population (and Theatre) at Risk: Battered Women in Henley's *Crimes of the Heart* and Shepard's *Lie of the Mind*," *Modern Drama*, 36 (March 1993): 87.
33 Brater, "American Clocks," 609.
34 Frank Rich, "Theatre: *A Lie of the Mind*," *New York Times*, 6 December 1985, Section c3.
35 Langer, *Holocaust Testimonies*, 173.
36 Adam Zachary Newton, *Narrative Ethics* (Cambridge, MA and London: Harvard University Press, 1995), 250.
37 Saul Friedlander, *When Memory Comes*, translated by Helen R. Lane (New York: Farrar, Straus, and Giroux, 1979), 57.
38 David Savran, "Sam Shepard's Conceptual Prison: *Action* and *The Unseen Hand*," *Theatre Journal*, 36 (March 1984): 72.
39 Gussow, "Sam Shepard Revisits the American Heartland," *New York Times*, 15 December 1985, Section 2:3.
40 Quoted in Freedman, "Sam Shepard's Mythic Vision," 1.

9

CARLA J. McDONOUGH

Patriarchal pathology from *The Holy Ghostly* to *Silent Tongue*

Shepard's plays have little to say about women outside of their role within the drama of male individuation. Yet, it is precisely in his focus on masculinity and its problems that Shepard's plays provide acute critiques of the destructiveness of patriarchy for both men and women. Shepard's early plays establish his interest in male individuation, especially in regard to the father/son conflict where the son's identity is at stake. In *The Rock Garden* (1964), for instance, the son's final monologue about his sexuality ends up "killing" the father who falls over, supposedly dead, at the end of the play. Again, in the 1970 play *The Holy Ghostly*, the son must "kill" the father, or at least the father's spirit, in order to assert his own identity, which he has been struggling to do after changing his name and running away from the "Old West" to New York City. But sons in Shepard's plays never escape the father's legacy, even after the father's death, because they inherit patriarchal ideas of violent masculinity from their fathers and have learned from them to stake their claim to manhood upon the body of a woman.

This last belief leads Shepard's men to search for completion of themselves in the body of a woman, reflecting how in many of Shepard's plays and films a man's sense of his control over his world and of his own identity is usually tied to his ideas of women. In the early play *Chicago* (1965), we witness Stu, whose self-image has been shattered by the imminent departure of his girl-friend (aptly named Joy), retreat into a childish land of make-believe as he refuses to leave his bathtub. In *Fool for Love* (1983), Eddie's inability to let Mae go – his perpetual seeking of her to return to old fantasies in contrast to her continued attempts to forge a new life for herself – demonstrates the differences between men and women's needs for each other in Shepard's world. Often when a man is most desperate in Shepard's plays, he turns to a woman for solace or grounding, a move made by Lee in *True West* (1980) when he frantically searches for the phone number of a woman he knows just so he can hear her voice. And most certainly in *A Lie of the Mind* (1985), Jake's violence toward his wife Beth is the result of his self-image being destroyed upon believing that she has "betrayed" him with another man. Jake can continue living in this play only after reestablishing his lie of the mind which is his fantasy image of her. Yet, it is precisely because women are not fantasies and thus always elude the narrow definitions allotted to them by the patriarchal ideology of Shepard's men that these men become so desperate and pathetic.

The tensions between the ideological positioning of women and the reality of women's lives in Shepard's work reflect that women clearly mean more than patriarchy insists they should mean. They are not fully captured or contained by the male-defined roles of sexual object or of mother (their main roles in Shepard's plays as in patriarchal society), and thus the male identity that insists on this narrow definition of women as being necessary for its own self-image is certain to be in continued peril. Shepard's plays end up portraying the conflict between the fantasy of patriarchal ideology and the reality of women, a conflict that is clearly detrimental to those male characters who cling most to that limited ideology. The men of Shepard's plays often end up resorting to violence in their desire to enforce the codes of this ideology. Because violence is directed toward women in Shepard's plays by men attempting to shore up their own sense of self, Shepard's plays tend to expose his male characters' weaknesses more than to empower them through this violence. This move is apparent in several of his plays and films, but I will focus on three of them here, one of his most often discussed plays, *A Lie of the Mind*, and two films that have received relatively little critical attention, *Paris, Texas* (1984) and *Silent Tongue* (1992). In all three of these works, male identity is explored through an examination of male/female relationships that are fraught with implications about the intersection of gender, power, and language.

My reading of these works is informed by the theories of Jacques Lacan in regard to a person's formation of identity, as posited in both Lacan's ideas of the mirror stage of development and the Oedipus complex he set forth in his *Ecrits*. Lacan divides the initial moments when an infant gains its first sense of self into the pre-mirror and the mirror stage of development, both associated with the mother as the primary object of identification. An infant passes through the mirror stage of development when he first learns to recognize his image in either the literal reflection of a mirror or the reflection provided by the mother whom the infant sees as an image of self. After this experience, the child progresses through the Oedipus complex that entangles his search for identity with the father. Jonathan Scott Lee explains the Lacanian version of the Oedipus complex thus:

> What Freud had understood as a struggle between instinct and the demands of civilization . . . Lacan describes as an entry into the "unconscious participation"

in the background "language" making "civilized" behavior possible and intelligible. The child, in passing through the Oedipus complex, learns the language of familial relations and thereby adopts a position within the culture of his family by taking on a *name*, itself made intelligible by the language of kinship . . . For Lacan, successful negotiation of oedipal conflicts is quite literally a matter of learning to speak properly.[1]

This name by which the child comes to identify itself within the structure of culture and of language is, in a patriarchal society, the name of the father, where the father stands as "the figure of the law."[2] Ellie Ragland-Sullivan further explains how Lacan's description of this stage as the Law of the Name-of-the-Father puns on the word "name," which in French is "nom" and which is similar to the French word "non" or "no." Thus the father's name is associated with the law that restricts a child's behavior according to social codes by providing the "no."[3] When children learn language, they enter the public code, the rules and regulations of society by which they are defined, a code that in a patriarchal society is logically connected to the law of the father. Despite this naming, however, Lacan argues that we remain incomplete, fractured, because language itself (the structure through which we learn to name ourselves) is merely a representation of what it is supposed to signify – it is the symbolic rather than the real. The name of the father does not, it seems, solve an individual's identity crisis but in fact introduces the individual into the struggle to maintain an identity that is always eluding him or her.

Lacan's connections between language, identity, and the gendering of roles are useful for examining Shepard's explorations of the power dynamic between men and women in the struggle for self-knowledge and individuation. Although Shepard is, as early feminist critiques of his work pointed out, most concerned with the male psyche, his explorations of the fractures and schisms within the male psyche lead his readers to consider the pathology of patriarchal ideology.[4] This ideology asserts a fantasy of control that cannot actually be maintained if one's identity is always only symbolically represented through language, or misrecognized through an image projected onto others. Following their fathers' modes of behavior, especially their behavior toward women, Shepard's men search for a solid marker of their manhood as key to their identity but can never grasp it.

Due to the feminist revolution, which it wouldn't be exaggerating to say has affected all aspects of intellectual and physical life in America, the speciousness of patriarchal stereotypes of women, of woman's "natural" subservience and helplessness, has long been exposed, though of course the effects of these long-standing myths about women are still being fought in courts, classrooms, and business offices. What has only more recently come to be seriously examined is the fact that traditional gender stereotyping has damaged and continues to damage men by way of its myths of male behavior. A recent bestseller by psychologist William Pollack, entitled *Real Boys: Rescuing Our Sons from the Myths of Boyhood*, that examines the troubled boys of American society, brings more fully into public consciousness the legacy of patriarchy's destruction in the lives of boys.[5] Pollack demonstrates through his research that when boys follow the traditional model of emotionally locked masculinity enforced upon them at often very young ages, they end up emotionally damaged, unable to express their emotions in productive ways. Thus, boys and the young men they grow into are more likely to participate in pathological behavior from suicide to murder, from specific physical violence toward those they know to indiscriminate violence such as grabbing a gun and shooting up their school. Acting out physically rather than relying on language is a key trait of traditional masculine behavior, ironic given that, according to Lacan, language itself is what moves us into the law of the father, into patriarchal law. The silencing of women by physical actions of men thus creates an interesting question. If we can speak only in the language of the father's law, of patriarchy, why do proponents of male power eschew language in favor of physical action? Perhaps the answer is that that law itself also limits and silences men. Increasingly as the works of Shepard's maturity move from exploring male–male relationships to explorations of romantic love between men and women, he explores the limits of language – where it fractures and erupts – and thus addresses many of these questions regarding the tenuous connection between language and the gendering of power.

Shepard's use of male violence, especially toward women, is best treated in the 1985 play *A Lie of the Mind*. Previous discussions of gender issues in this play have often focused on the image of Beth, whose ability to speak has been damaged by her husband's severe beating of her while in a jealous rage.[6] In beating Beth, Jake tries to regain his, supposedly, lost control over his wife (who, he believes, is sleeping with another man), yet he beats her so severely he thinks he has killed her and is devastated by this loss. Although Beth survives, she suffers brain damage that results in aphasia. How Beth has been interpreted critically demonstrates the range or perhaps the evolution of feminist criticism from seeing only victimization of women at the hands of men (and Shepard's limitations as a writer of women's roles) to an awareness of how a character such as Beth offers complexities that actually critique male power and even elude it.

An influential early article about the play by Lynda Hart argues that by "silencing" Beth, Shepard moves the focus of the play to Jake's plight, leaving

Beth with "no objective whatsoever; she is simply an image of a destroyed woman," and thus making her "not a real character in the play; she is a culturally constructed fantasy" who is a projection of Jake's psyche.[7] However, as accurate as this reading is for the early parts of this play, Beth is not so easily dismissed as simply a reflection of Jake's inner turmoil. Her speech and her behavior, rather than being cowed by this treatment, are freed to a level of greater understanding of the ideas that entrap Jake, and many men, leading them to defensive behavior about their masculinity, behavior that is usually violent and ultimately self-destructive. Beth's life and her effects on the play do not stop with the image of her beaten body in the hospital room. In fact, it is her actions and her words in Act 2, Scene 3 that provide this play with its greatest critique of male behavior.

Back at her childhood home, where her brother-in-law Frankie has come to check on her, Beth takes over control of Frankie and, in one scene, explains how she knows that men merely masquerade as being strong and in control. She understands traditional manliness as a costume or even a suit of armor that men put on to shield their actual vulnerabilities and weaknesses. Holding up her father's shirt she tells Frankie:

> Look how big a man is. So big. He scares himself. His shirt scares him. He puts his scary shirt on so it won't scare himself. He can't see it when it's on him. Now he thinks it's him. Jake was scared of shirts. You too?[8]

Putting on the shirt, she calls it a costume, saying,

> Now I'm like a man. (*Pumps her chest out, closes her fists, sticks her chin out and struts in the shirt.*) Just feel like the man. Shirt brings me a man. I am a shirt man. Can you see? Like father. You see me? Like brother. (*She laughs.*) (74–75)

Ultimately, Beth shows that the "power" of male gender is no more than a masquerade, just as later she plays with the masquerade of femininity when, wanting to marry Frankie, she appears in a stereotypically sexy outfit of black high heels, a tight pink skirt, a low-cut sweater, and heavy make-up, an outfit her father describes as making her look like "a roadhouse chippie" (111). This get up is clearly another costume, part of the role-playing she sees as defining gender.

Beth is not the only female character in this play whose critique of patriarchal ideology is worthy of consideration. Jane Ann Crum's 1993 article about *Lie* reads the play as an exploration of feminine writing that "rejects binary opposition and challenges the power structures which result from phallogocentrism."[9] Crum reads the women of this play as offering "two diverse models of feminine revolution, two methods by which the female characters liberate themselves from submissive roles and activities and achieve 'the landscape of the female body'" (197). These two models are embodied by two mother/daughter combinations: Lorraine and Sally who destroy their ties to the men in their life and prepare to move to the motherland of Ireland, and Meg and Beth who "resocialize the invalid men" of their lives (203). While Crum comments that "neither solution is without substantial cost" for the women,[10] she seems to favor the moves made by Meg and Beth to reintegrate their men, and to "save" them, so to speak. Yet, to call the behavior of these last two women revolutionary is a bit questionable. Not only do Meg and Beth seem to see their role as necessary for the resocialization and the saving of men, but it seems that Shepard's men most often consciously or unconsciously view "their" women that way, thus placing the women into a traditional role of helpmate for male individuation. How then does this role differ from the one that women have been expected to play by patriarchy for centuries – as the civilizing influence on men, their saving grace? The difference from this traditional role seems to lie in the self-awareness of the women, of their knowledge of their own independence and their willing choice to still be with men rather than compulsory enforcement of this behavior. Meg pointedly says to her husband Baylor when he complains of the burdens women place on him that women can and will "take care of [them]selves. We always have" (106). She further points out that men are dependent on women for their survival but don't recognize it due to a profound lack of self-awareness: "The male one goes off by himself. Leaves. He needs something else. But he doesn't know what it is. He doesn't really know what he needs. So he ends up dead. By himself" (105).[11] Through such characters as Jake and Baylor, who clearly cannot function without the women in their lives, A Lie of the Mind shows that male identity within a patriarchal structure is more dependent on women than is female identity dependent on men. In doing so, the play ultimately presents these would-be domineering men as the weaker party in the negotiation for individuation and selfhood within gender roles. They are a burden on the whole system, although traditionally it has been expected that the burden be carried for men by women. While this burden has in the past "victimized" women, it does not end up doing so in this play. In fact, the fracturing of Beth's language serves to uncover the precariousness of male power within the patriarchal system as we see the law of the father break down and the women escape its control, even as the men succumb to its destruction.[12]

While A Lie of the Mind is the most complex and rewarding of Shepard's stage works in regard to female subjectivity, Shepard's work is generally more concerned with the plight of men within and against patriarchy than it is with women. Yet he consistently grapples with the problem for men that their self-image is tied to their idea of women. By vividly recording the literal and psychic dead-ends of patriarchal ideology for both men and women, Shepard ends up recording the pathological nature of this ideology. While feminist theory has long talked about how women are silenced by male oppression and power, Shepard's plays demonstrate that men are often destroyed by this oppression as well. The question thus becomes how to elude this silencing – how to escape or to speak other than the destructive law of the father. Although he does not provide solutions to this dilemma, in his two most successful screenplays Shepard has focused on this issue of language and identity from a male point of view.

In *Paris, Texas*, a 1984 film directed by Wim Wenders and written by Sam Shepard, the familiar issue of the legacy a son inherits from his father is explored, along with the issue of the mother/wife's role as well. In some ways, sections of this screenplay seem almost a pre-script for *A Lie of the Mind*. In both scripts, the fractured family is the result of male obsession with having absolute power over a woman, and his violence toward her comes out of his unfounded suspicions of her sexual infidelity. Travis (Harry Dean Stanton), seen at the opening of the film wandering in the desert, and speechless for the first part of the film, is a self-exiled wanderer, we learn, due to his inability to maintain a reasonable relationship with his wife, Jane (Nastassja Kinski). Growing ever more obsessed with her, unable to leave her even for a few hours to work due to his constant fear that she is sleeping around on him, Travis drives Jane to leave him. After tying a cowbell around her leg at night, and still finding her trying to get away, Travis ties her to the stove one night, only to awake the next day to find her and his son gone and the house and himself in flames. His response is to wander aimlessly, so we are led to believe, for four years – absolutely lost. And in that time of wandering, his basic human markers disappear, most significantly his ability to speak.

The film opens with the image of Travis wandering into a small Texas town from the desert. Due to a card found in his pocket by the doctor who attends him, Travis's brother Walt (Dean Stockwell) is located and arrives from Los Angeles to retrieve him. Walt, a successful businessman, has been taking care of Travis's son Hunter (Hunter Carson) for the past four years after Hunter was left with Walt by Jane. Travis is thus reunited with his son, and it is through this reunion that he reconnects with life, starting to talk again, and to interact with the world around him. This reincarnation of Travis follows an interesting trajectory in regard to identity being created through mimicking a role. Hunter inspires in Travis a desire to communicate with others again, but Travis does not know how to interact with his son. One afternoon, while Hunter is at school, a maid finds Travis flipping through magazines. When she asks him what he is looking for, he inquires, "What does a father look like?"[13] Figuring out that Travis wants to "look" like a father, she helps to costume him in the appropriate outfit by finding a suit of clothes in Walt's closet. That afternoon, wearing the suit that transforms him into a father, he is at last successful in connecting with Hunter by walking him home from school. Although initially the two – father and son – walk on opposite sides of the street, Hunter ends up mirroring the actions that Travis makes such as walking backwards and bumping into a trash can. The entire sequence points out the way that proper costuming helps Travis to achieve his role of father, which is affirmed by Hunter accepting him as a model for his behavior. The father/son relationship becomes a mimicking or a reflection that leads, at the end of the walk, to Hunter's acceptance of his father's presence.

Once Travis has found his identity as a father, his mission soon becomes to locate Jane and restore her to the role of mother. He eventually finds Jane working in a peep show in Houston, a job that emphasizes the kind of sexual objectification of her that had initially caused Travis to mistreat her. In the peep show, she can never be touched by any of the men who come to observe her, and instead remains an image or an idea onto which they can place their fantasies. Travis's purpose in coming to see Jane at the peep show, however, is different. He seeks a kind of communication more akin to that of the confessional. Placing himself in the position of a disembodied voice by speaking to Jane through the two-way mirror of the peep show that obscures him from her, Travis retells the story of his obsession as a way to do penance for his behavior, acknowledging through this retelling that he is the cause of their disrupted lives. Thus he reestablishes contact with Jane only verbally, indirectly asking for her forgiveness by his confession. At the end of this conversation, he tells her that Hunter is waiting for her at a nearby hotel, and he leaves before she can make any physical contact with him outside of the peep show. Travis, again through a mirrored window at the hotel, witnesses Jane and Hunter's reunion before leaving. Realizing, evidently, that he would recreate the same problems if he joined them, Travis is last seen driving alone into the Texas night. Thus the film's ending offers no resolution to the issue of a man's successful integration into the roles of husband and father. This ending parallels the distance between men and family that Shepard's plays have often explored as time and again he offers portraits of men who disappear into the western desert rather than live with people. Perhaps the most stunning explanation of this move is made by Lee of *True West* when he explains to his brother that his choice to live in the desert is the result of a personal failing, his inability to live with people: "I'm living out there 'cause I can't make it here."[14]

In contrast to Travis's stunted relationship skills, the film offers the successful family life and career of his brother Walt. Rather like Austin of *True West* to Travis's Lee, Walt seems to have integrated successfully into the role of family man, being a good husband to his wife Anne (Aurore Clement) and a good father to Hunter. Nevertheless, Walt demonstrates no qualms at giving Hunter back to Travis, even though he has been raising Hunter as a son. Walt's seeming lack of emotional attachment to Hunter, especially when compared to that of his wife, perhaps reflects an expectation that the father-bond is simply not supposed to be as emotionally close as that of a mother. Walt, still, provides a stark contrast to the wayward Travis. Why one brother goes so terribly wrong and the other doesn't is a question that this film never really addresses, but which a viewer can't help but wonder, especially since we have seen this pattern elsewhere in Shepard's work. Particularly in the context of the present discussion of the pathology of patriarchy, it is important to note how Shepard's work will at times show women actively trying to escape the destructive legacy of patriarchal gender roles, but does not fully explore how it is that men might or do succeed in doing so. In fact, Shepard usually shows the futility of trying to escape a father's legacy because it is part of one's character. In an interview with Carol Rosen about this subject,[15] Shepard commented, "I think character is an essential tendency that can't be – it can be covered up, it can be messed with, it can be screwed around with, but it can't be ultimately changed. It's like the structure of our bones, the blood that runs through our veins" (8).

In the course of the film, Travis actually grapples with his past, and the issue of his roles and responsibilities, as well as where and how he went wrong. He tries to understand how he got where he is by thinking back to his origins – not where he grew up but where he was conceived, which he believes to be in Paris, Texas. He reminds his brother of the way their father used to say he met his wife in Paris, then he would pause before offering the clarifying bit of information, Texas. As a result of this story of where his parents fell in love, Travis comes to believe he was also conceived in Paris, Texas. His sense of connection to this town is revealed in the fact that he carries with him a picture of an empty parcel of land he bought there sometime in his past. Travis later tells his son, when the two are traveling to find Jane, about how his father got into his head confused ideas about his mother:

> My mother, was NOT a fancy woman. [. . .] Just plain and good. But my daddy, see, my daddy, he had this idea, he had this idea in his head that was kind of a sickness. [. . .] He had this idea about her and he looked at her, but . . . he didn't see her. He saw this idea. And he told people she was from Paris. It was

a big joke. But he started telling everybody all the time, and finally, it wasn't a joke anymore. He actually believed it. (87–88)

Although the film offers little explanation as to why Travis was unable to control his jealousy over Jane, his few comments about his father's treatment of his mother indicate that Travis inherited a pattern of not really seeing the woman he loved, but only his ideas about her. This is a pattern of behavior that Travis shares with Eddie of *Fool for Love* and Jake of *A Lie of the Mind* – men who, like Travis, have damaged themselves by their limited ideas of women. Notably, all three of these men – three of Shepard's most profoundly damaged men – grapple with troubled legacies from their fathers that have molded their patterns of behavior toward women.

The corruption of the father's law is apparent in the majority of Shepard's works of his maturity, where the father is usually a drunken, self-centered, worthless, violent, abusive lout (*Curse of the Starving Class, Buried Child, Fool for Love, A Lie of the Mind, Paris, Texas,* and *Silent Tongue*). The son's conflict with this father's legacy reflects his struggle, often an ineffective struggle, to escape that legacy. Some sons, usually the younger sons, manage to overcome this problem – Walt, Austin, Frankie – but others are profoundly and seemingly irreparably damaged by it – Travis, Jake, Lee. And it seems that for many of the elder sons (who are the traditional inheritors of their father's legacy according to the laws of patrilineage), their damage is then visited upon the women in their lives. Shepard's 1992 film, *Silent Tongue*, which he both wrote and directed, is a profound statement of the legacy of patriarchal violence as it is connected to both the treatment of women, and the myths of the American frontier, two ideas that become connected in the film. Yet most of the men of this play, far from embodying the image of the successful conqueror or ruler, are profoundly damaged – haunted by their past, and limited by their inability to survive without the crutches of either liquor or the nurture of a woman. In contrast, the victimized women in this film prove themselves to be the stronger parties, never fully owned or defined by the men who have sought to possess them.

Silent Tongue offers an interesting capstone to Shepard's many explorations not only of male confusion about women but also of the myths of the Old West and its legacies in modern day life.[16] This film, set in the New Mexico Territory of 1873, returns to many of the mythic images of the West that Shepard has explored in earlier plays, and that many of his critics have discussed as well.[17] This focus is apparent in plays such as *Cowboys, The Holy Ghostly, Operation Sidewinder, The Unseen Hand,* and *True West. The Holy Ghostly* is especially worthy of commentary here in that it offers a striking resemblance to certain elements of *Silent Tongue*. In this early play, Shepard explores the generational conflict between father and son as a reflection of the conflict between the past and the present, the East and the West, and the city and the country. A father, Pop, has called his son, Ice, to come to him for help. Having traveled from present-day New York City, Ice finds his father camped out in the Badlands and also, seemingly, still in the Old West. Pop is being haunted by a Chindi (a female ghost or witch) who wants to steal his spirit, and he wants his son to rescue him. Yet, by the end of the play, it becomes apparent that Pop is already dead and simply needs to accept that fact, as does the son. Given the ending, it seems that it may have actually been Ice who was haunted by the spirit of his father rather than Pop being haunted by the Chindi. Ice ends up throwing Pop's corpse on the campfire and freeing himself from his father's influence and from the past as he watches the corpse burn.

The legacies of the Old West that Shepard explores in his Western-themed plays from *The Holy Ghostly* to *True West* resonate with issues of patriarchal ideology. *Silent Tongue* also genderizes images of the American West, melding iconic images from the genre of the Western with what becomes ultimately a male/female conflict. This conflict between male and female is presented as an outgrowth of a patriarchal legacy that fathers have passed on to their sons, a legacy clearly connected in the film with the colonialism of the white man toward Native Americans. The white man/Indian conflict is presented in this film along gender lines that reflect the gender assumptions lying beneath the colonial mind-set.[18] The relationship between the colonizer and the colonized is that between dominator and dominated, a relationship that mirrors the vision of male/female intercourse in a patriarchal society. Thus, the colonized subject is viewed as a feminized subject in the sexist sense of being weak and in need of subjugation, while the colonizer is presented as masculine in the sexist sense of being powerful and a natural leader. The traditional narrative of colonial politics is a clash between men – the ones in power striving to maintain their control and thus protect their manliness, and the powerless seeking to gain their manhood by gaining power and control. Often this battle is fought symbolically or literally over the body of woman. Gayatri Spivak's well-known discussion of postcolonial discourse, "Can the Subaltern Speak?," examining the debates about the practice of widow sacrifice in India, reveals how the sati emblematizes the subaltern in colonial discourse and thus reflects how women's bodies are the sites upon which men's conflicts, discussion, arguments, and wars of national identity, independence, and autonomy are emblematically fought.[19]

These gendered issues of the colonial conflict are played out in fruitful ways in Shepard's *Silent Tongue* in which the main images offered of Native

Americans are women, and the story focuses on two father/son relationships between white men who exploit the women for their own selfish needs, much as they or their ancestors exploited the resources of the western frontier. While Shepard's film does not take on the larger canvas of national identity, its focus on the struggles of the men to maintain control over their women, lives, and sanity offers a microview of how colonialism's patriarchal ideology is ultimately a destructive force that fails to save even the white men who are supposed to benefit from it.

Silent Tongue opens on a desolate western landscape in which we see a young white man named Talbot Roe (River Phoenix) keeping watch over the corpse of a young Indian woman, protecting it from being eaten by scavengers. The scene quickly shifts to the film's second area of focus, Dr. Eamon MacCree's Kickapoo Indian Medicine Show run by the Irishman Eamon MacCree (Alan Bates) whose addiction to his alcoholic Kickapoo Indian Juice is quite apparent. MacCree's son, Reeves (Dermot Mulroney), seems to be the real energy behind the medicine show, keeping the outfit running. The show consists of a grab-bag of vaudevillesque entertainers, including comics, little people, a tap-dancing Negro boy, and the chief attraction, Eamon's "half breed" Indian daughter Velada (Jeri Arredondo) who entertains the crowd with impressive pony-riding tricks. Eamon, a drunken father typical of Shepard's stories, explains to the crowd how he learned the secret of the Kickapoo Indian Juice from "an authentic Medicine Man from the dreaded Kiowa/Comanche Nation" (140–41), thus emphasizing white exploitation of the "exotic" knowledge of the Indian nations. This medicine show is being witnessed not just by a crowd of locals but also by Prescott Roe (Richard Harris), a horse-trader who is Talbot's father. Prescott has returned to MacCree wanting to trade his horses for MacCree's daughter Velada. We learn that Prescott had earlier traded three horses for Velada's sister, Awbonnie (Sheila Tousey), as a wife for his son Talbot. It is Awbonnie's body that Talbot is guarding in the wilderness, driven mad by his grief over her death in childbirth. Prescott is convinced that the only way to save his son is to replace Awbonnie with Velada, thus revealing how the body of woman is a generic tool for him, to be used for the good of a man. While Velada's half-brother Reeves is angry over this treatment of his sisters – traded as if they were horses – their father MacCree is unfazed. He turns down Prescott's offer not out of disgust but simply because Velada is the medicine show's chief draw, and he believes it would be bad for business to lose her. Unable to trade for her, Prescott abducts Velada and sets off on the two-day ride to Talbot's camp. When Reeves discovers the abduction of Velada and the trick pony she was riding, MacCree becomes angry that his property has been stolen from him, exclaiming, "That paint was worth a hundred dollars!" (160). Once on the trail of Prescott and Velada, however, the drunken MacCree soon forgets his reason for the pursuit, having to be reminded and encouraged by the much more persistent Reeves to track down the two.

Prescott had originally bought Awbonnie in an attempt to save his already mentally deranged son, and while Talbot obviously fell obsessively in love with Awbonnie, she did not return the sentiment. Her ghost is the chief adversary that Talbot is fighting in order to keep some part of Awbonnie with him. Awbonnie's spirit wants the corpse burned or else eaten by scavengers so that she will at last be free from him, telling him "You keep me bound here out of your selfish fear of aloneness! I am not your life!" (150). The idea that women can be passed from one man to another as some kind of property, or that they have definition only as part of a man's life, is an assumption held by Prescott, Talbot, and MacCree, but called into question by both the women themselves, and (interestingly) their brother Reeves. Reeves offers the minority point of view among Shepard's men, which is similar to that of Frankie in *A Lie of the Mind*, that women deserve respect and that men must take responsibility for their actions toward the women in their lives. Inevitably, however, these men in Shepard's work prove ineffectual in altering the behavior of their brothers or fathers. MacCree keeps reminding his son that Velada and Awbonnie are only his half-sisters – and that they are themselves "half-breeds," their mother being a Kiowa Indian, and thus not worth as much concern as Reeves demonstrates toward them. MacCree explains about Velada, "She's an Indian. They were born to suffer" (172).

The difference in attitude between the older man MacCree and his son Reeves indicates a contrasting view of both women and Native Americans that is represented along generational lines. MacCree has taken on many of the clothes and accouterments of Native Americans, and claims to have spent enough time with certain tribes to have learned their medical secrets, but he clearly can see them only through his white prejudice as objects of exploitation or as savages to be feared rather than as people in their own right. When a group appears on the horizon as Reeves and MacCree track Prescott and Velada, MacCree loses his wits and panics, assuming they will attack and scalp the two white men with no provocation. He even shoots his mule and hides behind its body for protection in an iconic image of the cowboy's last desperate stand against the savage Indians reminiscent of so many of Hollywood's B-Westerns. Reeves observes this behavior noncommittally, and after calmly asserting they have nothing to fear from this hunting party because they have not done anything to them, he leaves his father and goes on tracking Velada, although he quickly becomes lost in the gathering darkness. The last he hears of his father are pleas coming to him from the dark: "Reeves! You can't abandon me to this! We're flesh and blood! Reeves!!!

Europeans! Don't forget that! . . . Masters of an empire! . . . We can't succumb to this barbarism! We have to cling together at all costs!" (189). Reeves is not swayed by his father's pleas in regard to their mutual mastery as Europeans. He does not return to his father, but simply makes a dismissive observation about his father's ideas before disappearing from the film, "Madness is a sorry thing" (190). Unfortunately, his rejection of his father's ways has no effect over the outcome of this film.

The image that MacCree has of Indians as savages and/or as victims is made apparent in a flashback to MacCree's younger days when he was hunting buffalo with ten-year-old Reeves and a fellow hunter. Through this flashback, we learn that Awbonnie and Velada are the result of MacCree having raped an Indian woman named Silent Tongue (Tantoo Cardinal). When the hunters come upon Silent Tongue picking up bones in a vast buffalo graveyard (a graveyard that is clearly the result of the white man's indiscriminate killing of buffalo for sport and thus another image of white exploitation of the West), the unnamed hunter tells MacCree that her name came from the fact that her tongue had been removed as punishment for lying to a chief of her tribe. Silenced for speaking falsely to a man, alone in the landscape, and a mere Indian woman, Silent Tongue is viewed as a ready victim for MacCree's lust, which he quickly acts upon. When he rapes her, she is completely powerless, unable even verbally to resist. Although MacCree asserts, after this flashback, "I made her my legitimate wife! Don't forget that!" (159), we recognize his actions as worthy of the guilt he evidently still feels for his treatment of her. She, like Awbonnie, was taken unwillingly and made the wife of a white man. Silent Tongue later ran away from MacCree, who indicates his profound misunderstanding of her when he tells Reeves, "Isn't that just like a Kiowa! They cut her tongue out and she rushes back to their fold, first chance she gets! I fed and clothed her all those years and she deserts me, back to her tormentors!" (185). We, of course, do not actually know Silent Tongue's story, despite her titular role in the film, except as it has been interpreted by the white hunter and by MacCree, two clearly suspect witnesses. She herself never gets to tell her own story due to her physical silencing as punishment for supposedly once speaking falsely to a man. Even Shepard limits her screen time, allowing us to see her only in the flashback scene of her rape, and briefly in MacCree's final scene.

This final scene of MacCree provides the film with some sense of justice, however misunderstood by MacCree. He is captured by the band of Indians he had so feared. MacCree referred to them as the "Dog Soldiers" that Silent Tongue had sent after him as payback for his treatment of her. Although initially, this fear sounded like the ravings of a drunk, the last we see of Eamon among this band of Indians, who have captured him and are marching him through the plains on foot, is from the point of view of Silent Tongue. She sits astride a pony, watching from a distance as Eamon is driven off. Silently, it seems, she has triumphed over her former captor through her connection to her own people, but again, we do not get her full story, and are allowed only a glimpse of her.

Rather like her mother, Awbonnie's power and person have not been diminished by her enslavement. Her spirit is clearly stronger than that of Talbot Roe, whose mental health was dependent upon Awbonnie's physical presence. His obsession with Awbonnie's body, even in death, is clearly pathological. Even as the corpse breaks into pieces, he keeps gathering it up and protecting it from the fire and from scavengers. Although he views his behavior as indicative of his love for her, Awbonnie more accurately describes it as a result of his fear and selfishness. We realize how Talbot has inherited his limited view of women from his own father, who buys women as if they are horses to be used by men. The abducted Velada, at first emblematic of helpless femininity in the face of a man's greater physical power, soon turns the tide on Prescott and runs away with his horses. Although he recaptures her through trickery, eventually they make a deal in which Prescott pays her the horses and gold coin he had first offered her father if she would just help his son. Setting her own terms for payment, she agrees. On the one hand, Velada could be seen as taking control of her own destiny, although Awbonnie's ghost derides her for selling herself and thus (Awbonnie believes) denying their mother. Awbonnie's ghost is clearly vengeful due to her treatment while alive and sees no reason to bargain with men like Talbot and Prescott. She threatens her sister, telling her

> You like bargaining with Whites, then you bargain with me, your sister. You move in close to this squirming dog. You pretend that you love him...and then take my body and you burn it. You owe this to our mother. If you run, I will hunt you down and cut your tongue out so you will never ever, never, never, never forget who gave you birth. (184)

If sons are bound to their fathers, it seems that for Awbonnie, at least, daughters are forever bound to their mothers. In fact, much of Awbonnie's story replicates that of her mother, and she, like her mother, rejects utterly the men who abducted her and seeks a violent revenge.

In the end, it is Prescott who finally throws Awbonnie's corpse into the fire, freeing her but doing so only in hope of saving his son from madness and death. With Awbonnie and Silent Tongue's stories rectified, the film moves quickly back to its focus on the male plight. The Roes, father and son, are last seen walking aimlessly across a desolate western landscape, the son's hand on the shoulder of his father who leads him. When they pass another lone traveler, headed in the opposite direction, who calls out to them, "Where to?" they do not answer. The scene thus leaves us with a final impression that these men are headed nowhere but are as lost as Travis was at the opening of *Paris, Texas*. Although they have maintained the central focus of this film, the men are left beaten, unresolved, or lost – MacCree being driven off by the Indians who have captured him, Reeves still searching for Velada, and the Roes wandering mindlessly in the desert landscape. The women who were seen by the men as objects of manipulation, as bodies to be traded or used, are the only ones whose stories have been resolved favorably, partly, it seems, because they refuse to validate the male point of view.

The failure of Shepard's male characters to find resolution or to escape destruction in his plays and films reflects a point of view about male dilemmas that is pertinent to the critique of patriarchy that has driven much feminist criticism. In Shepard's world, the patriarchal structure fails not only the women who are explicitly subjugated by it but also the men who are supposed to benefit from it. Thus his work provides a scathing look at the damages inherent in patriarchal ideology. As a writer, Shepard may care more about his male characters than he does his female characters, but he nevertheless provides excellent fodder for a critique of patriarchal ideals, a critique that places much of his work into pertinent discussions within gender studies, perhaps explaining one reason why his plays and films continue to resonate with such a wide audience.

NOTES

1 Jonathan Scott Lee, *Jacques Lacan* (Boston: Twayne, 1990), 64.

2 Jacques Lacan, *Ecrits: A Selection*, trans. Alan Sheridan (New York: W. W. Norton, 1977), 67.

3 Ellie Ragland-Sullivan, *Jacques Lacan and the Philosophy of Psychoanalysis* (Urbana: University of Illinois Press, 1986), 55.

4 For feminist readings that critique Shepard's tendency to ignore women characters, see Bonnie Marranca's "Alphabetical Shepard: the Play of Words," in her edited collection, *American Dreams: The Imagination of Sam Shepard* (New York: Performing Arts Journal Publications, 1981), 13–33, and Felicia Hardison Londré's "Sam Shepard Works Out: the Masculization of America," *Studies in American Drama, 1945–Present*, 2 (1987): 19–27.

5 William Pollack, *Real Boys: Rescuing Our Sons from the Myths of Boyhood* (New York: Henry Holt, 1998).

6 The best examples of this reading of Beth have been offered by Lynda Hart, whose work I discuss in the following paragraph.

7 Lynda Hart, "Sam Shepard's Pornographic Visions," *Studies in the Literary Imagination*, 21.2 (1988): 69–82, reprinted in Matthew Roudané (ed.), *Public Issues,*

Private Tensions: Contemporary American Drama (New York: AMS Press, 1993), 161–77.

8 Sam Shepard, *A Lie of the Mind* (New York: Plume, 1987), 74. Page references in parentheses within the text are to this edition.

9 Jane Ann Crum, "I Smash the Tools of My Captivity: the Feminine in Sam Shepard's *A Lie of the Mind*," in Leonard Wilcox (ed.), *Rereading Shepard: Contemporary Critical Essays on the Plays of Sam Shepard* (New York: St. Martin's Press, 1993), 196–214.

10 Ibid., 211.

11 For further analysis of Meg and Baylor's relationship, see my book, *Staging Masculinity: Male Identity in Contemporary American Drama* (Jefferson, NC: McFarland Press, 1997), 64–65.

12 For an extended discussion of the gender politics of this play, see my article, "The Politics of Staging Space: Women and Male Identity in Sam Shepard's Family Plays," *Journal of Dramatic Theory and Criticism*, 9.2 (1995): 65–83.

13 Sam Shepard, *Paris, Texas* (New York: Ecco Press, 1984), 42. Page references in parentheses within the text are to this edition. Film references are to *Paris, Texas*, Dir. Wim Wenders, Screenplay by Sam Shepard, 20th Century Fox, 1984.

14 Sam Shepard, *True West* in *Sam Shepard: Seven Plays* (New York: Bantam Books, 1986), 49. Page references in parentheses within the text are to this edition.

15 Carol Rosen, "Emotional Territory: an Interview with Sam Shepard," *Modern Drama*, 36.1 (1993): 1–11.

16 Sam Shepard, *States of Shock, Far North, Silent Tongue: A Play and Two Screenplays* (New York, Vintage Books, 1993). Page references in parentheses within the text are to this edition. Film references are to *Silent Tongue*, Dir. Sam Shepard, Screenplay by Sam Shepard, Le Studio Canalt, 1992.

17 For critical discussions of images of the cowboy and the West in Shepard's plays, see Tucker Orbison's "Mythic Levels in Shepard's *True West*," *Modern Drama*, 27 (1984): 506–19; Ellen Oumano's *Sam Shepard: The Life and Work of an American Dreamer* (New York: St. Martin's Press, 1986); Mark Siegal's "Holy Ghosts: the Mythic Cowboy in the Plays of Sam Shepard," *Bulletin of the Rocky Mountain Modern Language Association*, 36 (1982): 235–46, and Megan Williams's "Nowhere Man and the Twentieth-Century Cowboy: Images of Identity in Sam Shepard's *True West*," *Modern Drama*, 40 (1997): 57–73.

18 For a further discussion of the gendering of colonial issues and discourse, see Ania Loomba's incredibly lucid overview in *Colonialism/Postcolonialism* (New York: Routledge, 1998), 151–72 and 215–45.

19 Gayatri Spivak, "Can the Subaltern Speak? Speculations on Widow Sacrifice," *Wedge* (Winter/Spring 1985): 120–30.

10

JOHN M. CLUM

The classic Western and Sam Shepard's family sagas

I keep praying
for a double bill
of
Bad Day at Black Rock
and
Vera Cruz
> *Motel Chronicles*

"Cowboy my eyeball. He's a useless twerp. We shoulda canned
him right from the start."
> *The Mad Dog Blues*

At the beginning of *Vera Cruz*, Gary Cooper appears riding slowly from
the distance, a speck against the vast Mexican desert landscape. When Wim
Wenders's film from Sam Shepard's screenplay of *Paris, Texas* begins, we
see Harry Dean Stanton dressed in an old business suit with a baseball cap
on his head trudging aimlessly through the eerily white Mojave Desert. The
landscape looks as if it is covered in post-apocalyptic ash. Much of the
resonance of this moment of anomie comes from the echo of the classic
opening of the Western – the lone hero riding out of the wilderness for a
brief foray into society to perform a saving act. Shepard's Travis will also
perform such an act but, like the world in which it takes place, now more a
spiritual than physical wilderness, the act will be morally ambiguous.

While much has been written about the Western hero and Shepard's own
persona as actor and public figure and about the role of the cowboy in his
early works, I want to focus here on echoes of the classic Westerns Shepard
grew up with in the family sagas he wrote in the 1970s and 1980s. It is in
the echoes of the Western hero in Shepard's work that we see most vividly
what the contemporary American male has lost, a loss connected again and
again to the terrifying or ineffectual patriarchal wanderer always associated
with the desert.

I want to suggest that Shepard's feckless fathers are failures because the dream of the West, as depicted in Westerns, is dead. The conflict between the natural man and the social man continues to be played out in their crippled sons. Critics have noted the autobiographical aspects of Shepard's work, the way his own father circulates through a number of the plays, a man who himself embodies the split between domesticity and waywardness. As Shepard succinctly put it: "My Dad lives alone in the desert. He says he doesn't fit in with people."[1] I am interested more in the ideals of masculinity that circulated through American culture and that intersect with Shepard's own life to create his Western family sagas.

When David Savran discusses Sam Shepard at length in his intriguing study *Taking It Like a Man: White Masculinity, Masochism, and Contemporary American Culture*, he both links Shepard to the cowboy mystique and ignores its centrality in Shepard's work. Savran notes that: "Shepard's men are almost invariably locked into a system of intense competition less for power, glory, and the girl than for the distinction of being the toughest, most ornery, most angst-ridden, most rugged individual in the (true) West."[2] However, Savran is more interested in the "reflexive sado-masochism" he finds as the pattern of male relations in Shepard's plays than in Shepard's deep personal and artistic commitment to the mystique of the Western and its heroes, which is at the heart of his mature work. In his earlier book, *Communists, Cowboys, and Queers: The Politics of Masculinity in the Work of Arthur Miller and Tennessee Williams*, Savran dismisses the Western hero as a model of political incorrectness: "In many respects, the cowboy most clearly exemplifies the hegemonic masculinity of the late 1940s and the 1950s in all its violent contradictions."[3]

Nonetheless, to understand Shepard, born in 1943 and raised in the West during the heyday of the Western, one must understand how he used certain basic premises of the Western and its hero, not only in his more abstract earlier work like *The Unseen Hand, Cowboy Mouth, The Mad Dog Blues*, and *The Tooth of Crime*, but also in his family sagas, including *Curse of the Starving Class, Buried Child*, and *True West*. As Doris Auerbach writes, "Shepard has used as his paradigm for the family in crisis the overwhelming cultural myth of the American West,"[4] one expression of which is the Hollywood Western.

Shepard and the American male

"It sounds a little trite, but there's not a whole lot of men who know what a man is, and I always thought it weird that American men haven't resolved this; the American male is in conflict, uniquely in cultures of the West."[5]

Gender theorists would tell Shepard that there is no ontological definition of a man. Indeed, the frustration for Shepard's characters, and perhaps for Shepard himself, comes from seeking a non-existent essential, unified American masculinity. What his characters experience, instead, is division. In her book on the state of the contemporary American male, *Stiffed*, Susan Faludi writes:

> The man controlling his environment is today the prevailing American image of masculinity. A man is expected to prove himself not by being part of society but by being untouched by it, soaring above it. He is to travel unfettered, beyond society's clutches, alone – making or breaking whatever or whoever crosses his path.
>
> ...from the nation's earliest frontier days the man in the community was valued as much as the loner in control, homely society as much as heroic detachment. Even in the most archetypal versions of the original American male myth, a tension prevailed between the vision of a man who stood apart from society and the man who was a part of society; the loner was not the ideal.[6]

Faludi does not see, as Shepard does, that these contradictory goals can tear an individual male apart, split him into two figures, neither of whom can settle for his half of the ideal. For Shepard, the heart of his 1980 play, *True West*, is "this conflict between the intellect and the emotions, the physical wild man part and the reasonable, intellectual side. You know, what it really means to be a man."[7] Man's essence, then, is an irreconcilable split: "I think we're split in a much more devastating way than psychology can ever reveal."[8]

At the heart of the psychic split and crisis of masculinity that so interest Shepard is the central situation of American domestic melodrama: a powerful but failed father; an ineffectual but sensual mother; and two brothers in conflict. The central issue of these plays is the inheritance sons receive from a failed patriarchy. Tangential to this is the question of whether the sons' relationships with women are possible or even important. In *Buried Child*, Vince tells his girlfriend Shelly, "I've gotta carry on the line,"[9] but he is not speaking of producing progeny with a woman, but of reconnecting with his dysfunctional family history, particularly a physically and spiritually maimed male lineage, and absorbing it. The sons are compelled to connect with ideals of masculinity for which there are no real models and with myths of the American land that are no longer relevant. One important expression of those ideals was the classic American Western with which Sam Shepard grew up and on which, to some extent, he built his persona.

Fathers and John Wayne

Sam Shepard's domestic dramas present impasses. They end in inertia as men, aware of their incompleteness, violently reunite with their siblings and parents. Violence is the operative term here in families as destructive as any in Greek tragedy. How does a man assert himself in these violent family structures and how does the family isolate him from the rest of American society? Never is this separation more clearly seen than when placed against the Oedipal myth of the classic Western echoed in Shepard's work.

Shepard's story, "The Real Gabby Hayes," presents both a typical picture of the Shepard father-figure and the playwright's investment in Western movies. The story appears in the collection *Cruising Paradise*, which also contains two other tales which echo the Western, "Gary Cooper or the Landscape" and "Spencer Tracy is not Dead," which evokes the Tracy of *Bad Day at Black Rock*. In the quasi-memoir, "The Real Gabby Hayes," Shepard remembers his father trying to bond with him in the Mojave Desert. Shepard's father, like Weston in *Curse of the Starving Class*, has bought "a small patch of desert"[10] from a traveling salesman. The father's desert dream reflects the tensions between isolation and society central to the Western: "That's what I had in mind for this place. A little desert hideaway. Can't always be the family man" (7). For the father, this excursion with the son into the desert was to be a bit of male bonding – confidences and shooting rabbits in their hideaway – but the bonding was another fantasy: "He tried to get friendly with me. I could hear it in his voice. Trying to include me in something as though I were a conspirator. But the more he tried, the further I felt from him" (7). On the way home, Shepard's father takes him into an exclusive bar where, in a corner booth, Gabby Hayes, who appeared in scores of Westerns, "the subservient gummy-mouthed sidekick, slightly demented and always shy around women" (11), is being fondled by a couple of prostitutes.

In this short memoir, all echoes of the West are of diminution. The desert becomes a tiny tract of land sold by a con man. The alcoholic father dreams of building not a ranch, but a bottle house. Old western myths of treasure lead to a story about a black man being beheaded for leading Spanish explorers not to the Seven Cities of Gold, but to an Indian village that looked gold in the afternoon light: "My Dad walked away, leaving me with the image of decapitation" (9). The remnant of the mythic West isn't John Wayne or Roy Rogers, but toothless old Gabby Hayes, neither hero nor patriarch. Shepard's father–son scene is a reduction, even mockery, of the surrogate father's education provided in Westerns from *Shane* to *The Searchers*.

John Ford's *The Searchers* (1956, written by Frank S. Nugent), one of the greatest of Western films, provides a paradigm for two crucial family relationships found throughout Shepard's work; brothers who represent opposing concepts of masculinity and problematic patriarchy. John Wayne's Ethan Edwards is both renegade brother and surrogate patriarch. Ethan returns to the Texas homestead of his brother, Aaron, in 1868, three years after the end of the Civil War. While Aaron has taken care of his fragile homestead, which stands alone in the middle of hostile territory, Ethan, who has never accepted the Confederate surrender, has been engaging in suspicious activities before his return home. He arrives with bags of newly minted gold he may have stolen. Aaron has a wife and two daughters, though his wife seems to be enamored of Ethan. The first line in the film is "Welcome home, Ethan," but Ethan is anything but the domestic type. The film traces his four-year journey to find Aaron's daughter, who was taken away in an Indian raid that slaughtered the rest of the family. At the end of the film, having returned Debbie to a home, Ethan rides off again into the desert. His "good" brother, Aaron, is killed off fifteen minutes into the film. Ethan endures, but the domesticated, feminized society that is building up on the prairie is no place for him.

As brothers Ethan and Aaron Edwards represent a classic masculine split between anarchic spirit connected to the natural world and domesticated, feminized male we will see played out in Shepard's *True West*, so Ethan and Martin Pawley are one manifestation of the surrogate father–Oedipal son conflict at the heart of John Wayne movies. After Martin's parents were killed in an Indian raid, Martin was rescued by Ethan and brought to his brother's home to be raised. Though Martin, like Ethan, is initially visually associated with the outdoors, he is one of the next generation of men, comfortable in domestic settings but in need of harsh education to face the hostile environment outside the home. Much of *The Searchers* is Martin's education through Ethan into Ethan's world of practical knowledge. Yet Martin, one-eighth Cherokee, must fight Ethan's racism and his Ahab-like monomaniacal vengeance. Ethan is a tough, unyielding father, a personification of the landscape. Martin will master this world, but also learn to live indoors. At the end, the Oedipal conflict is resolved. Ethan and Martin gain mutual respect and grudging affection, but Ethan rides off leaving Martin in the domestic social space in which he belongs. Ethan's knowledge is necessary, but not enough.

The Western was a nostalgic genre in which the West was a time as well as a place. Its subtext was that men can only be men in a pre-industrial America where men fight for what they want and believe in. When the cabin door shuts on John Wayne's Ahab-like Ethan Edwards at the end of

The Searchers, it also shuts on the rough frontier he represented. The future is inside, domesticated, feminized. But something important has been lost. The patriarch is gone. The inside is dark, perilous without that protector. Yet the West of the Western was also a geography; arid, beautiful, yet hostile land. In *The Searchers*, as in so many classic Westerns, the land itself is a crucial character. Shepard has said:

> There are areas like Wyoming, Texas, Montana and places like that, where you really feel this ancient thing about the land. Ancient. That it's primordial. It has to do with the relationship between the land and the people – between the human being and the ground. I think that's typically Western and much more attractive than this tight little forest civilization that happened back East. It's much more physical and emotional to me.[11]

The patriarch understands and loves the land. He knows as well that human habitation is frail and impermanent against the land and human predators. The family, above all, seems constantly under siege, in need of protection from outsiders like Shane or Ethan Edwards.

By the 1950s, another sub-genre of Western developed, set in the West, but in the postwar, technological era. John Sturges's classic *Bad Day at Black Rock* (1955, screenplay by Millard Kaufman) begins with a diesel locomotive roaring across the desert right at the spectator, an invasion of the old West and of the spectator's space in the theatre. Tracy's MacReedy alights from the train at a desolate western town where outsiders are clearly not welcome. Dressed in a black business suit, one-armed, white-haired, and avuncular, MacReedy hardly looks like the Western hero able to defeat the sinister-looking bullies who people the town (played by the likes of Lee Marvin). By the end, MacReedy has enlisted the aid of the cowardly old-timers, his contemporaries (played by veterans Walter Brennan and Dean Jagger), but has also played surrogate father and taught young John Ericson the need for courage. In the classic Western, heroes aren't young men. Gary Cooper was over fifty when he made *High Noon* and *Vera Cruz*. John Wayne is decidedly middle-aged in his greatest Westerns. The Western hero may be a case of arrested development in his inability to conform to the norms and institutions of society and conventional heterosexual domestic partnerships, but he is also something of a sage, a remnant of an earlier age with wisdom and knowledge young men still need.

Against the surrogate fathers and heroic, if quixotic loners of the classic Western, Shepard's fathers, seeking refuge from the strictures of civilization in the desert, are usually absent or destructive; wandering drunks or embittered nihilists (Dodge in *Buried Child* seems to have walked out of Beckett's *Endgame*). While they are nominally progenitors, they are surrounded with images and accusations of impotence. Above all, they seem totally incapable of integrating into civilized society.

These images of failed patriarchy and its relation to a lost West are most vividly seen in Wim Wenders's film from Shepard's screenplay, *Paris, Texas* (1984). Travis Henderson, walking through a white Texas desert as a hawk watches him from a high rock, couldn't look more out of place, but we discover in the course of the film that he doesn't fit any better into contemporary American society. Lynda Hart rightly notes:

> this anomic scene projects the destiny that we suspect any one of Shepard's later heroes may succumb to. It is the likely fate of Weston in *Curse of the Starving Class*; it is the imaginary space out of which Lee emerges and will return in *True West*: it is a macrocosmic view of the barren garden in *Buried Child.*[12]

The desert in Shepard's work, according to Hart, is "that illusory, eminently male landscape that summons Shepard's heroes with a siren more seductive than Circe."[13] Like the landscape around him, Travis is silent. He is, for all intents and purposes, a vagrant, but that itself echoes Western heroes. In his classic essay on the Westerner, Robert Warshow observes, "The Westerner is *par excellence* a man of leisure. Even when he wears the badge of a marshal or, more rarely, owns a ranch, he appears to be unemployed . . . As a rule we do not ask where he sleeps at night and don't think of asking."[14] In contemporary society there is no place for a man outside the economic system. He is no longer a hero but, as Jack describes himself in *Lonely Are the Brave*, "a cripple."

Travis has a brother who is his opposite, a man who has adapted to his world. Walt has built a successful life for himself in billboard advertising (is there a greater desecration of the landscape?) and lives in that other favorite Shepard setting, the Los Angeles hills, once rugged nature and now suburbia, overlooking not valleys, but freeways. "No one walks," asserts Travis's son Hunter, now being raised by Walt and his wife. When Travis enters this suburban home, Walt's wife says, "Welcome home," an echo of Martha's opening line to brother-in-law Ethan in *The Searchers*. But this isn't Travis's home and home is an alien concept to Travis. At Walt's California home Travis gradually, reluctantly, regains language and memories of his parents and of his wife. Gradually, too, Travis builds a bond with his son, teaching him to enjoy walking. At the end, Travis restores his son, Hunter, to the boy's biological mother in a Houston hotel room and Travis moves on. Travis is incapable of living with the woman he loves and incapable of being anything but a fellow child to his son. The West is the Los Angeles hills and a Houston hotel. Even the Mojave Desert is decorated with highways, motels, and railroad tracks. As Shepard wrote in 1979:

> Poor Texas
> Carved into
> Like all the rest (*Motel Chronicles* 26)

Above all, in *Paris, Texas*, life is movement, whether it is walking or driving, but this is no longer a westward migration to build an agrarian utopia. Like Travis's walking at the beginning of the film, it seems to be constantly movement away from something. Other than Walt's home, the only other domestic spaces we see in *Paris, Texas*, are motel and hotel rooms, images of transience in this constantly moving society.

Travis asks Walt's Mexican maid, "What does a father look like?" To the maid, a father is a symbol of affluence, the good provider, so Travis decks himself out in his brother's three-piece white suit with a matching white fedora. He goes to walk his son home from school, but they walk home on opposite sides of the street. Fatherhood is a role Travis doesn't know how to play. Domesticated Walt and his wife love Hunter, but they don't seem capable of having children of their own. Travis is fertile but incapable of maintaining the social structure of family. Bringing Hunter back to his mother is an ambiguous act, a recreation of a family unit in which Travis cannot play a part, but also a destruction of the family Walt has created.

Few Shepard fathers are as benign as Travis. At the beginning of *Curse of the Starving Class*, young Wesley describes lying awake fearing invasion: "I listened like an animal. My listening was afraid. Afraid of sound. Tense. Like any second something could invade me. Some foreigner. Something indescribable."[15] The invasion Wesley fears is his drunken father Weston (*West*-on) beating down the door of the family house. The images in Wesley's speech are surprisingly feminine. Wesley lies on his back fearing a violent assault that has sexual overtones. The father can invade one, take one over. Wesley's father, Weston, was "infected" by his father:

> WESTON I never saw my old man's poison until I was much older than you. Much older. Then you know how I recognized it?
> WESLEY How?
> WESTON Because I saw myself infected with it. That's how. I saw me carrying it around. His poison in my body. You think that's fair? (168)

The poison passed on from father to son is violence: "He's not counting on what's in my blood. He doesn't realize the explosiveness" (171). Violence in *Curse of the Starving Class* is nature: what animals do to each other, what men do to animals, to each other, and to their own families. In a coming-of-age ritual, young Wesley tries to become his father, mimicking his actions:

> I started putting all his clothes on. His baseball cap, his tennis shoes, his overcoat. And every time I put one thing on it seemed like a part of him was growing on me. I could feel him taking over me . . . I could feel myself retreating. I could feel him coming in and me going out. Just like the change of the guards. (197)

By the end of the play, Wesley is being called Weston. The home has been invaded again, this time by men who claim the family's property as theirs, sold to them by Weston in one of his drunken moments. The violence that is one's birthright is not the only threat a man faces. The dream and reality of American materialism has crushed Weston and his family: "See, I always figured on the future. I banked on it. I was banking on it getting better. I figured that's why everyone wants you to buy things" (195).

Son Wesley knows that the threat to their home will not be not natural disaster or Indian raid, but bankers and land developers, men in suits who will take their home and land to build housing developments: "It's zombie invasion. Taylor [the lawyer his mother has hired and is probably sleeping with] is the head zombie. He's the scout for the other zombies. He's only a sign that more zombies are on their way. They'll be filing through the door pretty soon" (163–64). Losing the house to these developers is "losing a country" (163), the old West.

While dominated by a powerful, yet feckless father-figure, *Curse of the Starving Class* is filled with images of castration. Like many of Shepard's plays, it is funny, but a profound sense of anxiety pervades the piece. However violent and destructive, family is the only refuge, but family cannot really protect one. Wesley may have turned, through a kind of ritual mimesis, into his father, but like his father he is ineffectual, incapable of protecting his home. As his father has disappeared once more, Wesley dreams of going to Alaska, the last American frontier, but in Shepard, Alaska hardly seems a serious dream of the frontier:

> EMMA What's in Alaska?
> WESLEY The frontier.
> EMMA Are you crazy? It's frozen and full of rapers.
> WESLEY It's full of possibilities. It's undiscovered.
> EMMA Who wants to discover a bunch of ice? (164)

When *Buried Child* begins, Tilden has returned from a disastrous attempt to be independent in the mythic West, New Mexico. The old West required a self-containment of which Tilden was incapable: "I was alone. I thought I was dead" (23). So, like the sons in classic American drama, Tilden comes home, in this case to Dodge, a father who doesn't want him: "You're a grown man. You shouldn't be needing your parents at your age. It's unnatural. There's nothing we can do for you now anyway" (23).

Dodge is the embodiment of nihilism, never leaving the ratty sofa to which he seems physically attached: "I don't enjoy anything" (12). Tilden is physically intact, but "Something about him is profoundly burned out and displaced" (12), eerily calm in opposition to his brother, Bradley, who, though missing a leg, finds means of violent, if displaced, aggression. He brutally cuts off his sleeping father's hair and sticks his fingers in a young woman's mouth, displaced gestures of castration and impotence. Here is another symbolic fraternal split: passive and aggressive, loving and spiteful, fertile and sterile. Halie, Dodge's wife, is the typical Shepard matriarch. She is either occupying her room upstairs, filled with pictures of the past and expressing idealized images of her sons, or off having an affair with the ineffectual minister. Halie descends from her upstairs room dressed in mourning, but returns in yellow, her arms full of flowers, still an image of fertility, wife and mother to men who represent forms of sterility.

This family lives in Illinois farm country, in the middle of the American midwest. *Buried Child* gives us a dark vision of agrarian America in which the land, even the "catastrophic" weather, seem poisoned by the human inhabitants. Into this dysfunctional family comes a third generation, Vince, Tilden's son and Dodge and Halie's grandson, eager to reconnect to his family roots. Shelly, Vince's girlfriend, tells Dodge:

> I mean Vince has this thing about his family now. I guess it's a new thing with him. I kind of find it hard to relate to. But he feels it's important. You know. I mean he wants to get to know you again. After all this time. Reunite. I don't have much faith in it myself. Reuniting. (30)

Shelly expected "turkey dinners and apple pie and all that kinda stuff" (35), the stuff of American mythology. Instead she was brought into a primal American tragedy. Vince is traumatized by not being recognized by father or grandfather. While his very existence is denied by his progenitors, he is still haunted by his family ties. Driving west, he studies the reflection of his face in the windshield as if it were someone else's:

> And then his face changed. His face became his father's face. Same bones. Same eyes. Same nose. Same breath. And his father's face changed to his grandfather's face. And it went on like that. (71)

which echoes Tilden's glimmer of recognition of Vince, "I thought I saw a face inside his face"(44). Vince's vision turns him back toward the East. For him, as for his father, the West is too full of terrifying truth. Tilden, the only character in the play who expresses positive human attributes like love or loyalty, the only character who is tied to images of fertility, sees the family tie in someone other than himself. Vince's vision is a reflection, a form of narcissism. The family ties he seeks are inside and have nothing to do with positive human connection. As family ties in *Curse of the Starving Class* are described as "invasion" or "infection" here they are under the skin, faces beneath faces, an identity beneath the face we show the world outside the family. They are also once again invasion as Vince, singing the Marine hymn, drunkenly assails the ramshackle homestead. When Dodge dies, Vince takes his place as sterile patriarch, carrying on the line.

Brothers

True West takes place in another symbolic landscape, the hills outside of Los Angeles, also seen in *Paris, Texas*. The only West left is Alaska, where Austin and Lee's mother is vacationing when the play begins. Austin has left his wife and children to house-sit for his mother and write a love story for a Hollywood producer. At no point does he seem at all interested or concerned about his own nuclear family. Instead, he is engaged in a battle with his brother, Lee, who has just emerged from the desert, where he was looking for his father. Though the setting is the mother's suburban house, both parents are identified with less populated, less civilized places, the final frontiers. For the mother, the trip is a vacation she leaves early because she misses her house-plants; domesticated nature is more comforting to her than the glaciers she sees in Alaska. The father wanders drunkenly through desert and border towns, losing his teeth in a bag of Chinese food. Yet this absent father is still an object of sibling rivalry for brothers Austin and Lee.

Austin is writing his Hollywood love story, his "period piece," by candle-light, using pen and paper instead of typewriter or computer, itself an act of nostalgia:

> LEE Isn't that what the old guys did?
> AUSTIN What old guys?
> LEE The forefathers. You know.
> AUSTIN Forefathers?
> LEE Isn't that what they did? Candlelight burning into the night? Cabins in the wilderness?[16]

None of this means anything to Austin who seems, in his own way, as disconnected as his sociopath brother, Lee. Both feel remote from the landscape they now inhabit. Lee sees the country as "wiped out" and can only see the domestic behavior of the inhabitants from the outside, looking in the window at the "Blonde people movin' in and outa' the rooms, talkin' to each other. Kinda place you wish you sorta grew up in, ya' know" (12). But Lee and Austin did grow up in this neighborhood back in the fifties, when people believed in the mythology underlying the new suburban development. Now Austin sees his mother's neighborhood as a simulacrum of something he vaguely remembers: "Wandering down streets that turn out to be replicas of streets I remember. Streets I misremember. Streets I can't tell if I lived on or saw in a postcard. Fields that don't even exist anymore" (49).

Lee forces Austin to help him with his screenplay, "Contemporary Western. Based on a true story" (18). Austin counters: "There's no such thing as the West anymore! It's a dead issue!" (35). Lee's Western is a typical masculine myth: two men, husband and lover of the same woman, chase each other through the panhandle. The chase ceases to be about the woman, but is instead an endless, potentially violent bond of the two men: "And the one who's chasin' doesn't know where the other one is taking him. And the one who's being chased doesn't know where he's going" (27). The trouble with Lee's script is that it is endless, as is *True West* itself, as the two brothers continue their violent hold on one another: "I can't stop choking him! He'll kill me if I stop choking him!" (58). In a sense, Lee's screenplay comes true in the final mutual grip Austin and Lee have on each other, but there is no heroism in it, none of the nobility of the cowboy duel. As Bonnie Marranca writes: "The heroism and strength of the cowboy is revered by Shepard [and his characters] but in actuality the men he creates are ineffectual, fearful, and emotionally immature. They show no strength of character or will, yet they are allowed to dominate because it is their due as men."[17]

The only Western mentioned specifically in Shepard's *True West* is *Lonely Are the Brave* (1962, screenplay by Dalton Trumbo, directed by David Miller), a requiem for all the best aspects of the cowboy. It is worth examining in detail, for many of Shepard's Western scenes echo this classic film.

When the film begins, we see Jack Burns lying down in the New Mexico desert. The scene looks like the opening of a typical Western, albeit in black and white, used only in the early sixties for "serious" films, but on the sound track we hear the rumbling of jet planes. Jack looks up and sees the vapor trails of what are obviously military aircraft rushing to an unknown destination. This is New Mexico after all, home of the atom bomb. Jack, we find out later, was a decorated soldier in World War II and Korea, but was punished on several occasions for breaches of military discipline. He could be a hero, but not a follower.

Jack and his horse, Whiskey, who seems equally uncomfortable with the sights and sounds of contemporary life, ride off into the desert where they come across a barbed-wire fence put up by a power and water company. Jack cuts the fence (he later says that real Westerners hate fences) and rides on. Fences are easy, four-lane highways much more difficult. Whiskey, herself something of a free spirit who resents being tamed and ridden, panics but finally gets across safely. In a series of shots, Jack and his horse are contrasted visually with truckloads of abandoned cars, the detritus of modern America.

Jack's destination is the home of his best friends, Paul and Jerry Bondi. Though set in the middle of nowhere, the house looks like any suburban American house. Jerri is in the kitchen when she hears Jack ride up and a loving, expectant look shines on her face. As in *The Searchers* the hero is loved by a woman who has married someone close to him, knowing that the hero is not the type to settle down. And our hero, though in love with Jerri, is too noble to betray his best friend. Jerri is played by the usually worldly Gena Rowlands in her pre John Cassavetes days. With her perfectly bleached and set hair and fashionable clothes, Jerri hardly seems the frontier type. She is, however, the Traditional Woman, feeding and nurturing the men in her life and making sure their clothes are washed. Jerri's husband, Paul, is in jail for two years for helping illegal immigrants. Paul has put principle ahead of wife and family. Good Western women know that the rules are there to protect the family and society while their men try to maintain their freedom: "Oh, you men just make me sick. You act like children."

Jack decides that he is going to get Paul out of jail so that the family can be reunited. To get in jail briefly, he decides to get drunk (drunkenness is another sign of manliness) and disorderly at a local bar, but this bar isn't the large edifice with the swinging doors of the old Westerns. It's cramped and sinister, and the classic barroom brawl has degenerated into a very dirty fight with a one-armed psychopath. When the barroom brawl isn't enough to get Jack in jail, he punches a policeman and is given a longer sentence than he hoped for. In jail, he is beaten by a sadistic guard. Fortunately the jail is anything but high security and Jack finds a way to get Paul and himself out, but Paul, a man who has learned the value of living by the rules, decides to stay: "I've got a debt to pay off. If I break out tonight, they'd [his wife and son] be running beside me for the rest of their lives." Jack responds, "You grew up on me, didn't you." The price of maturity is bondage, but it allows one to live safely in society. Jack is constantly beaten up, constantly on the run. He may be the classic Western loner, but he knows that in the modern world a loner is "a cripple." It is interesting to note that, in the quirky but appropriate casting, Paul looks and dresses more like a character out of the city than a Westerner. The other men in the jail seem to belong in Jack's world, but not Paul. He has "grown up" into modern urban (or suburban) life. Jack and Paul are friends, not brothers, but their manifestation of the masculine division between good brother and renegade, a classic pattern in Westerns, is a benign version of what we see in *True West*.

From this point on, *Lonely Are the Brave* turns into a chase film as the police and the military are brought in to capture Jack as he and his horse slowly try to elude their captors. The chase is crosscut with the progress across New Mexico of a truckload of toilets. Finally, on a rainy night, when Jack's horse once again balks on crossing the highway, they are hit by the truck. The horse is shot, and Jack is taken off in an ambulance to an uncertain future. The final shot is of Jack's cowboy hat sitting on a rainy highway, a remnant of the Old West and the anachronistic cowboy who has no driver's license, no social security number, no address, but who has a mystical, spiritual connection to the land, which is being paved over, built up.

The postwar American Western was always an exercise in nostalgia. *Lonely Are the Brave* turns that nostalgia into grief. The bored Western sheriff who amuses himself by keeping track of how many times a stray dog can urinate on the same fire hydrant knows Jack embodies what he and his society are missing. The good woman knows that the cowboy is a case of arrested development, but she's also in love with him. The death of the horse and, symbolically at least, of the cowboy, takes place at night in the rain in a scene filled with black. Though Jack has no words (the cowboy has been silenced, if not killed), the bleak scene echoes classic tragedy.

In *True West*, Lee and Austin's battle over their father is a battle over a debased version of the Western loner, mourned in *Lonely Are the Brave*, but also the problematic father played by John Wayne. Unfortunately, their father is more like Gabby Hayes and the drunken fools who provide comic relief in a John Ford film than like Wayne or Kirk Douglas.

The battle between Lee and Austin, like that between protagonists in so many early Shepard cowboy plays, echoes one of his favorite films, *Vera Cruz* (1954, screenplay by Roland Kibbee and James Webb, directed by Robert Aldrich). Shepard remembers "trying to imitate Burt Lancaster's smile after I saw him and Gary Cooper in *Vera Cruz*. For days I practiced in the back yard. Weaving through the tomato plants. Sneering. Grinning that grin. Sliding my upper lip up over my teeth" (*Motel Chronicles* 14). What Shepard forgot was that his teeth were crooked and discolored, not at all the perfect pearly whites Lancaster flashes: "I'd forgotten how bad my teeth were." Girls were not impressed. This adolescent memory turns into a typically Shepard moment of despair: "I stopped grinning after that. I only did it in private. Pretty soon even that faded. I returned to my empty face" (*Motel Chronicles* 14). Still, in another version of this memory, Shepard credits this moment as the beginning of his career as an actor: "If I know anything about movie acting, it's from practicing my Burt Lancaster sneer – from *Vera Cruz* – at sixteen in front of a bedroom mirror."[18]

Vera Cruz opens with shots of Ben Trane (Gary Cooper right after the success of *High Noon*) riding alone through uninhabited wilderness. When his horse is injured, he meets up with Joe Erin (errant?) who will be his side-kick and nemesis throughout the film. While both Ben and Joe are soldiers of fortune out to kill for money in the midst of the Mexican revolution, they are distinctly different personalities. Ben is the classic Gary Cooper character, a loner with a strong code of honor. A descendant of Louisiana aristocracy, Ben has come to Mexico to find money to rebuild his family estate, destroyed by the Civil War. Like Ethan Edwards in *The Searchers*, Ben has never accepted the Confederate defeat. In this Western parable of good and evil, Ben wears the light-colored outfit. Joe Erin (Burt Lancaster) is always in black, like the villains of the old B-Westerns. If Ben Trane is the stereotypical Western loner with a code of honor, Joe Erin is the stereotypical Western sociopath, the man who lives outside of society because he can't live within its laws. Joe, whose motto is "There's no such thing as an innocent man," will kill friend and foe alike. His behavior toward the members of his own gang is as awful as his table manners (an aristocratic member of Emperor Maximilian's court says while watching Joe eat and drink, "Careful, you might get some of that in your mouth"). From their meeting until Ben kills Joe in a gunfight in the final minutes of the film, the two men have an uneasy love–hate relationship. Some critics who see more eroticism in Western male bonding than I do see, as Kate Buford does, *Vera Cruz* as a film in which "the villain falls in love with the quasi-hero as the only friend he's ever had and the hero lets him."[19] Ben may need to ally with Joe, but he can never trust him. Joe's trademark, in addition to his black outfit, is his smile, which is as much of a warning signal as a rattlesnake's rattle. Joe never seems more menacing than when he tells Ben, "You're the first friend I ever had." We see how Joe treats his friends. In his early films, that toothy grin was as much Lancaster's calling card as Cooper's stolidity and inarticulateness and Lancaster is clearly using the smile as a contrast to, even friendly mockery of, Cooper's famous taciturnity. In the wilderness, Ben must play by Joe's rules. One way or another everyone does, from aristocrats, holding on to colonial territory, to the Juaristas, who picturesquely and absurdly pop up by the hundreds throughout the film, to the women, who must play by the same rules of dishonor to survive, to the outlaws. Ultimately, Ben does the honorable thing and sees to it that the gold in question gets to the revolutionaries. Joe and what he represents have to be killed. Throughout the film Ben allies with Joe because he has to. Joe has the men and the firepower. But Joe seems to keep Ben alive out of fascination. We see him watching Ben to see what he'll do next. This kind of animal curiosity is as close as Joe comes to human emotion.

It is not surprising that Shepard loved *Vera Cruz*. The destructive partnership–rivalry of Cooper's Trane and Lancaster's Erin is echoed in early plays like *The Mad Dog Blues* and *The Tooth of Crime*. More important for our purposes, it is echoed in the relationship of Austin and Lee in *True West*. In Shepard's play, an elemental battle is being fought, not over Western values, but over the writing of a Western. Bounty is not gold, but television sets and toasters. Gunfights are replaced by golf matches. The territory to be fought over is astroturf in a suburban kitchen. The True West is their father, toothless and drunk in some desert border town. The idea of the father is worth fighting over because he is what's left of the West: anarchy, rootlessness, but also arrested development, "grown men acting like little boys" (35). In Shepard's vision of *Vera Cruz*, Ben can't kill Joe, because Joe is inside Ben. They are, at the end, eternally locked together in a comic, but potentially deadly fight.

Much has been written, including by Shepard himself, about Austin and Lee as two halves of a divided personality. It is also important to see them as brothers, family members, and family is every bit as violent in Shepard's plays as it is in Edward Albee's work: "You go down to the L.A. Police Department there and ask them what kinda people kill each other the most. What do you think they'd say? . . . Family people. Brothers. Brothers-in-law. Cousins. Real American-type people" (23). As hard as Austin may try to be different from his father, Austin and Lee, like other Shepard sons, have been "infected." Both are essentially loners who avoid even the human interaction demanded by their familial roles. Lee screams, "This is the last time I try to live with people, boy! I can't believe it. Here I am! Here I am again in a desperate situation. This would never happen out on the desert" (47). Austin decides he has to escape the unreality of his current situation and go to the desert. Their mother is skeptical:

MOM You gonna go live with your father?
AUSTIN No. We're going to a different desert Mom.
MOM I see. Well, you'll probably wind up on the same desert sooner or later.
(53)

The fact is, the desert Austin and Lee seek is exactly where there father is, in a limbo away from any social or familial demands. Lee and Austin at the end are still inside their mother's home. Like the Western, the desert they seek no longer exists in any meaningful way.

In the course of *True West*, Austin and Lee trash their mother's house. In *Buried Child* Vince cuts through the screen porch to invade his family home which has been strewn with vegetables and beer bottles. *Curse of the Starving Class* opens with a battered door being repaired. In the course of the play Wesley urinates on a poster on the kitchen floor and brings a live lamb into a temporary pen in the kitchen. The violent destruction of domestic space is the visual counterpart of the damage done to basic familial relationships. The men can only bring the violence and anarchy of their ideal wide open spaces inside, a corollary to the barroom brawls of the classic Western. The Western fantasy is not only fiction: it represents a masculine drive that is Shepard's *idée fixe*.

NOTES

1 Sam Shepard, *Motel Chronicles* (San Francisco: City Lights Books, 1982), 56. Page references in parentheses within the text are to this edition.

2 David Savran, *Taking It Like a Man: White Masculinity, Masochism, and Contemporary American Culture* (Princeton University Press, 1998), 187.

3 David Savran, *Communists, Cowboys, and Queers: The Politics of Masculinity in the Work of Arthur Miller and Tennessee Williams* (Minneapolis: University of Minnesota Press, 1992), 18.

4 Doris Auerbach, "Who Was Icarus's Mother? The Powerless Mother Figures in the Plays of Sam Shepard," in Kimball King (ed.), *Sam Shepard: A Casebook* (New York: Garland Publishing, 1988), 53.

5 Quoted in Bruce Weber, "An Unusual Case of Role Reversal," *New York Times*, 27 February 2000.

6 Susan Faludi, *Stiffed: The Betrayal of the American Man* (New York: William Morrow, 1999), 10.

7 Weber, 'An Unusual Case," 37.

8 Ibid., 8.

9 Sam Shepard, *Buried Child*, revised edn. (New York: Dramatists Play Service, 1997), 71. Page references in parentheses within the text are to this edition.

10 Sam Shepard, *Cruising Paradise: Tales* (New York: Vintage Books, 1997), 6. Page references in parentheses within the text are to this edition.

11 Don Shewey, *Sam Shepard*, 2nd edn. (New York: Da Capo Press, 1997), 5.

12 Lynda Hart, *Sam Shepard's Metaphorical Stages* (Westport, CT: Greenwood Press, 1987), 122.

13 Ibid., 105.

14 Robert Warshow, *The Immediate Experience: Movies, Comics, Theatre and Other Aspects of Popular Culture* (New York: Athenaeum, 1971), 138.

15 Sam Shepard, *Curse of the Starving Class*, in *Sam Shepard: Seven Plays* (New York: Bantam Books, 1981), 137. Page references in parentheses within the text are to this edition.

16 Sam Shepard, *True West*, in *Sam Shepard: Seven Plays*, 6. Page references in parentheses within the text are to this edition.

17 Bonnie Marranca (ed.), *American Dreams: The Imagination of Sam Shepard* (New York: Performing Arts Journal Publications, 1981), 30.

18 Quoted in Kate Buford, *Burt Lancaster: An American Life* (New York: Knopf, 2000), 138–39.

19 Ibid., 139.

II

JOHAN CALLENS

European textures: adapting Christopher Marlowe's *Doctor Faustus*

In 1974, either before or after Shepard's return from England, the Mark Taper Forum in Los Angeles commissioned from him a new adaptation of Christopher Marlowe's *Doctor Faustus* (1588–89), to feature in Edward Parone's New Theatre for Now series.[1] In due course the Taper declined to stage the finished script, *Man Fly: A Play, with Music, in 2 Acts*,[2] but ended up producing *Angel City* instead during its 1976–77 anniversary season. The script nevertheless invites comparison with John Whiting's *The Devils* (Royal Shakespeare Company, 1961), the Taper's very first and highly successful 1966 production,[3] based on Aldous Huxley's seventeenth-century tale of witchcraft and demonic possession, *The Devils of Loudun*, and resonating with Arthur Miller's *The Crucible* (1953). Insofar as Shepard's protagonist manifests his boundless aspiration by wagering his soul in return for the mind-altering (and highly profitable) capacity to speak in tongues, the adaptation also anticipates *Tongues* (1978), the collaboration with Joseph Chaikin resulting in part from the desire to have him direct *Man Fly* when the Taper abandoned the project.[4] To date *Man Fly* remains unproduced and unpublished. As late as 1986 Shepard was still enthusing about a possible film version of Marlowe's play, taken as he is by its "incredible language" marked by a strong musical quality.[5] During Shepard's stay in England, though, Faustus's dissatisfaction with the sciences of his day must have struck a sensitive chord in the playwright who was then suffering from a lack of inspiration.[6] Going by his other plays featuring artist figures struggling with the muses, from *Melodrama Play* (1967) via *Angel City* (1976) to *True West* (1980), that fearful condition even amounts to a chronic one. Small wonder Shepard turned the doctor of divinity disappointed by traditional academic disciplines into a writer. His acknowledged models are Whitman, Kerouac (B45), and Faulkner (B2), but his tale contains echoes of Kiowa lore, Hemingway ("The Snows of Kilimanjaro"), and the pessimistic late Twain ("The Man That Corrupted Hadleyburg").

At first sight *Man Fly* appears a fairly faithful adaptation of *Doctor Faustus*. The three-part structure is firmly in place – from the contract with the devil, to the evidence of the powers gained, and the subsequent damnation. So is the subtle fabric of images and motifs (the circle, the four elements, time, animal transformations, and so on), even individual lines, at times literally transposed. Separate scenes can easily be recognized, major incidents and passages retrieved: the apparent equivocation as to who is ordering whom or made the worst deal, the boons bargained for and the price settled, the signing and reading of the deed, the later renewal of the pledge, the probing for answers to the scholastic questions of the day, and the growing desperation running through it all. All the same, as the already mentioned models and intertextual echoes indicate, Shepard grounded the dramatic events of Marlowe's play in American soil at the time of writing. Hence he did away with the undefined "worldly" stage of early modernity, switching effortlessly between Rome and Germany, internal and external conflict. Instead he aimed for a "semi-realistic" (B1) setting, whose liminality still corresponds to the tense coexistence of the emblematic and illusionistic representational modes of early modernity.[7] Because the events are situated in the US, the dramatic method of *Man Fly* also differs from the contrastive one Shepard used in his adaptation of Middleton and Rowley's *Changeling* (1622). *The Bodyguard* (1973, 1978) indeed shifts the scene from Spain to Greece, England, and France, surroundings in which the eponymous American anti-hero stands out. Even so, *Man Fly* prolongs the earlier adaptation's exploration of national identity, triggered by Shepard's stay in England (1971–74) and equally evident in *Blue Bitch* (1973) and *Geography of a Horse Dreamer* (1974).

Man Fly is set at the foot of the snowcapped Rocky Mountains, where the Great Plains prairie crosses over from North Dakota into Wyoming, going by the contradictory provenance of the script's hero from Grey Bull, ND (B24). From lowly origins Skeetz was raised to the rank of doctor of letters and poet laureate but now he is "on the skids" (B7). *Nomen est omen*. Longing to become "conjurer laureate" (1.3.33), he calls upon Lucifer, king of the underworld, a familiar enough metaphorical designation for gangland. Through Lucifer's intermediaries (Jet, Scooter, and "top dog" [B4] Mustafo), Skeetz forfeits body and soul in return for twenty-four years of "constant ecstasy" (B16). With the mob's secret information and Mustafo's assistance, he blackmails a Reverend Green and replaces him at the head of his powerful Pentecostal congregation. Thus Skeetz is transformed into a gifted southern-style country preacher and nation-wide media star, business magnate, and minion of the president rolled into one. No emperors in sight on the American horizon, except naked ones, which in our televisual age means virtual ones, too. At the end of Skeetz's term payment is due, and irrevocably so. Neither his belated withdrawal into the anonymity of provincial America, signaled by some small talk with his barber, nor the urgings of his former poet friends, Billy Lee and Jackson Hooker, can prevent that.

Billy Lee and Jackson Hooker stand in for Marlowe's Good Angels, materializing whenever Faustus hesitates on the path of evil or despairs of his salvation. That these angels are portrayed as street punks conversing in idiomatic American English steps up the local color and the dramatic interest of the morality's allegorical characters. As in *The Tooth of Crime* (1972), the conflict had better not appear a foregone conclusion. With his baseball cap and glove, Billy Lee comes across as an All-American kid. But the rhythmic sound of leather slapped onto leather grants him punch and an inflammable coolness. Jackson Hooker as a child caused his mother's death by stealing her drugs to shoot up. This looks very much like Marlowe's systematic inversions of good and evil: of the saint's life (conversion, temptation, miracles, and holy death), the *Ars Moriendi* tradition (its contempt of the world), ritual exorcism (in Faustus's anagrammatizing of God's name), and Christ's Atonement (the blood shed for the sake of evil rather than redemption). At the same time, good and evil, still after Marlowe, are deliberately and tragicomically fused, as in Skeetz's preacherly persona of Anti-Christ or the presentation of his evil castigations as blessings-in-disguise (B50). By invoking God (much as Faustus does), the apostate chooses evil without letting go of good. As an irked Lucifer and Mustafo put it, for too long he has been "riding the middle rail" (B5) and playing both ends against it (B54). Mustafo knows his classics, for didn't T. S. Eliot argue that Marlowe's blasphemy necessarily implied a lingering belief,[8] causing what J. B. Steane later dubbed the play's fascinating "instability," its unresolved "to-and-fro motion"?[9] Unfortunately, Shepard belabors Billy Lee and Jackson Hooker's dramatic function of swaying Skeetz, thereby reintroducing some of the doctrinal morality's obviousness. Jet and Scooter, whose names convey the agility they require as turncoat apprentices and underlings of the devil, at least profess not to know whose side they are on (B8). This leaves the audience in suspense, too. All the same, their doubts about Skeetz's blackmailing scheme and newly gained powers make them easily eliminated challengers, abandoned on the prairie, if not killed by Green's bodyguard, Olson.

As a preliminary Jet is subject to some torture – a spell is cast on his foot, causing Skeetz's own to ache sympathetically. This situation recalls the angry horse-courser's pulling loose Faustus's leg because his horse turned into a "bottle of hay" when driven into the pond (4.1). Mustafo's impatience at Skeetz's "treading water" (B16) before committing his soul also resonates with this scene, presenting another foolish bargain. Earlier, Jet has a sexual fantasy of magically possessing some Radcliffe students during "a seminar on extra-sensory phenomena" (B17), which harks back to Robin's lewd visions at the prospect of becoming Wagner's apprentice. On the whole, though, Shepard did without the comic interludes composed by Marlowe's collaborator(s). This may indicate that the adaptor primarily went by the 1604 quarto because in the 1616 text these interludes have been expanded. Still, Shepard preserved their function of cutting down Skeetz's achievements, as in Jet and Scooter's double-edged excitement at hitting the road to "Indianapolis! Boise, Idaho!" (B16), a far cry from Faustus's flight across Europe (past Trier, Paris, Naples, and Venice). The comic reduction of miracles to magical tricks, show, and artifice is made explicit in Skeetz's mocking provocation of Green (B37), becoming a parodic "temptation" of Christ in the desert. But this reduction is already subsumed by Skeetz's double identity as priest *and* poet, besides a vocabulary reminiscent of Marlowe's, with its allusions to fading fashions, art, and performance.

Except for the script's centerpiece, an overpowering faith-healing, and the procession of poets offering Skeetz a final sanctuary, the diverse "entertainments" were also discarded. In Marlowe's play these insets are either meant to distract Faustus from his despair (the hot whore, courtesans, and Helen, the procession of the Seven Deadly Sins) or ought to prove his prowess and establish his fame and reputation (getting grapes in winter for the pregnant Duchess of Vanholt, conjuring Alexander and his paramour). In the adaptation their metatheatrical role has been maintained in the onstage observers framing the action proper (Jet and Scooter overhearing Skeetz's opening monologue [B3] or watching his being visited by Billy Lee and Jackson Hooker [B17–18], much as in the 1616 text the devils are watching Faustus's damnation). The insets' removal, however, does make for a tighter, more homogeneous play, offering less relief from the protagonist's tragicomic rise and fall, even if the "unity" and "comic synthesis" of the original play have been defended.[10] As a corollary, the presence of women is reduced to practically nothing. The token exception is the beautiful and smartly dressed Foxey, initially serving as Green's "jailbait" (B32) and rubbing Skeetz's aching foot, a menial role that foreshadows Meg's in *A Lie of the Mind*. This exception is made to confirm the rule once Skeetz turns against Foxey, too, for trying to prevent his revenge on Olson, Jet, and Scooter. In the end she is made to assume her "true" shape when transformed into a snarling demon dog (with mask) pursuing Reverend Green on all fours.

Jackson Hooker's disguise as an Old Lady, "tempting" Skeetz to do "good" by accepting her bag of "savings" so as to foil her cousins' vulture-like greed, accords with the Renaissance cross-dressing practice and Marlowe's inversions. Yet the near absence of female characters in *Man Fly* also prolongs Marlowe's patriarchal bias. As Sarah Munson Deats has demonstrated,

Doctor Faustus reduces women either to mothers or prostitutes. The one category represents in-law feminine values, the other outlaw ones, but neither has any substantial part or number of lines. Appearances notwithstanding, sensuous pleasure as well as mercy, compassion, repentance, and community constantly take a backseat to the masculine values of fame, power, and wealth. Consequently, this allegedly religious rebel upholds the Christian Patriarchy, which gendered and ranked these values accordingly. In Jungian psychological terms, Deats concludes, Faustus simply fails to achieve individuation by integrating his female anima.[11] The result is a "demonic" imbalance, constantly threatening his self, as the onslaught of Angels and the images of dismemberment reveal, a Dionysian "sparagmos" commensurate to Faustus's sin of male lust.

In pursuing this imagery, Shepard first alludes to Samson's symbolically disempowering haircut in the barber scene following the climactic faith-healing like a post-orgiastic low. The deadliness (also signaled by the empty stage and the funerary white sheet) is barely ruffled by the terse snipping of the scissors and the subdued chat, close to dreamy self-reflection. Toward the end the playwright then literalizes the dismemberment, like the 1616 text did. Upon closer inspection Jackson Hooker's bag of "savings" contains a severed arm with the titular inscription, "Man Fly." The bloody horror agrees with the modern crime setting (take the horse head in Francis Ford Coppola's 1972 *Godfather*) as well as the genre of revenge tragedy (witness the cut-off finger in *The Changeling*). Besides resuming the moment of the original pledge, the severed arm confuses Skeetz as to whether he is still alive or dead already, having a vision or being one, the ghost of his former self (B55–56). It is as if the play's events so far had been one prolonged dream. This impression is enhanced by the "smokey-blue quality" of the lighting, cut through by the follow spots marking the devils' apparitions (B1) or isolating the severed arm (B55, B57). In his opening soliloquy Skeetz already suspected his prospective power and knowledge would be pretense, a perceptive trick, black magic. Unless his rise and fall should be considered an unwitting demonstration of his writerly capacities, a hard-to-beat dramatic act of reinvention, ending in catastrophe when the play-within (Skeetz's adventures with the devil) encroaches upon and short-circuits with the frame (the writer who imagined them). After all, Skeetz measures time in "paragraphs" (B3).

As to Deats's conclusion: Shepard didn't exactly redress Marlowe's patriarchal bias. It would be another eight years before *Fool for Love* (1983) would present an independent female character challenging her male counterpart. Neither did Shepard, in *Man Fly* any more than in *Fool for Love* or so many of his other works, solve the vexed question of individuation.[12] On the contrary, Skeetz's opening soliloquy states the problem straightaway ("Me again.

Big whole man. Fractured into smithereens") and expands it to America at large ("Pieces of Americana") whose picture fails to cohere in his writings (B2). In its waverings and irregular tempo not unlike those of Faustus's final moments, this soliloquy forms a frantic gloss on his line "O, I'll leap up to my God. Who pulls me down? – " (5.2.77), which Shepard retained with minor changes (B59). As is well established by now, this line could have served as motto to the Renaissance emblem adorning the cover page of the 1604 Quarto of Marlowe's play and showing a man with one winged arm raised toward heaven, the other unwinged and pulled down toward hell. *Man Fly*'s split level stage – facilitating the sudden, "magical" entrances and exits of the devils from above – mirrors (hence inverts) this emblematic picture. Below are Skeetz's quarters, "a primitive structure of four poles," meant to suggest "a Plains Indian burial site"(B1) with the corpse abandoned to the sun on a simple platform. This set-up clearly anticipates *Silent Tongue* (1992). There Awbonnie's ghost or soul is prevented from soaring because Talbot Roe, the husband maddened by her loss, prevents her body from being dismembered and devoured by the birds. (Think, too, of Tamburlaine carrying about the balmed body of his dead queen, Zenocrate.) Among the southwestern tribe of the Kiowa, birds often function as protective and totemic spirits. Taboos exist against eating them, but being eaten is a way of sharing their avian powers.[13]

The funerary setting of *Man Fly*, like the severed arm, implies that Skeetz is dead already. Even without radically curtailing the comedy of Marlowe's alleged collaborators, Shepard's adaptation therefore possibly seals Skeetz's fate from the very start. There and then he abandons the throne-like "old Western saddle set on a horse tree" (B1) serving as his writer's seat and means of salvation. Faustus only "fliest the throne of His tribunal seat" (5.1.113) at the very end, after deciding to have intercourse with the "spirit" of Helen. This episode, which Shepard left out, has been said to make Faustus guilty of "demoniality" and the crime of bestiality it involves irrevocably to upset the tragicomic balance between salvation and damnation.[14] Granted, the 1616 text also loads the dice against Faustus, but retrospectively. As Mephistopheles gloatingly boasts, "When thou took'st the book / To view the Scriptures, then I turned the leaves / And led thine eye" (5.2.99–101),[15] which instills a bitter sense of Calvinist predestination. For his part, Mustafo underscores Skeetz's flawed character by refusing to wonder at his not feeling suddenly "polluted" upon signing the deed ("you weren't no angel up to now" [B25]). Coming from notorious liars, though, both statements may be false.

The ambiguous title of Shepard's adaptation encapsulates the emblematic point of *Doctor Faustus*. Strictly speaking "Man Fly" is a literal translation of the Latin inscription Faustus hallucinates on his arm after he has signed the deed with his own blood: "'*Homo, fuge!*' Whither should I fly? / If unto God, he'll throw thee down to hell. – " (2.1.77–78). This inscription in turn is Marlowe's quotation of the New Testament phrase, "Fly, O man!," with which Paul incites Timothy to abandon the pursuit of money, "the root of all evil," in favor of "eternal life" (1 Timothy 6.10–12). Bevington and Rasmussen add the (reverse) implication from Psalms 139.7–8, that man cannot escape God's omnipresence, neither in heaven nor hell.[16] The verb "to fly," then, connotes the fall and failed escape no less than the ascension (as in 5.2.91–95 and 5.2.108–9).

The adaptation's title (glossed on B23) preserves the Latin original's meaning. Yet it ingeniously adds the check to any misplaced human(ist) aspiration in a conceited attempt to replace God. Despite the magical powers granted him for twenty-four years, Faustus is still but a man (1.1.23; B54), ending up even less than one, as insignificant as a mayfly hectically living out its "restless course" of a mere twenty-four hours. Shewey's systematically erroneous spelling of Shepard's title in one word implies as much.[17] After all, "Homo, fuge" equally brings to mind the stock phrase "tempus fugit," referred to by Marlowe on several occasions (4.1.100–1; 5.2.74–75). When Faustus implores "Fair nature's eye" to "make perpetual day" (5.2.70–71) and the horses of the night to slow down (5.2.74) (in Shepard's rendition of the Latin phrase [B59]), Marlowe draws on ancient mythology by way of Ovid. His plea of ecstatic love from the *Amores* (1.13.40) is thereby recycled as a final though vain magic spell against human transience. Chronos, the god of time, used to be presented as a winged horse harnessed by the Hours into pulling the sun's chariot. It is this heavenly chariot which Helios' son, Phaeton, wrecked through reckless driving. Thus he became a warning against intolerable disruptions of the fixed chain of being, like the animal transformations from Marlowe's play which Shepard also recovered in *Man Fly*.

Another classic exemplum of such disruptions is Icarus (Lucifer is a third one). In *The Changeling* Middleton and Rowley also allude to the mythical figure and, when adapting that Renaissance play, Shepard followed his model in Slade's desire for his socially superior mistress and his love of piloting and the mountains.[18] That he only dies by drowning in the 1978 revision of *The Bodyguard* may well be ascribed to Shepard's working on *Doctor Faustus* in the intervening years. Surely there exists a remarkable parallel between the image of the blood-drenched sky above the Rocky Mountains during the finale of *Man Fly* and the close-up of Katrin's red "blood on the harsh blue water" ending the revised *Bodyguard*. True, the former image derives from Faustus's heavenly vision of Christ's Atonement (5.2.78–79) and the rebel's fiery retribution (since the mountains begin to glow as hell is discovered [B59]), whereas the latter image hails from the imprecation with which De Flores is sent back to his Beatrice, "the pilot / [who] Will guide you to the Mare Mortuum." But this is no objection. During the Renaissance the Dead Sea stood for the bottomless pit of hell in which the salt prevented one from ever sinking.[19] That meant appropriate enough punishment for highfliers of any kind. Similarly, Skeetz gets into "hot water" with Lucifer for invoking God's name (B53–54) and his final despair is an "endless sea" (B58).

Icarus of course features in Marlowe's very opening Chorus: "[. . .] swoll'n with cunning of a self-conceit, / His waxen wings did mount above his reach, / And melting heavens conspired his overthrow" (20–22). From Una Ellis-Fermor (1927) through Harry Levin (1952)[20] to Marjorie Garber (1975),[21] the overreaching figure of Icarus has played an emblematic role in critical interpretations of Marlowe's work. As such, Icarus embodies the dialectic between aspiration *and* limitation (Skeetz's "alchemical transformation" from "demon dog" to "angel cowboy" and back [B2]). The "cunning" (erudition, skill, deceit) in the above quote indeed conflates Daedalus with Icarus. The one made the confining maze and the wings, besides issuing the parental warning not to abuse them. The other fitted these wings to transgress boundaries, whether those between man and God (the Father) or man and beast (bird and minotaur in Ovid's tale). These interactions between man and beast Garber, like Deats (and Shepard on B58), construes as an individuation problem: the difficulty of civilized man to contain the subhuman within. But it is Camille Paglia who restricted the meaning of "man" when considering the Greek tragic pattern of hubristic self-assertion and downfall as a "male" drama.[22] Conditioned as they are by the natural menstrual cycle, women, says Paglia, never delude themselves into believing that much in free will. This is one meaning of Faustus's and Skeetz's necessary subjection to the inexorable cosmic rhythms in their final soliloquies. Paglia's insight also adds meaning to the drying up of the characters' blood during their deeds' signing. Mustafo knows it signifies the body is growing "wise" to the men's misguided aspiration (B22). So does Skeetz (B23), even if the mind's impotent reaction to what the body cannot help but "hunger" for, constitutes an equal "curse" (B58).

The talk of menstruation in *Curse of the Starving Class* certainly gives that play's title a gendered inflection. When Weston irritatedly wonders, "What happens when I'm gone, you all sit around and talk about your periods?",[23] he reaffirms the gender law of feminine domesticity, Ella's obligation to provide food, cook, and do the laundry, which "deprives" her of the right to run off with Taylor. Weston's drinking escapades and B. Traven's radical disappearance are meant to contrast with the women's failure to escape for good: Emma is first thrown off her horse and dragged through the mud, then killed when the car in which she wanted to flee explodes; nothing will come of Ella's trip to Europe. Going by Weston's soaring tale of the eagle and the cat, his hungry masculine flight has equally disastrous consequences (which may be why its victims, Ella and Wesley, finish it together). Even so, in Paglia's analysis, sky-cults, of which the monologue in *Curse* and the Icarian myth suffusing *Man Fly* partake, are typically male forms of resistance against female earth-cults. They are no less than a cultural displacement of the natural creative focus of the belly to the head, from which emanated patriarchal abstractions like logic and language.

Shepard's "True Dylan" (1987) expresses similar ideas in the context of its reflection upon artistic creativity and the mythical status it grants some. Not without some sexual innuendo and simplification, it ventures that "By nature" (66) the female rhythm is a horizontal and the male rhythm a vertical movement.[24] Throughout "True Dylan" the former rhythm is symbolically present in the "distant rhythmic splashing of waves" (59). The latter rhythm makes Dylan think of a "flying horse" (62), which provides a second, belated answer to the mock interview's programmatic opening question: whether the musician ever thinks of angels. His first answer is good whiskey, Weston's way of getting high. Dylan's recollection of his motorcycle accident offers a third response, insofar as its terms are clearly meant to recall Icarus' infringement upon the parental or social edict (68). In keeping with Jung's animus/anima theory, but in contrast to Freud's binary construction of gender, Dylan and Shepard ultimately agree that the male and female rhythms inevitably co-inhabit single men and women, "Like God and the Devil. [...] Like you feel the lie and the truth. At the same time, sometimes. Both, together" (66). The artist's challenge, therefore, the playwright told Kevin Sessums, is to remain smack in the middle of these contradictions, without taking sides.[25] For this reason, artists ought to be neither recorders of reality nor plain fantasists but mythmakers, since myths are lies that speak the truth,[26] fantasies as powerful as reality. For this reason, too, Sessums has likened Shepard's plays to images of Pegasus, "sweaty animals with nostrils and flanks," yet "able to sprout wings and take off."[27] Pegasus stands for "a hooved spirituality," if also for poetic creativity, since the impact of his powerful hooves causes the muse's spring to flow.

One of Shepard's earliest dramatic reflections upon creativity is already couched in the gendered mythic–symbolic terms pertaining to *Man Fly*. According to Albert Wilhelm, *Icarus's Mother* (1965) foregrounds the primordial struggle for (the son's, the present's) creative expression in the face of opposition (by the father-figure, the past) and the inaccessibility of the inspiring figure (the mother-figure).²⁸ Doris Auerbach has broadened that play's scope by attributing the American dream's decay to the female figures' being prevented from sustaining nurturing families in a patriarchal world.²⁹ Additional evidence for these critics' thesis is offered by Daniel Petrie's movie, *Resurrection* (1980), apart from its showing the close fit between Shepard's writing and acting stints. The attraction of Calvin Carpenter (played by Shepard) to the healer Edna Mae McCauley (Ellen Burstyn), who saved his life, indeed angers his preacher father. Because she denies the allegedly divine source of her gift, Calvin is deluded into taking her for the Anti-Christ and tries to assassinate her during a motorcycle sequence with which the one in "True Dylan" resonates.

Like "True Dylan," *Icarus's Mother*, and *Resurrection*, *Man Fly* ties artistic creativity to the conflict between genders and generations. The connection is really a staple in Shepard's work since *The Rock Garden* (1964). Skeetz certainly blames his (divine) "Father" for his personal insignificance (B16), which compounds the evidence for a double reading of the word "fly" in Shepard's title, and for the symbolic meaning of Skeetz's living quarters as funerary grounds. At last he hopes to turn the page ("Bury the poet" [B16]), engender himself ("My birthday is tonight" [B16]), and achieve fame. Foxey, more like a Good than a Bad Angel but in keeping with Marlowe's inversions, rekindles the poet's flame in Skeetz by voicing her rather patriotic regrets at the prospect of further corrupting America. A simple remark about the prairie's bracing smell opens up the yawning "everlasting space" within him and without (B35). For all that, Skeetz has staked his salvation on a life of crime. The choice automatically entails a rejection of the feminine, so he puts Foxey in her place, reminding her she is a spirit, no muse (B34). In the process true creativity is forsaken and salvation, too.

As a result, *Man Fly* approaches the generic category of "sit-trag," a term Toby Zinman coined to designate the perverted religious hunger, its systematic structural and thematic abrogation in Shepard's artist/saviors, from *Cowboy Mouth* (1971) to *States of Shock* (1991).³⁰ Skeetz's fate (like that of Faustus, as Fred Tromly has argued) indeed resembles that of Tantalus no less than Icarus. Magic "tantalizes" him with a fulfillment ever outstripped by his "hunger" (B10, B14), not to mention his thirsting for one drop of Christ's blood. Skeetz's Icarian downfall appears perhaps unusually conclusive for Shepard's work and sit-tragedy, but then the character's Tantalian torment (going by the 1616 text) is meant to go on obsessively, in a hell conceived along pagan rather than orthodox Christian lines.³¹ Sartre's *No Exit* (1944) dramatized a secular hereafter in similar terms, not to mention the life this side of the grave Beckett envisaged in *Waiting for Godot* (1953). Zinman has adduced plenty of causes for the perverted spiritual impulse in Shepard's work: from religion's failure to deliver and our skeptic secular times, to a corrupt system and ineffectual messianic figures too weak to sustain faith rather than overweening like Icarus.[32] Her etiology for the strained dialogue between self and soul which Shepard's plays, including *Man Fly*, externalize, runs the entire gamut. Almost, for on the evidence of *Man Fly* the neglect of feminine values should be added.

For a good understanding of the adaptation it is important to realize that the lost promise Foxey signals is also that of the equivocal "natural" sublime – silencing her (B39) makes the silence of "Ancient America" resound all the heavier (B29). The prairie to which Foxey pays tribute stands in for the desert, the unstable trope encountered elsewhere in Shepard's work,[33] as he reminds us by Scooter's confusion of these settings (B29–30). Here the prairie is of course dominated by the Rocky Mountains. Their majesty is commensurate with Skeetz's Wordsworthian ego when he has just signed away his soul and is still feeling "on top of the world" (B25). Lest it be forgotten that his superhuman grandeur is a vicarious emotion, the Mountains' later heartlessness (B60) expressly mirrors Lucifer's in the anticlimactic coda (during which he kicks the severed arm, the only thing remaining of Skeetz). According to the same principle, this natural scenery has served a legitimizing function within a nationalist rhetoric, which Shepard is said to invoke rather nostalgically and uncritically, "like the purple-mountain majesty of the nationalist lyric, 'God Bless America.'"[34] This seems much to the point in an American adaptation of a British classic written after a three-year stay abroad. Skeetz still comes across as an expatriate of sorts, aspiring to "full-blown citizen[ship] in [Mustafo's] native state" (B21). However, the bleeding Rocky Mountains ending *Man Fly* project both America's Manifest Destiny and the *loss* of redemption, whether in the Christian or national context. From Mustafo's mobster perspective, Christ is dead, and so is the frontier (B27), despite the notion's lingering Tantalian appeal.

A crucial index of this double demise is the emergence of a criminally figured postmodern sublime, marked by urbanization, commodification, and technology. Not that *Man Fly* ever moves to the city – whether Las Vegas (*Operation Sidewinder* [1970], *Seduced* [1978]), L.A., or Houston (*Angel City* [1976], *Paris, Texas* [1984]) – the desert's metaphorical counterpart and the *locus classicus* of the crime genre, for whose bright lights Jet and Scooter pine.[35] Nor does Lucifer exactly plan to cover all of America with concrete, as Bottoms has it.[36] But the phone booth along the abondoned highway where Skeetz awaits a call from Reverend Green already intuits the invisible power-lines, the communications network cross-cutting natural space, to which Mustafo promises a gateway: "the secret machinery [...] that makes things tick. The force behind the hidden police [...]" (B2). Skeetz's control over the media is the pay-off, allowing the alchemist's sublimation of lead into gold, if also entailing the commodification of his self. The dialectic of expansion and humbling to which the sublime (like Zinman's "sit-trag") subjects the self rehearses the Icarian attempt at overcoming boundaries and the subsequent fall. The spectacle of nature's (and God's) boundlessness may have been displaced by that of human(ist) power and wealth (which Timothy warned against), but the logic of infinitizing profit and economic performativity and the *mise-en-abîme* of power ("the force behind the hidden police") spell an endless deferral, a Tantalian lack of closure.

Considering the rhetorical means by which Skeetz works his magic (as opposed to the prairie's silence), success is even less guaranteed. In this regard *Man Fly* reenacts *Doctor Faustus*'s substantiation of the amply thematized (Icarian/Tantalian) sublime dialectic on the theatrical, tropological, and discursive levels. To Palmer, Faustus's study toward the end embraces the entire cosmos *and* shrinks to cramping dimensions, time opens out onto eternal damnation as it runs out, the poetry takes wing until a heavy caesura arrests the flight.[37] Just so, for Garber the magic circle (by extension the stage at large) protects *and* traps the conjurer. Spoken language proves capable of calling forth devils (by its blasphemous character), but also threatens the apparitions of Helen and Alexander (5.1.25), whose own inability to speak comes across as an extra flaw. Faustus's written deed allows him to burst his human confines yet binds him to his word till death ensues. Marlowe's flexible iambic pentameter, at last, reembodies the central tension – with its occasional "aspiring foot" or extra syllable disrupting the internal rhyme or meter. In the final analysis, Garber believes the playwright to transcend the play's antitheses in the act of (re)creating them.[38] Despite Eliot's somewhat disrespectful comparison of Marlowe's blank verse with an early derivative of "that astonishing industrial product coal-tar,"[39] its expressiveness gainsays for Garber the inexpressibility topos, so that Marlowe ultimately forges a rhetorical sublime.

To all appearances, Shepard proves Marlowe's equal in Skeetz's mesmerizing faith-healing, even if it is framed by a grotesque canvassing song. The audience's mood thus set, the subsequent *séance* justifies with a twist Eliot's claim that the Renaissance dramatist's savage style and mighty line occasionally skirt farce, caricature, and "huffe-snuffe bombast."[40] Nonetheless the scene is supposed to work its magic. Begun in the dark with the radio song before lights flood the televised Hollywood Bowl over which a crucified Christ towers, the staging mimes the speech's internal movement from darkness to enlightenment. Offering an alternative to Faustus's literal travels through Europe, Skeetz teletransports his audience by emotional, rhetorical, and technological means. Rallying the faithful by opposition to his detractors, this Anti-Christ invokes pity for his own pseudo-victimization, that of the two deaf-and-dumb girls about to be cured, and the mother who suffered from their fate. At the same time he arrogates the divine power to command the elements and, like an impudent, sharply dressed patriarch, pounds his listeners into a trance. The incremental repetition and cumulative buildup of his words brook no resistance, as they boom across the theatre's PA system in the evangelical priest's typical call-and-answer fashion.

At last the girls recover their speech, a "miracle" capped by Skeetz's bleeding hands and feet (B46). The single high-pitched note the girls utter to the accompaniment of a screaming saxophone is the foil to Skeetz's demonic eloquence, their respective lack and excess de-humanizing and de-personalizing both. If the color backdrop of the Rocky Mountains is supposed to be "photographic" (B1), that of the bleeding Christ on the cross, by taking after "the Dali painting" (B44), aims for surrealism. The whole set-up erupts into a dystopian scene in which people are weeping, writhing, and frenziedly falling to the ground as if seized by cataleptic fits. This violent madness is a far cry from Faustus's controlled ritual incantation of the devil (1.3.8–23), the friars' measured malediction (3.1.89–100), or the silent and decorous apparitions. The chaos rather exemplifies the crisis experience which baptism by the Holy Spirit in the Pentecostal belief is by definition.[41] It also rehearses the apocalyptic disasters on which Shepard's other artist/saviors stake redemption, unsuccessfully so.[42] "[S]oft" organ music and a "*mournful*" choir are heard underneath the exhausted preacher's more relaxed call upon his congregation's generosity – financial counters or "gifts" in exchange for verbal ones. But no sooner is his extortionist sales pitch over than the pandemonium resumes, this time with people singing and dancing amidst the floating greenbacks.

There is a profound lyricism and rhythmicality to this set speech (supported by sax, organ, and choir singing), this orchestrated mania with its seemingly uncontrolled ebb and flow of energy levels. Surely these warrant the subtitle's generic reference to music as much as the low-key saxophone accompanying Skeetz's opening soliloquy and facilitating the transitions between scenes, or the pounding, menacing music enhancing the devils' interventions. If in the earlier *The Tooth of Crime* (1972) Shepard recycled the registers of rock-and-roll, sci-fi, cars, and boxing to build his verbal riffs, he here draws on black gospel music, besides the Pentecostalists' glossolalia, holy dancing, and "joyful noise unto the Lord." Together these make for a spectacularity strangely at odds with the puritan antitheatrical prejudice documented by Jonas Barish,[43] which ought to be further exacerbated by the venality.[44] In Marlowe's play no less than in a late capitalist society, time is money – the term during which Faustus can amass wealth. The timing of Skeetz's faith-healing is all the more important then: to mesmerize the audience and avoid antagonizing it when calling upon its generosity.

Shepard's Reverend Green, a composite character, appears to be partly modeled on "Soul Survivor" Al Green, which may be one reason why the Taper Forum rejected the script or perhaps required further revisions, lest they be sued. Al Green was repudiated by his father for abandoning the religious music on which he was raised in favor of soul. Somehow compensating for the loss were his musical successes. His 1971 hit, "I'm So Tired of Being Alone," turned him into a superstar and is alluded to in the horror of Shepard's Reverend at being abandoned in the desert. After being "born again" – a revivalist experience the poet magician in Skeetz is addicted to (B2) – Al Green returned to traditional gospel. In the 1980s he kept bringing out award-winning albums while heading the Full Gospel Tabernacle in Memphis, Tennessee, a city with a large Pentecostal following.[45] By exemplifying the spectacularization and commercialization of gospel Shepard's Reverend Green and his proxy, Skeetz, definitely warrant the title's injunction against money, the "reward of sin" (1.1.39–41). In light of the playwright's other failed savior/artists, "televangelists" guilty of financial and sexual malpractices, like Jim Bakker and Jerry Falwell, are also targeted, even relatively honorable ones like Billy Graham. As a former friend of Eisenhower, Graham underwrote the 1960 presidential campaign of Nixon, portraying him in an unpublished article as "a Christian, moral leader." This was of course before Watergate, a scandal that dominated the papers throughout Shepard's stay in England, prior to his writing *Man Fly*. In 1973, Falwell, who went on to found the Moral Majority and help elect Ronald Reagan, was charged by the Securities and Exchanges Commission with "fraud and deceit." This did not prevent him from replacing Jim Bakker as head of the PTL television network, when in 1987 he admitted to a sexual indiscretion.[46] Such moral hypocrisy is obviously at issue in Skeetz's call to "cure" the "sick" and the "poor," the "dope fiend" and the "homosexual" (B47), as if all were equal evidence of perverted Christian values (health, wealth, and orthodox desire). In truth, the apocalyptic fervor of Graham's speeches possessed its own macabre obscenity at the expense of the so-called doomed, which recalls the sadistic overtones in the 1616 version of Faustus's damnation.

The fervor of revivalist preaching depends to a large extent on its belief in a one-to-one correspondence between the spoken word of God, the Gospel, and its referent.[47] A case in point is the equation of the Eucharist's wine and bread with Christ's blood and body, the transubstantiation doctrine much debated in Marlowe's days and infusing *Doctor Faustus*.[48] *True West* also resonates with its symbolism.[49] In fact, the (theo)logocentrism underlying Evangelism has appealed to Shepard for a long time. An unresolved tension between the written and the spoken permeates his work, one that finds nondramatic expression in the essay "Language, Visualization, and the Inner Library."[50] Similarly, Marlowe's play reflects the shift from an oral to a written culture under the influence of the growing mercantilism and the invention of book printing. This partly explains why Mephistopheles can no longer be satisfied with Faustus's oral promise but requires a written and signed contract forfeiting his soul. In a way, the contract offers a secular variant of the classic metaphors for the *vanitas topos* (skull [B58], hourglass, jewels, or flowers). By ever reminding Faustus of the term to his life, it gainsays Plato's fear that writing would undo memory. What the contract cannot prevent is that Faustus's soul, in the Aristotelian tradition still a divinely inspired organ of thought, now becomes a commodity in a secular economy of exchange, without any absolute value or "proper" being. (To Skeetz it "isn't worth a two day bus ride" [B20].) By the same token it has become an abstract currency on a par with the signifiers of literary language. According to Graham Hammill, Marlowe's inversions and play with emblems of power (Adrian's silver belt, Bruno's diadem) foreground the arbitrary link between signifiers and their signifieds, now making for insecurity and incredulity rather than an unwavering faith.[51] Hence the horse-courser doubts Faustus's words, though he speaks the truth, and Benvolio mocks Faustus's capacity to conjure Alexander the Great and his paramour before the German Emperor, Charles V. Both episodes demonstrate the emergence of a split between believers and disbelievers, orthodoxy and heterodoxy.

In his first draft Shepard did without either episode, though Jet's earlier mentioned doubts concerning the blackmailing scheme still resonate with the doubts voiced in *Doctor Faustus*. In the B-text Mustafo sends Skeetz off to hell with the rejoinder to "remember it's from hunting pleasure that you fall" (B59). In mythical terms the poet – already modeled after Icarus and Tantalus – is further identified with Actaeon, who was transformed into a stag, no longer able to tell what he had seen after stumbling upon Diana's grotto when she was bathing. In the *Metamorphoses* Actaeon's story culminates in his dismemberment by his own hunting dogs. Shepard, who also relied on the myth in *Fractured*, anticipates and conflates Skeetz's silencing and dismemberment in the severing of his arm, a synecdoche for his writings. Ovid's tale meant to warn against a subject's curiosity transgressing social boundaries, apart from gaining insight into the metaphorical or fraudulent nature of authority – Diana's nakedness without the signs of power. Skeetz's taste of power is all the more bitter for being fraudulent, like his rise from the ranks through his undeserved doctor's title.

To Hammill Faustus's transgression and its mercenary character allow for a reading in sodomitical terms of his relations with Mephistopheles, Helen, and the other devils in female disguise. This reading is independent of any actual intercourse but derives from Plutarch's version of Actaeon's story in which he is torn apart by his lovers. The anxieties over sodomy or the homosocial which *Doctor Faustus* registers are congruent with those *Man Fly* expresses about Foxey and the feminine. Both should be seen as "improper" to male entitlement or empowerment, except as means to an end. Foxey is exploited as "bait" (B32), dangled before Green's eyes but ultimately denied him. ("She'd dissolve in your mouth before you got the taste" [B42].) This fits Marlowe's extensive reliance on consumption imagery, the theology of communion perverted into gluttony and hunger, warranting the exemplarity of Tantalus for Skeetz and his victims. Jackson Hooker's disguise as an "old" lady (because of the intervening years) defuses the potentially erotic tension (in contrast to Faustus's enhancement of beauty by male standards [2.2.161–62; 5.1.106–9]). The hand kiss Skeetz receives inverts Judas's traitor's kiss. By violently wiping it away, the poet–preacher dismisses its redemptive power and potential homosocial connotations. For this reason *Man Fly* helps to arbitrate the debate about the alleged misogyny of Shepard's male characters as the result of homophobia[52] rather than homoeroticism.[53] Skeetz's sneer at the inappropriateness of Reverend Green's "feelings" for his "slave" of a bodyguard (B38, not in the A-text) point in the same direction. Presumably, the poet's wistful vision of several "bouncing Southern boys" (B58) is governed by Billy Lee's recent departure and his enthusiasm for baseball. Even if Skeetz's sending him off to avoid witnessing his damnation (like the scholars in *Doctor Faustus*) bespeaks emotional concern for his well-being.

Equally important, however, is the extent to which Hammill's reading emphasizes the discursive "impropriety" of *Doctor Faustus*, its refusal of closure. He thus disagrees with Garber, for whom Marlowe ultimately achieves complete "control over the realm of imagination and the world of the stage,"[54] "terminating" as he does, after the Latin phrase in the epilogue, his dramatic travesty of Christ's Atonement with "a new religion of the autonomous author," the one Faustus failed to achieve within the play proper.[55] Even Belsey's analysis tends toward closure through the historical momentum by which the fragmented medieval subject dependent on the Church and God made room for the autonomous humanist self, relying on empirical experience. But, as seen, Skeetz and his implied author are post-humanist selves, irrevocably shattered. From the fundamentalist perspective, the rambunctious faith-healing of *Man Fly* forms the paradoxical epitome of "propriety," in the sense of logocentric orthodoxy, embodied words sweeping the stage audience of the faithful off their feet in a dance of joy. Skeetz's words may well have a similar exhilarating effect on the more susceptible among the theatre spectators. Broadcast as they are through the PA system, they make for a minimalist version of Richard Schechner's environmentalism, a secular communion doubling the religious one. (This weakens Shepard's disavowal of the director's controversial environmental production of *The Tooth of Crime*.) However, to the average, more skeptical theatre audience the scene's meretriciousness and staged character undermine its orthodoxy, as with Marlowe's "miracles" (in Hammill's interpretation, not in Tromly's requiring the audience's tantalization).[56] The very excess of the faith-healing in *Man Fly* constitutes the scene's impropriety, like the outrageous spectacles of *The Tooth of Crime* and *States of Shock*.[57] Skeetz's own "impropriety" resides in his not being what he seems (i.e., the theme of the white devil in Renaissance drama), in his not being at all. The point is made extensively: Skeetz comes from "nowhere" and ends up "nowhere" (B50), longs for the power to shift-shape into "empty space" (B2), "airs" his sermons (B52), is "nobody to serve" (B35), or judges his life a dream vision that has come to "nothing" (B59). All exemplify his ontological insufficiency.

In the last resort, there is of course another heterodox audience, Shepard's incredulous readership at the Taper Forum withholding the play from production, exnominating it (like the feminine and homosocial in *Doctor Faustus*), and barring the community of theatregoers from attending it. That audience (Parone? Davidson?) prevented the play from achieving a tentative, provisional closure on stage, whether it judged *Man Fly* "unsatisfactory" by itself or as an adaptation of Marlowe's *Doctor Faustus*. In the latter guise, its protagonist pretends to be no foreshadowing of Christ's second and final coming, but its incarnation made virtually omnipresent to his audience through radio and television (B44). By now, however, we know Skeetz for the composite dramatic character he is, one recalling the historical figures of Billy Graham and Jerry Falwell, the literary one of Urbain Grandier in John Whiting's *Devils*, and the mythical ones of Icarus, Tantalus, and Actaeon. This is an altogether different dance of signifiers, the interminable performativity of intertextuality on which Skeetz's being and subjectivity depend, next to the performativity of written language *tout court*. "THERE'S NOTHING LASTING IN ME" (B12), he yells in despair. By being forgotten, the adaptation as a whole repeats the exemplary onslaught of time the Faustian type is made to suffer from, even if his inscription within the intertextual tradition has guaranteed his survival.

That *Man Fly* deserves to be salvaged from this forgetfulness, the present essay should have shown. Together with *The Bodyguard*, the script represents an independent generic category within Shepard's work: that of the adaptation. Its limitation to Renaissance classics may prove an asset when assessing the playwright's confrontations with the dramatic canon (comprising also figures like Ibsen and O'Neill). Because the upshot in both scripts has been a critical reappropriation of Shepard's American roots, they certainly remain indispensable to gauging the impact of his four-year stay in England. Beyond that *Man Fly* throws further light on the gender problematic and prolongs the self-reflection upon his craft so prominent in the plays featuring artist figures, notably in the tension between the oral and the written.

The adaptation's relevance to Shepard's career and work also exceeds the links here established with *Icarus's Mother*, *Curse of the Starving Class*, "True Dylan" or *Resurrection*. Traces of *Doctor Faustus* litter the plays written and produced shortly after *Man Fly*. *Angel City* (1976), which the Taper Forum ended up substituting for the Marlowe play during its anniversary season, in its title already recycles the Icarian flight symbolism, before dramatizing the artist's failure at transcendence when corrupted by evil. The disaster movie Wheeler wants Rabbit to produce clearly partakes of the controlled chaos Skeetz stages during his Pentecostal meetings. In California the Pentecostal Holiness movement incidentally spread from Azusa Street in Los Angeles (featuring also in *The Unseen Hand* and *Simpatico*) thanks to the early twentieth-century ministerings of William Seymour.[58] *The Sad Lament of Pecos Bill on the Eve of Killing His Wife* (Oct. 1976), an "operatic musical" commissioned by the Bay Area Playwrights' Festival to celebrate the US bicentennial, again features a larger-than-life Faustian character, just like Henry Hackamore in *Seduced* (1978). The latter hero, based on Howard Hughes (movie mogul, pilot, aircraft-builder, and personal friend of Nixon), is forced at gunpoint to leave his inheritance to his bodyguard/secretary. The contract written with an intravenous needle dripping the business tycoon's own blood comes straight out of *Doctor Faustus*. By signing away his life Hackamore seemingly provides a fitting conclusion to the Icarian pattern, but his legend survives Raoul's bullets. In fact, by recasting the Faustus myth in a national mold, from Hollywood producers to the legendary Pecos Bill, Shepard warns against its survival through lingering nationalist pride, as exemplified in *States of Shock*, written on the occasion of the Gulf War. "This country was hatched on witches' blood. It still goes on" (B3).

NOTES

1 Stephen J. Bottoms, *The Theatre of Sam Shepard: States of Crisis* (Cambridge University Press, 1998), 288.

2 There exist two typescripts of *Man Fly*, both in Box 2, File 15, of the Shepard papers in the Mugar Memorial Library, Boston University. The first text, numbered through 42, carries the holograph inscription "1st Draft/Jan '75." The second sixty-one-page text carries no date, just the holograph specification "2nd Draft." That it is crossed out possibly suggests that Shepard considered this a satisfactory second version. Besides integrating the typed and hand-written inserts to the first draft, this "revision" also contains some new material. This is the one referred to parenthetically in my text. References to Marlowe are to the A-text unless stated otherwise. Sincere thanks go to Sam Shepard and Judy Boals for permission to quote from the typescripts, and to the staff of Boston University's Special Collection for perusal of the material.

3 Katharine M. Morsberger, "The Mark Taper Forum," in John MacNicholas, (ed.), *Twentieth-Century American Dramatist*, Part 2: K–Z. DLB vol. VII (Detroit: Gale, 1981), 443.

4 Don Shewey, *Sam Shepard*, 2nd edn. (New York: Da Capo Press, 1997), 101, 113–14.

5 Jonathan Cott, "The *Rolling Stone* Interview: Sam Shepard," *Rolling Stone*, 18 December 1986–1 January 1987, 168, 170.

6 Ibid., 170.

7 Catherine Belsey, *The Subject of Tragedy: Identity and Difference in Renaissance Drama* (London: Methuen, 1985).

8 T. S. Eliot, *Selected Essays* (London: Faber and Faber, 1972), 133.

9 John Jump (ed.), *Marlowe. Doctor Faustus* (London. Macmillan, 1969), 177–87.

10 Robert Ornstein, "The Comic Synthesis in *Doctor Faustus*," and Cleanth Brooks, "The Unity of Marlowe's *Doctor Faustus*," in Jump, *Marlowe: Doctor Faustus*, 165–72 and 208–21. See also Fred B. Tromly, *Playing with Desire: Christopher Marlowe and the Art of Tantalization* (Toronto University Press, 1998), 19, 135.

11 Sarah Munson Deats, *Sex, Gender, and Desire in the Plays of Christopher Marlowe* (Newark: Delaware University Press, 1997), 202–24.

12 Bottoms, *Theatre of Sam Shepard*, 94, 144–47, 227, 234.

13 Paul D. Streufert, "The Revolving Western: American Guilt and the Tragically Greek in Sam Shepard's *Silent Tongue*," *American Drama*, 8.2 (Spring 1999): 32.

14 W. W. Greg, "The Damnation of Faustus," in Jump, *Marlowe: Doctor Faustus*, 71–88.

15 Christopher Marlowe, *Doctor Faustus*, ed., intro., and annot. David Bevington and Eric Rasmussen (Manchester University Press, 1993). References to act, scene, and line numbers in parentheses within the text are to this edition.

16 Bevington and Rasmussen, *Doctor Faustus*, 142.

17 Shewey, *Sam Shepard*, 101, 104, 113, 156, 264.

18 Johan Callens, *From Middleton and Rowley's "Changeling" to Sam Shepard's "Bodyguard": A Contemporary Appropriation of a Renaissance Drama* (Lewiston, NY: Edwin Mellen, 1997), 28, 112.

19 Ibid., 52–53, 55.

20 Tromly, *Playing with Desire*, 15.

21 Marjorie Garber, "'Infinite Riches in a Little Room': Closure and Enclosure in Marlowe," in Alvin Kernan (ed.), *Two Renaissance Mythmakers: Christopher Marlowe and Ben Jonson* (Baltimore: Johns Hopkins University Press, 1977), 3–21.

22 Camille Paglia, *Sexual Personae: Art and Decadence from Nefertiti to Emily Dickinson* (New Haven: Yale University Press, 1990), 8–10.

23 Sam Shepard, *Angel City, Curse of the Starving Class, and Other Plays* (New York: Urizen Books, 1976), 87.

24 Sam Shepard, "True Dylan," *Esquire*, July 1987, 59–68. Page references in parentheses within the text are to this edition.

25 Kevin Sessums, "Sam Shepard: Geography of a Horse Dreamer," *Interview*, September 1988, 78.

26 Amy Lippman, "Rhythm and Truths: an Interview with Sam Shepard," *American Theatre*, 1.1 (April 1984 [1983]): 9.

27 Sessums, "Sam Shepard," 78.

28 Albert Wilhelm, "*Icarus's Mother*: Creative Transformations of a Myth," in Kimball King (ed.), *Sam Shepard: A Casebook* (New York: Garland Publishing, 1988), 21–30.

29 Doris Auerbach, "Who Was Icarus's Mother? The Powerless Mother Figures in the Plays of Sam Shepard," in King, *Sam Shepard: A Casebook*, 53–64.

30 Toby Silverman Zinman, "Shepard's Sit-Trag: Salvation Subverted," in Johan Callens (ed.), *Sam Shepard: Between the Margin and the Centre. Contemporary Theatre Review* 8.3 (1998): 41–54.

31 Tromly, *Playing with Desire*, 12, 20, 22, 25, 145–46.

32 Zinman, "Shepard's Sit-Trag," 51–53.

33 Leonard Wilcox, "The Desert and the City: *Operation Sidewinder* and Shepard's Postmodern Allegory," in Leonard Wilcox (ed.), *Rereading Shepard: Contemporary Critical Essays on the Plays of Sam Shepard* (New York: St. Martin's Press, 1993), 42–57.

34 Rob Wilson, "The Postmodern Sublime: Local Definitions, Global Deformations of the US National Imaginary," *Amerikastudien/American Studies*, 43.3 (1998): 521.

35 See Leonard Wilcox, "The Desert and the City," 42–57, and "West's *The Day of the Locust* and Shepard's *Angel City*: Refiguring L.A. *Noir*," *Modern Drama*, 36 (March 1993): 61–75.

36 Bottoms, *Theatre of Sam Shepard*, 143.

37 D. J. Palmer, "Magic and Poetry in *Doctor Faustus*," in Jump, *Marlowe: Doctor Faustus*, 200–2.

38 Marjorie Garber, "'Infinite Riches,'" 19–20 and "'Here's Nothing Writ': Scribe, Script, and Circumscription in Marlowe's Plays" (1984), in Richard Wilson (ed. and intro.), *Christopher Marlowe* (London: Longman, 1999), 40.

39 T. S. Eliot, *Essays on Elizabethan Drama* (New York: Harcourt, Brace and World, 1960 [1956]), 57–58.

40 Ibid., 62–64.

41 Charles Reagan Wilson and William Ferris (eds.), *Encyclopedia of Southern Culture* (Chapel Hill: University of North Carolina Press, 1989), 1296.
42 Zinman, "Shepard's Sit-Trag," 44–47.
43 See Jonas Barish, *The Anti-Theatrical Prejudice* (Berkeley: University of California Press, 1981).
44 See Robert Sacré, *Les negro spirituals et les gospel songs* (Paris: Presses Universitaires de France, 1993), 39, and Wilson and Ferris, *Encyclopedia of Southern Culture*, 1012–14, 1296.
45 Sacré, *Les negro spirituals*, 113–14.
46 Wilson and Ferris, *Encyclopedia of Southern Culture*, 1317–19.
47 Ibid., 1272–73.
48 Garber, " 'Here's Nothing Writ,' " 41–48.
49 See Zinman, "Shepard's Sit-Trag," 49, and Jeffrey D. Hoepper, "Cain, Canaanites, and Philistines in Sam Shepard's *True West*," *Modern Drama*, 36 (March 1993): 76–82.
50 Johan Callens, "Introduction," *Sam Shepard: Between the Margin and the Centre*, 1–17.
51 See Graham Hammill, "Faustus's Fortunes: Commodification, Exchange, and the Form of Literary Subjectivity," *English Literary History*, 63 (1996): 309–36.
52 Alan Shepard, "The Ominous 'Bulgarian' Threat in Sam Shepard's Plays," *Theatre Journal*, 44 (1992): 59–66.
53 Florence Falk, "Men Without Women," in Bonnie Marranca (ed.), *American Dreams: The Imagination of Sam Shepard* (New York: Performing Arts Journal Publications, 1981), 90–103.
54 Garber, " 'Infinite Riches,' " 19.
55 Garber, " 'Here's Nothing Writ,' " 30, 48.
56 Hammill, "Faustus's Fortunes," 320; Tromly, *Playing with Desire*, 142.
57 Callens, "Diverting the Integrated Spectacle of War: Sam Shepard's *States of Shock*," *Text and Performance Quarterly*, 20.3 (July 2000): 290–306.
58 Wilson and Ferris, *Encyclopedia of Southern Culture*, 1296.

12

KIMBALL KING

Sam Shepard and the cinema

Few great playwrights are as inextricably bound to film as Sam Shepard. Personally, he has possessed a "star" quality since his earliest days as a would-be actor, musician, writer, and amateur playwright. Handsome enough to be a male model, Shepard's face had an even stronger impact on his public than his talent as a writer. It seems that he first wrote plays almost as a compensation for his not being a top-notch musician. As a boy he imagined himself as a film star, often Gary Cooper, and would act out scenes from favorite films as he did his chores, often to the astonishment of onlookers. Almost incidentally he was commissioned by Antonioni to write the screenplay for the Italian director's *Zabriskie Point* (1970) a few years after Antonioni had gained international recognition with his acclaimed movie, *Blow-Up* (1966). Antonioni was drawn to Shepard for his alienated but dangerously appealing manner, the very American nasal twang of his southwestern accent, and his irreverent and inchoate early plays, often performed in coffee houses or totally noncommercial venues. Somehow he perceived that Shepard stood for all disenchanted young Americans who could capture the loathing for contemporary capitalistic decadence while at the same time projecting old-fashioned, anarchistic longing for the carefree American individual of an earlier century. Shepard's first encounter with a movie production was something of a debacle. Although the playwright has claimed authorship of the *Zabriskie Point* screenplay, he abandoned the project before the movie was ever completed and Antonioni chose Fred Gardner to rewrite most of the script. Few of Shepard's lines of dialogue or artistic imaginings remain in the completed work. Yet *Zabriskie Point* had a traceable influence on Shepard's *Operation Sidewinder* (1970), which he completed after his resignation from the Antonioni film. In fact many of Shepard's best stage plays have been enriched by his primarily negative reaction to contact with mainline Hollywood films. Not only *Angel City* (1976) with its specific exposé of Los Angeles and Hollywood, but also *True West* (1980), where two brothers vie to write a better screenplay, and *Seduced* (1978), where a dying Henry Hackamore describes his disastrous liaisons with female stars and a movie industry which robbed him of personal identity at the same time it turned him into an American icon, dissect a gangrenous Hollywood milieu. Then, too, it would be impossible to disprove that Shepard's many turns as a movie idol conferred on him a celebrity status that resulted in Americans having a peculiar reverence for his stage plays. A good-looking movie star, projecting a strong heterosexuality in all of his performances, earning what must have seemed to many, huge amounts of money, chose nevertheless to write for the stage. Shepard is not a dilettante and his plays are not indulgences of a mediocre talent, but his originality of mind, his unerring ear for speech rhythms, his wildly imaginative characterizations were possibly less relevant to many theatregoers than his celebrity status. Always distrusting Hollywood's artificiality and distortion of what the playwright considers honest values, he nevertheless is fully aware that success in this area of his life has enhanced his reputation in other areas.

Shepard as film star

Shepard's reputation as a brilliant young playwright led to his being discovered as an actor and, conversely, his international recognition depends in large part upon the familiarity of his face in more than twenty films he has appeared in over thirty years. He was first an amateur playwright, then a professional though hardly "mainstream" writer for the stage. He has also been a stage actor, a screenwriter, a director, and a film star, even playing the lead in his own movie, *Fool for Love* (1983). He never seems to have conceived of himself as a professional stage actor. Such an actor would have been cast in a variety of roles and, out of a necessity to survive, would have developed several stage personae and would have accepted parts in works he failed to admire or which forced upon him the need to depict a character unlike himself. Shepard is not haughty, but he is aloof and independent, hardly the sort to be molded by a director with an incompatible vision. It is difficult to separate the playwright from the filmmaker from the actor. Shepard is unswervingly male, unaffected, and bright – but never polished or super-educated. Financial considerations may have led him to accept certain parts in films, and there are subtle differences in his characterizations; but primarily he has been selected for and/or has agreed to participate in projects in which the Shepard persona remains intact. He is the lean, handsome man of mystery with crooked teeth who seems to flaunt his distrust of artificiality. When he joins the cast of a movie, that film tends to be shaped by his presence, rather than absorbing him into it. Maybe because he has juggled several related careers successfully, the actor/writer has been more careful than most to choose projects that reflect his interests and display his talents to advantage. Shepard was asked to act the role of a wealthy Texas farmer in *Days of Heaven* (1978). Approached in 1976 to begin work in the movie, Shepard drove himself to Alberta, Canada, where the film was being shot. He might have written the script himself although, in fact, it was partly inspired by Hamlin Garland's *Boy Life on the Prairie* written in 1899.

In the movie Shepard plays a terminally ill Texan who is plotted against by a rebellious young day-worker and his girlfriend, Abby, who see the opportunity of an ample inheritance for Abby, if she can seduce "the boss." Of course, she falls in love with him and thwarts her boyfriend's plan. The plot in that sense is similar to Kate Croy's and Merton Densher's deception of Milly Theale in Henry James's novel, *Wings of the Dove* (1902), although there is no reason to believe the makers of *Days of Heaven* were ever aware of the Jamesian novel, nor that James, in turn, knew about the Garland journal. Shepard was a "natural" at performing cinematic "tasks" that were a part of his childhood. He enjoyed riding horses, shooting game, and knew exactly how a farmer would test a sheaf of wheat grain. Always his long-legged swagger and vocal twang added authenticity to his portrayals. They were, of course, natural assets. Shepard is not a narcissistic artist, but the male characters who interest him are ones similar to himself – rugged individualists at home riding the range in period pieces, or driving Chevy pick-up trucks in a more modern milieu. Timing is important in the movie industry. A youth in the sixties, Shepard entered the film industry at a time when the polished, almost artificial good looks of a Robert Taylor or Tyrone Power were being replaced by the "natural" man. Shepard the actor, like Shepard the writer, projects self-confidence, sex appeal, and a mysterious detachment, which suggests intelligence without intellectual pretense. Although *Days of Heaven* also featured a very young Richard Gere and Brooke Adams, Shepard took the lion's share of applause when critics discussed the movie at the Cannes film festival.

Shepard's successful acting turn in *Days of Heaven* led to his being recruited for the scruffy hero of *Resurrection* (1980). Cast this time as a rowdy, often drunken poor man in greasy clothes, he merely exposed what seemed to be a different side of the earlier character – equally authentic yet winsome, in a way. In this way the two protagonists resemble Austin and Lee in *True West* or Carter and Vinnie in *Simpatico*, paired first in stage plays and later in movies based on those plays, sharing an almost symbiotic relationship and literally experiencing role reversals, as if they were two parts of the same person. Ellen Burstyn plays a faith-healer in *Resurrection* and Shepard is cast as her lover who is divided by his belief in her powers of healing and by the fundamental prejudices of his background, which are exacerbated by the presence of his testy, self-righteous father. Some credited versatility to Shepard's performances as two very different men in *Days of Heaven* and *Resurrection*. It is easier to note the similarities, however, and to gain a sense of an immutable personal vision in all of the artist's endeavors.

For many, of course, Shepard's most memorable film opportunity was his contract to play Chuck Yaeger in a movie adaptation of Tom Wolfe's book on astronauts, *The Right Stuff* (1983). Like the title of Shepard's play, *True West*, Wolfe's use of "The Right Stuff" is ironic. Both works emphasize the artificial labels which society assigns to the genuine and the worthwhile. Image becomes more important than reality in a public relations-oriented society. Most Americans perceive the West as a Hollywood product, a legacy of films like *Stagecoach* (1938). In the same way, they glorify the over-hyped heroism of astronauts, ignoring the hard work and frequent discouragement that have under-girded their eventual successes. The character of Chuck Yaeger had been written out of the original screenplay of *The Right Stuff* but Phil Kaufman, the movie's director, insisted on Yaeger's inclusion in the movie. Yaeger is "the real thing," a no-nonsense test pilot who despises vainglorious publicity-seeking. Pretending to be a test pilot is a far cry from being a farmer or a hick roustabout, but Shepard conveyed his same unyielding persona – the manly loner without a façade who discovers a role for himself and accepts it somewhat stoically. Thus, it seems that a certain stolid unity in Shepard's own personality gives shape to all of his creative experiences. From playing the dynamic lover of Frances Farmer in the movie, *Frances* (1982), to performing quite minor roles in *Crimes of the Heart* (1986), *Steel Magnolias* (1989), and *The Pelican Brief* (1993), Shepard seemed to select films which permit him to affirm his favorite themes: the difficulty of romantic relationships, the frustrations and disappointments of everyday life, and the competing emotions of anger and compassion in ordinary men. His screenplays and stage plays become amplified explorations of these same interests. In the spring of 2000 a modern version of *Hamlet* was released with Shepard playing the ghost of Hamlet's father. Denmark is now a multinational corporation and the murdered king its former CEO. The play's setting and action have been moved to New York City after the millennium. Shepard is well cast as Hamlet's father appearing to his bemused son in a video arcade and on the balcony of the Hotel Elsinore. His stern masculinity blends well with his understated but appropriate recitation of Shakespeare's familiar lines. When he appears as an apparition standing in Hamlet's room or sitting in a chair by Gertrude's bed, Shepard's presence is natural, expected. The subject of murderous feelings between brothers recalls *True West* and the flighty wives with wavering loyalties have appeared in *Buried Child* (1978), *Curse of the Starving Class* (1977), and other of the actor's stage plays. He continues to select screen roles which reflect his own views on life. And like many other twentieth-century artists, Shepard has written several stories for the screen that to this day remain unproduced.

Unproduced screenplays

When he was still in his twenties Shepard had gained a reputation as an off-beat playwright of great promise. It was logical that he would also begin to write screenplays. One of his first was called *Maxagasm*, which he called "a distorted Western for the Soul and Psyche."[1] The screenplay had been based on one of Anthony Foutz's stories and Shepard gave the characters archetypal names: Child, Princess, Peach, Cowboy, etc. Shepard's contact with the musical group, the Rolling Stones, at the time of his association with Antonioni, had led him to dream of a movie in which he and the Stones would all participate. But the Stones went on to fame and fortune in other arenas about the time Antonioni replaced Shepard as a writer on *Zabriskie Point*. Still, merely because Antonioni had originally signed him up for work on his screenplay, and ultimately gave Shepard some screen credit for his time on the set, offers to write screenplays continued to reach Shepard. In one case he collaborated with Tony Richardson, director of *Tom Jones*, on a rewriting of Middleton and Rowley's Jacobean masterpiece, *The Changeling*, which was to be re-named *The Bodyguard*. Soon, too, he joined forces with Murray Mednick to write a screenplay called *Ringaleevie*, which contained elements of his slightly earlier stage play, *Operation Sidewinder* (1970). There was an amateur flavor to the whole project and he and Mednick dedicated the play to various Shepardian characters, including Crazy Horse and the Holy Yehudi, as well as to their wives, Kathleeen Mednick and O-Lan Shepard. Shepard began several screenwriting projects; in some cases he was an "idea" man, in others he rewrote scenes by previous writers. Eventually he completed a screenplay called *Seventh Son* that concerned feuding gangsters in a child-pornography operation. Shepard recoils from pornography and, in fact, a blackmailer who has used pornographic photos gets his just deserts in both the stage play, *Simpatico*, and the film based on it.

At several points in Shepard's career critics have noted what they perceived as autobiographical elements in the artist's work. For example, *Curse of the Starving Class*, *True West*, and *A Lie of the Mind* are often interpreted in this vein. In films the same is said of *Fool for Love*. The unpublished screenplay, *Fractured*, also appears to contain autobiographical elements. Shepard, who lived with his wife and son at the time in California while attempting to earn a living in Hollywood, describes a suburban rancher who supports his family by posing as a model for the Marlboro Man. The husband and wife in the screenplay are called Massey and Lu-Anne (near anagrams for Sam and O-Lan). One scene, in particular, has the potential power of Shepard's best films. In it a wild Appaloosa mare rampages through Massey's suburban house, providing a frightening image of untamed nature that emphasizes suburbia's recent, shallow origins. The runaway horse, Mel, in *Far North* (1988) or the horses in *Silent Tongue* (1992) possess some of the same vital mystery of the rogue Appaloosa in *Fractured*. Still, Shepard would have to wait several years before he would take full control of a film project. Meanwhile he saw several works he had written for the stage transformed by others into movies.

Filmed versions of Shepard's stage plays adapted by others

The video film of Shepard's *True West* (1984) is an anomaly. While Shepard wrote *True West* as a stage play, generally considered to be one of his best, the video version was taped by PBS. The Cherry Lane theatre production of the play stars John Malkovich and Gary Sinese. Therefore, while Shepard had essentially nothing to do with producing the film, it is an accurate representation of his theatre piece. Although it was not intended to be a feature film, such as Shepard's *Fool For Love* (1985) which was also based on one of his stage plays, it is available at video stores and is considered by many as a Shepard "movie." It is worthwhile to examine its production values. Literally filmed on a stage set, *True West* avoids the monotonous and claustrophobic atmosphere one might expect of a drama filmed in a single room. And while the absurdities of Hollywood's financial exploitation of writers and their audiences become its principal subject matter, the city of Los Angeles, the environmental rape of California, and the corrupt milieu of major studios are never witnessed first-hand. The impact of these elements on two estranged brothers provides all the proof we need of their existence, apart from two brief scenes with a Hollywood "idea" man, Saul Kimmer, who plays the role of an *idiot savant*, who recognizes the commercial possibilities of the sociopathic brother, Lee's, improbable saga of adventure in the modern West.

The simple plotline of *True West* is equally well-suited to stage or screen. Austin, a semi-successful, college-educated screenwriter from north California has taken occupancy of his mother's house while she is traveling to Alaska. He is interrupted in his attempts to lead a quiet life as a writer when his brother, Lee, a boorish, uneducated bum who has been leading a hand-to-mouth existence in the desert (he claims) and who has a reputation for thievery and brushes with the law, alluded to by his disapproving brother, appears unexpectedly and demands asylum. After unsuccessfully canvassing his mother's neighborhood for robbery prospects, Lee directs his energies to becoming a screenwriter like his brother. A chance meeting with Austin's Hollywood sponsor, Saul, results in Lee's being assigned to write a screenplay rather than Austin. There is the suggestion that Hollywood professionals like Saul have no appreciation for art and see involvement in culture as a business and also that Saul has selected Lee's project over Austin's as a result of gambling on a golf game, as well as a hint of a possible homosexual assignation.

Horribly disillusioned and crushed by the rejection of his own screenplay, Austin begins eventually to "exchange" roles with his brother, in time stealing from neighbors' houses (admittedly toasters, with limited monetary value) drinking excessively, and bemoaning his discomfort in "civilized" surroundings. Yet Lee, though he attempts to choose writing as a career for a few minutes, is ultimately defeated by his impoverished vocabulary, inability to type, and utter lack of self-discipline. Increasing hostility between the two brothers and their atavistic reversion to infantile behavior suggest the intolerable pressures which sap the strength and talent of ordinary people.

When PBS officials decided to videotape the Cherry Lane production, they hired Malkovich and Sinese to recreate their stage roles on film. Both actors were experienced by this time with cinematic acting techniques and their close-ups, somewhat less theatrical gestures, and slightly accelerated patter contribute to an impressive "movie." The film's cinematography adds to its appeal, especially in scenes where close-ups of the actors' faces are distorted by light and shadows into almost symbolic manifestations of the play's cultural conflicts. A good example is the closing shot focusing on the face of John Malkovich, whose make-up emphasizes the lupine cast of his face, and the eerie lighting, combined with the sound of coyotes' howling on the soundtrack, transforms him into a kind of indestructible beast, who has survived strangulation to reign again as a predator.

Along with the cameo appearance of Saul Kimmer, satirized as a plump, effeminate, polyester-clad representative of studio system crassness, is the unexpected return home of Austin and Lee's mother at the play's conclusion. Stereotypically middle-class, orderly, and almost inhumanly passive, the mother startles viewers with her tidy but inexpensive-looking carefully matched travel outfit and suitcases. Arriving amidst the squalor of her sons' transformation of a once pristine suburban ranch-style house, she brings events to a simultaneously comedic yet frightening conclusion. When she speaks to her sons, they revert to childhood poses, partially hiding behind screens and talking in small-boy voices, as if they were accustomed to defending themselves against accusations of unacceptable behavior. As she slaps Austin in the back of his head, the audience immediately recognizes the connection between Lee's irritating "swats" at his brother's head and the physical abuse the boys, now grown men, received from at least one of their parents when they were growing up.

Typically, the film of *True West*, a recapitulation of the playwright's words for the stage, features role reversal, atavistic behavior, a longing for a simpler life and for an America which perhaps exists only in myths of the past. It is a macho, male-dominated world and the one woman who enters it has inscrutably surrendered any attempt to impose order or meaning upon it. There is a thematic connection, both psychological and philosophical, among all of Shepard's works. Although the movie of *True West* is not the playwright's adaptation of his own play, it shares with his films topical similarities which legitimize its inclusion among his movies.

Ten years after the effective film production of *True West*, a cable TV film of *Curse of the Starving Class* resulted in the unsatisfactory adaptation of one of Shepard's finest plays. The cable movie's screenplay was written by Bruce Beresford, who had directed Shepard in the film of Beth Henley's *Crimes of the Heart* (1986). Shepard perceived Beresford as a controlling man who misunderstood his theatrical intentions. Director Michael McClary missed much of the play's understated humor and tended to sentimentalize the story as well. In fact, Roy Loynd wrote in the *Los Angeles Times* that "McClary's direction misses Shepard's rhythms and Bruce Beresford's screenplay fails to highlight the playwright's tone and idioms."[2] More damningly Loynd asserts that Shepard had been writing "metaphorically" about a "'starving class' hungry for moral and physical sustenance" but claims that in the movie "they're just snarly, messy farmers."[3] The Big Name power of Kathy Bates and James Woods as actors in the film was intended to draw viewers. It did, but the actors' interpretations of the original stage roles diverged from Shepard's intentions. While Kathy Bates effectively depicts the exhausted but noisy mother who dreams of leaving the farm and going to Paris, James Woods over-acts his part as the sulky alcoholic father and turns him into an abusive monster. A highly suspect real-estate agent who wants to get the family off potentially valuable land, a son who seems mentally disturbed rather than rebelliously adolescent, and a daughter entering womanhood who is clearly self-destructive rather than confused and questing, create an unhealthy ménage of dysfunctional characters. With such overstated depiction of entrepreneurial destroyers of the environment and with such hopelessly neurotic family members, the movie of *Curse* becomes a predetermined tragic melodrama, rather than a cautionary tale of declining American values.

Along with *True West* and *Curse of the Starving Class*, *Simpatico* (1999) is a movie made from a Shepard play without the playwright's direct involvement. The stage play, *Simpatico*, written four years earlier, contained

familiar Shepardian motifs. Horse owners and horse-racing were central to
the plot. The opening scene of the play takes place in a tawdry western motel
room and its occupant is an eccentric, seemingly outcast loner, who refuses
to look at television sets or to drive cars that are manufactured in Japan.
Although he appears to be agoraphobic, he surprises audiences by visiting
his former partner, now a wealthy Kentucky horse-farmer, in a successful attempt to stir up past troubles. A complicated plot involves pornographic pictures, the framing of a supposed friend whose life was consequently ruined,
and an almost inevitable role-reversal of the major characters: the poorer
partner virtually exchanges roles with the formerly wealthy one, who is left
at the play's conclusion, huddled in the stark motel room's bed. Justice has
been served in the process and the play's message is more affirmative than
many of the author's previous works.

Unfortunately, the transformation of *Simpatico* into a movie is only partly
effective. Nick Nolte, Jeff Bridges, Albert Finney, and Sharon Stone bring
major Hollywood names to the production but the wide-screen treatment
of the story fails to capture the nuances of the original. Nolte, as Vinnie,
who lives in the cheap Los Angeles motel, possesses the masculine persona
and potential for violence one associates with Shepard's protagonists, but
he lacks the fidgeting edginess of Vinnie on stage. Bridges, as Carter, is too
sophisticated to imagine as Vinnie's former partner and Stone is too stylishly
beautiful to be cast as the down-to-earth Rose, Vinnie's former girlfriend.
Lavish Kentucky settings provide an overly bold contrast to the stage's confined in-door spaces with their hint of vulgarity and modest expectations.
G. D. Schmitz, in a generally negative review, believes only "more horse-
racing and more tightly edited scenes"[4] could rescue the film. Its major fault
is, in fact, English director Matthew Warchus's inability to capture the essentially western American quality of Shepard's original work, with its wry
wit and homespun philosophy, so typical of the author's bizarre mixture of
authentic details in unexpected situations.

Although Shepard has written successfully for the stage since the 1960s,
has created movie scripts since the 1970s, and has often appeared as a movie
actor in important films, it was not until the 1980s that the author and film
star would realize his dream of creating important feature films.

Shepard's filmed screenplays

Paris, Texas

Paris, Texas (1984) is the first of Shepard's four feature films. At a cost of
3 million dollars it was considered a low-budget production, even in the

early 1980s. Harry Dean Stanton, who would later play Shepard's father in *Fool for Love*, is cast as a loner and drifter named Travis, whose secret past is not completely revealed until the last moments of the movie. Travis's ravaged face is more manly than handsome, but his soulful eyes possess a gentleness that keeps him from being frightening. He shares many qualities with the playwright: he's a heavy drinker, refuses to fly in airplanes, and enjoys driving pick-up trucks. He seems anxious not to repeat the child-rearing mistakes of his parents when he returns to his abandoned son after a four-year absence. He is obsessed with the notion that he was conceived in Paris, Texas. Clearly Paris, France, is prominent in the playwright's personal iconography. Travis's wife is a Frenchwoman and characters in Shepard plays often dream of escaping to Paris (for example, the mother in *Curse of the Starving Class*). Paris, Texas, seems to represent some idyllic combination of an authentic American southwestern town and an ideal modern community, where families can communicate freely and trustingly.

Travis's nearly eight-year-old son, Hunter, is played by Hunter Carson. Hunter seems instinctively to trust his long-lost father enough to leave the benevolent Aunt Anne and Uncle Walt who have raised him in his parents' absence. Father and son travel to Houston where they discover the boy's mother, Jane, played by Nastassja Kinski, working in a peculiar sex-games parlour. When Travis enters a booth, Jane appears at the other side of a two-way mirror, offering to remove her blouse while she listens to her "customer's" tale of woe and/or sexual fantasies. Horrified, Travis leaves Jane and takes Hunter to a hotel, but later he returns to Jane's "club" and reveals himself in a dark narrative of the couple's life together. Acknowledging his obsessive love for his young wife, he begs forgiveness for his drinking and carousing and tying her to a stove in their trailer home. Simultaneously, he forgives her for setting the trailer on fire when escaping with their small son. All along his intention was to reunite Hunter with his mother. One supposes he will relinquish custody to the aunt and uncle who have raised him so lovingly and that the boy's birth mother will play a more active role in his life. Travis will probably disappear again, sacrificing his own needs to those of his son and former wife. In one of the film's most interesting shots, Travis, looking through the one-way mirror, sees his own face transposed upon his wife's. The long gaunt face of Travis surrounded by Jane's dyed-blonde pageboy is strangely androgynous and suggests the futile and even grotesque attempt of two people to become a single being. The symbiotic pairing of the brothers in *True West*, the incestuous brother and sister in *Fool for Love*, and the Indian woman and her young husband's obsessive devotion in *Silent Tongue* are recalled for a moment. The artist's preoccupations with doubling, role reversals, and a kind of permanent human bonding appear to be constant thematic concerns. And while a lack of money has contributed to the failure of Travis's marriage, his son's initial discomfort at reuniting with him, his brother's need to finance his expedition to Houston, and his wife's employment in a kind of soft-core sex-game parlor, the film, like Shepard's stage plays, primarily emphasizes the division of good and bad, masculine and feminine, and active and passive qualities within a single individual. The importance of a loving family and the need for human kindness must ultimately prevail over the material limitations placed upon us by modern society. Vincent Canby argues that while *Paris, Texas* begins "so beautifully and so laconically," it eventually "begins to talk more and say less." He believes that Shepard's "art – and his temperament – do not seem to adjust well to the sort of long, collaborative process by which movies are made."[5] However, the film's affirmation of long-term loyalty, the need for forgiveness, and the willingness to make sacrifices for others provide a unique example of idealistic film-making.

Fool for Love

Shepard's next screenplay was based on a play he had staged in 1982, *Fool for Love*, two years after *True West*. The successful filming of *True West* for a made-for-television movie preceded by a year the filming of *Fool for Love*, which was the first Shepard play that the writer himself adapted to the big screen. It was directed by Robert Altman and its premiere was originally timed to coincide with the opening of Shepard's *A Lie of the Mind* in New York City. Critically, the film was not a success. Reviews were mainly negative, often scathingly so, although it is possible to glimpse a grudging recognition of Shepard's skill as a playwright in both John Simon's review for the conservative publication, The *National Review*, and Stanley Kauffman's more liberal essay in the *New Republic*. Simon claimed that the "impinging of reality and fantasy" gave the stage play "much of its interest," adding that in the movie Shepard "devised a scenario that the past takes place currently behind and around the present, with present selves mingling with the past ones." He added that the solution is "ingenious, especially as abetted by Pierre Argnot's extremely flexible camera work and Robert Altman's most successful direction in years."[6] Simon nevertheless concludes that the movie fails to satisfy the audience. Kauffman, slightly more upbeat in his assessment, claims that "somewhere inside . . . the electric Shepard was struggling to emerge and almost made it."[7] Several changes were required for *Fool for Love* to be transformed from stage play into a movie. On stage, the continuous appearance of a silent father, sitting in a chair, stage forward, emphasizes the psychological impact of the father's past actions on his hapless children. Eddie and Mae are lovers but they are also half-brother and -sister, sired by a father with two wives. Repeatedly they try to escape their "fatal attraction" to each other but while pursuing more "acceptable" relationships, they always appear to reconcile with each other. The silent father in an onstage chair reminds theatre audiences of Anna, sitting in the rear of a naked stage in Pinter's *Old Times*. As a friend of a youthful Kate, now coupled with Deeley, a needy male, Anna's silent presence suggests to audiences that she has played a significant role in the woman Kate has become. In the same way Eddie and Mae's father has, unintentionally perhaps, burdened them with the sin of incest, a legacy of his own irresponsible philandering.

Again the cramped interior of a cheap motel room adds to the intensity of the play's atmosphere. When one of Eddie's jilted lovers, "the Countess," drives insanely around the motel in her Mercedes Benz, firing at Mae's room with a shotgun, Shepard's dark humor captures the spectator's attention. When Mae asks how "crazy" the Countess is, Eddie's wry response, "pretty crazy" elicits a hilarious reaction from the audience. The necessity in a film to move outside a single room, to display the entire motel complex, to locate it visually in a New Mexican oasis adds a dimension of reality at odds with the subtler theatre piece. In the movie the errant father is an almost voyeuristic motel-owner. Played by Harry Dean Stanton who had starred earlier in *Paris, Texas*, he conveys little of the sensitivity of Travis in the earlier film. Shepard himself plays Eddie and one feels he truly enjoys driving a truck and lassoing furniture. As Mae, Kim Bassinger, while not admired by many critics, manages to project successfully both vulnerability and sensuality. In spite of Shepard's and Bassinger's fine performances, however, *Fool for Love* exaggerates the tense, confined subject matter of the play and seems more like an absurd melodrama than a tragic glimpse at unhappy siblings trapped by a parent's indiscretion.

Far North

Following the production of *Paris, Texas* and *Fool for Love*, Shepard turned director as well as screenwriter in *Far North*. The thought-provoking comedy was shot in northern Minnesota, near where his companion, the film's protagonist, Jessica Lange, had grown up. The story line is simple, which gives Shepard ample opportunity to comment on the changing nature of rural life in America, the death of the pioneering spirit, and the somewhat alarming urban growth of the twentieth century. An aging father, Bertrum, played by Charles Durning, is thrown from his horse at the onset of the movie and ends up in a hospital bed. His daughter, Kate (Lange), returns home from New York City to check on him and is startled when he asks her to shoot the horse that unseated him. Ahab-like, he seeks vengeance on the dumb brute who caused his injury. The horse runs away, however, and Kate, though at first resolved to do so, is unable to carry out her father's wishes. Eventually, Bertrum escapes from his hospital bed and walks the many miles to his rural home with an alcoholic male relative, Uncle Dave, played by Donald Moffat. The two old men see the horse, nearly get run over by a speeding car, and Bertrum collapses on the roadside, possibly of a heart attack. One is never sure whether or not he has died but his two daughters and granddaughter, who have been lost in the woods, come upon the father's body and transport him home on the horse. The film concludes with a birthday party for Kate's one-hundred-year-old grandmother, and its final shot appears to reveal the father with a gun in one hand and the horse's reins in the other marching out through snowy woods to the horse's possible execution. Perhaps the figure we see is not Bertrum, however, or the whole scene is a fantasy on the part of Bertrum's wife and daughters.

Such fantasy elements punctuate most of Shepard's plays and screenplays, but as with many other twentieth-century artists, imagined or surreal scenes are played naturalistically, in the manner of Harold Pinter's work or Samuel Beckett's. Not only is the audience uncertain as to whether Bertrum is living or dead at the film's conclusion but it seems highly unlikely that two men could "escape" so easily from a hospital, walk down empty city streets, and complete a walk of many miles back into the countryside.

In another scene, Kate's bemused mother prepares an enormous breakfast and conjures up a kitchen table crowded with men who work on the farm. Only one of these men any longer lives on the farm, yet the mother's imaginings are filmed realistically with husky, hearty eaters crowding the table so that she can barely reach her arms through them to pour them coffee. Similarly, while it is not difficult to get lost in the woods, the fact that the three women and an overly frisky horse end up at dawn in the same spot of road with Bertrum and Uncle Dave seems like a more fitting ending for Shakespeare's *Midsummer Night's Dream* than the tidy finale to a plot emphasizing credibility.

Throughout *Far North* the artist's favorite themes resonate in the crisp rural landscape. Americans are depicted as having abandoned the countryside, and the constant complaint of the many women and few men who inhabit it is the question, "Where are the men?" Obviously, they have left their homes to seek better jobs and more exciting lives in the city. *Far North* is yet another of Shepard's elegies for the death of rural America. The close, often hostile, relationship between man and animals is emphasized, as well as the strength of female survivors in a male-dominated world, the love of traditions (at Granny's one-hundredth birthday her female descendants and friends sing a Norwegian folk-song), and the regrettable loss of religious faith.

Again, Granny, distressed that her birthday falls on a Sunday, keeps asking, "Doesn't anyone go to church anymore?" Such thematic concerns are commonplace in Shepard's plays as well. In *Far North*, however, the artist is able to add visual concepts and episodes inappropriate to the stage. The artist's love of nature is, of course, particularly apparent.

Shepard has always been moved by larger images that cannot be contained in a stage setting. His picture of man fighting the forces of nature recalls Hemingway's adventurous episodes, although Shepard's landscape is more distinctly American, glorifying the unique rock formations of the Southwest or Northwest, silver-treed forests, wild horses, and grain-covered fields. Movies provide an excellent opportunity to reveal visual experiences that can only be captured on the wide screen. The sheer beauty of the settings in the playwright's films is arresting. One can almost feel the cold air in *Far North* and enjoy the sunsets and full moon against a backdrop of trees, or shudder at the bleak snowscapes. Filming also permits naturalistic representation of surreal events, more convincingly than they can be presented on stage. Movie audiences tend to believe what they see on film is actually happening, whereas unlikely or distorted episodes on stage become more blatantly theatrical. The "tricks" of the camera are more difficult to detect.

In *True West*, both the stage version and the filming of the Cherry Lane Theatre production hint at the look of the desert. But the actual desert is described mainly by Lee. Primarily, the howling of coyotes on a sound track suggests the usurpation of the wilderness by a metathesizing suburbia. In films, though, the majesty of the country's remaining geographical beauty lingers. A play hasn't been written where a horse can enter the stage and become a major character. Yet, Mel, the horse in *Far North*, frequently takes possession of our attention and suggests that he is more than an animal – in fact, he may well represent something pure and untamed from an earlier era.

The loneliness of rural life is palpable in *Far North*. People are separated by vast spaces, country roads are empty, and tangible evidence of a declining population is visually depicted throughout. The rugged individualism of an earlier America, the fundamental conflicts between people and animals can only be hinted at microscopically on the stage. Furthermore, Shepard's personal fetishes need to occupy the wider landscape. His habit of driving old pick-up trucks on country roads, his love of walking through forests or over stony paths can be facilitated by the cinematographer's skills. The filmmaker can indulge urges that must be expressed differently, if at all, in a theatre. In his next movie, *Silent Tongue*, Shepard also blends the real with the surreal, using the visual impact of natural scenery to enhance his almost mythical narrative.

Silent Tongue

Although he had already written nine screenplays when he created *Silent Tongue* in 1993, it is only the second film which Shepard both wrote and directed as an original movie. Like its predecessor, *Far North*, *Silent Tongue* provides deep insights into the artist's underlying philosophy and world view. It accomplishes on the screen certain effects that cannot be easily conveyed on stage. The combined majesty and starkness of the desert and of outlying fields of grain underscore the daunting combination of usurpation and challenge encountered by our forebears in a newly discovered country. The imagined rampaging female warriors on horseback who are occasionally interspersed with a realistic plotline express the astonishment and outrage of Native Americans who were forced to confront pioneers who claimed an inexplicable right to their property. Caryn James, writer for the *New York Times*, entitled her review of the film "Sam Shepard's Spiritual, Majestic Vision of the Old West." She calls the film "uncompromisingly good" and argues that it deals with "mysticism, history and a kind of profound family tangle that echoes his best plays." Elsewhere she refers to *Silent Tongue* as "eerie, inventive, poetic,"[8] citing it as a noncommercial film which deals less with specific issues than with underlying anthropological conflicts and personal enigmas. Recognizable issues that mirror the plays, of course, abound. An alcoholic father, who engenders two daughters with an Indian woman he rapes, one of whom he sells to another pioneer, provides the typically destructive parent one expects to find in a Shepard play. Performed by Alan Bates, this character named Eamon McCree operates a circus of sorts, sells patent medicine, scorns his son by a previous relationship, and eventually flounders in the desert like a mad King Lear who, deservedly perhaps, lacks even one loving child to rescue him.

Eamon was not the first white man to injure the mother of his daughters. She had been previously raped by another white man and her tongue had been ripped out so that she couldn't accuse her attacker verbally, hence giving her the cognomen of Silent Tongue and the movie its title. Eamon's counterpart is actor Richard Harris, who plays Prescott Roe, a devoted father who's willing to risk his life and fortune for the well-being of his son, mad with grief over the death in childbirth of his part-Indian wife. The dark side of Prescott's character is a willingness to disregard the humanity of others as he attempts to satisfy his son's needs. It seems he originally purchased the now deceased Indian woman from McCree and seeks to purchase her surviving sister as well, to distract his own flesh and blood from self-destructive mourning. The bond between parents and children or the severing of this bond becomes subject matter for much of Shepard's work. Also, the bonding of siblings, who often need to protect themselves against a hostile or controlling parent, is shown in the relationship of McCrce's two half-Indian daughters who remain resolute in their hatred of the man who abused their mother. Believably, as with Austin and Lee in *True West* or Kate and Rita in *Far North*, siblings squabble and compete as frequently as they support each other.

Although Shepard avoids overtly political issues in *Silent Tongue*, the white invaders of Indian territory appear to possess the larger share of vices and to provide the major cause of conflict. The gigantic issue of man's proper place in the natural world, the perilous encroachment of civilization upon the wilderness, and the dangerous solipsism of ethnocentric Western culture pervade Shepard's universe.

Enjoying as he does the music of the Red Clay Ramblers, Shepard employs them again in *Silent Tongue* (as he had in *Far North* and the stage play, *A Lie of the Mind*) to compose original songs, with a blend of country music, jazz rhythms, and, perhaps, even resonances of rock-and-roll, which complements the mystical and primitive elements in the plot and the photography. A musical "medicine show," supervised by the drunken Eamon as a prelude to this sale of patent "medicines," suggests the outbursts of energy and joy which both enliven and shatter the otherwise silent and foreboding landscapes. Performing dwarfs hint at the exploitation and abnormalities of supposedly "civilized" life. The carnival atmosphere of Eamon's traveling sideshow as well as his verbal virtuosity, expressed in a poetically exaggerated Irish brogue, offer a diversion from monotony and a painful reminder of the human cost of pleasure-seeking.

With such devices as a dead woman whose face is half-beautiful and half-decaying, who is still able to berate her grieving husband and to demand that she be burned on a traditional Indian funeral pyre, Shepard indicates his sincere fascination with the spiritual world. From Lee in *True West*, who recoils from his brother's suggestion that destroying a typewriter is a "sin," to the hundred-year-old granny's complaining that no one goes to church anymore in *Far North*, to the vision of a dead woman restored to beauty, and tranquility, as she emerges ethereally from the blaze that consumed her corpse in *Silent Tongue*, issues of good and evil, honor and ritual, sin and redemption take their places as recurring motifs of otherworldliness in Shepard's cosmology. What distinguishes *Silent Tongue* most importantly are the deft suggestions of nature's mysteries and greatness. The appearance of young elks on a barren plain, the twisting of shimmering, curled-up rattlesnakes on two occasions, the startling contrast of a white wolf against lush green grass make watching *Silent Tongue* a treat for the eyes. And then there is the totally unexpected approach of a camel led by a circus lady, the former as comfortable on a New Mexico set as in the shadow of Egypt's pyramids, and the sight of a white horse fording a stream, or of four horses turned gold-colored by the twilight. All of these images deepen one's sense of primal forces that are alluded to but infrequently depicted on a small stage.

As a director, Shepard selects masterfully effective final shots as conclusions to his films. In this case a field of waving golden grain against a blue sky is framed like an abstract painting and its black borders become wider and more intrusive, leaving viewers with what resembles an abstract expressionist composition.

Conclusion

While most of the chapters in this volume assess various facets of Shepard's literary achievement, this one has attempted to examine his relationship to the cinema. The subject is complex because the ideas and attitudes which shape Shepard's canon define his achievements as a movie actor, director, and screenwriter, just as they do his reputation as a major twentieth-century dramatist. His vision and his accomplishments cannot be contained by a single medium.

NOTES

1 Quoted in Don Shewey, *Sam Shepard*, 2nd edn. (New York: Da Capo Press, 1997), 65.

2 Roy Loynd, "*Curse of the Starving Class*," *Los Angeles Times*, 4 February 1995, 17.

3 Ibid., 16.

4 G. D. Schmitz, "Simpatico," http://upandcomingmovies.com/simpatico/html.

5 Vincent Canby, "*Fool for Love*," *New York Times*, Section 1, part 2, 14 October 1984, 14.

6 John Simon, "Love's Fools," *National Review*, 30 June 1986, 3.

7 Stanley Kauffman, "Fooling Around with Love," *New Republic*, 23 December 1985, 24.

8 Caryn James, *New York Times*, Section c, col 2, 25 February 1994, 3.

13

DAVID J. DeROSE

Sam Shepard as musical experimenter

Alternate Tracks

In 1998, when rock musician Bruce Springsteen released his boxed set, *Tracks*, he offered up the previously unreleased songs and recorded materials as "an alternate route to some of the destinations"[1] his career as an artist had taken him. Springsteen's words remind one that as an artist amasses a body of work and acquires a lasting artistic identity, critics and the public may view him in an increasingly narrow light. Consequently, the artist sometimes steers, or is perceived as steering, a straighter and straighter course, ceasing to explore the side roads, the alternate tracks, of his personal and artistic interests. As the character Hoss says in Sam Shepard's *Tooth of Crime*: the artist becomes "stuck in [his] image" and can no longer, as Crow says in that same play, "[run] flat out to a new course."[2]

Gathering together some of the marginalia of playwright Sam Shepard's career, the material that has been pushed to the perimeter of his public image to make way for "the Shepard myth," there arises an alternate route through that career which has all but disappeared from critical perceptions of Shepard's work as a playwright. That route includes an accomplished body of music plays and musical experimentation which, for many other dramatists, might have been a satisfying life's work. With the exception of *The Tooth of Crime* (1972), Shepard's experimentations in music and theatre have appeared, in the larger scope of his writing career, to be minor diversions, both in the sense that they are not at the center of most critics' appraisal of his work as a writer, and in that the best of these works have been collaborative pet projects among and between friends, dependent for their impact upon specific people and a specific production rather than a substantial literary text by Shepard as playwright. And yet, when attempting to map the landscape of Shepard's work as a dramatist and theatre artist, alongside the terms myth-maker, pop-culture chronicler, and poet laureate of the American West, would have to be "percussionist, jazz aficionado, and one-time, would-be rock star."

This chapter follows the impact of music and the course of musical experimentation in Shepard's career. The rock star as American pop archetype; Shepard as rock-and-roll playwright; jazz improvisation as a model for playmaking and for the perception of reality; an equal expression between music and the actor; and, the rhythmic and percussive qualities of Shepard's language: these are the alternate tracks that music has cut through the landscape of dramatist Sam Shepard.

"Rocking to Bethlehem to be born . . . "

First off let me tell you that I don't want to be a playwright, I want to be a rock and roll star. I want that understood right off. I got into writing plays because I had nothing else to do. So I started writing to keep from going off the deep end.[3]

When the twenty-seven-year-old Sam Shepard included this passage in the Program Notes for *Cowboy Mouth* in 1971, he had already seen twenty of his plays produced, been proclaimed the most gifted playwright of his generation, been commissioned by Italian film director Michelangelo Antonioni to write the screenplay for *Zabriskie Point*, and watched his first production in a major venue – the Lincoln Center production of *Operation Sidewinder* – bomb with the press and public. Within weeks of premiering *Cowboy Mouth* – a play in which Shepard himself played the role of a would-be rock star – he left New York and was on his way to London to pursue a career as a rock musician. Such a move might seem naive at best, sheer foolishness and self-delusion at worst, for a playwright of such promise; but Shepard's belief in himself as a musician was both sincere and not without some grounding in reality. Shepard was no different from any other young American growing up in the 1960s. As biographer Don Shewey has noted, "Rock 'n' roll was the heartbeat of American youth in the 1960s, and Sam Shepard felt the pulse."[4] Rock music was playing, at this point in Shepard's life, an increasingly important role. Seven of his last nine plays had included a rock band on stage in some form,[5] either performing musical numbers between scenes or accompanying the action of the plays. Shepard himself played drums and occasionally guitar with many of those bands.[6] He was an accomplished percussionist and had recorded two albums with the folk-rock band, the Holy Modal Rounders. He had also been commissioned to write a screenplay for the Rolling Stones.[7]

That Shepard would aspire to rock stardom was also understandable when one considers the place of highest honor he reserved for rock-and-roll in his pantheon of pop culture mythology. Shepard's plays of this period are peopled almost exclusively by popular culture stereotypes: cowboys and

Indians, gunslingers, pirates, gangsters, sugar daddies, sex kittens, mad scientists, space invaders, two-headed bog beasts, and, most importantly, rock stars. Whatever pop genealogy Shepard's plays inhabit during this period and from whatever milieu he lifts his characters, he inevitably turns them into rock stars, as when a character in *The Mad Dog Blues* dreams of cinematic sex symbol Mae West "singing like Janis Joplin."[8]

Shepard's work in the late 1960s and early 1970s demonstrates a search, on his part, for a genealogy of American myth and, particularly, an archetypal American character who was both outlaw and messiah, and who spoke to a contemporary youth audience. That search culminated with what is broadly considered Shepard's pop mythic masterwork, *The Tooth of Crime*, and with the modern-day tragic hero of that play, Hoss. A cross-section of American sub-cultures, Hoss is part gangster, part racecar driver, and a rock star through and through. His mysterious profession, known only as "the Game," is populated with "hit men, astrologers, disc jockeys, souped-up cars, and rock and roll music."[9] The oracles of this culture are the record charts which, as one reviewer put it, the characters study "like the entrails of animals."[10]

Shepard's concept of the rock star as a new messiah, a figure who "reach[es] out and grab[s] all the little broken, busted-up pieces of people's frustrations" and "takes all that into [him]self,"[11] is best articulated in one of Shepard's most frequently cited plays, *Cowboy Mouth*. This play, written immediately before *The Tooth of Crime*, is a transparently autobiographical one-act created collaboratively with poetess (and, later, rock star) Patti Smith.[12] Smith's character, Cavale, has kidnapped Shepard's Slim, and wants to turn him into the ultimate rock star as savior: what she calls "a rock-'n'-roll Jesus with a cowboy mouth" (*Cowboy Mouth*, 157).

> People want a street angel. They want a saint but with a cowboy mouth. Somebody to get off on when they can't get off on themselves ... A sort of god in our image ... It's like ... well, in the old days people had Jesus and those guys to embrace ... they created a god with all their belief energies ... and when they didn't dig themselves they could lose themselves in the Lord. But it's too hard now. We're earthy people, and the old saints just don't make it, and the old God is just too far away. He don't represent our pain no more. His words don't shake through us no more. Any great motherfucker rock-'n'-roll song can raise me higher than all of Revelations. We created rock-'n'-roll from our own image ... It's like ... the rock-'n'-roll star in his highest state of grace will be our new savior ... rocking to Bethlehem to be born. (156)

When Shepard toured in 1975 with Bob Dylan's "Rolling Thunder Review," he observed firsthand the rock star's potential for near-messianic stature. In his journal from that tour, *Rolling Thunder Logbook*, Shepard writes of the landscape Dylan creates and the mythic aura he achieves as a performer:

> Myth is a powerful medium because it talks to the emotions and not to the head. It moves us into an area of mystery. Some myths are poisonous to believe in, but others have the capacity for changing something inside us, even if it's only for a minute or two. Dylan creates a mythic atmosphere out of the land around us. The land we walk on every day and never see until someone shows it to us.[13]

In Shepard's account, Dylan as performer becomes a powerful shaman of sorts, a self-created mystery into which his audience attempts to enter, from which they draw a sense of spiritual wonder, and upon which they can project their own aspirations.

> Dylan has invented himself. He's made himself up from scratch. That is, from the things he had around him and inside him. Dylan is an invention of his own mind. The point isn't to figure him out but to take him in.[14]

> All [the audience] can do is imagine what he's like. You see them staring hard into his white mask, his gray-green eyes, trying to pick at the mystery. Who is he anyway? What's the source of his power? An apparition?[15]

Shepard's observations of Dylan as mysterious, self-invented apparition and myth-weaver would suggest that the playwright had found his real-life rock-and-roll Jesus. However, the messianic ideal articulated by Cavale in *Cowboy Mouth* isn't realized either in *Rolling Thunder Logbook* or in any of Shepard's dramatic works. The Rolling Thunder Tour ends anti-climactically, not with the ascension of Dylan into a state of divine glory, but with Shepard wandering the backstage halls of Madison Square Garden. In *Cowboy Mouth*, Slim walks out on Cavale, unable to believe any longer in her rock fantasy. Cavale, in desperation, attempts to transform the mute lobster deliveryman into her rock messiah. But, when she hands him a gun and he puts it to his head, it is clear that only suicide will complete his transformation. Likewise, in *The Tooth of Crime*, the outlaw rocker Hoss – whose musical and artistic identity, like Dylan's, is created out of the American landscape – is defeated by the empty stylist, Crow. Hoss's one "true gesture" (249) is to put a bullet through his brain, as if only in death, frozen in memory, can he acquire mythic stature. In this, he is like "Johnny Ace," the rock star against whom Cavale, in *Cowboy Mouth*, measures all others. But Johnny Ace recorded only one hit song; his claim to immortality was to play Russian Roulette in front of his adoring fans and blow his brains out on stage. In the end, Shepard's writings would suggest that the rock messiah is an unattainable ideal, the pursuit of which leads to self-delusion or self-destruction.

"The band would come out and make this noise . . ."

At the same time Shepard was exploring the possibilities of the rock star as mythic hero, he was generating a great deal of rock music himself, and including it in his plays. The earliest of Shepard's plays to incorporate live rock music was *Melodrama Play* (1967). A blunt, one-dimensional account of rock stardom, the play examines the woes of Duke Durgens, a singer/songwriter who has produced a single big hit, and who is now being held captive by his manager until he writes a follow-up success. Shepard's interplay of music and dramatic action in *Melodrama Play* is not particularly sophisticated. The first time the band begins to play, the actors simply stop and "do the frug onstage." When the song is over, the actors "finish dancing and applaud the band, the band bows and the play continues."[16] Between *Melodrama Play* in 1967 and *The Tooth of Crime* in 1972, rock music becomes a central element of Shepard's dramaturgy. *Forensic and the Navigators* (1967), *The Unseen Hand* (1969), *Operation Sidewinder* (1970), *The Mad Dog Blues*, and *Back Bog Beast Bait* (both 1971), all employ rock scores. In the latter three, musical numbers were written into the texts of the plays, sometimes to be sung by the characters either as segues between scenes or as bits of character development or emotional exposition. While Shepard grew increasingly comfortable with rock music scores and the presence of live bands on stage, it must be said that, for someone with Shepard's true gift for language and rhythm, he was a pedestrian songwriter at best. Compared to the ground-breaking nature of the plays into which they were written, the songs are utterly reliant on conventional modes of musical expression with frequently banal lyrics. The music in *The Mad Dog Blues*, for example, may be appropriate for the comic book characters and B-movie plot line, but it is extremely bourgeois in sentiment, filled with cookie-cutter laments for lost love and homesickness. Songs like *Operation Sidewinder's* teen sex fantasy, "Do It Girl," and the play's ode to teen drug use, "Euphoria," are equally conventional in form and adolescent in sentiment. Even *The Tooth of Crime* has suffered from the limitations of Shepard's musical numbers. Most later productions boast an "updated" or "original" score.[17] Even Shepard himself, when reworking the play – now called *The Tooth of Crime (Second Dance)* – for a 1996 revival at New York's Signature Theatre, called upon blues composer T-Bone Burnett to write new music and lyrics.

But songs are not the only musical contribution Shepard makes in these plays. In *The Tooth of Crime*, when the rock star / warlord Hoss must face off against his nemesis, Crow, their weapon of choice for the ultimate showdown is neither knives nor guns, but language: that is, chanted, intoned language accompanied by rock-and-roll music.[18] Shepard employs music in two fashions in *The Tooth of Crime*: (1) as has already been mentioned, in the form of songs which serve as "emotional comment on what's taking place in the play,"[19] and (2) as an emotional "amplifier" in the form of accompaniment to and backdrop for some of the spoken speeches. In particular, when the characters Hoss and Crow engage in their duel of words, Shepard calls, in his stage directions, for a spontaneous interplay between language and music:

> HOSS *and* CROW *begin to move to the music, not really dancing but feeling the power in their movements through the music. They each pick up microphones. They begin their assaults just talking the words in rhythmic patterns, sometimes going with the music, sometimes counterpointing it. As the round progresses the music builds with drums and piano coming in, maybe a rhythm guitar too. Their voices build so that sometimes they sing their words or shout. The words remain as intelligible as possible like a sort of talking opera.* (234)

This use of music does not replace or interrupt dialogue or dramatic action, as song does; instead, it complements and heightens the ongoing play.

This call for the musical enhancement of spoken language – the scoring of speech without turning it into song – formally articulates an application of sound and music which had appeared sporadically in Shepard's earlier plays. In interviews, Shepard has always exhibited a keen awareness of the emotional and physical power that music exerts over an audience. "[W]hen you play a note...," he once explained, "there's a response immediately – you don't have to wait to build up to it through seven scenes."[20] Elsewhere, he has commented that "music communicates emotion better than anything else I know, just anything! Just bam! And there it is. You can't explain exactly how the process is taking place, but you know for sure that you're hooked."[21] Bits and pieces of Shepard's musical scoring from the period leading up to *The Tooth of Crime* appear in stage directions. In *The Unseen Hand* he notes that a climactic speech should be backed with rock-and-roll guitar chords.[22] In other plays, music and sound are noted in stage directions as means of heightening the already high level of psychic agitation that Shepard's characters experience and project. In *The Holy Ghostly*, an escalating drumbeat and bells played by offstage characters are employed to enhance the surreal qualities of a character's dying moments.[23] In *Back Bog Beast Bait*, one of the characters screeches on a fiddle while the others rant wildly in drug-induced hallucinations.[24] But such stage directions are fairly rare. Most instances of Shepard's early use of sound and music to induce mood or heighten emotions – many of them created in rehearsal – were never recorded, or exist only in reviews of the productions or in personal accounts of the performances such as director Ralph Cook's recollection of the Theatre Genesis productions of *The Rock Garden* (1964) and *Forensic and the Navigators* (1967). The printed texts of these plays mention no sound effects or musicians at all, but Cook clearly recalls specific musical effects, such as a rock band whose harsh discordant sounds Shepard used to irritate and drive the audience out of the theatre at the end of *Forensic and the Navigators*:

> [When the smoke cleared,] you had the Holy Modal Rounders...Sam was playing drums in the band, and the band would come out and make this noise that was so bad that all you wanted to do was get out...There was a woman who was singing with them...she was just screeching at the microphone as loud as she could, everybody playing in dissonance against her...People were just outraged...But, Sam wanted it that way.[25]

Cook further recalls that during *The Rock Garden* Shepard employed a subsonic oscillator which created a kind of white noise that the audience did not hear, or were not conscious of hearing, but which made people very physically agitated nevertheless. According to Cook, when the play ended, and the machine was turned off, the audience would noticeably slump with relief. Primitive though they may be, these uses of music and sound to evoke a visceral response are significantly different from the traditional role of lyric-driven music which Shepard articulates elsewhere as a "sounding-board" that helps the audience "step out of the play for a minute."[26] By contrast, this scoring is part of the overall sensory fabric of the plays, drawing the audience further into the plays' emotional texture.

Shepard must have eventually seen the limitations of rock music – and in particular of songs – to create this kind of visceral effect. The tension between Shepard's use of rock music in his plays and his desire to use sound and music to evoke emotion and atmosphere is most apparent in *Operation Sidewinder*, Shepard's most ambitious musical production. The play's musical score, which includes eleven pop and rock songs, mostly performed by an onstage band between scenes, is eventually overpowered at the play's conclusion by an entirely different style of music: Hopi Indian chants. The rowdy, playful electric rock that gives a youthful, sometimes satirical quality to the play suddenly seems trivial and inappropriate in light of the highly spiritual Native American ceremony that Shepard painstakingly recreates as part of the final scene of the play. The play leaves no clue as to whether or not Shepard is aware of the disparity between the two forms of musical expression; however it does foreshadow his eventual rejection of rock music for less rigid and more emotionally pliable avenues of musical expression.

"Form in a formless sense..."

Having failed to find rock stardom in London, but having won great acclaim for *The Tooth of Crime*, Shepard returned to the United States in 1974. He moved to the San Francisco Bay Area and began collaborating with a small group of local musicians and actors on "ways in which 'character development' might evolve directly from music and sound."[27] This experimentation resulted in a string of theatre works, starting with *Inacoma* in 1977. Inspired by the real-life "right-to-die" court case of Karen Ann Quinlan, a young woman who lapsed into a coma under uncertain circumstances, *Inacoma* was a collaboratively and improvisationally developed musical fantasy about a comatose teenage girl who has fallen from the speaker towers at a rock concert.

Inacoma was built upon the synthesis of music and language Shepard had exhibited in *The Tooth of Crime*; however, it differed from *The Tooth of Crime*, and introduced a new period of musical experimentation for Shepard, in two significant ways: (1) the play was composed improvisationally and collaboratively, in rehearsals, with the contributions of musicians playing an equal role to the spoken word and dramatic action, and (2) with *Inacoma*, Shepard rejected rock-and-roll with its strong, percussive rhythms in order to explore the more amorphous, less formally shackled qualities of improvisational jazz. Shepard was no stranger to jazz. His father had been an amateur Dixieland drummer; his first roommate in New York City was the son of jazz great Charlie Mingus; and Shepard had worked as a busboy at the Village Gate, a Manhattan jazz club where he nightly cleared tables to the sounds of improvisational jazz's masters. In short, Shepard had been exposed to and appreciated jazz for much of his life; but, as he explained in a 1983 interview, he pursued rock-and-roll in the 1960s because jazz carried with it an aura of urban "sophistication" against which he felt compelled to rebel. Rock-and-roll, by comparison, was a "back-to-a-raw-gut kind of American shit kicker thing."[28] So, Shepard became a rock musician and a rock-and-roll playwright.

In San Francisco in the mid-1970s, Shepard began taking music lessons and, consequently, engaging in discussions of musical theory with local jazz composer, Catherine Stone. According to Shepard, "jazz could move in surprising territories, without qualifying itself... You could follow a traditional melody and then break away, and then come back, or drop into polyrhythms... But, more importantly, it was an emotional thing. You could move in all these *emotional* territories, and you could do it with *passion*... There was a form in a formless sense."[29] With Stone supplying local musicians and Shepard gathering a troupe of actors from the Magic Theatre, work on *Inacoma* began as a series of improvisational exercises in "an attempt to find an equal expression between music and the actor."[30] The performance ensemble was comprised of eight actors, some of whom, like Shepard's wife, O-Lan, were also accomplished musicians. Eight musicians were also involved. Each played a variety of instruments, creating a broad range of orchestral possibilities. According to Stone: "We started meeting, all of us, in my house. [Sam] brought around all these actors . . . and we started 'jamming' the way musicians jam, but with actors . . . "[31] From the beginning, music in the form of improvisation and jamming played an essential role in the play's composition. Shepard took improvisational exercises learned from his old friend Joseph Chaikin of the Open Theatre and adapted them to include musicians. The "Sound and Movement" exercise, in which a sound/movement is developed by one actor and then handed off to another who develops or expands upon it before handing it off to another, was modified to create a dialogue between musicians and actors. According to Stone, "an actor would step out and a musician would step out. And the musician would make the music and the actor would make the movement and the sound. And then the actor would go over and hand it off to another actor, and the musician would go over and hand it off to another musician." *Inacoma* rehearsals also employed "Music Puppet" exercises in which a musician, acting as a puppeteer of sorts, manipulates the actor/puppet with music or sound serving as "the strings." According to Stone, "A musician would get behind one actor and play. And the actor couldn't do anything except if the musician did something." This exercise could be reversed, so that the musician became the puppet, responding to the performance of the actor, with the musical accompaniment commenting upon the performance.

> We would take a specific character and that character would step forward like a soloist with a back-up, like a soul singer with a back-up orchestra. And we'd say, OK, this is the doctor . . . and he would step forward . . . It was like the actor would step up and the musicians would gather something just from knowing what the character was, and knowing who the actor was. And they would start to play something. (Stone)

The majority of *Inacoma* was created in this improvisational manner. Shepard might raise either issues or situations as jumping-off points for improvisation; but, according to Stone, the only written materials he brought into the rehearsal process were lyrics to be set to music.

Although the musical experimentation of *Inacoma* was quickly overshadowed by the success of Shepard's first family plays, *Curse of the Starving Class* (1977) and *Buried Child* (1978), it nevertheless began a string of experiments that continued, as a secondary track of Shepard's career, throughout the time he was making a name for himself as a chronicler of the American family. In 1978 and again in 1979, Shepard collaborated with Joseph Chaikin on *Tongues* and *Savage/Love*. These pieces were far smaller in scale than *Inacoma*, with Chaikin as the solo vocal performer and first Shepard himself and later a trio of musicians offering accompaniment. Shepard also collaborated again with Catherine Stone's Overtone Theatre (whose members included Shepard's wife O-Lan and other members of the *Inacoma* company) on *Superstitions* (1981). None of these three pieces follows a conventional dramatic action. Instead, they are collage-like in structure, incorporating monologues, poems, dialogues, even chants in a variety of voices and characterizations. Each piece is unified, not around character or action, but around a specific theme such as human identity, love and hate, or our little habits, rituals, and superstitions. Motifs are introduced, as in a musical composition, and then repeated and commented upon in different voices and variations. In the Program Note to *Superstitions*, the members of the Overtone Theatre describe how they approached the individual segments of that work:

> We worked with each piece until we found its particular musical nature. It became clear that the role of the music was as varied as the drama it surrounded. At times its presence initiates action, at other times it echoes and reflects the action. The music can be the natural sounds around the characters or the moods inside them. It can also be an equal participant in conversations, or an entry point to parts unknown.[32]

Shepard's contributions on these music theatre pieces varied. On *Tongues*, he supplied the entire musical score himself, actually sitting back to back with Chaikin on stage, with a broad collection of percussive instruments spread out around him. On *Superstitions*, Shepard contributed the many short written texts, allowing Stone and the actors to serve as equal collaborators to stage the piece, offering a physical and musical contribution equal to Shepard's written one.

Superstitions[33] offers an excellent example of those equal contributions. The piece consists of three performers: a man and a woman who speak or sing the texts and a musician (Catherine Stone). The music and sound-effects sometimes serve as a response to or enhancement of the language or mood of the two performers; other times, Stone's musical contribution seems to initiate an environment of sound and emotion which gives rise to the performer's thoughts or words. In a monologue about insomnia, Stone creates an ominous middle-of-the-night aural and emotional soundscape by sporadically dropping objects such as marbles, silverware, and small blocks of wood on the stage floor. These unidentified nocturnal sounds lead the actor to contemplate exactly what he's heard in his house in the middle of the night: "is it a rooster/or some woman screaming in the distance."[34] His anxiety, in turn, is articulated by one of the actors with the screeching of fiddle strings and the rhythmic scraping of a fork on a metal hubcap. To use Shepard's words, the performers attempt to create and employ sounds that "cut through space without having to hesitate for the 'meaning.'"[35] Jarring thoughts are punctuated with a blow to a tambourine; physical discomfort is recorded in discordant piano chords or fingers scraped across piano strings; static on a radio evokes the desperation of doubts that have arisen in a stagnant marriage. Music can also counterpoint rather than reinforce speech, as when melodramatic, silent-movie chords played on the piano comically undercut a paranoid speech about vampires. Likewise, a cowboy's confusion over which of his six pairs of boots to wear is mocked by turning the ritual into a bluegrass waltz. In creating the musical environment for this collection of dialogues, monologues, and prose poems, Stone and the actors utilize conventional musical instruments – piano, fiddle, tambourine, guitar, saxophone, synthesizer, xylophone, cymbals – as well as unconventional instruments – rattling coins, wood blocks, silverware, radio static; they also use conventional instruments in unconventional ways – plucked and scraped piano strings, droning sustained fiddle notes, a rasping, spitting saxophone – in order to create the emotional space in which the speakers' thoughts take place. Although many of the texts in *Superstitions* are published in Shepard's volume *Motel Chronicles*, it is impossible, having seen them performed, to imagine them as a separate literary text without the musical landscape in which the production and Shepard's collaborators place them.

"The world is a highly ordered place..."

At the same time Shepard was collaborating and experimenting with music theatre composition, he was also incorporating a jazz world view and jazz musicians as characters in his plays. In the mid-1970s, jazz musicians were under the sway of the so-called "outside" musicians such as Charlie Mingus, John Coltrane, and Ornette Coleman. These innovative jazz improvisers "played out": that is, they played improvisational music that was well outside of – that shattered – the conventional structural and formal boundaries of musical composition, even earlier jazz composition. For those who "played out," improvisation meant more than a means of musical expression, it was a means of perceiving and experiencing life. "Playing out" was a way of being in the world, of interacting with the world, and of perceiving the world. Thus, if conventional music gave you the feeling that "the world is a highly ordered place, it's safe and peaceful, and beautiful" (Stone), then "playing out" could evoke a whole new experience of reality as an existential landscape, a place both free from the impositions of ordered existence and at the same time potentially terrifying in its lack of order.[36] In two of Shepard's plays from this period, *Angel City* and *Suicide in B-Flat* (both 1976), that ambiguity is embodied by a rift between characters who wish to embrace the rational world and musicians whose "playing out" embraces the irrational.

The characters in *Angel City*, which is set in the office of a film industry executive, have allowed themselves to become the voluntary prisoners of an industry which offers them security and wealth, but which seals them off from any contact with "the world out there." The only character in the play that is not coopted by the Hollywood dream machine is a shadowy, faceless saxophone player. Catherine Stone tells an amusing anecdote which sheds light on the origins of this liminal character. During the time that Shepard was taking music lessons with Stone, one of her housemates was a saxophonist:

> [Sam] loved the saxophone player because he would come down the hall and play "Misty" in the corner... Sam would be sitting there playing at the lesson and [he] would be in the kitchen with the door to the fridge open, playing to the vegetables. I didn't realize that the fact that this guy was the kind of guy he was – outside of society, playing this beautiful music all around – was all part of Sam's mythology... It was right after that he started rehearsing *Angel City*.

In *Angel City*, the unnamed saxophonist hovers on the periphery of the play, seeming to live in thin air. He wanders in and out of the play, his saxophone – sometimes mellow, sometimes writhing – enhancing moods or adding emotional color to the hallucinatory speeches of the characters in the play. The speeches in *Angel City* are also enhanced by the percussive accompaniment of a young drummer appropriately named Tympani who has been hired to create a rhythm structure "guaranteed to produce certain trance states in masses of people."[37] While Tympani's drumming allows other characters in the play to explore expanded states of consciousness, his own attempt at relinquishing conscious control, letting the music go where it wants, has been too frightening and has left him unable to duplicate the experience. As he recounts it, "I'd never had quite that kind of feeling enter into a simple four-four pattern before... Then I looked straight down at my hands and I saw somebody else playing the pattern. It wasn't me. It was a different body. Then I got scared. I panicked when I saw that, and right away I lost it" (79). Shepard recounts a similar sensation when he was playing drums with the Holy Modal Rounders in the late 1960s:

I begin to get the haunting sense that something in me writes but it's not necessarily me. At least not the "me" that takes credit for it. This identical experience happened to me once when I was playing drums with the Holy Modal Rounders, and it scared the shit out of me. Peter Stampfel, the fiddle player[,] explained it as being visited by the Holy Ghost, which sounded reasonable enough at the time.[38]

Acting as well as music arises out of jazz-like improvisation in *Angel City*. In a "Note to the Actors," Shepard encourages the performers to relinquish some of their conventional ideas of character, of motivated action, and of conscious control:

The term "character" could be thought of in a different way when working on this play. Instead of a "whole character" with logical motives behind his behavior which the actor submerges himself into, he should consider instead a fractured whole with bits and pieces of character flying off the central theme. In other words, more in terms of collage construction or jazz improvisation. This is not the same thing as one character playing many different roles…If there needs to be a "motivation" for some of the abrupt changes which occur in the play they can be taken as full-blown manifestations of a passing thought or fantasy. (61–62)

While Shepard does not allow his actors to improvise, he does encourage them to perform his characters in a manner that manifests the improvised fashion in which he has apparently written them: that is, as "riffs" and "bits and pieces of character flying off the central theme," just like a jazz musician stepping forward to "jam" or perform an improvised solo. This reconsideration of character implies a radical reinterpretation of the human psyche, arising out of the concept of improvising oneself and implying that there is no central self, no core, only a fragmented collage of selves.

In *Suicide in B-Flat*, that collage of selves is manifest in the form of a suicidal jazz musician who must kill off his various artistic identities in order to write truly original music. In his absence, his band members must fight with the police over the nature of improvisation as a lifestyle. *Suicide in B-Flat* begins with a faceless body, found in the apartment of improvisational jazz pianist, Niles. Two gumshoe detectives have been sent to investigate what appears to be Niles's suicide. When the detectives are joined by members of Niles's band, the dialogue turns to the relationship between improvisational jazz and ways of seeing and being in the world. If the detectives represent a world of certainties, where truth "lap[s] your face like a Bloodhound's tongue"[39] and verifiable facts and data inevitably lead to the resolution of any mystery, then the musicians represent a world of ambiguity and "free-form stuff" where the rules of life, as of music, can be improvised. Pressed to elaborate upon the nature of their collaboration with Niles, the musicians offer only vague metaphysical theories of improvisation to which the detectives respond with panic. According to one of the detectives, improvisation leads to a "breaking off with the past," which in turn "distort[s] the very foundations of our cherished values!" (130–31). Improvisation is nothing less than a subversive means of political revolution. As one detective puts it, "[It leads to] rubbing up against the very grain of sanity and driving us all to complete and utter destruction! To changing the shape of American morality!... You're not strong enough to take us over by direct political action so you've chosen to drive us all crazy!" (131). The longer the two detectives remain in Niles's apartment, the more they are overtaken by the dreaded dissolution of their safe world. While the musicians are unaffected, one detective rolls about the floor fighting off the butcher knife he holds in his own hands, while his partner screams out that they are the victims of "AN UNSEEN ENEMY" (149). The enemy, Shepard's play seems to suggest, is nothing more than the threat to the detectives' rational, ordered world posed by an improvisatory lifestyle and an unexplained suicide.

"Rhythm discoveries in space and time..."

Writing is very rhythmic, there's a rhythmical flow to it – if it's working. I've always been fascinated by the rhythm of language, and language is musical, there's no way of getting around it, particularly written language when it's spoken. The language becomes musical, or at least it should in one way or another...[40]

Even when there is no band, no musical score, no songs: there is a rhythmic, frequently percussive, quality to the language of Shepard's characters that makes music of his plays. Words as percussion, as vibration and breath which hit and move the air, have been a trademark of Shepard's work since his earliest plays. Shepard once described his writing process as experimentation "that led to rhythm discoveries in space and time... packing up words and stretching them out along with their size and shape and sound."[41] This statement is applicable to the hallucinatory language of the early play, *Red Cross* (1966), for which Shepard wrote this note. But, it is also applicable to language from nearly all of Shepard's writing. In Shepard's 1977 family drama, *Curse of the Starving Class*, a teenage boy describes his drunken father's late-night homecoming in a speech composed entirely of sounds heard from his bedroom. The speech starts with the young man, awake in his bed, listening to the sounds outside his room, expanding his consciousness to "feel the space around me like a big, black world."[42] When, from a great distance, he hears his father's Packard "coming up the hill," the speech intensifies and the rhythm of the prose moves from long, contemplative sentences to short percussive bursts of sound as the boy's drunken father tries to force his way into the house.

> Then I hear the door of the Packard open. A pop of metal. Dogs barking down the road. Door slams...Feet walking toward the door. Feet stopping. Heart pounding. Sound of door not opening. Foot kicking door. Man's voice. Dad's voice. Dad calling mom. No answer. Foot kicking. Foot kicking harder. Wood splitting. Man's voice. In the night. Foot kicking hard through door. One foot right through door. Bottle crashing. Glass breaking. Fist through door. Man cursing. Man going insane. (138)

The images mirror the emotional intensity of the event, coming in short, panted breaths and harsh, explosive beats, like the pounding of the boy's heartbeat. Eventually, the father stumbles away and drives off into the night. The scene slowly returns to its previous silence.

> No sound. Mom crying soft. Soft crying. Then no sound. Then softly crying. Then moving around through the house. Then no moving. Then crying softly. Then stopping. Then, far off the freeway could be heard. (138)

The gradually increasing length of the sentences, the increasing gaps of silence, and the mother's intermittent crying, reflect the gradual slowing of the speaker's breath and heartbeat. Ears, attuned minutes earlier to the specific sounds of the father's arrival, are now free to wander back to the distant noises of the freeway. The speech's near-ejaculatory build toward a climax and release exemplifies Shepard's strong sense of the physical impact of language as a form of expression which has the ability to quicken the heartbeat and jump-start the emotions as does the intensified beating of a drum. This speech does not fall into the more commonly recited standards of poetic language: it is not iambic pentameter, nor does it possess the natural poetic rhythms of modern spoken English notable in the loquacious urban fast-talkers of a playwright like David Mamet. What it contains is a percussive pulse – the quickening heartbeat and shallow breath of the speaker – that intensifies the pulse of the listener as powerful music does.

Actors and directors who have worked with Shepard, or who have acted in or directed his plays, find similar rhythms in everything he writes. His language begs for musical or percussive accompaniment. New York-based director George Ferencz, for instance, when directing several of Shepard's "musical" plays at Columbia University and La MaMa Theatre between 1979 and 1984,[43] took the musical accompaniment of the plays a step further than Shepard's stage directions indicated by creating a near-continuous score to serve as mood-evoking backdrop to the dialogue. On several of the plays, jazz drummer Max Roach served as musical director, with a full jazz ensemble present from the very beginning of rehearsals to score each moment of the plays, both where the plays called for music and where they did not. According to Roach, "The music [becomes] another character in the play. It speaks almost as much as the actors do."[44] While this effect was similar to that Shepard himself pursued when working on *Inacoma* and the music pieces which followed, here the scoring was being applied to pieces for which Shepard had indicated only an intermittent desire for musical accompaniment. In 1992–93, while directing at Yale University, Ferencz applied the same near-continuous rhythmic and percussive scoring to two Shepard plays that had no explicit connection to music whatsoever. In his productions of *Action* and *Icarus's Mother*, entire beats, passages, and scenes would either emerge out of a metronomic pulse or would build around simple percussion created by the actors themselves. In rehearsals, Ferencz encouraged actors to establish a base line or beat to which they would then play an entire speech or scene. In his production of *Icarus's Mother*, Ferencz and his actors employed choreographed movement and rhythmic, sometimes chanted, speech to create a somber, unnerving ritualism which heightened the play's already bizarre and irrational dramatic action. His production of *Action* started with one of the characters tapping a spoon on a table to set a beat. For several minutes, the actions and spoken lines of the characters were more synchronized dance than drama. When one of the characters finally broke the established rhythm, the audience could immediately feel the existential desperation and isolation as the other characters scrambled to reestablish a protective rhythm of living.[45] What George Ferencz and many other artists recognize is that all Shepard's work is based on a keen sense of the rhythmic, percussive, and musical qualities of language and dramatic action. Whether playing to their own musicality or working in counterpoint to it, the speeches, beats, and scenes in Shepard's plays frequently cry out for a performance treatment that underscores their rhythmic and musical qualities.

Converging Tracks

The days of on-stage rock bands may be over for Shepard as a dramatist, but the various tracks of his musical experimentation all lead back, eventually, to the main course of his writing and work as a theatre artist. Since the early 1980s, Shepard's taste in music has moved toward bluegrass and country, and his work, for the most part, has moved in directions which do not involve the type of intense musical experimentation he engaged in during the late 1960s and 1970s. If anything, it might be said that he has grown comfortable with the subtler possibilities music has to offer his plays. His keen sense of the use of music and sound to enhance the emotional texture of even his most realistic plays is evident in his direction of many of his plays' premiere productions. Recent works, such as *Simpatico* (1994) and *Eyes for Consuela* (1997) have been produced with original musical compositions and musical scoring. *States of Shock* (1991) used two dueling drummers to add percussive intensity to the characters' apocalyptic descriptions of warfare. In *When the World Was Green: A Chef's Fable* (1996), Shepard "worked very closely with [the composer]," using music as "a sort of suggestive underscoring" with the piano becoming "almost another character."[46] Shepard's work with the bluegrass band, the Red Clay Ramblers, on *A Lie of the Mind* (1985) led him to include a note with the published script that, while it would be "stretching the limitations of this publication to include all the lyrics and music notations that were such an integral part of that production," the band's work left him "no doubt that this play needs music. Live music. Music with an American backbone."[47] Finally, in what must be one of the most original uses of percussion ever made in a dramatic play, Shepard amplified the walls and doors of the set to *Fool for Love* (1983) "so that each slamming of a door, each pounding of a wall, each blow from an elbow, knee, and fist"[48] in this lover's battle was captured and broadcast on speakers placed beneath the audience.

As Shepard continues to employ live music as accompaniment to performance, he demonstrates that music – but not necessarily formal music or song – can be an integral part of any theatrical presentation. His involvement in the productions of his plays has resulted in an increasingly understated incorporation of musical scores that blend seamlessly with the other elements of the text and performance. What were once alternate routes have now become converging tracks moving toward the same artistic destinations.*

* Professor DeRose gratefully acknowledges the support of Saint Mary's College's Faculty Development Program.

NOTES

1 Bruce Springsteen, [Liner Notes,] *Tracks* (New York: Columbia Records, 1998).

2 Sam Shepard, *The Tooth of Crime*, in *Sam Shepard: Seven Plays* (New York: Bantam Books, 1981), 224, 250. Page references in parentheses within the text are to this edition.

3 Quoted in Don Shewey, *Sam Shepard* (New York: Dell, 1985), 47.

4 Shewey, *Sam Shepard*, 62. Shewey's excellent literary biography of Shepard paints a detailed picture of the playwright's personal life in the 1960s, arguably

demonstrating that music played every bit as important a role in Shepard's daily existence at that time as theatre did.

5 Between *Melodrama Play* in 1967 and *Cowboy Mouth* in 1971, only *The Holy Ghostly* and *Shaved Splits* (both 1970) did not contain live rock music in some form. *Forensic and the Navigators* (1967), *The Unseen Hand* (1969), *Operation Sidewinder* (1970), *The Mad Dog Blues*, and *Back Bog Beast Bait* (both 1971), all had live bands and, to some extent, musical scores. The last three contained songs written into the texts of the plays.

6 Shepard played drums mostly with spin-off bands from the Holy Modal Rounders. The bands that performed with Shepard at his plays included the Moray Eels on *Forensic and the Navigators* and Lothar and the Hand People on *The Unseen Hand*. Shepard went by the name Slim Shadow when he led the (unnamed) band, playing tambourine, electric guitar, and sound effects on *The Mad Dog Blues*. Lou Reed is credited with the music for *Back Bog Beast Bait*.

7 Shewey, *Sam Shepard*, 71–72.

8 Sam Shepard, *The Mad Dog Blues*, in *The Unseen Hand and Other Plays* (New York: Bantam Books, 1986), 260.

9 David DeRose, *Sam Shepard* (New York: Twayne, 1992), 53.

10 Irving Wardle, "Return of Theatrical Fireball," *The Times* (London), 6 June 1974, 9.

11 Sam Shepard, *Cowboy Mouth*, in *Fool for Love and Other Plays* (New York: Bantam Books, 1984), 156. Page references in parentheses within the text are to this edition.

12 Shepard's affair with Smith, and their mutual influence on each other's artistic careers, is well documented in Shewey, *Sam Shepard*, and in Patricia Morrisroe, *Mapplethorpe: A Biography* (New York: Random House, 1995).

13 Sam Shepard, "Big Stakes," in *Rolling Thunder Logbook* (New York: Viking Press, 1977), 62.

14 Sam Shepard, "The Inventor," in *Rolling Thunder Logbook*, 100.

15 Sam Shepard, "Audience," in *Rolling Thunder Logbook*, 79.

16 Sam Shepard, *Melodrama Play*, in *Fool for Love and Other Plays*, 121, 123.

17 As composer Stephen LeGrand diplomatically put it when writing a new score for the 1985 Berkeley Repertory Theatre production: "Stuff that was maybe experimental then has now become old-hat." Quoted in Calvin Ahlgren, "A New Rock Bite for *The Tooth of Crime*," *San Francisco Chronicle*, Datebook, 21 April 1985, 42.

18 Shepard derived the war of styles in *The Tooth of Crime* from music theatre innovator Bertolt Brecht's *Jungle of Cities* (1923). For more, see DeRose, *Sam Shepard*, 72–74.

19 Kenneth Chubb, et al., "Metaphors, Mad Dogs, and Old Time Cowboys" (1974), reprinted in Bonnie Marranca (ed.), *American Dreams: The Imagination of Sam Shepard* (New York: Performing Arts Journal Publications, 1981), 201.

20 Chubb, "Metaphors," 202.

21 Pete Hamill, "The New American Hero," *New York*, 16 (5 December 1983): 88–89.

22 Sam Shepard, *The Unseen Hand*, in *The Unseen Hand and Other Plays*, 27.

23 Sam Shepard, *The Holy Ghostly*, in *The Unseen Hand and Other Plays*, 194–96.

24 Sam Shepard, *Back Bog Beast Bait*, in *The Unseen Hand and Other Plays*, 323–24.

25 All observations and quotations from Ralph Cook are taken from an interview with the author conducted in Berkeley, California, 12 December 1984.

26 Chubb, "Metaphors," 201.

27 Sam Shepard, "Proposed Project," an undated, typewritten document in Magic Theatre publicity archives.

28 Hamill, "New American Hero," 88.

29 Ibid., 88–89.

30 "Program Note," *Savage/Love* and *Tongues*, Eureka Theatre, San Francisco, 1979. Shepard conducted other musical experiments with Stone, including his cowboy opera, *The Sad Lament of Pecos Bill on the Eve of Killing His Wife* (commissioned by the Bay Area Playwrights' Festival to celebrate the bicentennial, 1976), for which Stone wrote the music. In an attempt to reverse the usual order of composition and to abolish the reliance of music upon "book," Shepard also asked Stone to write an hour's worth of music, around which Shepard was to afterwards write a play. The project was never realized.

31 All observations and quotations from Catherine Stone are taken from an interview with the author conducted in San Francisco, California, 14 March 1985.

32 The Overtone Theatre, "Program Note," *Superstitions* and *The Sad Lament of Pecos Bill on the Eve of Killing His Wife*, Magic Theatre, San Francisco, 1984.

33 The Overtone Theatre production of *Superstitions* was broadcast on KQED (San Francisco PBS Channel 9), 18 December 1984.

34 Sam Shepard, *Motel Chronicles* (San Francisco: City Lights Books, 1982), 20. Several of the spoken texts from *Superstitions* are published in *Motel Chronicles*.

35 Sam Shepard, "Language, Visualization, and the Inner Library" (1977), reprinted in Bonnie Marranca (ed.), *American Dreams: The Imagination of Sam Shepard* (New York: Performing Arts Journal Publications, 1981), 217.

36 Well before Shepard incorporated the vocabulary of jazz improvisation and "playing out" into his work, he had created characters, such as those in *Action* (1975), caught between a perception of reality and of the self which was fixed, safe, and rational (but also imprisoning), and a perception which was unfixed, terrifying, and irrational (but also liberating). See DeRose, *Sam Shepard*, 63–71.

37 Sam Shepard, *Angel City*, in *Fool for Love and Other Plays*, 72. Page references in parentheses within the text are to this edition.

38 Shepard, "Language, Visualization," 217.

39 Sam Shepard, *Suicide in B-Flat*, in *Fool for Love and Other Plays*, 155. Page references in parentheses within the text are to this edition.

40 Matthew Roudané "Shepard on Shepard: an Interview," chapter 3, 67.

41 Sam Shepard, "Playbill for the Premiere Production [of *Red Cross*]," in Robert J. Schroeder (ed.), *The New Underground Theatre* (New York: Bantam Books, 1968), 80.

42 Sam Shepard, *Curse of the Starving Class*, in *Sam Shepard: Seven Plays* (New York: Bantam Books, 1981), 137. Page references in parentheses within the text are to this edition.

43 Ferencz's productions were widely documented in the New York press; however, regarding his rehearsal process, two journal articles are of specific interest: George Ferencz, "Directing Shepard," *The Journal of the Society of Stage Directors and Choreographers* (Winter 1968): 48–69, and Toby Silverman Zinman, "Shepard Suite," *American Theatre* (December 1984): 15–17.

44 Quoted in Carol L. Cleaveland, "Shepard Sets' Music 'Another Character,'" *Syracuse Post Standard*, 12 January 1985.

45 I saw George Ferencz's production of *Action* in 1992 at Yale University. In 1993, Ferencz and I team-taught a course on Sam Shepard at Yale; it was during this course that I observed Ferencz's rehearsal process and saw his production of *Icarus's Mother*.

46 Alvin Epstein, quoted in Gideon Lester, "Unlikely Human Beings," American Repertory Theatre webpage, updated 20 March 1997. [www.fas.harvard.edu/~art/green1.html]

47 Sam Shepard, "Music Notes," in *A Lie of the Mind* (London: Methuen, 1987), viii.

48 DeRose, *Sam Shepard*, 121.

14

ANN C. HALL

Sam Shepard's nondramatic works

It will come as no surprise to those familiar with the dramatic works of Sam Shepard that he believes that "all good writing comes out of aloneness." His plays are peopled with loners, renegades, and the pathologically independent. It might, however, cause some alarm to learn that he does a good deal of his writing while driving alone: "It's a good discipline because sometimes you can only write two or three words at a time before you have to look back at the road, so those three words have to count. The problem is whether you can read the damn thing by the time you reach your destination."[1] There are, of course, other problems, and the highway patrol would probably be very interested in Shepard's plate number, but the image of Shepard frantically writing while maneuvering the US Interstates is a fitting one for his three collections of nondramatic works, *Hawk Moon* (1981), *Motel Chronicles* (1982), and *Cruising Paradise* (1996). Many of the short stories, monologues, poems, and rantings, for lack of a better word, contain roadway imagery: characters hit the highway to leave or to return home, to lose or to find a job, or to drift. The focus on automotive imagery has led Robert Brustein to note, "Shepard may be the most inveterate chronicler of motel culture since Nabokov made Humbert Humbert chase Lolita through the backlots of America. (Both writers recognize that nothing better suggests the bleak rootlessness of American life than a rented room.)"[2] And both recognize that nothing suggests the American ethos quite so well either – the frontier, the restlessness, the quest, and the fierce independence. As in his stage plays, the characters who inhabit these anthologies are dynamically desultory, sometimes searching for specific answers, and sometimes shifting identities as frequently as a truck driver shifts gears along the hills of Pennsylvania in the desperate hope to find a new persona that will result in understanding. Many of the pieces beg autobiographical readings, so it is tempting to interpret the three collections as an archive of Shepard's development as a writer and man.[3] *Hawk Moon* is best characterized as a work of a young man and writer; *Motel Chronicles* by its haunting and maternal emphasis; and

Cruising Paradise by its reflections on professional concerns, the concerns of a mature writer, actor, and man. All three offer insights into Shepard's life, work, and familiar dramatic themes: the frontier, gender relationships, and creation, both physical and artistic. What is most compelling, however, is Shepard's repeated attempt to address the question of identity, a quest that characterizes his stage work.[4] Both he and his characters seem torn between two dialectical extremes: there is an insatiable desire for individual freedom and an equally strong desire for almost unrealistic connection to others, particularly in heterosexual relationships.[5] There are opposing desires for isolation and communication, vitality and obliteration. And it is with *Cruising Paradise* that Shepard seems to offer solutions to these paradoxes.

Michelle Huneven describes *Cruising Paradise* as a collection of "'tales,' a genre that seems more inclusive, oral, and ancient than the contemporary short story."[6] And this description could easily be applied to all three anthologies. All have a ritualistic rhythm, and all begin with a mythic tale of creation, an inaugural signpost along the highway of self-discovery. Like the births of Buddha or Christ, Shepard's birth stories indicate, if not greatness, a sense of the unusual, a uniqueness that is at once celebrated and lamented but always somehow connected to some superhuman force.

Hawk Moon, for example, opens with Shepard recalling the day of his birth "under a November moon," a "Hawk Moon," characterized by "secrets" and "prayer" (11).[7] *Motel Chronicles*, which does not provide titles to the individual pieces, begins with a story about a teething Shepard and his parents who stop at a roadside motel. Unlike other motels, this one has huge plaster dinosaurs on its grounds, and Shepard recalls, "there were no people around. Just us and the dinosaurs."[8] Both opening images clearly establish a sense of isolation and alterity. In this isolation, however, there is a sense of pride in the uniqueness of self – it is out here, under the moon or out in the desert, that the individual truly is.

The birth imagery of *Cruising Paradise* offers an opposing view to the previous works' celebrations of individuality. The opening selection, "The Self-Made Man," charts one man's growing awareness of his unavoidable connection to the past and his lack of personal identity: "it began in a moment of shattering stillness. Something separated and fell away. Instinctively his heart understood this 'something' was the long cherished notion of himself as a distinct individual; an American entity called 'The Self-Made Man.'"[9] He is overcome by this awareness and seeks solace in the night, only to discover that even the boundaries between himself and nature dissolve: "There was no border suddenly between his skin and the night, between his own breath and surrounding thick air" (5). In effect, the man is borne into oblivion. On the one hand, the loss of self and boundaries is frightening, but on the other, it is important that this man, and perhaps Shepard himself, realize that he is not entirely autonomous and omnipotent; the individual is part of a whole. In this way, Shepard contradicts the American myth of autonomy, one that cherishes the attributes and contributions of the "Self-Made Man." The man is clearly influenced by the past, culture, and even the forces of nature.

Such a conclusion alters the dissolution of self prevalent in some of the earlier nondramatic writings. In *Hawk Moon*, for instance, individuality is also frequently dissolved, but in this case, the individual voluntarily enters group anonymity, unlike the "Self-Made Man" who has his connectedness thrust upon him. "Back in the 70's" in *Hawk Moon* presents a brief description of life during the Vietnam War and the fate of draft dodgers in Canada: "There was no way of telling a Canadian kid from an American. Everybody fucking and sucking and smoking and shooting and dancing right out in the open. And far off you could hear the sound of America cracking open and crashing into the sea" (12). Here, the loss of personal identity creates a superhuman force; it is not a victim of it, and this new group entity creates revolutionary consequences for an entire culture. The anonymous group does not destroy the individual; it empowers individuals which, in turn, challenges other groups, in this case the American *status quo* and the institutions, other powerful group entities, supporting the Vietnam War. Here, then, individuals relinquish identity in order to insure personal freedom for themselves and others later.

"The Phantom Trailer," on the other hand, illustrates chilling consequences for the individual when such group anonymity occurs. "The Phantom Trailer" is a mobile brothel. And men compete to be first in line, thinking that being first will somehow gain them a sense of identity. But the narrator tells us that being last has its rewards and recalls a particularly moving night of sex with one young prostitute who pities him for his last place in line. Later, he learns that the prostitute, having been given a drug with aphrodisiac qualities, has bled to death.

Likewise, in "Sleeping at the Wheel," driving becomes a metaphor for the Socratic unexamined life. As two men travel down a highway, one says, "once in a while I'm just amazed when I catch a glimpse of who I really am . . . And I ask myself, 'where have I been all this time? Why was I blind?' Sleeping. Just the same as being asleep. We're all asleep. Being awake is too hard" (17). Under these circumstances, the loss of the self has disastrous consequences. Both selections suggest that identity requires effort; without tending to ourselves, we lose ourselves.

At this point, it would appear that Shepard is calling for a return to individuality, a call to wakefulness or mindfulness. But in the other transformation pieces, Shepard seems to doubt humanity's ability to discard its somnambulant state, and this inability leaves humanity vulnerable. In "Left-Handed Kachina," for example, a husband and wife vacation in the American West where they decide to purchase a tribal American Indian doll. After many negotiations with the natives, they purchase one, and return home. While listening to Native American chants in the presence of the doll, the husband is overtaken by the magical power of the Kachina. His wife arrives in time to save him from oblivion. Like the figures in "The Self-Made Man," the characters in this piece are forced to accept the limits of their own autonomy, but in this piece, the man is merely foolish, not enlightened. He toys with mysteries that are beyond him and comes to no conclusions about his own existence; he is merely a tourist on the existential highway. Similarly, in "The Curse of the Raven's Black Feather," a man finds a dead raven, takes a feather, and assumes it will bring good luck. He soon discovers, however, that the feather is cursed, and he is destined to drive north indefinitely.

In many selections from *Hawk Moon* perceptions are frequently suspect. Characters are unaware of the weaknesses in their own behavior, the vagaries of fortune, or the forces of nature. In one of the most poignant pieces, "The Sex of Fishes," Shepard illustrates our flawed perceptions regarding gender. A man and woman have had a child, and the woman's mother wants to know the gender immediately. This question sends the narrator into a reverie that illustrates how his experience violates social stereotypes: his wife "looked like a little boy doing dishes. His hands looked long and slender like a woman's."[10] In this story and in others, it is clear that what we impose upon reality may, in fact, not reflect reality. There is, for Shepard, a reality above and beyond us, one that influences our identity and frequently violates social conventions.

Many have tried to categorize Shepard's dramatic style, particularly the chameleon-like nature of his characters, explaining it in terms of jazz improvisation, rock-and-roll, the influence of Joseph Chaikin's Open Theatre, a reflection of postmodernism, or his own personality.[11] Marc Robinson notes, "The simplest explanation for the unpredictability of Shepard's art, however, is also the most likely. Like any good spectator, Shepard has a fierce aversion to boredom – or at least the pace of his plays suggests that he does – and so he has made a theatre to surprise himself."[12] What is so compelling about Robinson's assessment is that it acknowledges a universal quality that pervades Shepard's works, in this case, the desire for entertainment. Such an explanation suggests the reason for Shepard's appeal beyond the specific explanations of the aforementioned critics. It is not just jazz, postmodernism, or theatrical movements that explain Shepard's appeal; there is something more. For Robinson, it is the entertainment. But this collection and the other two demonstrate that his dramatic strategy is more than entertainment, more than postmodernism, more than his own personal preferences. Shepard writes about disjointed, frantic, and desperate characters and situations because this is life as he sees it – unpredictable, misleading, torturously quick, and frequently indifferent to personal desires. The driving metaphor, as well as the very chaotic structure of these nondramatic collections, enables him to communicate the joy, the despair, and the absolute confusion surrounding existence and our attempts to understand it.

The transformations in *Motel Chronicles* persist, but there is a decidedly maternal or feminine focus in this collection that distinguishes it from the other two. Clearly, the quest for identity must address the maternal, but, more importantly, women in this collection are presented in an important and powerful way. This is significant because Shepard has frequently been criticized for creating invisible or stereotypical female characters in his dramatic works.[13] Further, for those who see a shift in Shepard's female representation in his plays, this collection cannot be ignored as part of that process.[14]

In addition to the opening image, Shepard and his mother among the plaster dinosaurs, *Motel Chronicles* concludes with the story of his mother-in-law's stroke, a subject that is reminiscent of *Inacoma* (1977) and prefigures *A Lie of the Mind* (1985). According to Don Shewey, the opening and concluding pieces in *Chronicles* were written at the same time, but Shepard chose to frame the collection with these stories, rather than presenting them chronologically.[15] Such a decision demonstrates the important power and even omnipresence of women: they participate in birth, sickness, and death.

Between the maternal frame are more maternal stories. In one, Shepard's mother carries a gun with her to ward off Japanese snipers on their drive to a movie on an Air Force base. Shepard makes it clear that his mother and the other women on the base were fearless in their use of firearms: "later I found a Japanese skull / out by the reservoir / ants were crawling / out of a bullet hole / right through the temple" (32). Clearly, there is ambivalence here – she has the capacity to give and take away life indiscriminately, for Shepard mentions that the women frequently fired upon one another accidentally.

In another piece, Shepard recalls the moment of his birth which contradicts what he has been told by an unnamed woman about his birth. According to his version, he was mobile postpartum, and he attempted to look out the window:

> When I reached the wall I began to get my first taste of what it is to suffer. The
> windows were directly overhead but too high to reach in my condition. Pale
> green light poured through them, casting a double beam on my unconscious
> mother across the room. I watched her body. I knew I'd come from her body
> but I wasn't sure how. I knew I was away from her body now. (53)

Again, ambivalence prevails in this image. First, Shepard feels the need to
retell his version of his birth, perhaps in an attempt to reclaim his birth narrative from the family, particularly from the female storyteller. Second, Shepard
is fascinated by the realization he has regarding himself and his mother; he
is simultaneously connected to her and separated from her. Through the
character of the infant in this story, Shepard presents a struggle frequently
enacted in his dramas: the need for communion, and its attendant anxiety
regarding the loss of self, versus the need for the solitary journey and its
attendant loneliness.

Almost as if to underscore the oedipal images, Shepard raises the image
of his father. In one vignette, Shepard tells a story about pretending to sleep-
walk, just to be near his parents at night. He uses a pretense to gain communion, but his efforts are foiled. He is caught and sent back into his own
bedroom, by his father. He explains he did it "for the thrill of having a relationship with them outside the ordinary. A different kind of encounter. Now
it was over. Now it was just a humiliating silence lying in the dark" (19). His
pretense does not bring him an extraordinary connection with his parents.
Rejected and humiliated, he is left to face solitude, and it would appear that
Shepard and many of his characters remember this isolation bitterly and
rather than risk connection again, they make some kind of peace with the
darkness.

The struggles Shepard had with this father are no secret, but in this collection, he describes the father/son relationship with curiosity and confusion,
not rage. On some level, he understands his father completely: "My Dad lives
alone in the desert. He says he doesn't fit with people" (56). In this way, his
father represents that fierce independence seen in *Hawk Moon* and other
writings. Isolated and marginalized, Shepard's father can only be himself
completely when he is alone in the desert.

While Shepard does not attempt to explain his father's behavior, he is like
many of the other men in the collection, motivated by inexplicable forces.
The collection, like *Hawk Moon*, is filled with thinkers and dreamers. One
character, for example, obsesses about the threat of nuclear holocaust. Another pleads for a respite from his raging, but unspecified, thoughts: "Let me
hit the road / empty-headed / just once" (20). And in one of the most haunting
pieces, a farm-hand's chores include standing "transfixed for 1/2 hour" (15).

For Shepard, even the most common people are subject to moments of extraordinary epiphanies. What the characters conclude as a result of these transformative moments, however, is unspecified.

Such characters are never condemned, no matter how bizarre their actions. A character may believe that he has been banned from Radio Land, "doomed to prowl the air waves forever, seeking some magic channel that would reinstate him for his long-lost heritage" (39). Or a group of people may believe that a wicker chair in someone's front yard signifies death (60). Shepard merely records and respects these oddities of human behavior, perhaps cherishing their uniqueness as his own.

Shepard only harshly judges those who have ceased their quest for identity and understanding in favor of the security of the status quo, particularly the static personae manufactured by marketers. His Hollywood pieces are caustic: "they ooze and call each other 'darlings'/they hire fortune tellers who lie/they frame pictures of the kids they've sent away...their loneliness is covered with grins/their loneliness is smothered in a circle of 'friends'" (63). In two other pieces, Shepard condemns "men turning themselves into advertisements of men" and "women turning themselves into advertisements of women" (81). Even those who attempt to manipulate the Hollywood Dream machine cannot escape. One character, for example, attempts to live between San Francisco and Los Angeles in order to avert the corruption of the southern city. He believes that the middle ground will protect him. But Shepard concludes, "It was a vain scheme. Already things were pulling him in two directions. Already he was moving when he wanted nothing but stillness" (121). Manufactured images provide no salvation.

Strangely, however, Shepard implies that there may be redemption in a "tiny piece of cellophane" (81). In this vignette, a little girl chases the transparent paper, speaking to it; she "feels no separation between herself and the cellophane. Both being blown. Both being together at the same moment" (81). Again, there is this mythical connection sought after, but at the same time, the little girl wants to pin it down, to catch or retain or secure the connection. The little girl says to the cellophane, "Just let me step on you" (81). The difference, of course, is that the little girl is trying to control the piece on her own terms. She is being "natural"; she is not succumbing to media stereotypes or cultural roles, so her desire to pin something down, to stop the restlessness is approved. Of course, the natural is not always positive. As in *Hawk Moon*, there are times that the natural overcomes the human, but according to Shepard, it is worth the risk. It is better to face the forces of nature, the primitive, and risk the loss of self than settle for the socially contrived.

Shepard's *Cruising Paradise* is much denser than the other two collections. There are fewer poems, and the stories are longer and more complex, but the restlessness persists. The opening piece, for example, is about the death of the "Self-Made Man." But the concept of the self is not settled here. Subsequent pieces raise questions regarding perceptions, the nature of reality, and their effects on the individual.

In "The Real Gabby Hayes," a young Shepard accompanies his father into a bar where Gabby Hayes is drinking with several young women, and this image contradicts the young Shepard's perception of his Western idol. In "A Man's Man," Shepard relates one of his first work experiences. Hoping to teach him the value of work, Shepard's father forces him to hard labor. Shepard, though, discovers that one of the men he works with is a pedophile. Shepard does not condemn the man, but instead asks, "What is it about certain men?" (33). In these and other pieces, Shepard exposes idealized versions of reality.

In "Day of Blackouts" Shepard seems to abandon all philosophical ponderings when he admits that he was "born without a clue" (20). The other stories offer insights into his adult experiences: loves, friendships, and one-night stands. But these pieces are clearly part of the struggle. It is only with "The Hero Is in His Kitchen" that Shepard seems to resolve the questions of identity that have plagued him throughout not only these collections but his entire body of creative work. Here, Shepard describes the revelation of a fellow drifter. The character says he no longer dreams of being somebody else. He claims he is

> the person in my day dreams...The fact is, that I'm actually here, and this adventure is mine...I suddenly see my life as a real adventure. I actually experience it the way you experience a movie...You see what I mean? We're actually the heroes in our own kitchens...Don't buckle under the weight of a heavy heart! That's my advice to you. Never surrender! (161–63)

With this realization, the collection of essays seems to find its sense of direction. There is an answer; identity is personal, private, and liberating. It need not demand the grand gesture, ironically, coming from the dramatist who is noted for the grand gesture. More surprising still, given the criticism of Shepard by feminist critics, Shepard sets this revelation in the kitchen, not on the frontier. The quest for identity appears to have been solved by a return to home.

While the remaining pieces take place on the road, frequently chronicling his experiences with movie-making, there is a sense that Shepard has found himself, though the world is still chaotic and frenzied. Shepard tells amusing anecdotes about the film industry, his distaste for flying, and the absurdity of a culture controlled by the media. In "Spencer Tracy is Not Dead," for example, he lies in order to get across the Mexican border; he pretends to be Spencer Tracy. Star-struck, the Mexican officials grant him access.

The stories very literally come to rest with a final piece on his mother. In "Place," Shepard, his eldest son, and his mother visit the unmarked grave of her parents in order to place a limestone marker there. Shepard explains that his mother wanted to "place a native stone from the very same beach where her father had built his cabin, back at the turn of the century" (237). Again, there is a mythic return to origins here. Once the stone is in place, however, Shepard's mother thinks that it is the wrong place. They decide to leave the stone where it is, and one year later, Shepard's mother dies, and while they are working out burial arrangements for her, they discover that the limestone marker was in the wrong place. Now, however, "it lined up right behind my mother's grave. Everything was in its place now, and we left it just like that" (239).

Shepard's sense of humor is never far from even the most poignant moment, and the scene he creates with his mother, his son, and the gravestone is very similar to a scene from an absurdist drama. We may be "born astride a grave," in the words of Beckett, but Shepard's characters cannot even find it. In the end, the grave is our destination, and it would appear that in this final anthology Shepard has resolved many of his questions regarding identity: the place to find it is in the home, not outside of it. And through this final piece, it appears that Shepard has found peace, a "place." Shepard, his characters, and his writings seem to have discovered themselves. The quest for identity has ended. But this solution does not lead to stasis, for at this moment, it is difficult to ignore the title of the collection, *Cruising Paradise*. And with the title, Shepard implies that we may find solutions, we will die, but that does not mean we have to stop driving.

NOTES

1 Quoted in Ben Brantley, "Sam Shepard, Storyteller," *New York Times*, 13 November 1994: 1, Section 2.

2 Robert Brustein, "*Cruising Paradise*: Book Review," *The New Republic*, 215 (15–22 July 1996): 27–29. *FirstSearch*, 10 December 1999.

3 Don Shewey's biography, *Sam Shepard*, 2nd edn. (New York: Da Capo Press, 1997), presents numerous parallels between Shepard's life and work, similarities that appear in the nondramatic works as well.

4 See, for example, my chapter on Sam Shepard in *"A Kind of Alaska": Women in the Plays of O'Neill, Pinter, and Shepard* (Carbondale: Southern Illinois University Press, 1993), 91–116.

5 According to Shepard, "I think we're split in a much more devastating way than psychology can ever reveal." Quoted in David Wyatt, *Out of the Sixties: Storytelling and the Vietnam Generation* (New York: Cambridge University Press, 1993), 53.

6 Michelle Huneven, "Fathers Drink, Women Leave, Mistresses Combust: *Cruising Paradise* by Sam Shepard," review of *Cruising Paradise*, *Los Angeles Times Book Review*, 28 July 1996: 6. *Lexis-Nexis*, 10 December 1999.

7 Shepard had a Hawk Moon tattooed on his left hand during his affair with singer Patti Smith according to Jennifer Allen, "The Man on the High Horse: on the Trail of Sam Shepard," *Esquire*, November 1988: 141–51.

8 Sam Shepard, *Motel Chronicles* (San Francisco: City Lights Books, 1982), 9. Page references in parentheses within the text are to this edition.

9 Sam Shepard, *Cruising Paradise: Tales* (New York: Vintage Books, 1997), 3. Page references in parentheses within the text are to this edition.

10 Sam Shepard, *Hawk Moon: A Book of Short Stories, Poems, and Monologues* (Los Angeles: Black Sparrow, 1973), 77. Page references in parentheses within the text are to this edition.

11 See C. W. E. Bigsby on Shepard and Chaikin, *A Critical Introduction to Twentieth-Century American Drama*, vol. III (Cambridge University Press, 1985), 244–48. For jazz comparisons, see Michiko Kakutani, "Identity and its Absence, by Way of Sam Shepard," review of *Cruising Paradise*, *New York Times*, 17 May 1996: 23, Section 2, Col. 1. *Lexis-Nexis*, 10 December 1999. And Leslie Wade, *Sam Shepard and the American Theatre* (Westport, CT: Greenwood Press, 1997), for rock-and-roll comparisons.

12 Marc Robinson, *The Other American Drama* (New York: Cambridge University Press, 1994), 66.

13 Lynda Hart, "Sam Shepard's Pornographic Visions," *Studies in the Literary Imagination*, 21.2 (1988): 69–82, reprinted in Matthew Roudané (ed.), *Public Issues, Private Tensions: Contemporary American Drama* (New York: AMS Press, 1993), 161–77. Hart argues that Shepard's depiction of women is not only pornographic but representative of a patriarchal culture that silences women. Given Shepard's incredible popularity despite his, according to Hart, sexist representation of women, he continues to be lionized: "the 'true' spokesperson for America seems to necessarily speak from a masculine space where the feminine is always the absent Other" (69).

14 Felicia Hardison Londré, "Sam Shepard Works Out: the Masculization of America," *Studies in American Drama: 1945–Present*, 2 (1987): 19–27. Londré calls Shepard's early plays his "mindless macho period" (20).

15 Shewey, *Sam Shepard*, 129–30.

15

LESLIE A. WADE

States of Shock, Simpatico, and Eyes for Consuela: Sam Shepard's plays of the 1990s

The career of American dramatist Sam Shepard merits acclaim for many reasons, not the least of which may be his remarkable endurance. Dating back to the tumultuous days of the early Off-Off-Broadway movement, Shepard's work first fascinated counter-culture audiences with its frenetic, lyrical outbursts and unrelenting energy. However, unlike the legion of Off-Off-Broadway playwrights whose notoriety was followed by an all too sudden eclipse, Shepard's renown continued to ascend as the coffee-house theatre scene declined. Always prolific and inventive, the playwright found persistent success despite the changing economics, production approaches, and audience tastes of the American theatre. In the three decades (and counting) since his debut at Theatre Genesis, Shepard has emerged as a phenomenon of cultural fascination, a playwright now widely produced and taught as a canonical author, an iconic figure often praised in hyperbolic terms (one critic has extolled Shepard as "after all the most original and vital playwright of our age.")[1] If one were to invoke metaphors drawn from Shepard's obsession with the racetrack, the playwright over the years has proven sure of stride, game and tireless, endowed with a dramatic gift comprising equal parts imagination, drive, and stamina.

From the vantage point of the mid-1980s, when Shepard's status in the American theatre reached its apogee, the trajectory of his career engendered assumptions that he would continue to produce the challenging, often daunting works expected of the country's most prominent playwright. In the 1990s these expectations went unfulfilled. To all but the most loyal of Shepard devotees, it seems that the playwright has entered a state of decline, at best a state of transition. This is not to imply that Shepard has not been busy. He has written and directed a feature-length film, *Silent Tongue*, collaborated on another experimental piece with Joseph Chaikin, *When the World Was Green*, and published a book of short stories, *Cruising Paradise*. And in the last decade he has appeared in nearly a dozen film roles. Nonetheless, dating back to 1986, he has penned only three new stage plays: *States of*

Shock (1991), *Simpatico* (1994), and *Eyes for Consuela* (1998). In 1997 he failed to deliver a new script commissioned by the Signature Theatre Company – this from a playwright once considered prodigiously prolific, who authored almost thirty plays within the first decade of his career. In virtue of his sporadic productivity, one might conclude that Shepard has willfully spurned the role of Great American Playwright, that he has eased into an emeritus mode. However one might assess the recent artistic activity of Sam Shepard, I suggest that he is no longer perceived as the most important dramatist working in America today.

Though his past achievement remains unquestioned, magnified in some quarters, Shepard's fall from grace has not gone unnoticed. Following the 1994 production of *Simpatico*, John Lahr wrote: "It gives me no pleasure to report this. For almost thirty years, Shepard's plays . . . have been a defining part of American theatre. So what's happened?"[2] Jeremy Gerard likewise lamented: "it's been disheartening to watch this writer spin further and further out of the dramatic center."[3] One notes various tones and attitudes in such commentary. Frequently admissions of sadness or regret are sprinkled in reviews, as though the subject might be a famous athlete at the end of his career. Those who never admired Shepard's work take the opportunity to confirm their suspicion that Shepard was never a playwright of any accomplishment but rather the product of hype and uncritical adulation. And there are conversely those apologists invested in Shepard criticism who recognize no decline and labor to manifest the writer's ingenuity and brilliance, despite the unremarkable impact of his recent work.

This chapter offers a chronicle of Shepard's career during the 1990s, an analysis of each of the three plays he has written in the decade, and speculation as to why Shepard has come to be regarded as something of a man out of time. It is not my intent to deliver a eulogy. Though I believe *States of Shock*, *Simpatico*, and *Eyes for Consuela* by and large to be failed attempts, I find that Shepard's work retains vitality and spurs curiosity (though not satisfaction). What most interests me is the introduction of a meditative, even ethical element to Shepard's dramatic vision. The graying of the dramatist has brought with it a diminished output, a less volatile and explosive theatrical realization, but one may find in Shepard's work a new introspection, a sensibility less prone to tantrums than conciliation.

If one had to choose a playwright of the moment, whose work at the beginning of the twenty-first century best represents the "serious" drama of the American theatre, a case could be made for Paula Vogel. After having written numerous plays from the late seventies to the present, Vogel in 1992 won an Obie for *The Baltimore Waltz*, and, of course, *How I Learned to Drive*, recipient of the 1998 Pulitzer Prize, has with wild-fire rapidity spread throughout the regional and university theatre circuits. I would contend that Vogel's cresting visibility owes much to a marginalized sensibility that emphasizes compassion, empathy, responsibility – a standing-in-the-place-of the other. Prominent dramatists of the decade reflect a wide array of racial, ethnic, sexual, and gender categories (August Wilson, Tony Kushner, Suzan-Lori Parks, José Rivera, Terrence McNally, among others), suggesting a general critique of what has been termed white, male hetero-normativity. However, in Vogel's work, one does not find an impulse toward divisiveness or enclave-building. Rather, her vision is infused with a desire for inclusivity, what one critic has identified as "a Whitmanesque generosity."[4] Vogel's popularity attests to a growing fascination with new forms of community and confederation that do not operate under the rubric of "the same" but which nonetheless privilege empathetic relations. In light of the continued decentering of cultural consciousness that has been the consequence of identity politics (affiliations along the axes of race, ethnicity, gender, etc.) and the post-structuralist critique of identity categories, ethical regard for the other has been problematized in extreme fashion but revealed as a more-than-ever-vital matter of concern. We are thus challenged – by a sort of Levinasian ethic – to regard the face of difference and to respond to its call. This insistence on "relational" thinking is typified in the recent writing of the African–American feminist, bell hooks, whose *Stories of Love: New Visions* calls for the discarding of conventional paradigms in favor of emancipatory models that seek bonding in view of extreme otherness.[5]

Shepard has been grouped – often with unflattering implications – with David Rabe and David Mamet as a white male playwriting triad. Susan Harris Smith has characterized Shepard's writing as a "Baedeker to modern American male neuroses,"[6] and, indeed, Shepard's long-held interest in (if not valorization of) male aggression, alienation, sexual conquest, and violent display runs counter to the sensibility celebrated in the work of Vogel. However, though they inhabit worlds easily recognized as Shepard-inspired, his plays of the 1990s demonstrate an attitude that distinguishes them from his more famous work. In short, *States of Shock*, *Simpatico*, and *Eyes for Consuela* express a concern for interconnectedness that is new to his writing, one that militates against individualism and ego assertion. These plays expose the deleterious effects of self-absorption, of masculinist power-grabs, and reveal a yearning for mutuality. Shepard has evidenced interest in new explorations, permutations beyond male protagonists at each other's throat (and has in interviews admitted as much). This element in Shepard's work begs several questions. Is his decline in critical regard a result of his meager output, or the result of audience fatigue with his high-octane machismo? Or is there an implicit desire for the old Shepard, which prejudices reception of his more recent work? Has his interest in new relational modes been as yet unable to find compelling dramatic form? Can Shepard successfully develop his dramatic vision in a way that recognizes the hauntings of the American male without feeding the very demons he wishes to expel?

To illuminate the relational concerns of Shepard's recent plays, a brief look backward proves helpful, especially since the greater body of his work regards communal attachment and intimate involvements with keen suspicion. It is a commonplace of Shepard criticism to cite the author's obsession with rock stars, gangsters, jazz musicians, rodeo-riders, those who writhe under social constraint and seek liberation through either physical flight or identity transformation. For such characters, emblems of community are perceived as inhibiting if not tyrannical. In these plays one finds the impulse to shatter, a persistent drive to break social, familial, and cognitive structures, leading to an experience of "the self and the world as unfixed."[7]

In his review of *Simpatico* Eric Grode in a shorthand way describes the "typical" Shepard play as "men talking poetic between breaking stuff,"[8] and without doubt what has interested audiences has been the germ of destruction in Shepard's work. Critics early on recognized Shepard's propensity toward dismantling sets and props. For many, this sort of libidinal expenditure has come to essentialize Shepard's dramatic technique. If one invokes the hermeneutics of father/son contestation, this energy is principally transgressive. His plays dramatize an impulse to overthrow or escape the dominant order – all that goes under the aegis of the father (national mythologies, corporate capitalism, stable identities, attachment to the nuclear family, and so on) – and violence is frequently the outcome. In this light the Shepard hero executes what Georges Bataille would call an act of nonproductive expenditure.[9] In defiance of constraining social and identity structures he enacts a gesture of excessive expense, discharging an energy that defies mediation and utility. What we witness in a Shepard play is often a spell-binding "performance of waste,"[10] in which desperate characters act to negate the economy of the father, inaugurating in its place an order without equilibrium or any balance of exchange.

Shepard has on more than one occasion voiced his dislike of endings, and scholars writing on his work often frame this aspect in congratulatory terms, indicating the playwright's reluctance to follow conventional narrative structure. His irregular endings also reveal something rudimentary about his suspicion of communal relations. His works as a rule shatter without restoration. The central figures of Shepard's plays never find a harmonious balance. The gesture of Kent in *La Turista* typifies the avenue of wholesale flight. This path is followed by Eddie in *Fool for Love*, by Weston in *Curse of the Starving Class*, and by Hoss in *The Tooth of Crime*, who escapes via self-immolation. Another ending finds characters locked in an attenuated moment, bound in an antagonistic relation – note *Curse of the Starving Class*. Another common response is that of catatonic withdrawal, or slippage into dementia or infantilism (for example, Vince and his blanket in *Buried Child*).

In recently discussing Bach's melodies, Shepard disclosed an aspect of his own aesthetic/ethical inclination when he underscored that *fugue* "means to flee,"[11] for the trope of flight well illuminates the disposition of Shepard's drama and its dispersive tendencies, evident in his improvisatory aesthetic, his disavowal of realist psychology, and his preoccupation with shifting states. Such formal features have been privileged by many scholars, who laud the plays' many textures, emotional evocations, destabilized identities, and elliptical plotting. The impulse to break or flee seen in Shepard's dramatic technique and in the grain of his characters no doubt makes for compelling confrontations and riveting theatrical effects. But this impulse can serve not just as a motive force but as a constraint, rendering engagement difficult for his characters, especially in the matter of emotional intimacy and connection.

Shepard may be a master at conveying a sense of postmodern fracture, but admitting destabilized identities and fluid positionalities does not negate an ethical responsibility between self and other. Feminist criticism of Shepard's work has an ongoing history,[12] and chief among the charges made against him, outside of his peripheral interest in women characters, has been his inability to rethink human relations.[13] The playwright too frequently seems enmeshed in the economy of the father, with its dynamic of conquest and subjection, or intent on its overthrow (which produces fracture and estrangement). What his plays fail to deliver is any vision of reconstituted community, of an interconnectedness that operates outside of the sacrifice/exchange of the paternal order.

A Lie of the Mind (1985) stands as a pivotal play in Shepard's career, and its ambitions and shortcomings shed important light on the plays that would follow in the 1990s. The work on one level operates as a sort of self-critique, indicating the playwright's increasing awareness of the debilities attending masculinst codes and postures. In *A Lie of the Mind* the writer attempted to dramatize reconciliation, to explore what he once termed "the female side of things."[14] The play presents in the actions of Jake a performance of waste, yet the work looks toward appeasement, to an allaying of the "black hate" that stirs male paranoia and precipitates aggression and/or flight.

I would imagine that the moment in *A Lie of the Mind* most prized by Shepard involves Jake's prostrate confession before his estranged wife: "Everything in me lies. But you... You are true. I love you more than this life."[15] Such an expression of intimate feelings had not been witnessed before in a Shepard play. Jake appears vulnerable, defenseless, relieved of his machismo posturing. And the figure of Beth was read by many as a break-through character for Shepard, a different kind of woman, who speaks pre-sciently about the constructedness of gender. Despite what may have been Shepard's best intentions, the play strained and labored for effect. And de-spite the "feminist possibilities" some viewers detected, others took Shepard to task for inviting sympathy for and identification with Jake the wife-beater, who hands his wife over in chattel fashion to his younger brother. It was duly noted that Beth's insightfulness comes as a result of brain-damage consequent to her battering. One scholar in fact identified this work as "the most dis-turbing of the family plays" in its "treatment of women."[16] Coupled with an unusually mawkish moment – the flag-folding ritual between Baylor and Meg – Jake's closing sequence in *A Lie of the Mind* thus indicates a desire for reconciliation, without credible dramatization.

In retrospect, *A Lie of the Mind* seems Shepard's last attempt to write on the grand scale, to produce what might be considered a great American play. And with distance, the play's weaknesses become more evident. Yet one would be remiss to overlook the gestural attitude of the play and the play-wright's novel attempts to investigate the masculinist aversion to emotional intimacy, for this facet would prove the touchstone of the plays to follow in the 1990s. Perhaps Shepard himself recognized *A Lie of the Mind* as a failure on some level, either structurally or emotionally, and viewed this time in his career as suitable for a shift in orientation and focus. Whatever the reason, the playwright entered a hiatus after *A Lie of the Mind*, and six years would elapse before he would again bring a new play before the American public.

It was thus with much curiosity that audiences anticipated the opening of *States of Shock*, which premiered in the spring of 1991. Several aspects of the production indicate a tempered attitude on the part of the dramatist – this was no attempt to reach a theatrical mainstream, to score any great popular or commercial success. For this production Shepard returned to the familiar, smaller confines of the American Place Theatre, a venue whose history of collaboration with the playwright dated back to the 1967 production of *La Turista*. The size of the play itself expressed a shift in aim and ambition, as one-acts seldom garner the attention of full-length works.

States of Shock is an antiwar play, written upon the public euphoria at-tending the American military success in the Gulf War. The play is dominated by the figure of the Colonel (played by John Malkovich), who voices hawk-ish allegiance to jingoistic "principles" and "codes."[17] He is dressed in a pastiche of military styles and marks the anniversary of his son's death in combat by bringing a crippled war veteran, Stubbs, to an all-American style diner for ice cream. The establishment is populated by a waitress, Glory Bee, and two pallid customers, the White Man and White Woman, who remain at the edges of the play as cadaverous embodiments of mainstream consumer consciousness. Through the course of the piece, it becomes apparent that an unspecified war rages outside, threatening to intrude upon the sanctuary of the diner.

The emotional landscape of *States of Shock* is familiar to Shepard audiences, and the work's propelling tension issues from the interchange between the Colonel and Stubbs, who frequently lifts his shirt to expose a gaping red wound. The Colonel insists on learning the truth of his son's death and relentlessly questions Stubbs as to the details of the situation. What the Colonel cannot tolerate is Stubbs's continued assertion that he is in fact the Colonel's son, injured by "friendly fire," that is, shelling from his own forces (the play never confirms the truth of the blood-relation, though it is strongly implied). As the work progresses the Colonel's fury escalates, indicating his inability to accept the incapacitated state of his son and the dubious nature of the war enterprise.

The stylistic devices of the one-act, subtitled "a vaudeville nightmare," represent a radical shift from the lyrical realism of *A Lie of the Mind*. Frequently the action of the play comes to a halt; the audience is assailed by percussive blasts from offstage drummers and sound effects signaling the encroaching war, including explosions, tracer fire, and the whistle of rockets. Beyond this acoustic assault, the audience witnesses a succession of bizarre and comic enactments, as when the Colonel models for Glory Bee how to properly carry a tray of glasses, and when he later tosses spoonfuls of chocolate sundae maniacally about the stage. At one point the White Man masturbates beneath a napkin then falls to the floor in a delirium. Any pretense of a realistic frame is given over in the play's conclusion, when the characters in unison sing "Good Night, Irene."

Although such antics provide considerable humor, the play's attitude to war and its masculinist codes is deeply serious and condemning. Shepard recounted watching TV in a Kentucky bar, viewing images of the Gulf War on the screen, and feeling acute outrage: "I could not believe the systematic kind of insensitivity of it . . . the notion of this being a heroic event."[18] Perhaps more than any other of his writings, *States of Shock* exhibits a crusading fervor; the play is forthright in its indictment of militaristic enterprise and nationalistic allegiance. The Colonel serves as the perverse embodiment of this viewpoint. He expounds on "American virtue" and extols a panoply of national heroes, from the Pioneer to the Lone Ranger (24). In the name of the nation he justifies the bloodshed of history and argues the necessity of aggression.

Stubbs emerges as a challenger to the war mentality and the many denials of his father. He is frequently given Christ-like associations and speaks broodingly of his injury, which endows the world of the play with metaphoric fracture and disconnection. He utters: "The part of me that goes on living has no memory of the parts that are all dead. They've been separated for all time" (14). Curiously, his injury is often conveyed in terms of his sexual impotence. On more than one occasion he looks down at his lap and refers to his "dead meat" (12). And it is only when his libido returns that he can cast off his subordination; Stubbs regains his manhood by mounting and writhing on top of a supine Glory Bee. The ending of the play gives the audience an unsettlingly violent image, of Stubbs rising up and overthrowing the Colonel, sword drawn; the image is frozen though the expectation is obvious – the son will literally sever the head of the father.

While the play envisioned itself as an extravagantly theatrical (and passionate) polemic on the masculinist mind-set, its impact was muted. *States of Shock* received some tempered praise, though its run at the American Place Theatre was undistinguished and disappointing. Richard Hornby cited the "endless tedium" of the piece and how a theatregoer actually booed at the play's conclusion.[19] Mimi Kramer pronounced the production "strictly for those who remain convinced that Shepard is a genius."[20] Many were rather surprised by the sentential nature of the writing. The play was criticized for its heavy-handedness, propagandistic intent, leaden symbols, and "oped declamations."[21]

Susanne Willadt has written insightfully on *States of Shock* and locates its failure in different terms. For Willadt, the play demonstrates that Shepard has "become a victim of his most prominent personal and artistic obsessions,"[22] trapped by his preoccupation with machismo and his overriding interest in male-to-male relations. In this view Stubbs rightly rebels against the injurious attitudes of the father, yet his only recourse is an embrace and perpetuation of aggression. According to Willadt, "to achieve a male identity, and this is what the play is primarily about, Shepard still sees no other way than to continue the ancient male tradition of competitiveness, machismo and violence which finally leads to war."[23]

Questions stirred by *States of Shock* have far-reaching implications and in a pointed way indicate an aesthetic and intellectual dilemma for the playwright, who in this play clearly wished to forward a statement against economies of domination. As Shepard has moved from a rather uncritical dramatization of male interaction to a more self-aware exploration of masculinist postures, one may justifiably ask what insight has been gained. Something of an impasse arises if no alternative relations are conceived or modeled, especially in light of the fact that Stubbs must employ violence to quell the violence of his father. Beyond the intellectual or ethical aspects of this matter, questions of aesthetic form come to the fore. How can Shepard dramatize eruptive masculine power-plays (his bread and butter) without valorizing, or at least making entertaining, those demonstrations? Are those features the very elements that audiences wish to see – expect to see – in a Shepard play?

The willful experimentation of *States of Shock* also merits consideration. One reading interprets the play's stylistics as a retrogressive move on Shepard's part, a kind of anxious groping, as though creative doubt had afflicted the playwright and had precipitated a return to once-fruitful devices and strategies. This view is implied by Frank Rich, who suspected Shepard of "hibernating since his East Village emergence in the Vietnam era."[24] To the contrary, David DeRose welcomed this turn in Shepard's writing as a much-desired departure from the more conventional style of his family plays. For DeRose, the exuberant experimentation confirmed Shepard's "renegade" spirit. In this light *States of Shock* indicated a "rejuvenation" of the dramatist's "impassionate (and somewhat reckless) theatrical genius"[25] and portended better days ahead.

For Shepard and his admirers this prognostication was somewhat off-base, as Shepard would offer only two other new plays in the decade. It was 1994 when Shepard's next work appeared, the full-length *Simpatico*, and the play experienced inauspicious complications before ever reaching an audience. For years many observers of the American theatre had noted – with frequent dismay – that its greatest practicing playwright had never witnessed his work on a Broadway stage (save for a segment in *Oh! Calcutta!*). In the early 1990s Shepard, exhibiting a restoration of ambition, set about rectifying this situation and worked to showcase his new play *Simpatico* in the Broadway market. However, the playwright, while still recognized as a luminary among American dramatists, was unable to raise the $800,000 needed to launch the production.[26] Shepard experienced considerable logistical frustration, complained openly about financial constraints, and finally aborted the venture. He agreed to have the work produced at the New York Public Theatre under his own direction.

Set amid the world of racetracks and high-stakes horse breeding, *Simpatico* represents Shepard's return to a broader canvas and a more realistic frame. At its heart the story of *Simpatico* is one of blackmail and betrayal, much in the tradition of *film noir*. Constructed chiefly in the form of two-person scenes, the play focuses on the contestation of its two male principals, Vinnie and Carter, long-time friends bound by a past crime. The pair, with the aid of Rosie, then wife of Vinnie, now wife of Carter, once lured a racing official into an adulterous situation, with blackmail pictures resulting. The action of the play begins many years after this scheme, and we see that Carter has become a successful businessman in Kentucky, with all the trappings of affluence – "Green swimming pool. White Mercedes. Blue car phone,"[27] as Vinnie reminds him. Supported by Carter, Vinnie lives in near destitution in Cucamonga, California. The dramatic turbulence of the play stems from Vinnie's sudden desire to come clean with Simms, the victim of the blackmail scheme, and overthrow his former buddy. The play's action moves fitfully, often with a cultivated ambiguity, as we view the characters in vertiginous states, moving from one set of provisional coordinates to another.

Simpatico generates much of its dramatic tension from its geographical bifurcation, and Shepard's handling of locales serves to contrast relational options and identity commitments. Cucamonga's desert remove represents a nexus of relations, of personal histories, that has receded into the past. Vinnie resides near to where he grew up, but his present situation serves less to connect him with his former life than to highlight the gap between then and now. The location, a sort of no man's land, signifies Vinnie's unmoored condition and reflects his profound isolation. According to stage directions the windows of his domicile "look out into black space. No trees. No build-ings" (5). Vinnie describes where he has been living as the "edge of nowhere" (16).

Kentucky conversely conveys an ostensible sense of centrality and connect-edness. It is presented as the locus of the American heartland, functioning much like the home-site of *Buried Child*. The Kentucky Derby proves a useful synecdochic device, linking the race to a complex of wider signifi-cations of American identity. It evokes notions of native tradition, agrarian wholesomeness, and national pride. Carter, however, regards the event rather sardonically and mocks those who attend: "They all want to be part of it. They're all dying to belong to something old and rooted in the American earth" (62). Such commentary points to the hollowness of mythic emblems, to the layers of nationalistic simulacra which finally offer no foundation for identity of communal involvement. The two locales together convey a bleak prospect, suggesting that commitments and belonging are tenuous, provisional, and often illusory.

As seen in such works as *La Turista*, *The Tooth of Crime*, and *True West*, one of Shepard's most utilized dramatic devices involves setting two male characters in opposition and precipitating a reversal. In *Simpatico*, Vinnie travels to Kentucky, hoping to undermine Carter's status and win back his former wife. Threatened with disclosure, Carter emotionally unrav-els and takes up residence in the Cucamonga hovel. At the play's conclusion, when Carter begs to remain in Vinnie's bed, Vinnie severs their relationship, snarling: "You can die with your tongue hanging out. I don't give a shit" (94). He summarily puts on his detective accouterment and steps into his imaginary life as a private investigator. Carter convulses on the floor, in a fetal position, laboring to ignore the cellphone ringing in his briefcase.

A few of the early reviews of *Simpatico* offered tempered praise; Vincent Canby believed the work revealed Shepard's writing "at his distinctive, savage best."[28] While some reviewers found elements both to commend and censure, a repeated line of criticism cited the play's narrative murkiness and its lack of payoff; the work tantalized but remained obscure, causing the play to lumber and ultimately wear down its viewers. Richard Zoglin's comment typifies the general disappointment experienced by critics and audiences alike: "[This is] Sam Shepard country, all right, a place of blasted American dreams and macho power games . . . there was a time when that country was an essential stop on any tour of the American theatre. No longer. *Simpatico*, Shepard's first new full-length play in nearly a decade, is a pretty arid stretch of land."[29]

Michael Feingold observed that *Simpatico*, which is perhaps too reminiscent of *True West*, sets forth material seen in earlier plays though in a less satisfying, somewhat "pallid" manner. He likened the drama to a "B-movie script by someone who's read a lot of Shepard."[30] Such criticism underscores the difficulty Shepard faced as a maturing playwright and the perception that a snuffing of his creative fire had forced him to reach into his bag of playwriting tricks and offer familiar material retooled. It is moreover curious that critics frequently employed euphemisms for impotence (slow, flabby, lazy, lugubrious, flaccid) to characterize Shepard's writing, as if the playwright's imagination had become afflicted with a sort of erectile dysfunction.

Though Shepard has certainly presented recycled material in his recent plays, these works operate somewhat differently, offering a more incisive degree of masculinist critique, a feature which may ironically work to the detriment of the play's theatrical and dramatic allure. That the playwright has concerned himself with social bonding and the ethics of relations is indicated by the very title *Simpatico*, with its associations of connectedness and harmonious alliance. The title of course generates ironies, inasmuch as the play is nothing if not a chronicle of dissolution. Still, the notion of empathetic relations hovers about the work in specter-fashion, desired though never materialized.

Simpatico replays the standard Shepard dynamic that propels his male characters to radical postures or states of consciousness that rend communal bonds. Recalling Bataille's concept of nonproductive expenditure, we see Shepard orchestrating, through Carter especially, the overthrow of the productive economy and the utilitarian ethic that measures social interaction according to a calculus of accumulation. Carter undertakes a performance of waste – jettisoning the rewards and retributions of Kentucky – and proceeds to a state of absolute loss. Carter declares to Vinnie, "I'm going to disappear" (92), and, shivering under his blanket, on the floor in Cucamonga, Carter has, on some level, succeeded.

What distinguishes *Simpatico* and serves to introduce a new element to Shepard's vision of human relations is the intriguing character of Simms, described by one critic as "the play's benign conscience."[31] Ever circumspect and watchful, Simms resides in Lexington, makes a modest living for himself, and has seemingly overcome the tragic turn that befell him earlier in his California life, when blackmail cost him his career, family, and name. When Vinnie comes to his Kentucky office, offering the means to release him from Carter's control, Simms behaves most cautiously. He discusses casual sexual impropriety and how "justice" operates according to no rightful system of balance and exchange, yet he admits no desire for recompense or restitution. What Vinnie cannot understand is Simms's lack of animus, his withdrawal from the logic of revenge. Simms asks his visitor: "Why is blood more appealing than re-birth?" (46), and the latter cannot respond. While the play dramatizes Carter's absolute loss in the present tense, in Simms we see a character who, despite his former loss, which he describes as "a powerful elixir" (40), has proceeded elsewhere, eschewing paralysis, dementia, or infantilism. Simms has denounced the economy of competition and profit and the violence it breeds, but does not allow the seed of vengeance to find ground in himself.

A strangely affecting moment occurs when Cecilia, an attractive though impressionable grocery clerk from Cucamonga, comes to Simms's office, believing that he has the negatives of the incriminating photos (she has been cajoled into the visit by Carter). Simms first prostrates himself before Cecilia in mocking fashion, believing her to be party to another entrapment. However, through a sometimes awkward and painful exchange the two come to a revelation of truth about one another and their intentions. Cecilia realizes that she has been duped by Carter. Simms verbalizes his longing for companionship. A clarity results and the two share an odd emotional intimacy. The moment is brief but conspicuous in its singularity. Though Cecilia does not consent, Simms proffers a poignant option – that next year they should join each other at the Kentucky Derby; he states: "I'll meet you at the Clubhouse Turn" (85). Simms executes a gesture that is uncommon in Shepard's world – he leaves open the possibility for connection, for involvement that admits no coercion or domination.

Though he continued to write new plays, albeit on an infrequent basis, public and critical attention in the mid-1990s focused less on Shepard the still-practicing playwright than Shepard the icon (with established persona and repute). Two events following soon after the run of *Simpatico* contributed significantly to this retrospective regard of the dramatist: the revival of *Buried Child* and the 1996–97 Signature Theatre season.

In 1996 the Steppenwolf Company, which had been responsible for salvaging the reputation of *True West* after its troubled New York début, brought its energetic and engaging production of *Buried Child* to Broadway, proving the first occasion in the playwright's thirty-some year career that one of his plays was showcased in a Broadway venue. The play was in fact nominated for a Tony award for best new play. Directed by Gary Sinise, this production demonstrated once again the great compatibility of Shepard's drama and the Steppenwolf performance aesthetic. The effort was abetted by Shepard himself, who revised the play's script, alternately clarifying or omitting some of the original's narrative obfuscation. The success the production experienced in Chicago was replicated in New York, and critics wrote almost unanimously of the play's merit and achievement. It was cited as the best of Shepard's family dramas and hailed as a classic, "a play for the ages."[32] The effusive praise gave confirmation that the work had securely found its way into the fold of American canonical drama.

Renewed adulation was heaped upon the dramatist. Shepard, who had for decades been represented as an avant garde experimenter, found himself in the company of those dramatists mentioned most often and most casually as the great American playwrights of the post-World War II era. An unintentional aspect of this phenomenon, however, was the tendency to view Shepard's career as a concluded event, representing a distinctive phase in the history of the American theatre. Shepard's past work and achievement were brought to the fore, which served to marginalize his plays after *A Lie of the Mind*. The Steppenwolf production thus helped trigger a reconsideration of Shepard's accomplishment, and his career was rightfully celebrated in many quarters, but the effect was something like that of a retirement party; Shepard had become a grand old man of the theatre.

This perception was galvanized by New York's Signature Theatre, which selected Shepard as its featured playwright for 1996–97. Led by James Houghton, the Signature Theatre had earned great respect for its practice of dedicating an entire season to the works of an individual playwright. The company had previously honored such writers as Adrienne Kennedy, Romulus Linney, and Lee Blessing. The two dramatists, however, who gained most from the Signature's endorsement were Edward Albee and Horton Foote. In both instances, the attention each playwright received proved instrumental in the artist's resurgence and consequent rise in critical reputation. For Albee, the Signature season helped bring an end to a long drought that had seen scant production activity in New York. The attention he received helped set the stage for the following, highly praised *Three Tall Women*, which won Albee his third Pulitzer in 1994, and the acclaimed revival of *A Delicate Balance*. Similarly for Foote, the Signature season placed his work and lengthy career in the limelight. Foote offered his new play, *The Young Man from Atlanta*, as an entry in the Signature season, and shortly thereafter the piece was awarded the 1995 Pulitzer Prize for drama.[33]

The Signature Theatre also succeeded in bringing Sam Shepard and his work into critical conversation. The company chose to highlight an array of Shepard's efforts, not simply his more famous family plays. The season involved four installments: (1) a double bill of *When the World Was Green* and *Chicago*; (2) *The Tooth of Crime*; (3) a triple bill of *The Sad Lament of Pecos Bill on the Eve of Killing His Wife*, *Action*, and *Killer's Head*; and (4) *Curse of the Starving Class*. The productions generated much discussion about the achievement of Shepard's career, the different stylistic phases of his writing, and his representation of various moments in American cultural history. Reviews were mixed. Many critics enjoyed the opportunity to see his early work staged again, though some viewed these efforts as puerile and inconsequential. The greatest disappointment came with *The Tooth of Crime* (staged in the Lucille Lortel Theatre, a prominent commercial Off-Broadway house), which was almost universally recognized as a disaster. No runaway hits ensued from the Signature season, but the overall undertaking was credited as a success, offering a provocative range of pieces, staged with varying degrees of accomplishment.

While one can in part attribute the resurgence of Albee and Foote to the Signature Theatre company's endorsement and promotion, the revival of Shepard's work did not yield a similar harvest. In the cases of Albee and Foote, the season not only celebrated past accomplishment but helped bring attention to new works by the authors, pieces which found favorable reception on their own terms. In the instance of Shepard, the playwright's status as a still-active dramatist was minimized. In fact, the company had commissioned Shepard to produce a new play for the last installment of the season; when no new script materialized the company inserted *Curse of the Starving Class* in its place. Moreover, Shepard became something of an elder by association. The ages of Foote and Albee – with whom Shepard was often mentioned – gave the impression that the triumvirate were senior members of the American playwriting elite, graying statesmen from another time and era. Though unintended, the retrospective nature of the undertaking brought with it something of a commemorative effect.

The attention and adulation Shepard received during the mid-1990s failed to inspire any major new work. If one contrasts the ambition of *A Lie of the Mind* a dozen years earlier – evidenced in its high-profile commercial staging, with star actors and national publicity – to the rather unpretentious appearance of *Eyes for Consuela*, Shepard's final new play of the 1990s, the modest dimension of his current writing seems striking. Opening in February of 1998, this production utilized actors with no great Hollywood visibility. Showcased at the Manhattan Theatre Club, an establishment with repute as a playwright's laboratory, the piece was staged in the theatre's smaller studio space. And the play is an adaptation of another writer's work, *The Blue Bouquet*, a short story by Octavio Paz. Though Shepard's drama varies significantly from the source material, the effort signifies a novel turn for the author. The exercise can be understood in different ways. Given that Shepard has always taken pride in his originality and the adventurous aspect of the creative enterprise, the move to adaptation could be viewed as a symptom of a faltering muse. The modest scope of the play also may indicate the playwright's unwillingness to assume the burden of writing as some sort of playwright laureate. The drama has the appearance of a diversion, a curiosity piece undertaken as a lark. But it may be that this sort of creative exercise and the lesser degree of expectations it engenders offered the playwright a new freedom, and new territory for the investigation of modalities and attitudes not developed in prior work.

A synopsis of *Eyes for Consuela* reveals elements recognizable to those who have followed Shepard's career. The play's action occurs in a rustic hotel deep in the Mexican jungle, where a beleaguered American wages emotional battle with a spectral presence and a maniacal villager. Hints of *La Turista*, *Back Bog Beast Bait*, *Seduced*, and other earlier work lurk in the piece. As one critic explained, the play "appears to have the right formula for a wild Shepard adrenaline-pumper: a tropical jungle, a bottle of tequila, two desperate men and an angry ghost."[34] Yet, the piece in tone and impact varies significantly from Shepard's earlier work. It finally veers away from the volcanic moment that would send the play into some fevered surreality; the piece at end is quiet, contemplative, more philosophical than percussive.

At the center of *Eyes for Consuela* one finds Henry, the American businessman who has taken refuge in a Mexican hotel to wrangle with his life choices. As the play opens he awakens from a nightmare and speaks of his dislocation, his disquietude. He later confesses to feeling "completely alone."[35] In this jungle solitude, he regrets the dissolution of his marriage (his estranged wife is stationed in the wintery blanket of Michigan). He also questions his career and the venality of the capitalist marketplace. With some self-loathing he identifies his God by the names "prestige," "power," "real estate," and "the Dow" (32). The dramatic tension of the play is incited by the arrival of Amado, a native of the area, who confronts Henry and holds him captive, threatening from time to time to cut out his eyes. Though the interchange between these two takes turns toward the violent, their discussion is chiefly reflective. They talk of life, of love, and the things that stir passion and commitment.

Henry fears his captor yet is fascinated by his utterly different world view. Amado, who once illegally crossed into the US for the lure of commodities – such as tennis shoes, televisions, even gringo women – expounds upon America's dispiriting effect: "In America everything is easy. Sex. Movies. Drugs. It becomes easy to forget yourself. To eat candy. To move farther and farther away from your heart" (24). Henry at times takes the prerogative of asserting American supremacy, though he finally gives over patronizing postures and recognizes the validity of Amado's pronouncements. He works to engage Amado, astonished by his passion, which he has in abundance, and questions him about his remarkable surety. Amado obliges and identifies his need to honor Consuela's peculiar whim; as Amado explains, "She wants a bouquet of blue eyes" (10).

Near the end of the first act Henry voices an admission of guilt and attempts to explain the faltering relationship with his wife: "She was her own person. And I – wanted that – that thing – whatever it was she had. I wanted to take it away from her and make it my own" (33). These sentiments echo feelings of jealousy experienced by Jake in *A Lie of the Mind*, though Henry is more conscious of his tendencies and more articulate in expression. Quite simply, he has come to an emotional impasse, unable to find any detour around the compulsion to control that has crippled his relations.

Recognizing Henry's tortured condition, Amado remarks: "Love is outside your language. You have lost the word" (19). In large measure the play is about Henry's bereft state and his subsequent emotional awakening. It should not, however, be thought that Amado's example is put forth as one to emulate. He tells Henry early on how he shot and killed Consuela's father in a reckless moment of celebration; later, Viego, the innkeeper, relates the truth, that Amado accidentally killed Consuela herself and seeks men's eyes as propitiation for his own inner turmoil.

Henry's redemption follows upon an encounter with Consuela, with whom he has come to feel an intuitive bond. He claims to know the pain that feeds her unusual desire, and when asked why he wishes to come face to face with Consuela, Henry answers: "Because I'm in sympathy with her!" (44). Though a spirit, Consuela appears, and just at the point of the victimage ritual, the knifing of the eyes, she relents and Henry is released. He steps away changed. The elder Viego offers the prediction: "When you return to Michigan, you will see the snow with new eyes" (47).

The deployment of the Consuela figure does not prove any new facility in Shepard's drawing of female characters or any seismic shift in his understanding of female consciousness. Consuela speaks only a few lines in the play and most often dances mysteriously in the jungle shadows. She is chiefly a cipher, representing an unknowable, alternate mode of perceiving. And her call for the eyes of men certainly links her with a castratory threat, exacting from men the organ of sight and emblem of the gaze. But in his encounter with Consuela, who takes pity on him, Henry does experience an emotional conversion; he determines to trek to Michigan and seek reconciliation with his wife.

This turn in Henry is unusual for a Shepard character. Though he is less vivid and engaging than Simms in *Simpatico*, the two men share similar experiences. Each undergoes a traumatic loss that reorders his world. Each flees the contexts of a former identity and lives in something of a schizoid suspension. Each at end manages an attempt at reconnection. Had *Eyes for Consuela* been written earlier in Shepard's career, it is likely that the play would have carried no further than the end of the first act, with a benighted Henry propelled to a point of dissociation, drunk on tequila, and curled up on the hotel-room floor. It is perhaps a sign of Shepard's shifting interest as a playwright that he continues the action of the play into a second act, allowing Henry to redirect his emotional compass and to seek a new order of commitment and intimacy.

Carla McDonough has observed how Shepard's women reside at the edges of his plays while the men take center stage. Yet, according to McDonough, it is only "in the margins that any hope for survival is offered."[36] All too commonly in Shepard's plays men allow themselves to be consumed by their compulsions, their fantasies and paranoias, always to their peril. The end of *Eyes for Consuela* is an anomaly in Shepard's writing, for it demonstrates the male's movement toward the female's space; Henry will exit his jungle seclusion and meet with his wife in the north. The play leaves the audience with pregnant expectation, of emotional fruition never before imagined in a Shepard play. The ending is optimistic, strangely affirmative. Critics noted this turn and what it might presage. Ben Brantley speculated that "the humble spirit of forgiveness" and "the emotional change at work" in the drama might "lead this playwright, one of America's best, into a new fertile territory."[37]

Though intriguing and novel in many respects, *Eyes for Consuela* is no great play. Critics were surprised by its meditative tone and lengthy reflective passages. The play was chided for its "self-consciousness." It was reported that the drama "only occasionally blooms into something alive."[38] What *Eyes for Consuela* delivers is a philosophical Shepard, who at times rambles over-long (the ensuing production at the Magic Theatre in San Francisco was compressed into a one-act). The play's lead figure is rather vague and somewhat antiseptic. The work's comment on love and emotional involvement can seem trite, and the jungle remove all too easily yields a romantic primitivism. Still, Shepard does tread new dramatic and emotional terrain, weighing in on the side of conciliation rather than that of anger and estrangement. It is a new vision, a story of love.

In attempting to contextualize Sam Shepard in the last decade of American theatre history, one finds that he is rather a man out of time. What has brought him fame and success as a dramatist have been his high-octane explorations of the American male psyche, conveyed in dazzling spectacles of ego anarchy. This mode of performance perhaps better suited the sensibility of the 1980s, an era marked by keen institutional suspicion, pro-market individualism, feminist backlash, and gunslinger politics, an era known more for its selfishness than its empathy (it is no coincidence that Shepard came to national prominence in the 1980s, a time recognized as the highwater mark of republican conservatism). But the American theatre of the 1990s embraced new concerns, new orientations, and consequently favored different imaginings of cultural consciousness. One may consider Paula Vogel and Tony Kushner as the decade's book-end dramatists, Vogel the representative of the decade's conclusion, Kushner its beginning. In his monumental *Angels in America*, Kushner castigates Reagan's America and its individualistic preoccupations. It is telling that in a 1994 interview he characterized Reagan as an "ego-anarchist,"[39] a phrase that in an uncanny way identifies something essential in Shepard's dramatic imagination. If I were to choose one image that best represents the theme of empathy and interconnectedness in the 1990s, it would be Harper's visionary monologue at the end of *Perestroika*, when Harper tells of seeing all the dead of the earth, from all times and nations, rising up and joining hands – forming "a great net of souls" – which fills the ozone hole and protects future generations.

This moment is no doubt visionary and utopian, but the ethical bonding – the responsibility for the other – that is evident in both the works of Vogel and Kushner signifies a conceptual transition in the American theatre. Their plays dramatize generosity and inclusivity, the often painful and troubled achievement of reaching beyond borders and the preoccupations of the self. These writers have responded to the profound dilemma of extending outward, of offering empathetic association in the face of difference, without appeal to ontological foundations, without appeal to fixed categories of identity. And in this light, the plays that have brought Shepard his fame can seem limited, ethically stunted. We see the explosion of communal connection, the Shepardian hero seeking liberation and open horizons. For the greater part of Shepard's writing, an adolescent sensibility prevails. His plays succeed in generating terror in virtue of the destruction unleashed – the dismantling of identities, attachments, and familial structures (something akin to an

Artaudian cruelty), and hence his often cited rapport with "the mythic." Yet the world Shepard establishes offers no reimagined possibilities, ethically or socially. And given the preponderance of destruction – that is often gleeful – in his work the effect is as much farcical as tragic.

Shepard's plays of the 1990s have incorporated attitudes and dramatizations that run contrary to the dynamic described above. The playwright is nonetheless celebrated for his pre-nineties work; note the lavishly praised revival on Broadway in 2000 of *True West*. Setting this production of *True West* alongside the Manhattan Theatre Club offering of *Eyes for Consuela*, one can see two Shepards – the then and now – which represent two distinct points in the playwright's maturation. This coupling also suggests something of the double-bind in which the playwright finds himself. *True West* has come to represent the quintessential Shepard, with its feuding brothers, its articulation of Western lore (and its evacuation), and its spectacular destruction of the suburban home-site. It may be that many theatregoers and critics assess any other of Shepard's works according to this arbiter, which by and large casts his plays of the 1990s in unflattering light, in that they fail to summon the explosive energy and the detailed nuance of the male psychology under extreme duress. Any new work by the playwright – especially as it models new relationships or philosophical concerns – may be consequently viewed as suspect, as a falling away from Shepard's more passionate and inspired writing. It may be thought that Shepard has somehow lost his nerve, lost his edge.

In pursuing a more self-conscious masculine critique and new relational modes, with novel power differentials and engagements with otherness (and I do believe this to be the direction of Shepard's plays of the 1990s), Shepard has undertaken a new path in his playwriting career, one that is certainly more in line with the sensibility of the decade. One may applaud Shepard's daring in his attempt to move beyond his former work, but the fact remains that these pieces – *States of Shock*, *Simpatico*, and *Eyes for Consuela* – have not been perceived as important works, or even good theatre. That could be in part due to critics' and audiences' inability to allow for a new sensibility in Shepard's writing, their insistence on judging Shepard according to his past efforts. The tepid response to these plays could also be attributed to a genuine failure of these works to successfully dramatize the issues and perspectives Shepard wishes to evoke; the great variance in styles between the three plays may suggest a kind of creative stammering. Frequently a writer's gift is also what proves that writer's limitation, and it is perhaps Shepard's lot to be a dramatist of male assertion and anxiety; in moving beyond this purview the muse for Shepard may vanish. His plays of the 1990s may evidence a wiser, more reflective, more philosophical playwright, one more open to ethical responsibility, but that sort of rumination – in Shepard's case – may simply not translate into the creation of compelling drama.

Two instances in Shepard's recent work bear mention as supportive evidence for the playwright's reflective turn. The first is *When the World Was Green*, subtitled *A Chef's Fable*, which presents conversations between a woman interviewer and an old man, a former chef, now on death-row, sentenced for poisoning a presumed enemy – the woman's father. The play argues against ancient hostilities and blood feuds and upholds the curative power of forgiveness. Stephen J. Bottoms provocatively describes the effort as "a kind of culinary prayer for the next millennium."[40] The second concerns Shepard's revision of *The Tooth of Crime* (subtitled *The Second Dance*) which appeared in the Signature Theatre season. Though the production was not regarded as a success, the changes Shepard introduced to the text are illuminating. Don Shewey points to Shepard's refashioning of Hoss and how the play's conflict between the elder rocker and his gypsy-challenger Crow becomes less an agonistic struggle between two embattled, overweening egos than a process of becoming, a process of connecting, in which Hoss awakens to see himself in Crow. Shewey writes of these changes in spiritual terms and concludes that the revision achieves a Buddha-like perspective.[41] What these instances underscore is Shepard's increased attention to questions of human relations; in his graying as a dramatist he thus reveals himself as a more meditative writer, one perhaps more concerned with connecting than disrupting. Shepard has never been particularly adept at conveying emotional intimacy, of dramatizing any sort of compassion or charity that transforms interpersonal bonds, that revisions the economy of relations – this may be the challenge the playwright has set for himself.

If one wishes to be generous with the playwright, this feature of Shepard's recent work should be highlighted, and applauded. And audiences of Shepard's plays may perforce alter certain expectations. And at the risk of keeping Shepard folded within the narrative of great master playwrights, one might allow him the possibility to evolve. It might yet be that Shepard can in Prospero-fashion conjure new modalities in the breach of the American male psyche. For Shepard and his audiences, one can hope for braver, newer worlds to come.

NOTES

1 Carol Rosen, "Emotional Territory: an Interview with Sam Shepard," *Modern Drama*, 36.1 (1993): 1.
2 John Lahr, "The Theatre: Review of *Simpatico*," *The New Yorker*, 5 December 1994, 128.

3 Jeremy Gerard, "Review: *Simpatico*," *Daily Variety*, 21 November 1994, 44.

4 Christopher Bigsby, *Contemporary American Playwrights* (Cambridge University Press, 1999), 329.

5 bell hooks, *Stories of Love: New Visions* (New York: William Morrow, 2000).

6 Susan Harris Smith, "En-Gendering Violence: Twisting 'Privates' in the Public Eye," in Matthew Roudané (ed.), *Public Issues, Private Tensions: Contemporary American Drama* (New York: AMS Press, 1993), 116.

7 David J. DeRose, *Sam Shepard* (New York: Twayne, 1992), ix.

8 Eric Grode, "Review: *Simpatico*," *Back Stage*, 28 February 1997, 48.

9 See Georges Bataille, *Visions of Excess*, trans. by Allan Stoekl (Minneapolis: University of Minnesota Press, 1985), 116–29.

10 This term is used by Joseph Roach in "Mardi Gras Indians and Others: Genealogies of American Performance," *Theatre Journal*, 44.4 (1992): 461–83.

11 Shepard, quoted in Mona Simpson, Jeanne McCulloch, and Benjamin Howe, "Sam Shepard: the Art of Theatre XII," *Paris Review*, 142 (Spring 1997): 222.

12 For a collection of feminist analyses and contentions on Shepard, a good sampling can be found in Leonard Wilcox (ed.), *Rereading Shepard* (New York: St. Martin's Press, 1993). See essays by Ann C. Hall, Susan Bennett, Jane Ann Crum, and Felicia Hardison Londré. A review of the feminist criticism of Shepard is also given in Susanne Willadt, "States of War in Sam Shepard's *States of Shock*," *Modern Drama*, 36.1 (1993): 147–66.

13 See Lynda Hart, "Sam Shepard's Spectacle of Impossible Heterosexuality: *Fool for Love*," in June Schlueter (ed.), *Feminist Rereadings of Modern American Drama* (Rutherford, NJ: Farleigh Dickinson University Press, 1989), 217.

14 Shepard, quoted in Kevin Sessums, "Sam Shepard: Geography of a Horse Dreamer," *Interview*, September 1988, 76.

15 Sam Shepard, *A Lie of the Mind and The War in Heaven* (New York: New American Library, 1987), 129.

16 Carla McDonough, "The Politics of Stage Space: Women and Male Identity in Sam Shepard's Family Plays," *Journal of Dramatic Theory and Criticism*, 9.2 (1995): 75. For another negative reading of the play, see Sue-Ellen Case, "Towards a Butch–Femme Aesthetic," in Lynda Hart (ed.), *Making a Spectacle: Feminist Readings on Contemporary Women's Theatre* (Ann Arbor: University of Michigan Press, 1989), 297.

17 Sam Shepard, *States of Shock*, in *States of Shock; Far North; Silent Tongue: A Play and Two Screenplays* (New York: Vintage Books, 1993), 27. Page references in parentheses within the text are to this edition.

18 Shepard, quoted in Rosen, "Emotional Territory," 9.

19 Richard Hornby, "Broadway Economics," *Hudson Review*, 44 (1991): 458.

20 Mimi Kramer, "Theatre: Toxic Shock," *The New Yorker*, 3 June 1991, 78.

21 Jack Kroll, "Sam Shepard Tosses Grenade," *Newsweek*, 27 May 1991, 57.

22 Willadt, "States of War," 148.

23 Ibid., 162.

24 Frank Rich, "Review/Theatre: Sam Shepard Returns, on War and Machismo," *New York Times*, 17 May 1991, Section C, 1.

25 DeRose, *Sam Shepard*, 137.

26 For more on the problems attending the effort to bring *Simpatico* to Broadway, see Mel Gussow, "A Play Lies Fallow," *New York Times*, 27 December 1993, Section C, 11.

27 Sam Shepard, *Simpatico* (New York: Dramatists Play Service, 1995), 12. Page references in parentheses within the text are to this edition.

28 Vincent Canby, "Sam Shepard Goes to the Races and Wins," *New York Times*, 20 November 1994, Section 2, 5.

29 Richard Zoglin, "Arid Country," *Time*, 28 November 1994, 82.

30 Michael Feingold, "Loner Stars," *Village Voice*, 22 November 1994, 77.

31 Canby, "Sam Shepard goes to the Races," 5.

32 Ben Brantley, "Theatre Review: Sam Shepard Revival Gets Him to Broadway," *New York Times*, 1 May 1996, Section C, 15.

33 For information on the Signature Theatre see Liz Welch, "Theatre: Choosing the Playwrights Who Can Go Home Again," *New York Times*, 17 November 1996, Section 2, 8.

34 Ben Brantley, "Theatre Review: When Love Is Blinding As Well As Blind," *New York Times*, 11 February 1998, Section E, 1.

35 Sam Shepard, *Eyes for Consuela* (New York: Dramatists Play Service, 1999), 9. Page references in parentheses within the text are to this edition.

36 McDonough, "Politics of Stage Space," 65.

37 Brantley, "When Love is Blinding," 1.

38 Greg Evans, "Review: *Eyes for Consuela*," *Variety*, 16 February 1998, 68.

39 Kushner, quoted in David Savran, "Tony Kushner Considers the Longstanding Problems of Virtue and Happiness," *American Theatre*, October 1994, 27.

40 Stephen J. Bottoms, *The Theatre of Sam Shepard: States of Crisis* (Cambridge University Press, 1998), 266.

41 Don Shewey, "Sam Shepard's Identity Dance," *American Theatre*, July/August 1997, 16.

16

MATTHEW ROUDANÉ

Sam Shepard's *The Late Henry Moss*

Sam Shepard's last work of the twentieth century, *The Late Henry Moss*, returns to the first subjects that long ago shaped the playwright's moral imagination. The play, Shepard says, "concerns another predicament between brothers and fathers and it's mainly the same material I've been working over for thirty years or something, but for me it never gets old."[1] The familiar material, of course, negotiates the problematic condition of the American family and its wayward inhabitants. As seen in so many Shepard plays, questions of heredity, legacy, and legitimacy animate the stage, as do the status of the real and the ways in which the individual subjectivizes his or her own version of reality. Competing versions of reality, conflicting accounts of what precisely happened to Henry Moss and others who came within his orbit in the days preceding his demise fill the stage. The drama raises debates about individual, familial, and cultural identity and memory, as it does about the relationship between abstract and concrete experience, fiction and reality, and, ultimately, about coming to terms with death itself. Shepard layers such debates with additional complexity and ambiguity by presenting the play's lead character as a ghost. As Shepard explains, *The Late Henry Moss* concerns "the father, who is dead in the play and comes back, who's revisiting the past. He's a ghost – which has always fascinated me."[2] This is a play about a dead man walking. It is equally a play about a family afflicted by the inevitability of their lamentable biological and spiritual fate. Whereas in the earlier Pulitzer Prize play the buried child never had a chance to live, the about-to-be buried father in *The Late Henry Moss* lived for nearly seven decades, though his phantasmic presence redefines antiheroism.

Apparitions, waif-like beings, and corpses occasionally infiltrate Shepard's stages. They assume, of course, differing forms: as Ghost Girl in *The Mad Dog Blues* (1971); or as the Old Man in *Fool for Love* (1983), who "exists only in the minds of Mae and Eddie";[3] or as Henry Hackamore in *Seduced* (1978), who, murdered at play's end, keeps repeating, "I'm dead to the world but I never been born."[4] In the brief one-act *The Holy Ghostly* (1970), spectral presences are even more direct. Witches inform the father, Stanley Hewitt Moss the sixth (surely a relative of Henry Moss), "You're already dead, Mr. Moss";[5] "You're a ghost, Mr. Moss" (189). By the end of *The Holy Ghostly,* his transubstantiation complete, Moss sees himself only as an anesthetized, "bloodless critter" (195). *The Late Henry Moss,* however, represents a turning point within Shepard's *oeuvre.* The play, Shepard notes, differs from his earlier dramas in that "it specifically deals with death. I've never directly dealt with that. The other [plays] have that peripherally, but this is the centerpiece of it."[6]

Shepard, who directed the Magic Theatre's 14 November 2000 premiere (staged at a larger venue, the 750-seat Theatre on the Square in San Francisco), assembled a memorable cast, many of them Hollywood friends. Nick Nolte and Sean Penn starred as the troubled sons, the elder booze-weary Earl and the edgy younger Ray, respectively, and James Gammon played their beleaguered father and title character. Woody Harrelson, as a humorously reluctant and frightened cab-driver named Taxi, and Cheech Marin, as a benevolent neighbor named Esteban, emerged as humorous figures who, when appropriate, worked the crowd for laughs. In an evocative performance, Sheila Tousey was Conchalla Lupina, Henry's mysterious and voracious Indian girlfriend. T-Bone Burnett provided quiet Spanish-inflected acoustic guitar solos, which complemented Anne Militello's haunting lighting effects. The play sold out for its seven week run. The night I attended a pair of tickets went for $900 on the street. The play drew mixed reactions, though most of the reviewers, apparently unable to address the play's complexities, wrote mainly about its stars.

When theatregoers settled into their seats, they saw a stage that at first glance seemed fairly unremarkable. As a framing device, though, Andy Stacklin's set provided a richly symbolic point of entry into Shepard's play. Within the yellowish "rough plastered walls," as Shepard specifies in his stage directions, there are a "mesquite door" and a "cot-like bed" which contains the corpse of Henry Moss.[7] In addition to the claw-footed bathtub upstage, there is the kitchen, with "a sink, stove, and small refrigerator set against the upstage wall." Downstage are "two metal S-shaped chairs" next to a Formica table, on which sit a bottle of bourbon, plastic cups, cigarettes, and an ashtray "in the shape of a rattlesnake." While most reviewers simply overlooked the stage arrangements, one commenting on the set diminished its importance: "Whatever the audience paid to get in," John Lahr wrote, "it was more than the producers seem to have shelled out for the set: a run-down adobe dwelling, with a bathtub on a platform and little else."[8] Whatever the cost of the set, Shepard worked carefully to ensure a semiotic of play space that reveals much about the hardscrabble life of its occupant. It is not for nothing that Shepard insists that above Henry's corpse is "a small barred window" that makes part of the home look "like a jail cell."

The Late Henry Moss revolves around the recent passing of the play's title character. His two estranged sons find themselves reunited after years apart, drawn by the death of their alcoholic father to his simple adobe located near the outskirts of Bernalillo, New Mexico. As the play begins, Earl thumbs through a family photograph album while Ray examines a wrench in an old red tool chest. Their father's body lies in rest in a small anterior bedroom. While taking care of burial arrangements, the brothers immerse themselves in present confrontations and past recollections, sometimes reconstituted through flashback sequences, that reveal not only what may have happened to Henry Moss during his last days but also what transpired years ago within the Moss family. Thus spatially and temporally, the play at times unwinds in a nonrealistic, and nonlinear, form. Moreover, the authority of Shepard's text and its performance is negotiable. Brothers immediately contradict each other. Accusations of "mis-remembering things" fly. There is, if you prefer, a rupture between the signifier and the signified. Whose version of reality do we accept? Whose version seems legitimate? This organic contingency of what Michael Issacharoff and Robin F. Jones would call the "performing text"[9] – its openness to theatrical and textual negotiations, the poignancy of its conflicting dialogues, its shifting accounts of past action and present consequence, the ways in which Shepard arranges language and nuances stage directions, its very performativity – not only gives *The Late Henry Moss* its classic Shepardian texture, but its theatrical largess and, most significantly, its currency and purchase on a postmodernist culture.

The Late Henry Moss, for some, may be viewed as autobiography. The parallels between Shepard's father and Henry Moss – the alcoholism, the shattering of doors and windows, the violence against wives and the attendant emotional injuries exacted upon children, the move from Illinois to New Mexico, the sheer implacable sense of anger that so consumes them, fathers who served in the air force, patriarchs who do not recognize their own children, the ignoble deaths of the fathers, and so on – invite such linkages. And Shepard limned personal experiences for imaginative materials both before and after his own father's death in 1984. Yet, despite the allure of interconnecting autobiography with *The Late Henry Moss* and the other "family" plays, Shepard has never been "an autobiographical writer in the simple sense of dramatising his own experiences."[10] In fact, the most remarkable feature about *The Late Henry Moss* is its compelling presentation of a series of events which suddenly broaden to encompass experiences felt by too many audiences: the never-seen mother, the father, and the sons emerge as bewildered figures, in the specifics of whose confrontations Shepard sets forth the entropic condition of the American family. Shepard's play, while regionally specific and very much about the Henry Jamison Moss family, is also informed by a larger cultural critique of the family in any part of the United States. Our conflicted sensory perceptions and experiences interfuse with Shepard's scripted performance and conflicted performers. *The Late Henry Moss* invites the audience to explore an extratheatrical reality as Shepard plays, and replays through flashbacks, public and private structures of theatricality itself and the society it reflects.

On the surface, the drama's past events seems simple, if horrific, enough. One fateful evening a quarter of a century ago, Henry assaulted his wife, kicking her into a bloody husk. Clearly the family never recovered from this defining moment. Henry recalls, "She was on the floor...I remember the floor – was yellow – and – her blood – was smeared across it like – orange butterflies. She was surrounded – by butterflies and – I thought I'd killed her...She kept – peering out at me through her swollen eyes. She just stayed there – under the sink. Silent. Balled up like an animal. Nothing moving but her eyes." Stunned by his own savagery, Henry abrogates claims to familial duty and Emersonian self-reliance: "I ran. I ran to the car and I drove. I drove for days with the windows wide open." Despite his howling that reaches a metaphysical poignancy by the third act, the fact remains that Henry Moss never apologizes for nearly murdering his wife. She remains "that little shit" who "caused me to leave! She caused me to pack on outa' there! Whatdya' think? You think I wanted to wander around this godforsaken country for twenty some years like a refugee? Like some miserable fuckin' exile? That's what she did to me! She banished me! She turned me out! [....] SHE LOCKED ME OUT!!!!" Only at the final curtain will Henry gain perspective regarding his exiled condition and the depth of his idiocy. Henry fathoms only seconds before lapsing into his final death that, at the precise moment he assaulted his wife, he transformed himself from the *present* Henry Moss to the *late* Henry Moss. Within the imaginative logic of Shepard's play, physical death twenty-five years later is a mere formality.

The Mosses emerge as characters whose very identities are under assault. For the blood-soaked mother nearly beaten to death, "identity" has been rendered invisible by a wayward husband whose anger gains its demented energy from drink and insecurity. In text and performance, she never appears in a flashback scene. Nor does she speak for herself in the present. She remains nameless. All the audience learns is that Henry used and abused her. We learn nothing else about her. For Earl, the elder son who lacked the courage to protect his mother, who ran in terror that fateful evening, and whose actions eerily replicate his father's throughout the play, "identity" is submerged by guilt over his mother's demise and, now, by alcohol that keeps at bay his shame. With their mother lying near death, Earl sped off in his 1951 Chevy, never to be heard from for years. Shepard provides few other details about his past. In the present, the hulking and besotted Earl exudes a sad world-weariness. He seems content to ignore his own fallibility and to forgive and accept his father – and his passing – at face value. As he says to his brother, it is "not like we're inheriting a legacy here."

He is wrong. "We're bound up!" Henry Moss screams. "We're flesh and blood, you idiot!" These brothers are the beneficiaries of their family's history. So for Ray, the skittish younger son, "identity" has been under pressure from the (de)formative experience of watching the family disintegrate and his own subsequent withdrawal. Too young to defend his mother and traumatized by the beating and subsequent abandonment of family by his elder male figures, he also ran from home. He used to work on cars with his father's tools; now he makes ends meet by playing the clarinet at a Ramada Inn. Although he wears a Hawaiian shirt, black leather jacket, and blue leather-tipped shoes, Ray appears withdrawn and paranoid. Ray seems consumed by a desire to stand up for a mother he could not protect as a boy, as if now he might make amends for the sins of the past. At best, however, he can only mop the kitchen floor in the third act with his older brother, just as the father mopped the bloody floor with their mother before. Within Ray's world of attenuated options, retribution comes too late. Expiation remains a distant force. These family members emerge as damaged figures whose only remarkable feature, Shepard suggests, is their own insignificance in the universe. As Ray says to Taxi, "You're nothing. Just like me. An empty nothing. A couple of nothings whose lives have never amounted to anything and never will."

For Henry, "identity" seems buried in a maze of denials and rationalizations. After all, he reasons, "What did I ever do to deserve this? I've led an honorable life for the most part! Few slip-ups now and then but – for the most part – I've served my country. I've dropped bombs on total strangers! Paid my taxes. Worked my ass off for idiots. There's never once been any question of my – existence. It's humiliating!" Defining his identity, however, remains as problematic as it is disturbing. Henry lives for years in his adobe, remaining drunk enough to blot out a past that forever emotionally paralyzes him. Only outsiders – Esteban, the kindly Mexican neighbor who long ago befriended and still feeds Henry, and Conchalla, Henry's enigmatic girlfriend he met while both were in the local jail's drunk tank – know much about Henry's recent existence.

The genesis of Henry's character in part came from Shepard's desire to write about his father's death. He wanted, apparently, to put his felt experiences onto page, and then stage, before too much time intervened. Aesthetically, inspiration for *The Late Henry Moss* may be traced back to a short story written by Frank O'Connor, "The Late Henry Conran," which appeared in the Irish writer's first collection of fiction, *Guests of the Nation* (1931). In O'Connor's piece, Henry Conran, having "the biggest appetite for liquor of any man,"[11] quarrels with his wife, Nellie, and finds himself locked out of his own home. Conran exiles himself to Chicago, where he lives for twenty-five years until learning that, in a marriage announcement for one of his sons, he has been pronounced dead. His pride wounded, character defamed, reduced to a spectral presence, Conran returns to Ireland, ready legally to charge Nellie with a defamation of character suit unless she restores, as he bellows, "the character ye took from me."[12] Whereas the Shepard play oscillates between mystery and menace, laughter and loss, while building toward an indeterminate ending, the O'Connor piece embraces more directly comedy and acceptance, resolution and closure. The story ends with implied renewal, for upon seeing her husband finally home and in their bed, Nellie's eyes shine "in her head with pure relief."[13] Conran lives. It is difficult to locate "pure relief" in Shepard's work. The play ends ambiguously. Moss dies. This is not, by design, the well-made fable.

Despite differences in narrative complexity and closure, *The Late Henry Moss* and "The Late Henry Conran" share important qualities. For O'Connor's fiction, like Shepard's play, is not merely about a lush who runs away from home, but about the condition of the individual who, once exiled from his familiar surroundings, becomes a stranger, a cosmic drifter, an apparition in his own diminished ether world. Both O'Connor and Shepard present voracious protagonists who cannibalize themselves and family by a willful relinquishment of moral nerve. Seeking spiritual fulfillment, or at least understanding, they instead fill themselves with spirits. They are, to use Shepard's phrase, "professional drunk[s]."[14] These are men tormented by a dimly perceived inability to maintain contact with those with whom they could, or should, be intimate. In effect, they transform psychologically and spiritually to ghosts, suspended between a kind of heaven and hell, at least until a secular or cosmic reckoning may brook purgation, a cleansing of the soul so that soul may find its rightful place in the universe.

In addition to the O'Connor influence, traces of *The Late Henry Moss* reveal themselves in a short story Shepard initially wrote in 1989, "See You in My Dreams." Appearing in his remarkable collection of fiction, *Cruising Paradise* (1996), the story unwinds in the same small town as the play and features similar characters and narrative patterns – the drunkard father, a Mexican neighbor named Esteban, a large, mysterious Indian girlfriend who goes trout fishing with the father during his last days on earth, abandoned offspring, the father's death, and so on. Significantly, the story foregrounds central issues that underpin *The Late Henry Moss*: an unresolved past, the violent history between the father, mother, and son, and the attendant over-whelming terror – "The same fear that invaded me at his [the father's] door when he was alive," as the narrator reports.[15] After working intermittently on *The Late Henry Moss* for ten years, Shepard revisited these origins while shaping his new play. Not surprisingly, Ray reflects, "I remember the very last thing he [his father] said to me . . . 'See you in my dreams.'"

In the manuscript draft of the play, Shepard provides a pre-text to his text, a revelatory epigraph from O'Connor's story: "'Tis no crime to be dead." This richly encoded epigraph appears at an emotional highpoint in the short story, and to understand this moment in the narrative is to dis-cover the broader personal and cultural dynamics of O'Connor's work and, by extension, Shepard's play. Henry Conran, furious that he has been pro-nounced dead and thus denied a voice, listens to his friend Larry Costello explain: "'And anyway, as I said before, 'tis only a manner of speaking. A man might be stone dead, or he might be half dead, or dead to you and me, or, for that matter of that, he might be dead to God and the world as we've often been to ourselves.'"[16] O'Connor's reflections are variants of the well-known spiritual death-in-life motif saturating the fictions of many of his Irish contemporaries, including George Moore, Seumus O'Kelly, Daniel Corkery, Liam O'Flaherty, Darrell Figgis, Brinsley MacNamara, Peadar O'Donnell, Elizabeth Bowen, and, of course, Joyce and Beckett. This motif has always appealed to Shepard's imaginative instincts. O'Connor theorized that truly engaging fiction radiates a "glowing center of action," an organic nerve cen-ter from which a work's mimetic energy pulsates, a point which Shepard embraces.[17] The problem afflicting Henry Conran and Henry Moss is that the "glowing center of action" long ago absented itself from their very ex-istences. This central problem underpins the play's essential theatricality. Henry Moss, like Henry Conran before him, finds himself suspended in some nether-world between the living and the dead. This in-betweenness produces an ongoing predicament in which Henry Moss is, in poststructuralist terms, "always already" dead. Like his Irish predecessor, Moss feels as if he is "stone dead." Henry Moss experiences an ongoing cosmic torture, feeling dead to the world though he cannot lapse into death itself.

Shepard spotlights the point during a tragicomedic scene in which Henry implores Taxi to gaze "past the outer covering" of his eyes in a search for some spark, ember, or "glowing center of action." Although a browbeaten Taxi claims his eyes look fine, their repartee suggests otherwise:

> They're dead eyes! Any horse's ass can see they're dead! Don't lie to me, moon-face! [. . .] So – So you think there just might be a little spark inside there, huh? (*pointing to his eyes*) A little ember glowing? [. . . .] But you think there might

be just a little bit of a glimmer? You saw something in there that led you to
believe there was some – potential? Some – hope?

The answers remain open to question. Henry, immobilized because of his
ghost-status, needs a substitute speaker to take up the question of his essence.
Shepard's script takes the audience to the nerve center of the play, for Henry
must raise, as he says, "the question of my being! My aliveness! My actuality
in this world! Whether or not I'm dead or not! [. . .]You can argue my case for
me. I've got no one else." Not surprisingly, Taxi finds himself accompanying
Henry and Conchalla on their suddenly announced trout-fishing excursion.
Shepard, however, is not merely dramatizing Henry's quest to discover if he is
"to be" or "not to be." For the play quickly deepens as Shepard interrogates
the highly contested site between the real and the imaginary.

Shepard's conflating of the real with the imaginary assumes particular
resonance through the subtle use of the family photographs throughout the
play. They function, in a minor key, like the films in *True West*: through
the ostensibly minor stage props of photographs, *The Late Henry Moss*
explores a number of epistemological questions about the ways in which the
individual apprehends, distorts, and then internalizes that distorted image
of the real to such an extent that the distortion – an abstracted replication of
actual experience – displaces reality itself. The photographs are connections
to the past, tangible objects, however inadequate or illegitimate they might
be. If, as Susan Sontag claims, "the camera's twin capacities" enable the
photograph to "subjectivize reality and to objectify it,"[18] the pictures Ray
and Earl gaze upon become outer manifestations of the inner distortions of
the eye that perceives them. The family pictures that Ray gives away to a
stranger are, for him, sentimental reprints of the original imprint. For Earl,
however, "There were photographs in there going back to the turn of the
century! . . . Those photographs are irreplaceable."

Even here, though, Shepard subverts the value of such objects, for the
photographs are of a prehistory, shots of a young Henry Moss "standing in
a wheat field," clueless about "what's in store for him." Ray senses that the
photographs are substitutes for a current reality, a recalling and framing of
a time past. Ray, Earl, and Henry try "to picture" (a term each man repeats
during the three-hour play) earlier events but remain frustrated throughout
because they only encounter various images, accounts, snapshots, as it were,
not real life moments. This explains why, for Ray, photography and heredity
interlink themselves through their potential falsification of outer experience.
And it's the falsification, not the image per se in the photo, that has been
passed down from generation to generation, that reduces the American family to "a pack of liars." For the Moss family as for the American family,

Shepard implies, the photographs collapse into oversimplifications of past events precisely because the camera eye was never privy to the beatings and alcoholic destruction of the Moss home. An even greater danger appears if the perceiving eye of each new generation examining the photographs inevitably confers upon them the impression of objectivity, reliability, and, indeed, reality itself. Then they become part of the family's folklore, its legitimized history. Thus the photographs in *The Late Henry Moss* (which, ironically, the audience never sees; we only see characters seeing other photographed figures) become nothing less than the true story, an authentic metanarrative of the family legacy.

Hence photographs, for Ray, remain suspect. They are co-conspirators and co-authors of frozen moments that are inadequate re-presentations, mere traces, of reality. This also explains why Ray berates a total stranger. After Taxi relates (in all sincerity as far as the audience can tell) that Comanche Indians killed his great-great-grandmother, Ray menacingly approaches, saying:

> Sounds like a story to me [...] Thing about that kind of story, Taxi-man, is that the very first fabricator – the original liar who started this little rumor about your slaughtered Great Great Grandma – he's dead and gone now, right? Vanished from this earth! All the ones who knew him are dead and gone. All that's left is a cracked tin-type, maybe; a gnarly lock of bloody hair, some fingernail clippings in a leather pouch. So there's really no way to verify this little story of yours, is there? This little history. No way to know if there's even the slightest germ of truth to it. It's just something you've grown to believe in. Something you've become convinced of because it ... gives you a sense of belonging, somewhere in time. A pathetic, sad little sense of belonging – out here in the black, black open-ended plains.
>
> (*Pause. Ray stops very close to Taxi's face, chewing on the pepper.*)

TAXI You're not calling me a liar are you?
RAY Your whole family's a pack of liars. They were born liars. They couldn't help themselves. That's why it's important to try to get at the heart of things, don't you think? Somebody, somewhere along the line, has to try to get at the heart of things.

Throughout the drama, metaphoric experience vies with actual experience for a purchase on human memory and consciousness. Ray distrusts the family album enough to give it, and Henry's "swap meet" (rather than genuine quality) ratchet wrench, to Taxi. Perhaps Ray thinks he can transfer his family's blighted past to someone else's. Maybe Taxi can refurbish falsehoods about heritage, substituting the Moss photographs for his own family's and encoding and developing them in new prints, new fictions: "Well, he can always make up some kind of story about them ... He can tell people they're pictures of *his* family. *His* ancestors . . . Maybe he's got no family. Maybe he needs to make one up."

Shepard finished much of *The Late Henry Moss* by the premiere of Michael Almereyda's *Hamlet* (2000), yet another film version of Shakespeare's tragedy. Shepard plays King Hamlet in the film. The Ghost in Shakespeare's *Hamlet* may or may not gain release from purgatory; but the Ghost in *The Late Henry Moss* gains release, though in accord with Shepard's postmodernist cosmology, his spirit will rise to heaven only after Conchalla, who appears as a *memento mori*, pours booze into his mouth, eases Henry to his death, and speaks the play's closing lines, "Henry is going to bed now. Henry is going to heaven." During his transfigurations from Living Man to Ghost Man to Dead Man, Henry Moss achieves transcendence of sorts. In his epiphanic moment, Henry Moss realizes that *he* always has been the source of his exile, the patriarch responsible for this family's collective state of shock, and the one who died a quarter of a century ago. His lines represent some of the strongest of the entire script:

> HENRY (*on his knees*) I remember – The day I died – she was on the floor.
> CONCHALLA (*stroking Henry's head*) Now, he sees.
> HENRY I remember the floor – was yellow – and – her blood – was smeared across it like – orange butterflies. She was surrounded – by butterflies and – I thought I'd killed her – but it was me. It was me I killed [. . .] She kept – peering out at me through her swollen eyes. She just stayed there – under the sink. Silent. Balled up like an animal. Nothing moving but her eyes. She must have seen me. She must have seen me – dying – right there. She knew! I ran out into the yard and I remember – I remember feeling – this – death. Cut off. Everything – far away. Birds. Trees. Sky. Everything. Removed! Removed from me! I ran. I ran to the car and I drove. I drove for days with the windows wide open. The wind blowing across my eyes. I couldn't stop. I had no map. No destination. I just drove. Drove until the money ran out [. . .] That's how I got here, wasn't it? I just – ran out. Ran out of gas.

These are Henry Moss's last words, heartbreakingly bellowed by Gammon. Shepard of course ironizes those last lines: Henry just – and the pause is telling – "ran out" of much more than fuel for his car, for this is a man who "ran out" of his marriage, relationship, home, fatherhood, and any meaningful connection with a larger community. Henry lies near death, a blanket shrouding him. Shepard's stage directions here are significant, for Henry's body is covered in "a yellow, orange, and red Mexican blanket," colors precisely matching those used to describe his wife lying on the kitchen floor, blood pouring from her beaten body.

At last Henry Moss understands his source of spectral terror, discovers its etiology. The power to terrorize can no longer be blotted from the landscape because such power has actually been carried into the landscape by his limited imagination in the first place. Shepard so successfully internalizes the terror – through inner webbings of heredity, legacy, and legitimacy – that the outer tensions of the public disappear into the inner anxieties of Henry. His fears become the conditions and consequences of his psychic state of mind. For Henry, as for his sons, the stimulus for terror ultimately comes from within. Thus there can be, in the lives they lead, no real survivors, no remissions of the terrible, and little chance to escape their fates. More often than not, it seems, the Mosses have been their own executioners. Self-afflicted and self-victims, Shepard dooms them to enact their downward journey, drifting further and further into voluble wonderment at themselves. The play, for Henry, has been a self-murder mystery.

In the Moss family's pursuit of the truth, the initial investigative question – what happened to father? – shifts to include a broader range of possibilities – what happened to father, mother, and children? What happened to other families suffering similar fates? What happened to communal decency? Thus Ray involves himself in much more than an obligatory plane trip to take care of funeral arrangements. When he decides to move into his father's home, he embarks on a symbolic homecoming of sorts. The return is not featured as extensively as the homecoming was in *Buried Child*, and Shepard elects not to develop this family as fully as the ones in *Curse of the Starving Class* and *True West*. But when Earl presses, "just go back home, Ray. Back where you came from," Ray can only respond, "Where was that? I've been trying to figure that one out ... Where I came from." Ray fills the refrigerator, that appliance which is symbolic in many Shepard plays, with food and Coca-Cola (which in America was for a time advertised as the "Real Thing"). He feels, he says, a "connection." While it would be wishful thinking to suggest that Ray's nourishment will replace Esteban's *Menudo*, the soup that cures hangovers in the play, his gesture is his way of moving closer to the truth about the Moss birthright.

The Late Henry Moss, then, concerns more than two brothers and a father engaged in a fateful and fatal reunion. This is a play in which the errant Mosses debate notions of honor, duty, and responsibility, ideas for years banished to the margins of their impoverished social world as they struggled with various "tokens of guilt." Like those in *Curse of the Starving Class*, *Buried Child*, and *A Lie of the Mind*, the family members of *The Late Henry Moss* experience the pressures of a dimly perceived scourge. The buried truths of the past, repressed through years of denial and subterfuge, are sources of disconnection in the family. No wonder the father claims that he does not even recognize one of his sons. Love is absent in *The Late Henry Moss*. Isolation is the norm. Denial becomes both a source of comfort and anguish. A willed ignorance stabilizes this family. The curse must be passed on, especially as seen in Earl, who has in effect become his father (much as when Nolte, playing the son of an alcoholic, became, like his father, a drunken misanthrope in the film *Affliction* [1999]).

Shepard refuses to construct a neat ending to *The Late Henry Moss*. Despite the father's and sons' intentions, they do not atone for their sins. There is no expiation, and the past legacies remain vibrant forces in a family long ago drained of its vibrancy. Henry, Earl, and Ray can only ponder the inevitability of their biological and spiritual destiny. Their father was, after all, Henry Jamison Moss, *Jr.* (my emphasis). They remain, at best, vaguely aware that a replicating process ensures that the heritage propagated by their grandfather to their father has been transferred to the sons through an ungovernable Darwinianism. The threat to future generations, Shepard implies, is a given. It seems unlikely, in light of the ending Shepard has scripted, that they will ever come to terms with their identities. No wonder Shepard has commented, "To me, one of the strangest and most terrifying things about being human is the need to come up with an identity. It has always bewildered me, and I can say that even now it's still mostly unresolved . . . 'Who am I?' As hackneyed and simplistic as the question might sound to us of the dot-com e-mail computer age, it may still remain the most important one we can ever ask."[19]

Still, there is, in the end, something oddly consoling about Henry Moss's coming to terms with his plight – and his death – as a son covers him with the Mexican blanket while the lights and music fade. Now he can leave a home Shepard described as "a jail cell." The play has been, for a baffled Henry Moss, a valediction encouraging mourning. It is a play filled, as Patti Smith once reflected, with "all those special dialogues of the heart."[20] To allude to the epigraph Shepard invokes, Henry learns that since living, for him, has been a crime, " . . . 'tis no crime to be dead." In Shepard's latest incarnation of the depleted American family, the "real" finds its authenticity in death. Henry soon dies after Conchalla, in a paradoxically cajoling and comforting gesture, pours liquor down his throat. Henry slips into the familiar stupor that has been his life. But he also slips, finally and incontrovertibly Shepard implies, to another and possibly more hospitable world.

NOTES

1 Matthew Roudané, "Shepard on Shepard: an Interview." See chapter 3, 79.
2 Ibid., 79.
3 Sam Shepard, *Fool for Love*, in *Fool for Love and Other Plays* (New York: Bantam Books, 1984), 20.

4 Sam Shepard, *Seduced*, in *Fool for Love and Other Plays*, 276.

5 Sam Shepard, *The Holy Ghostly*, in *The Unseen Hand and Other Plays* (New York: Bantam Books, 1986), 182. Page references in parentheses within the text are to this edition.

6 Edward Guthmann, "Shepard Talks a Bit about His Latest," *San Francisco Chronicle*, 5 November 2000, 2.

7 Sam Shepard, *The Late Henry Moss*, manuscript draft of the play. All further references are to this manually typed version Shepard gave to me before the play went into rehearsal. I base my speculative essay, then, on this reading version and on seeing the world premiere of the play in San Francisco. Because quotations come from a manuscript draft, I have not furnished page numbers after each citation. As this volume was in its final production, plans were underway for the Signature Theatre Company in New York City to launch its 2001–2 season with *The Late Henry Moss*, under the direction of Joseph Chaikin.

8 John Lahr, "Giving Up the Ghost," *The New Yorker*, 4 December 2000, 108.

9 See Issacharoff and Jones's edited collection, *Performing Texts* (Philadelphia: University of Pennsylvania Press, 1988).

10 Christopher Bigsby, *Modern American Drama, 1945–2000* (Cambridge University Press, 2000), 183–84.

11 Frank O'Connor, *Collected Stories* (New York: Knopf, 1981), 13.

12 Ibid., 18.

13 Ibid., 19.

14 Sam Shepard, *Cruising Paradise: Tales* (New York: Knopf, 1996), 142.

15 Ibid., 145.

16 O'Connor, *Collected Stories*, 16–17.

17 Quoted from Richard Ellmann, "Introduction," O'Connor, *Collected Stories*, VII; see also Roudané, "Shepard on Shepard," chapter 3, 78–79.

18 Susan Sontag, *On Photography* (New York: Farrar, Straus, and Giroux, 1978), 178.

19 Sam Shepard, "Foreword," in Mary Motley Kalergis, *Seen and Heard: Teenagers Talk about Their Lives* (New York: Stewart, Tabori, and Chang, 1998), 6–7.

20 Patti Smith, "Sam Shepard: 9 Random Years [7 + 2]," in Sam Shepard, *Angel City, Curse of the Starving Class, and Other Plays* (New York: Urizen Books, 1980), 244.

17

SUSAN C. W. ABBOTSON

Sam Shepard: a bibliographic essay and production overview

Biographies

Three texts which offer detailed biographical information on Shepard are Don Shewey's *Sam Shepard*, Martin Tucker's *Sam Shepard*, and Ellen Oumano's *Sam Shepard: The Life and Work of an American Dreamer*. All cover Shepard's life from childhood through to their publication dates, and consider both his playwriting and film work. They offer numerous and often illuminating anecdotes about Shepard culled from interviews and reports.

Shewey's *Sam Shepard* was originally written in 1985 when Shewey saw Shepard as being at the peak of his career. The book was updated in 1997 with two additional chapters, but is clearly not as enamored with Shepard's more recent work in film or theatre. Although hard to shake the impression that Shewey is more concerned with Shepard the "beefcake" movie star than the serious playwright, he does use this double life to point out a duality which is the cause of both tension and creativity throughout much of Shepard's work. Shewey's picture of Shepard as a rebellious innovator, inspired by popular culture to create a new kind of theatre, may, at times, seem overglamorized, but is intrinsically sound. There is no deep analysis of the plays, beyond pointing out autobiographical elements, but as biography the book offers insight, and its chatty style makes it an accessible introduction to Shepard the man. Shewey gives the facts – who did what, where, and when – allowing us to glimpse the process by (and conditions under) which Shepard writes.

Tucker's 1992 study, *Sam Shepard*, is closer to a critical work, and offers straightforward explanations of the central themes and ideas in Shepard's plays from *Cowboys* through *States of Shock*, seeing Shepard as working from experimental drama toward realism. However, because there is little reference to other critical views, and because Tucker places such a strong emphasis on the biographical impetus behind the plays, this reads more like a biography. What Tucker tells us is how Shepard's life and the plots of his plays fit together, while being conscious of a separation in Shepard's work between truth and reality. Tucker sees Shepard as a nonconformist who is ironically a political conservative; a loner rather than social activist. The tension between Shepard's public world and private life influences both how he writes, and what he writes about. This is a good introduction to Shepard, but there is little here for the advanced scholar.

In *Sam Shepard: The Life and Work of an American Dreamer* (1986) Oumano calls Shepard an "American hero" who "personifies our cultural ambiguity" (1). Thus she, too, organizes her biography around tensions in Shepard and his work. Shepard is described as a writer with a divided nature, caught between savagery and innocence, wanderlust and the security of home, transcendence and crass myth; who writes to stay sane. Again, limited in scholarship, with little analysis of the plays, but this is a very readable book. Oumano seems most interested in how and why Shepard's plays have come to be performed, and offers numerous quotes and anecdotes from key people involved.

Sam Shepard: Stalking Himself (1997), the product of a British Broadcasting Corporation's program, is now available in an hour-long video version. Throughout the program are performance excerpts from *Curse of the Starving Class*, *The Tooth of Crime*, *Buried Child*, and *True West*. Shepard reads from his own work and such theatrical talents as Edward Albee, Joseph Chaikin, Joyce Aaron, Ethan Hawke, Gary Sinise, and Ed Harris appear as well. It is worth seeing, although there is much more that could, or should, have been shown, footage that would have given viewers a much fuller perspective of Shepard's career.

Even though only a few distinct biographies of Shepard have been published, there are numerous biographical references in much of the critical work which has been produced. Many critics find it difficult to explain Shepard's plays without referencing the life of the man who created them. His plays are not necessarily autobiographical, they just often seem more accessible through the lens of their creator's life and experience.

Bibliographies

Bibliographic works like Charles Carpenter's *Modern Drama Scholarship and Criticism 1966–80: An International Bibliography* (1986), James Salem's *A Guide to Critical Reviews: Part I: American Drama. 1909–1982* (1984), Kimball King's *Ten Modern American Playwrights: An Annotated Bibliography* (1982), and Floyd Eddleman's *American Drama Criticism: Interpretations, 1890–1977* (1979), naturally include sections on Shepard. The best of these works is King's, which includes a list of early editions of plays which are no longer in print, as well as an annotated list of other primary and secondary material. Salem and Eddleman concentrate on reviews and critical articles, but beware of some of the gaps and inaccuracies in Salem's dates for key New York productions. Carpenter is more up to date, but limited. There are also brief sections on Shepard in volumes such as the Gale Research New Revision Series, *Contemporary Authors* (1988), and *Current Bibliography* (1979). There is also a detailed bibliography by Jürgen Wolter, which covers productions and writing on Shepard in German-speaking countries. This was published in the journal, *Studies in American Drama 1945–Present*, in 1991.

There are no book-length bibliographies on Shepard, to date. The useful *File on Shepard* compiled by John Dugdale (1989), part of the Methuen series on modern dramatists, offers production details, and a collection of excerpted commentaries on Shepard's plays, combined with comments from Shepard. It includes a brief chronology of Shepard, and culminates in a selected bibliography. The bibliography is no more detailed than those which exist at the end of several full-length books on Shepard, including Stephen Bottoms's *The Theatre of Sam Shepard: States of Crisis* (1998), Martin Tucker's *Sam Shepard* (1992), or Lynda Hart's *Sam Shepard's Metaphorical Stages* (1987). Even more useful bibliographies of this type are those which have been annotated, as in David DeRose's *Sam Shepard* (1992), and Ellen Oumano's *Sam Shepard: The Life and Work of an American Dreamer* (1986). DeRose also includes a useful (though incomplete) list of play-by-play production reviews. Also worth mentioning is Christopher Bigsby's annotated checklist for *Theatrefacts* (1974). This early attempt to record critical writing on Shepard, and annotate his plays through *Little Ocean*, remains useful, mostly for its descriptions of earlier and unpublished plays.

Johan Callens is working on an annotated bibliography on Shepard for ABES, an on-line and CD-ROM bibliographic source. An ongoing project, there are already well over a hundred entries on various articles and books going up to 2000. Callens's annotations can be a little obtuse, but he covers the material in detail. Another ongoing project is Gary Grant's Shepard web site at <http://www.departments.bucknell.edu/theatre%5Fdance/Shepard/shepard.html>. To date, it contains a detailed primary bibliography, a filmography, notes on current and upcoming productions, and various other information on Shepard, but remains under construction.

The best print bibliographic sources to date are those written by Lynda Hart for Matthew Roudané's *American Dramatists: Contemporary Authors Bibliographical Series* (1989), and William Kleb for Philip Kolin's *American Playwrights Since 1945: A Guide to Scholarship, Criticism, and Performance* (1989). Although there are some inaccuracies in Hart (mostly regarding dates), her bibliographic essay provides a thorough covering of earlier scholarship on Shepard. Particularly useful are her surveys of interviews, and major reviews and articles to that date. Kleb authoritatively lists primary and secondary material, and offers useful extras, such as his production history through to *A Lie of the Mind*, and a survey of secondary sources. Both, of course, effectively only take us as far as 1987.

Critical studies

Books

In their 1989 bibliographic essays, both Kleb and Hart bemoan the dearth of full-length critical studies on Shepard, but there has been an increase of interest in the intervening years, and a number of new books have appeared. This production has been an ironic contrast to the reduced output of plays by the playwright during this period.

1999 saw the publication of Michael Taav's *A Body Across the Map: The Father–Son Plays of Sam Shepard*, which focuses on the character conflict most central to Shepard's plays: that between fathers and sons. Beginning with *The Rock Garden* and concluding with *A Lie of the Mind*, Taav analyzes Shepard's evolving world view over a period of twenty years. With close reference to a number of plays, he concludes that Shepard's initially pessimistic view of genetic determination, angry miscommunication, and self-interest, has been disavowed in favor of the possibilities of spiritual generosity, cooperation, and an acceptance that truth can prevail.

Stephen Bottoms sees Shepard as a distinctive and culturally important writer, who often dissatisfies audiences and critics by his determined irresolution; it is this open-ended aspect of Shepard's plays which most fascinates Bottoms, allowing for a variety of interpretations. He describes Shepard's writing as a series of crises regarding the playwright's ambivalence toward writing aesthetics, identity, gender, and performance. *The Theatre of Sam Shepard: States of Crisis* (1998) is an intelligent assessment of Shepard's work from its beginnings through to 1996 with *When the World Was Green* and the Signature Theatre Company's season of Shepard. Bottom's chapters are subdivided by headings which point the reader toward central motifs in Shepard's work, as Bottoms considers the paradoxes, tensions, and uncertainties he sees at the heart of the plays, which he suggests are rooted in an "unresolved conflict between modernist and postmodernist perspectives" on self, society, and the act of creativity itself (ix). Bottoms has done his research, and there is plenty of archival material here, as well as references to other criticism on the playwright, and the author's own experience in staging Shepard.

In *Sam Shepard and the American Theatre* (1997), Leslie Wade works within a consciously developed critical framework inspired by Bakhtin to show how Shepard's work gives voice to the other and contributes to a new definition of national character. In an attempt to explain Shepard's rise from "counterculture to cultural icon" (5), Wade approaches Shepard dialogically, and considers how he has addressed the nation, and how that nation has helped fashion him as an agent of communal desire. Shepard's vision of America and what it means to be an American are at the heart of this scholarly work, which views his plays as a kind of "theatrical Smithsonian" (2), documenting contemporary American history and culture. Wade includes extensive notes, has done much research (especially on the earlier plays), and offers an interesting chronology which sets events in Shepard's life against those in the arts and public life of America.

As part of a comparative literature series, *From Middleton and Rowley's "Changeling" to Sam Shepard's "Bodyguard": A Contemporary Appropriation of a Renaissance Drama* (1997) is largely centered on Shepard, and a consideration of his preoccupation with national identity, myth, and symbol. Its author, Johan Callens, presents Shepard's unpublished and unproduced 1970s screen adaptations of Middleton and Rowley's *The Changeling* as important stepping-stones between Shepard's earlier, lighter works, and the more violent passions and love–hate relationships of later works. Between detailing two versions of Shepard's film script alongside *The Changeling*, Callens's analysis tries to depict the tension Shepard sees between national ideals and a multicultural reality, and how this is reiterated in his postmodern fusion of high and low culture.

There are also Laura Graham's *Sam Shepard: Theme, Image, and the Director* (1995) and Jim McGhee's *True Lies: The Architecture of the Fantastic in the Plays of Sam Shepard* (1993), both studies for the more advanced scholar of Shepard. Graham tries to ascertain Shepard's contribution to the evolution of American theatre, focusing on the theatrical milieu which embraced him, and Shepard's relationship to several movements, ideologies, and forms of artistic presentation. She determines that Shepard is a "disappointed" Romantic who places performance ahead of rhetoric in a presentational theatre which is imagistic, antirational and nonrealistic (5). Graham points to the intertextuality of Shepard's work, showing how earlier plays prepare us for the later. The first section of the book considers the development of Shepard's style, themes, and vision of the mythic, while the second section looks at details of performance, to consider what sound and vision contribute to Shepard's texts. Based on definitions of the fantastic formulated by Eric Rabkin and Tzvetan Todorov, McGhee's attempt to determine a responsive critical vocabulary and strategy of discourse to use on a dramatist who so frequently defies categorization, considers Shepard's satirical use of the fantastic in his work. He sees Shepard's importance as lying in the way he transforms rather than represents reality, and looks at how he does this in all the published plays through *States of Shock*. His analyses are plot-heavy, as he covers the plays' structures in close detail, as well as characters, themes, and staging. His depiction of Shepard's theatrical devices is limited in scope, and his closing biographical chapter seems extraneous, but he provokes discussion regarding Shepard's tendency toward a surrealist aesthetic, and the ways in which he tries to disrupt audience expectation.

Frederick Perry's 1992 study, *A Reconstruction-Analysis of "Buried Child" by Playwright Sam Shepard*, is an interesting approach, being the product of a computer-aided text analysis of the play. Perry has created full-sentence part-files for every character and one for stage directions, followed by individual concordances of these files. We do not see these files, but Perry's analysis of what he discovered in reading them. The character files lead Perry to assess the motivations, objectives, attitudes, and emotions of each character, while the stage direction file gives insight into the structure and visual elements of *Buried Child*. He concludes with an analytical essay comparing the project's findings with those of published critical analyses. Perry views the play as being built around Dodge's atonement for his murder of the incestuous child of Halie and Ansel, and his findings support such a view.

Another book from 1992 is David DeRose's *Sam Shepard*, which suggests that Shepard is a postmodern playwright, who writes in response to an unsettling fragmentation of self and society. DeRose pays close attention to direction, language, and stage imagery, and offers meticulous readings of plays from *Cowboys* through *States of Shock*, including a number which are unpublished and, therefore, rarely discussed. He also quotes extensively from initial, critical reactions to the plays, and his closing bibliographic information is nicely detailed. DeRose is not interested in Shepard as the chronicler of America or the American family, but in a playwright who is chasing his own personal demons, a man who seems simultaneously to relish and mourn the loss of older American myths. DeRose demonstrates how Shepard's work exhibits the playwright's "sense of the world and the self as unfixed" (138).

Lynda Hart analyzes Shepard's growth as a writer who has achieved a unique blend of naturalism and expressionism, through the study of ten key plays. Working backwards through major movements of modern drama, *Sam Shepard's Metaphorical Stages* (1987) maps Shepard's development from personal to social expressionism, through absurdism, to a "modified realism" (5). Despite the plays' resistance to categorization, Hart wants to place Shepard within a dramatic tradition, and offers some worthwhile connections between the playwright and European innovators, including Brecht, Pirandello, Artaud, Ionesco, and Beckett, who influenced the American avant-garde in the 1950s and 1960s.

Vivian Patraka and Mark Siegel's booklet, *Sam Shepard* (1985), insists on Shepard's roots in Western American drama, linked to Native American ritual, and suggests that his plays explore the efficacy of American myths of the cowboy and the West, which Shepard alternately justifies, elevates, and debunks in an effort to recover a sense of value. After giving some biographical background, they divide Shepard's plays, from *The Rock Garden* to *True West*, into five categories – plays depicting a cultural wasteland, investigations into survival tactics, false idols and heroes, apocalyptic exorcisms, and failed attempts at reintegration – each of which they explore. They conclude that in his collaborations with Chaikin, Shepard seems more optimistic that community can be recreated, which is borne out by more recent works.

The earliest full-length critical text on Shepard is Ron Mottram's *Inner Landscapes: The Theater of Sam Shepard* (1984), which concentrates on the family plays, and, most importantly, earlier works which are either out of print or unpublished, summarizing the plots of the plays, extracting recurrent themes, and noting typical stylistic devices. Mottram makes a good case for Shepard the intellectual over Shepard the sensationalist, pointing out the connection between works of Shepard and those of Beckett and Brecht, and giving a critical overview of Shepard's career to *Fool for Love*. He sees Shepard's work as culturally rich in images from "myth, history, and contemporary reality," by which the playwright "explores the simultaneous alienation and integration of the individual" in twentieth-century American society, using himself as model (viii–ix). Thus, there is much biographical material included in this study.

Despite Shepard's supposed Americanness, there is a strong interest in his work abroad, and a number of publications in both English and foreign languages. In English, Johan Callens, from Belgium, receives a number of mentions in this essay, and there is also Carol Benet's *Sam Shepard on the German Stage: Critics, Politics, Myths* (1993), which discusses German language productions of Shepard's work from 1968 through 1991 in Germany, Austria, and Switzerland. This contains no appraisal of the plays, but is a reception study exploring why German audiences find Shepard so puzzling and problematic. Benet suggests it is due to difficulties in translation, misleading publicity and program notes, a negative critical reaction from a small number of critics, and the intrinsic American ethos of the plays which often clashes with Germanic ideology. Prior to Benet's book are other works, published in German, indicating a Germanic interest in Shepard, including Ulrich Adolphs's *Die Tyrannei der Bilder: Sam Shepard's Dramen* (1990) and Michael Krekel's *Von Cowboys bis True West: Sam Shepard's Dramen* (1986). Wolter's bibliography, mentioned above, is a useful resource for studies in this area. There is also interest in Shepard in South America with Isaac Chocrón's *El Teatro de Sam Shepard: de Imágenes a Personajes* (1991), a Spanish-language text published in Venezuela. These suggest that Shepard's work may have resonances beyond the overtly American, as which he has often been defined.

Essay collections

There is a growing number of published essay collections on Shepard. The proceedings of a 1993 conference on Shepard held in Brussels, edited by Johan Callens, entitled *Sam Shepard: Between the Margins and the Center* was published in 1998. Divided into two parts, although each book is less than a hundred pages, it is a scholarly collection aimed at people with a working knowledge of Shepard and his work. Leonard Wilcox's *Rereading Shepard* (1993), a collection of original essays covering Shepard's career from its beginnings through *Lie of the Mind*, goes into more depth and detail. Wilcox's selection is clearly biased toward postmodern, poststructuralist, and feminist explorations of Shepard's work. After a useful introduction, which outlines the concerns of each essay within, the book is divided into three sections, beginning with two essays on the early plays. We move on to a group of pieces that are primarily concerned with the problem of origins in the plays. The final, larger section, concentrates on the "family plays," individually or together, and presents a variety of often conflicting viewpoints, including assessments of the plays as realistic or expressionistic works, and as challenging or supporting patriarchal values. 1993 also saw a special issue of *Modern Drama* devoted to Shepard, which prints an interview with the playwright, and twelve essays covering a variety of single plays, broader themes, and comparative studies.

Sam Shepard: A Casebook (1988), edited by Kimball King, is another collection of original essays, which are grouped thematically. King does not provide as detailed an introduction to the essays as Wilcox, neither is the standard of writing as consistent. The essays cover plays individually or in natural groupings, and explore such issues as Shepard's innovation, sense of myth, comedic spirit, relation to gender, Romanticism, and other aspects of theme, style, and technique. A number of the essayists draw on personal experiences producing Shepard's work, which nicely reminds us that these are plays to be performed and not just dry texts to be studied.

The earliest collection is Bonnie Marranca's *American Dreams* (1981) which offers a far more diverse mix with essays from critics, directors, actors, and Shepard himself. Some of these pieces have been published elsewhere, some are original, and they are organized into sections which relate to the writer's relationship to Shepard's work. Marranca's introductory essay is a quirky piece she has published in journal and book form elsewhere, which compartmentalizes her views on Shepard into alphabetized subheadings, rather than offering any indication of what will appear in the volume. Marranca's commentary covers Shepard's sense of privacy and family, how he creates character and flouts the rules of conventional theatre, and what she sees as his close relationship to Gertrude Stein. The remainder of the collection is as various, though its publication date means it says little regarding the family plays. The critical section contains assessments of Shepard's character, techniques, and obsessions in a variety of plays, as well as reprints of some reviews. This is followed by interviews with directors and actors who have worked with Shepard or his plays, as well as pieces written by the directors and actors themselves. The collection concludes with Kenneth Chubb and the editors of *Theatre Quarterly* interviewing Shepard, and three short essays on theatre by the playwright himself.

Book sections

Although there are exceptions, it is has become increasingly the case that most surveys of contemporary drama or collections of essays on modern drama issues contain a chapter on Shepard. Given the constraints of space, the following can only represent a selection, loosely organized by reverse chronology, and the type of text in which they appear.

A number of books consider Shepard in the company of other playwrights within a sustained critical framework. Such is Carla McDonough's *Staging Masculinity: Male Identity in Contemporary American Drama* (1997), which considers masculine representations in August Wilson, Rabe, Mamet, and Shepard, although she draws no direct comparisons between them. Viewing Shepard's work as displaying "overt masculinity" (1) through his fascination with patriarchal frontier mythology, she analyzes the men in *The Tooth of Crime* and the family plays, to ascertain what it means to be male in America, and the problems which ensue. In *American Drama since 1960* (1996), a cultural and critical exploration of how American drama has invented itself, Matthew Roudané balances Shepard against the later plays of Arthur Miller, in a chapter which looks at versions of the American Dream mythology as reflected in each playwright's work. While Miller's work is shown to contain an intrinsic optimism, Shepard's dramas, despite their humor, are viewed as disturbing studies in entropy. Roudané returns to Shepard in his chapter on "American Drama Since 1970," in *The Cambridge History of American Theatre*, vol. III (2000), edited by Don Wilmeth and Christopher Bigsby. Meanwhile, in *"A Kind of Alaska": Women in the Plays of O'Neill, Pinter, and Shepard* (1993), Ann Hall looks at female characters in the family plays. Asserting that Shepard exposes female stereotypes to elicit a reassessment of how the culture perceives women, she also draws brief comparisons between the studied playwrights.

Earlier longer analyses of Shepard are found in John Orr's *Tragicomedy and Contemporary Culture: Plays and Performance from Beckett to Shepard* (1991), which devotes three chapters to the playwright. Orr describes Shepard as "a child of modernist revolt in an age of mass culture" (109), and explores his relationship to American myth, community, and family. Viewing Shepard's plays as examples of modernist, American tragicomedy, Orr draws useful connections to Pinter and Beckett. There is also Doris Auerbach's study *Sam Shepard, Arthur Kopit, and the Off-Broadway Theater* (1982) which finds that, despite their work sharing common elements, Shepard and Kopit are diametrically opposed in style. Auerbach uses this as evidence of the variety within Off-Broadway theatre, though never directly compares the two. Her discussion of Shepard is elementary, reading like a series of annotated summaries of the plays, although her study of Shepard's relationship to Brecht, and the numerous excerpts from her unpublished correspondence with Shepard, are useful.

A number of essay collections include comparative studies, such as *Realism and the American Dramatic Tradition* (1996), edited by William Demastes, where Michael Vanden Heuvel compares Shepard to David Rabe, and applies chaos theory to the later plays; *O'Neill and the Emergence of American Drama* (1989), edited by Marc Maufort, where James Robinson compares Shepard to O'Neill, centering his discussion on *Buried Child* and *Desire Under the Elms*, to show the difference between postmodernism and modernism; and *Beckett Translating/Translating Beckett* (1987), edited by Alan Friedman, Charles Rossman, and Dina Scherzer, where Susan Brienza suggests that Shepard transposes Beckett's work into an American key, as the two playwrights share similar outlooks, techniques, and subject matter.

Other books contain multiple chapters on Shepard, such as *Feminist Rereadings of Modern American Drama* (1989), edited by June Schlueter. Here, Lynda Hart and Rosemarie Banks write essays regarding gender in *Fool for Love* and *A Lie of the Mind*. While Hart feels that Shepard tries, but fails, to transcend his innate maleness, and so perpetuates traditional gender stereotypes, Banks sees Shepard as presenting a heterotopic world of gender doubling and transformation that challenges such stereotypes. The four essays on Shepard in *Essays on Modern American Drama: Williams, Miller, Albee and Shepard* (1987), edited by Dorothy Parker, were originally published in *Modern Drama*. Charles Bachman discusses the inability of Shepard's early plays to reach a dramatic climax, Thomas Nash relates *Buried Child* to the western mythology expounded in Frazer's *The Golden Bough*, Tucker Orbison considers the use of myth and Jungian archetypes in *True West*, and Bruce Powe looks at Shepard's use of music and songs in *The Tooth of Crime*, *Operation Sidewinder*, and *Cowboy Mouth*.

Christopher Bigsby has published a number of pieces on Shepard, which refine his arguments as they go along, beginning with a chapter in his third volume of *A Critical Introduction to Twentieth-Century American Drama* in 1985, continuing with an essay in *Critical Angles: European Views of Contemporary American Literature* (1986), edited by Marc Chénetier, and culminating in 1992's *Modern American Drama*. Bigsby's insightful overviews of Shepard discuss the playwright's use of language, image, music, and technique in most of his plays, and tie Shepard to modern literary and cultural influences, most interestingly, to Tennessee Williams, David Mamet, and Walt Whitman. Ruby Cohn has similarly published two overlapping pieces. Her essay in *Essays on Contemporary American Drama* (1981), edited by Hedwig Bock and Albert Wertheim, describes Shepard as an "improbable blend of nature lover and media freak" (161), which she develops in a chapter on Shepard in her book *New American Dramatists: 1960–1990*, originally published in 1982, but updated and reprinted in 1991. Here she gives an overview of Shepard's contributions to contemporary drama, thematically and stylistically through *True West*, dividing his work into three phases: early collages, satiric fantasies, and realism.

A number of edited collections contain single essays on Shepard, including *Staging Difference: Cultural Pluralism in American Theatre and Drama* (1995), edited by Marc Maufort, where Johan Callens compares Shepard to O'Neill and argues that Shepard has the same universal appeal and lack of commercial concern. Essays by Callens also appear in two 1991 collections, *American Literature and the Arts*, edited by Callens himself, and *Belgian Essays on Language and Literature*, edited by Pierre Michel, Diana Phillips, and Eric Lee. The first is an analysis of the play and film of *Fool for Love*, in an attempt to assess why the film does not work, and the second combines a performance analysis of *Action* with a discussion of the play's postmodern features. In *Aesthetic Illusion: Theoretical and Historical Approaches* (1990), edited by Frederick Burwick and Walter Page, Susan Brienza explores the way Shepard blurs the boundaries between reality and art by drawing links to contemporaneous art and music, notably Jackson Pollock. *New Essays on American Drama* (1989), edited by Gilbert Debusscher and Henry Schvey, contains an interesting exploration, by Luther Luedtke, of Shepard's depiction of family from the earliest plays, noting the organic development of Shepard's notion of the nuclear family. Finally, *Melodrama* (1980), edited by Daniel Gerould, has James Leverett considering how *Melodrama Play* experiments with the conventions of melodrama.

There are also many books by a single author which offer a chapter on Shepard. Among these are *The Other American Drama* (1994) by Marc Robinson, who builds on Marranca's suggestion that Shepard writes in the tradition of Gertrude Stein in the way he de-emphasizes plot and concentrates on language, gesture, and presence in a variety of his plays. In 1993, Deborah Geis published *Monologue in Contemporary American Drama*, which includes a detailed survey of the monologuic mode in Shepard's plays through *Lie of the Mind* as part of her larger argument regarding postmodern dramaturgies. From 1992 is Jeanette Malkin's *Verbal Violence in Contemporary Drama: From Handke to Shepard*. Centering on *The Tooth of Crime*, Malkin considers little of what has been previously published on the play, but makes some interesting connections between Shepard and a host of other playwrights, mostly European. She offers a blow-by-blow account of the discourse battle raging between Hoss and Crow, and detailed descriptions of the threatening atmosphere created in *The Tooth of Crime*, showing how Shepard actively involves and emotionally disorients his audience, as his characters lose, destroy, and recreate identities, which end, ultimately, beyond their control.

Michael Vanden Heuvel's 1991 *Performing Drama/Dramatizing Performance: Alternative Theater and the Dramatic Text* describes Shepard as a postmodern playwright, and studies his relationship to performance theatre strategies as an alternative to conventional drama, and a more effective way of conveying the chaos of contemporary life. Published in 1989, Estelle Manette Raben's *Major Strategies in Twentieth-Century Drama: Apocalyptic Vision, Allegory and Open Form* draws parallels between *La Turista* and Pinter's *The Birthday Party*. 1988 saw the publication of Duncan Webster's *Looka Yonder: The Imaginary America of Populist Culture*, and William Demastes's *Beyond Naturalism: A New Realism in American Theatre*. The former provides an interesting reassessment of Shepard's gender depictions in a variety of plays, seeing them as cultural performance rather than embodiments, while the latter, concentrating on the later plays, depicts Shepard as a postmodernist who has developed a new kind of realism to challenge outdated naturalist thought, and create a fresh theatrical perspective. William Herman's 1987 overview, *Understanding Contemporary American Drama*, intended as a student guide, offers some biography, and a sketchy analysis of Shepard's plays, but relies heavily on Bigsby, without the insight or thoroughness.

Earlier studies include Rodney Simard's *Postmodern Drama: Contemporary Playwrights in America and Britain* (1984), which describes Shepard as an "existential realist" (xi), an American counterpart to Tom Stoppard, and the first totally postmodern voice in American drama. Also, *Dramatic*

Dialogue: The Duologue of Personal Encounter (1983), written by Andrew Kennedy, points to an affinity between Shepard and Brecht in the way they use dialogue, centering, for Shepard, on *The Tooth of Crime*. While *American Playwrights: A Critical Survey* (1981), gives us Bonnie Marranca's useful overview of Shepard's style, themes, career, and critical reception up to *Buried Child*, describing Shepard's essence as his interest in how people perceive themselves in the world. Arthur Ganz contributes an essay to *The Play and Its Critics: Essays for Eric Bentley* (1986), edited by Michael Bertin, and devotes his afterword in *Realms of the Self: Variations on a Theme in Modern Drama* (1980) to Shepard. The former compares Shepard to Pinter, casts doubt on his humor, and analyzes a number of plays to show how personal, psychological, and moral concerns dominate Shepard's work. The latter looks at *La Turista*, as proof that Shepard writes about the divided self in the romantic tradition of playwrights from Wilde through Pinter.

Finally, three books which touch on Shepard in terms of collaboration are *REAL: Yearbook of Research in English and American Literature* (1993), edited by Herbert Grabes, Winifred Fluck, and Jürgen Schlaeger; Eileen Blumenthal's *Joseph Chaikin: Exploring at the Boundaries of Theater* (1984); and *Theatres, Spaces, Environments: Eighteen Projects* (1975) by Brook McNamara, Jerry Rojo, and Richard Schechner. In the first, Johan Callens argues against the view that Shepard has become more conservative by using *Savage/Love*, Shepard's collaboration with Chaikin, to validate his opinion that Shepard remains an experimental artist, then Blumenthal covers pretty much the same territory as her earlier essay in Marranca's collection regarding the collaboration of Shepard and Chaikin from inspiration through performance of *Tongues* and *Savage/Love*. The third offers transcribed conversations by the collaborators on Schechner's "environmental" production of *The Tooth of Crime*.

Production overview

Sam Shepard's theatrical career has had its ups and downs, and about the only predictable aspect of his work has been its unpredictability. Bouncing between critical acclaim and disdain, it seems as if each time we try to fix who Sam Shepard is as a playwright, he shows us yet another face. His output has been prodigious but inconsistent, containing high points of creative activity interspersed by prolonged periods of silence. At times his writing seems to have sprung from prevailing artistic movements, at others, it seems to have run counter to such. Although a number of his plays have never been published, Shepard has produced around fifty plays, many of which have had substantive revivals, and often with a considerably altered script.

He has also won numerous Obies, a Pulitzer Prize for the original *Buried Child*, and the New York Drama Critics' Circle Award for Best Play for *A Lie of the Mind*. Due to space constrictions, this overview must focus only on Shepard's better-known plays.

Shepard's earliest work was marked by its improvisational force and ability to shock. Performance oriented, mostly brief, some of these plays were never published in their original form, so unless we attended their original presentation, all we have to go on are the reviews from the time. If we happen to be reading the *Village Voice*, then those reviews are mostly favorable, and thankfully detailed, but critics other than Michael Smith and Ross Wetzsteon were far less sure of Shepard's talent, and if not indifferent, were actively hostile.

Shepard fell into theatre through a series of fortunate connections. Ralph Cook was the head waiter at the Village Gate nightclub, where Shepard had been bussing tables to finance his interest in acting. Cook was given the use of a local church and converted it into Theatre Genesis, to focus on producing new plays. Cook chose to produce Shepard's short plays *Cowboys* and *The Rock Garden* in October 1964, directing them himself, and using waiters from the nightclub to play the parts. This was Shepard's first public airing, and for the first two weeks of the run the audience was sparse, due to bad reviews. Jerry Tallmer dismissed *Cowboys* as unoriginal (16), and did not even stay for the second play. However, Michael Smith chose to give the plays a glowing review, calling them "provocative and genuinely original." Praising Shepard's "intuitive approach to language and dramatic structure" (13), Smith's review led to better audiences for the plays' final week, and encouraged Shepard to continue writing.

Cowboys was never published, reputedly written on a napkin and lost, so Shepard later attempted to recreate this play with *Cowboys #2* in 1967. Meanwhile, *The Rock Garden* earned Shepard his first steady income from drama as it was included as the final scene in Kenneth Tynan's long running, risqué revue *Oh! Calcutta!* (1969). Shepard timed his theatrical debut perfectly with the onset of Off-Off-Broadway; but it was more than being at the right time and place. His was also the right voice. For the next three years, he had a succession of rapidly composed one-act plays produced at theatres such as La MaMa, Playwrights Unit, and Caffe Cino, to establish his position as Off-Off-Broadway's leading writer. These plays would typically dispense with traditional ideas of character and plot, addressing their audiences as a kind of abstract collage. Most notable among these were *Chicago* and *Icarus's Mother* in 1965, *Red Cross*, Shepard's first Off-Broadway play in 1966, his first longer play, *La Turista*, and *Melodrama Play* in 1967. All of these won Obies for Shepard, and a growing respect from the critics.

Melodrama Play tends to be viewed as the first of Shepard's "rock-and-roll" plays and, some would say, the first play he wrote which had any sense of plot, although the action still descends into chaos by the close of the play.

His reputation now established, Shepard changed gear and spent much of 1968 involved in the script of the movie *Zabriskie Point* and touring with his band, the Holy Modal Rounders. His next two plays, *The Unseen Hand* and *The Holy Ghostly*, were not produced until late 1969 and 1970. *The Unseen Hand* is an early example of Shepard's interest in the mythical, and one which uses more complex language, but it was poorly received. Although admired by some celebrities, including Andy Warhol and Abbie Hoffman, it was generally judged to be too camp, and closed after four weeks. In his review of the play, Clive Barnes suggested that Shepard's work seemed as disposable as Kleenex ("Double Bill" 43). But it was not until 1970 that Shepard had his first total critical disaster, *Operation Sidewinder*. Although optioned by Yale Repertory Theatre, Shepard withdrew the play after protests from black students over the play's stereotyped presentation of black men. The play eventually premiered at Lincoln Center, but in a production Shepard hated so much he was unable to attend the rehearsals. It was the first chance mainstream critics had to review him, and they were universally scathing. Walter Kerr declared the play to be fanciful, overproduced, and uninteresting; only John Lahr defended it, describing the play as "a grotesque spectacle of our psychic death and the possibility of rebirth" ("On-stage" 44). The play swiftly closed.

In 1971 Shepard wrote *Cowboy Mouth* with Patti Smith, seemingly a poeticized documentary account of their time together. They had intended to perform the piece together; however, Shepard pulled out after a single preview performance, and shortly escaped New York with his wife and son to live in England. His first play to premiere in London was *The Tooth of Crime* (1972), which many consider to be his first major play, although it fared better in later American productions than the London premiere. The work evidences a change in style, with its more distinctive characters, lyricism, and linear plot, alongside a reduction of visual images and obsession with real time. Richard Schechner directed a performance of this with the Performance Group in 1973 which Shepard disliked, but the play still won him an Obie. Critics warmed to the epic feel of the conflict between Hoss and Crow, seeing this as a more serious play, despite its humor. Barnes called it "splendidly provocative," and felt its "mythic subject" held tantalizing implications among the play's "depths and layers" ("*Tooth*" 34).

Remaining in England, 1974 was a productive year for Shepard. Directing the two-act *Geography of a Horse Dreamer* himself may have caused Shepard to recognize certain theatrical limitations in his work, and we see a reduction of his trademark long, spontaneous monologues. Critics were undecided about the efficacy of both play and director, but most agreed, as Harold Clurman suggested, that it was not his best work ("*Geography*" 27). Another atypical piece produced at this time was the revue-style *Little Ocean* he wrote for his wife and her female friends about childbirth. This is Shepard's only play to have an all female cast. But there was also *Action*, which seems to return to an earlier style, in which Shepard explores the concept of pure action without motivation. Initially unpopular, Lahr declared the play a "dead end" for the playwright, with "no mystery, only obfuscation, no characters, only fragments of speech" ("*Action*" 90). However, it won Shepard yet another Obie after its American showing the following year (now on a double bill with *Killer's Head*), on Shepard's return to America.

In 1976, Shepard directed *Angel City*, a two-act play with music, which premiered at the Magic Theatre in San Francisco, which was becoming a favorite venue with Shepard. The play was largely Shepard's disappointed response to having toured with Bob Dylan in the fall of 1975. An interesting mix of traditional and experimental, there are clear allusions to *Dr. Faustus*, while Shepard boldly experiments with on-stage jazz and character theory to produce a kind of collage of sound, word, and image for his audience. That year, the experiments continued with the pulp fiction improvisation, *Suicide in B-Flat*, and an operetta, *The Sad Lament of Pecos Bill on the Eve of Killing His Wife*.

1977's *Curse of the Starving Class* marked a major movement toward realism, with the first of Shepard's "family plays." In it he mixes his trademark monologues, visual images, and distinct stage actions with more traditional characters and plot. Although this was probably his most accessible play to date, many critics, at its London opening in particular, were strongly negative, seeing it as weakly derivative and clichéd. Although it had won a controversial Obie in 1977 based on the published version alone, its initial production was problematic and it remained unproduced in America until 1978 (evidence of Shepard's growing wariness of other directors and producers). Its eventual reception in America was less negative and the play uncovered some defenders, including Gerald Rabkin, who supported the way the play was structured (4), and Clurman who applauded its rough-hewn quality ("*Curse*" 349).

With the mixed reception of the Howard Hughes-inspired *Seduced* in-between time, *Curse of the Starving Class* was followed in 1978 by a second "family play," *Buried Child*, which was a more definite success, gained some excellent reviews (although it still had its detractors), and won Shepard both an Obie and a Pulitzer Prize in 1979. Shepard later revised this play and achieved further acclaim with it in 1995. 1978 had also been the year of

Tongues and *Savage/Love*, the first of Shepard's collaborations with Joseph Chaikin. Both pieces were designed for voice and percussion, with Chaikin supplying the voice, and Shepard, initially, the percussion. They were greeted with an enthusiastic response from the critics.

In 1980, *True West*, the play for which Shepard is possibly best known, first saw light. This was the first play Shepard admits to rewriting until it felt right. Although the initial West coast run had been praised, Shepard was unhappy with the cast which had been forced on the play's New York opening, and with Joe Papp taking over as director after Richard Woodruff had resigned during the previews. He disclaimed the whole play, was very outspoken against the production, and its run was brief. The subsequent West coast revival was disappointing, and it did not become a hit until the Steppenwolf Company produced it in 1982, with Gary Sinise and John Malkovich, transferring to a lengthy Off-Broadway run (762 performances), and videotaping it for American Playhouse on PBS in 1984. Mel Gussow declared the Steppenwolf production "an act of theatrical restitution and restoration" (c18).

Shortly after Shepard left his wife O-Lan in 1983, and got together with Jessica Lange, he directed a new play at the Magic Theatre, *Fool for Love*. This was another of his "family plays," and it was a substantial hit on its transfer to New York, playing for 1,000 performances and winning Obies for each cast member, director, and playwright. Even Douglas Watt, a long-time detractor of Shepard's work, called this his "purest and most beautiful play" (16). Shepard adapted *Fool For Love* into a screenplay for Robert Altman in 1985, and played the role of Eddie himself, but the movie was generally panned. In 1985 Shepard was again collaborating with Chaikin on *The War in Heaven*, the product of a workshop sponsored by the American Repertory Theatre. Due to Chaikin's recent stroke, it was not performed at this time, though it was recorded for the radio. Chaikin did some staged readings of the monologue, and eventually performed it as intended in Los Angeles in 1988, followed by a refined version at American Place Theatre in 1991.

1985 had also been the year of the most recent of Shepard's "family plays," *A Lie of the Mind*, and his first play to premiere in New York since the early seventies. This production used big name actors, including Harvey Keitel, Amanda Plummer, Aidan Quinn, and Geraldine Page, it was directed by Shepard, and got great reviews. Frank Rich described the play as "the unmistakable expression of a major writer nearing the height of his powers" (c3), and Gordon Rogoff declared Shepard to be "a playwright willing to be big, epic, demanding and ironic without ever quite knowing how to contain his visions and desires in the recalcitrant limits of theater" and the play as "consistently enthralling and explosively funny" (117). At the close of the season it won the New York Drama Critics' Circle Award for Best Play.

Ironically, after such mainstream acclaim, for the rest of the eighties Shepard was involved in his more lucrative film career and nothing new was produced for the theatre, until 1991, and *States of Shock*. In style, something of a return to his work in the 1960s, Shepard says the play was his response to the Persian Gulf War with all of its jingoism and false heroism. Starring John Malkovich, the play was sold out in advance of its run, but its absurdism had an ambivalent critical response. Shepard stayed out of the theatre for another three years, and then returned with a three-act play, *Simpatico*. Unable to raise the funds to open on Broadway or even Off-Broadway, Shepard asked George C. Wolfe for help in mounting a production, and he agreed to include it in the Public Theatre line-up for 1994. Shepard directed, the cast was good, but the critics hated it, calling it "rambling," "lazy," and "tired." It sold out in its run at the Public, but there was no transfer as hoped, although it fared better in London the following year.

As critical interest in Shepard rose in the nineties, his output slowed. Shepard continued to collaborate and experiment with Chaikin over extended periods of time. Their most recent piece, *When the World Was Green: A Chef's Fable*, was three years in the making. Unlike their previous work, this is a dramatic dialogue between a young female reporter and an old man on death row. It was directed rather than performed by Chaikin, and had its world premiere at the Olympic Games in Atlanta, Georgia, in 1996. 1996 was also the year in which the Signature Theatre Company decided to produce a season of Shepard, for which he gave them a revised version of *The Tooth of Crime (Second Dance)*. 1999 briefly witnessed a new short work by Shepard, *Eyes for Consuela*, then 2000 saw *The Late Henry Moss*, directed by Shepard in San Francisco with an all-star cast playing to decidedly mixed reviews. Reprising Shepard's perennial fascination with problematic father–son relationships, this play was rewritten for its 2001 off-Broadway opening, and so Shepard continues his evolution in pursuit of his own and society's demons.

WORKS CITED

"Theater: Shepard's *Tooth of Crime*." *New York Times* 8 March 1973: 34.

Barnes, Clive. "Theater: A Sam Shepard Double Bill." *New York Times* 2 April 1970: 43.

Clurman, Harold. Review of *Curse of the Starving Class*. *Nation* 25 March 1978: 348–49.

Review of *Geography of a Horse Dreamer*. *Nation* 10 January 1976: 27–29.

Gussow, Mel. "Stage: Shepard's *West* Revived and Restored." *New York Times* 18 October 1982: C18.

Kerr, Walter. "I Am! I Am! He Cries – But Am He?" *New York Times* 22 March 1970, Section 2: 1

Lahr, John. "*Action*." *Village Voice* 31 October 1974: 90.

"On-stage." *Village Voice* 19 March 1970: 43–44.

Rabkin, Gerald. "Like One Whole Thing." *Soho Weekly News* 16 March 1978: 4.

Rich, Frank. "Theater: *A Lie of the Mind*, by Sam Shepard." *New York Times* 6 December 1985: C3.

Rogoff, Gordon. "America Screened." *Village Voice* 17 December 1985: 117–18.

Smith, Michael. "Theatre: *Cowboys* and *The Rock Garden*." *Village Voice* 22 October 1964: 13.

Tallmer, Jerry. "Tell Me about the Morons, George." *New York Post* 12 October 1964: 16.

Watt, Douglas. "*Fool For Love* Shows Shepard at His Starkest, Bleakest Best." *New York Daily News* 27 May 1983: 16.

SELECT BIBLIOGRAPHY

Primary works

[In chronological order]

Books

Five Plays. Indianapolis: Bobbs-Merrill, 1967; London: Faber and Faber, 1969. Reprinted as *Chicago and Other Plays*. New York: Urizen Books, 1981; London: Faber and Faber, 1982. Contains *Chicago, Icarus's Mother, Red Cross, Fourteen Hundred Thousand, Melodrama Play*.

La Turista: A Play in Two Acts. Indianapolis: Bobbs-Merrill, 1968; London: Faber and Faber, 1969.

Cowboys #2. In *Collision Course*. Edward Parone (ed.). New York: Vintage Books, 1969.

Operation Sidewinder: A Play in Two Acts. Indianapolis: Bobbs-Merrill, 1970.

Maxagasm: A Distorted Western for Soul and Psyche. 2nd draft. Los Angeles: Creative Managment Associates, 1970.

The Unseen Hand and Other Plays. Indianapolis: Bobbs-Merrill, 1971. Reprinted New York: Urizen Books, 1981. Contains *The Unseen Hand, Forensic and the Navigators, The Holy Ghostly, Back Bog Beast Bait, Shaved Splits, 4-H Club*.

Zabriskie Point. With Michelangelo Antonioni, Fred Gardner, Tonino Guerra, and Clare Peploe. New York: Simon and Schuster, 1972.

Mad Dog Blues and Other Plays. New York: Winter House, 1972. Contains *The Mad Dog Blues, Cowboy Mouth* with Patti Smith, *The Rock Garden, Cowboys #2*.

Hawk Moon: A Book of Short Stories, Poems and Monologues. Los Angeles: Black Sparrow, 1973. Reprinted New York: Performing Arts Journal Publications, 1981.

The Tooth of Crime and *Geography of a Horse Dreamer*. New York: Grove Press, 1974; London: Faber and Faber, 1974.

Action and The Unseen Hand: Two Plays. London: Faber and Faber, 1975. Variant text of *Action*.

Curse of the Starving Class: A Play in Three Acts. New York: Dramatists Play Service, 1976.

Angel City, Curse of the Starving Class, and Other Plays. New York: Urizen Books, 1976. Reprinted as *Angel City and Other Plays*. London: Faber and Faber, 1978. Contains *Angel City, Curse of the Starving Class, Killer's Head, Action, Mad Dog Blues, Cowboy Mouth* with Patti Smith, *The Rock Garden, Cowboys #2*.

Rolling Thunder Logbook. New York: Viking Press, 1977; New York: Penguin, 1978. Reprinted New York: Limelight, 1987.

Suicide in B-Flat: A Mysterious Overture. New York: Berman, 1978.

Buried Child and *Seduced and Suicide in B-Flat*. New York: Urizen Books, 1979; Vancouver: Talon Books, 1979; London: Faber and Faber, 1980.

Four Two-Act Plays. New York: Urizen Books, 1980; London: Faber and Faber, 1981. Contains *La Turista, The Tooth of Crime, Geography of a Horse Dreamer, Operation Sidewinder*.

Sam Shepard: Seven Plays. New York and Toronto: Bantam Books, 1981; London: Faber and Faber, 1985. Contains *True West, Buried Child, Curse of the Starving Class, The Tooth of Crime, La Turista, Tongues* with Joseph Chaikin, *Savage/Love* with Joseph Chaikin.

True West. New York: French, 1981.

Motel Chronicles. San Francisco: City Lights Books, 1982; London: Faber and Faber, 1985.

Fool for Love and *The Sad Lament of Pecos Bill on the Eve of Killing His Wife*. San Francisco: City Lights Books, 1983; London: Faber and Faber, 1984.

Fool for Love. New York: Dramatists Play Service, 1984.

Fool for Love and Other Plays. New York and Toronto: Bantam Books, 1984. Contains *Fool For Love, Angel City, Melodrama Play, Cowboy Mouth* with Patti Smith, *Action, Suicide in B-Flat, Seduced, Geography of a Horse Dreamer*.

Paris, Texas. Berlin: Road Movies, 1984; Nordlingen (Bavaria): Greno, 1984. Adaptation L. M. Kit Carson.

Paris, Texas. New York: Ecco Press, 1984.

A Lie of the Mind: A Play in Three Acts. New York: Dramatists Play Service, 1986; London: Methuen, 1987.

A Lie of the Mind. New York: Plume, 1987.

A Lie of the Mind: A Play in Three Acts and *The War in Heaven: Angel's Monologue* with Joseph Chaikin. New York: New American Library, 1987.

The Unseen Hand and Other Plays. New York and Toronto: Bantam Books, 1986. Reprinted New York: Vintage Books, 1996. Contains *The Rock Garden, Chicago, Icarus's Mother, 4-H Club, Fourteen Hundred Thousand, Red Cross, Cowboys #2, Forensic and the Navigators, The Holy Ghostly, Operation Sidewinder, Mad Dog Blues, Back Bog Beast Bait, Killer's Head*.

Joseph Chaikin and Sam Shepard: Letters and Texts 1972–1984. Barry Daniels (ed.). New York: New American Library, 1989. Reprinted New York: Theatre Communications Group, 1994.

States of Shock. New York: Dramatists Play Service, 1992.

States of Shock; Far North; Silent Tongue: A Play and Two Screenplays. New York: Vintage Books, 1993; London: Methuen, 1995.

A Lie of the Mind: Play in Three Acts. San Francisco: Arion, 1993.

Simpatico. New York: Dramatists Play Service, 1995.

Simpatico: A Play in Three Acts. London: Methuen, 1995; New York: Vintage Books, 1996.

Cruising Paradise: Tales. New York: Knopf, 1996; New York: Vintage Books, 1997.
Buried Child. Revised version. New York: Dramatists Play Service, 1997.
Eyes for Consuela. New York: Dramatists Play Service, 1998.

Shepard's personal archives are housed in the Mugar Library, Boston University. They include numerous unpublished and unproduced plays, monologues, screenplays, and fragments; variant scripts of published plays; poetry, short prose, journals and notebooks.

Other library collections which house Shepard material are the Magic Theatre archives in the Bancroft Library, University of California, Berkeley; the Toby Cole collection in the Shields Library, University of California, Davis; and the Yale Repertory Theatre archives in the Yale School of Drama Library.

Essays

[This section does not include pieces which appear in books listed elsewhere in this bibliography.]

"Sam Shepard." In *The New Underground Theatre.* Robert J. Schroeder (ed.). New York: Bantam Books, 1968: 79–80.
"OOB and the Playwright (Two Commentaries)." *Works* 1.2 (Winter 1968): 70–73.
Untitled autobiographical statement. *News of the American Place Theatre* 3.3 (April 1971): 1–2.
Untitled comment. In *Contemporary Dramatists.* James Vinson (ed.). London: St. James, 1973.
Untitled statement. In "Symposium: Playwriting in America." *Yale/Theater* 4 (Winter 1973): 26–27.
"News Blues." *Time Out* [London] n. 222 (31 May–6 June 1974): 17.
"Less Than Half a Minute." *Time Out* [London] n. 228 (12–18 July 1974): 16–17.
"Emotional Tyranny." *Theatre Quarterly* 4.15 (August–October 1974): 22.
Letter. *Village Voice* 13 June 1977: 44.
"Peter Handke's Inner Self." *Vanity Fair* (September 1984): 106–7.
"True Dylan." *Esquire* (July 1987): 57–68.

Interviews and articles based on interviews

Gussow, Mel. "Sam Shepard: Writer on the Way Up." *New York Times* 12 November 1969: 42.
Khan, Naseem. "Free Form Playwright." *Time Out* [London] (13–17 July 1972): 30–31.
White, Michael. "Underground Landscapes." *Manchester Guardian* 20 February 1974: 8.
Chubb, Kenneth, et al. "Metaphors, Mad Dogs, and Old Time Cowboys." *Theatre Quarterly* 4 (August–October 1974): 3–16. Reprinted in *American Dreams.* Marranca (ed.): 187–209.
Oppenheim, Irene, and Victor Fascio. "The Most Promising Playwright in American Today is Sam Shepard." *Village Voice* 27 October 1975: 81–82.
Downey, Roger. "Inside the Words." *Time Out* [London] (22–28 April 1977): 11.

Drake, Sylvia. "Sam Shepard: A Play for Every Lifestyle." *Los Angeles Times* 21 October 1977, Calendar section: 1, 58, 62.

verMeulen, Michael. "Sam Shepard, Yes, Yes, Yes." *Esquire* 93 (February 1980): 79–81, 85–86.

Wren, Scott Christopher. "Camp Shepard: Exploring the Geography of Character." *West Coast Plays* 7 (Fall 1980): 75–106.

Ansen, David. "The Reluctant Star." *Newsweek* 17 November 1980: 117–18.

Coe, Robert. "The Saga of Sam Shepard." *New York Times Magazine* 23 November 1980: 56–58, 118–24. Reprinted as "Sam Shepard – Playwright Laureate of the West." *San Francisco Chronicle* 21 December 1980, Datebook section: 35–38.

McBride, Stewart. "Sam Shepard." *Christian Science Monitor* 23 December 1980: B2–3.

Goldberg, Robert. "Sam Shepard – Off Broadway's Street Cowboy." *Rolling Stone College Papers* (Winter 1980): 43–45.

Dark, John. "The 'True West' Interviews." *West Coast Plays* 9 (Summer 1981): 51–71.

McFerran, Ann. "Poet of Post-War Americana." *Time Out* [London] (4–10 December 1981): 24–25.

"Joe Chaikin Going On." [Conversation between Shepard and Chaikin] Film, 1983. Performing Arts Research Center, New York Public Library at Lincoln Center.

Weiner, Bernard. "Waiting for a Western." *San Francisco Chronicle* 9 February 1983: 54–55.

Lippman, Amy. "A Conversation with Sam Shepard." *Harvard Advocate* (March 1983): 2–6, 44–46. Reprinted *Gamut* 5 (1984): 11–27. Reprinted as "Rhythm and Truths: an Interview with Sam Shepard." *American Theatre* 1.1 (1984): 9–13, 40–41. Reprinted as "An Interview with Sam Shepard." *Dialogue* (April 1985): 50, 58–59.

Goodman, Joan. "The Good Shepard." *US* 11 April 1983: 76–77.

Dark, John. "A Conversation with Sam Shepard about a Very Corny Subject." *San Francisco* (September 1983): 68–72.

Hamill, Pete. "The New American Hero." *New York* 16 (5 December 1983): 75–76, 78, 80, 84, 86, 88, 90, 92, 95, 96–98, 100, 102.

"Playwright Shepard: On the Set... and Behind the Scenes." *Boston Globe* 23 December 1983: 38–39.

Kakutani, Michiko. "Myths, Dreams, Realities – Sam Shepard's America." *New York Times* 29 January 1984: B1, B26–28.

Vincent, Jean-Pierre (ed.). "A Long Ride: Interview with Sam Shepard." *Paris, Texas* press kit. Berlin: Road Movies, 1984: 15–17.

Goldberg, Robert. "Sam Shepard, American Original." *Playboy* 31 (March 1984): 90, 112, 192–93.

Peachment, Chris. "The *Time Out* Interview: American Hero." *Time Out* [London] 731 (23–29 August 1984): 14–17.

Fay, Stephen. "Renaissance Man Rides Out of the West." *Sunday Times Magazine* [London] 26 August 1984: 16, 19.

McCrary-Boyd, Blanche. "The Natural." *American Film: Magazine of the Film and TV Arts* 10 (October 1984): 22–26, 91–92. Reprinted as "True West!" *The Face* [London] n. 59 (March 1985): 22–26.

Fay, Stephen. "The Silent Type." *Vogue* 175 (1985): 213–18.

Kroll, Jack. "Who's That Tall Dark Stranger?" *Newsweek* 106 (11 November 1985): 68–74.

Freedman, Samuel G. "Sam Shepard and the Mythic Family." *New York Times* 1 December 1985, Section 2: 1, 20.

Wetzsteon, Ross. "Unknown Territory." *Village Voice* 10 December 1985: 55–56.

Cott, Jonathan. "The *Rolling Stone* Interview: Sam Shepard." *Rolling Stone* (18 December 1986–1 January 1987): 166, 168, 170, 172, 198, 200.

Sessums, Kevin. "Sam Shepard: Geography of a Horse Dreamer." *Interview* (September 1988): 7–78.

Allen, Jennifer. "The Man on the High Horse." *Esquire* (November 1988): 141–44, 146, 148, 150–51.

Rosen, Carol. "Silent Tongues: Sam Shepard's Exploration of Emotional Territory." *Village Voice* 4 August 1992: 34–42.

"Emotional Territory: an Interview with Sam Shepard," *Modern Drama* 36.1 (1993): 1–11.

Almereyda, Michael. "Sam Shepard: The All-American Cultural Icon at 50." *Arena* (May/June 1994): 62–69.

Brantley, Ben. "Sam Shepard, Storyteller." *New York Times* 13 November 1994: H1, H26.

Coen, Stephanie. "Things at Stake Here." *American Theatre* 13 (September 1996): 28.

Simpson, Mona, Jeanne McCulloch, and Benjamin Howe. "The Art of Theatre XII: Sam Shepard," *The Paris Review*, 142 (Spring 1997): 204–25.

Roudané, Matthew. "Shepard on Shepard: an Interview," in *The Cambridge Companion to Sam Shepard*, Matthew Roudané (ed.). Cambridge University Press, 2002: 64–80.

Secondary works

Biographies

Oumano, Ellen. *Sam Shepard: The Life and Work of an American Dreamer*. New York: St. Martin's Press, 1986.

Shewey, Don. *Sam Shepard*. 2nd edn. New York: Da Capo Press, 1997.

Tucker, Martin. *Sam Shepard*. New York: Continuum, 1992.

Sam Shepard: Stalking Himself. BBC Video Production (dir. Oren Jacoby), 1997.

Bibliographies and checklists

Bigsby, C. W. E., Kenneth Chubb, and Malcolm Page. "Theatre Checklist No. 3: Sam Shepard." *Theatrefacts* 3 (August/October 1974): 3–11.

Bottoms, Stephen J. In *The Theatre of Sam Shepard: States of Crisis*. Cambridge University Press, 1998: 293–96.

Callens, Johan. "Bibliography on Sam Shepard." ABES, Swets & Zeitlinger (On-line and CD-ROM), 2000.

Carpenter, Charles A. *Modern Drama Scholarship and Criticism 1966–80: An International Bibliography*. University of Toronto Press, 1986.

DeRose, David J. In *Sam Shepard*. New York: Twayne, 1992: 151–64.

Dugdale, John (ed.). *File on Shepard*. London: Methuen, 1989.

Eddleman, Floyd E. *American Drama Criticism: Interpretations, 1890–1977*. Hamden, CT: Shoe String, 1979.

Hart, Lynda. In *Sam Shepard's Metaphorical Stages*. Westport, CT: Greenwood Press, 1987: 149–52.

In *American Dramatists: Contemporary Authors Bibliographical Series*, vol. III. Matthew Roudané (ed.). Detroit: Gale Research, 1989: 325–60.

King, Kimball. In *Ten Modern American Playwrights: An Annotated Bibliography*. New York: Garland Publishing, 1982: 197–213.

Kleb, William. "Sam Shepard." In *American Playwrights Since 1945: A Guide to Scholarship, Criticism, and Performance*. Philip C. Kolin (ed.). New York: Greenwood Press, 1989: 387–419.

Oumano, Ellen. In *Sam Shepard: The Life and Work of an American Dreamer*. New York: St. Martin's Press, 1986: 163–70.

Salem, James. *A Guide to Critical Reviews: Part I: American Drama. 1909–1982*. 3rd edn. Metuchen, NJ: Scarecrow, 1984.

"Sam Shepard." In *Contemporary Authors*. New Revision Series, vol. XXII. Detroit: Gale Research, 1988: 422–29.

"Sam Shepard." In *Current Bibliography*, 40, 4 (April 1979): 33–37.

Sam Shepard Web Site. Ed. Gary Grant. 27 March 2000. Bucknell University. 17 June 2000 <http://www.departments.bucknell.edu/theatre%5Fdance/Shepard /shepard.html>.

Tucker, Martin. In *Sam Shepard*. New York: Continuum, 1992: 168–72.

Wolter, Jürgen C. "Sam Shepard in German-Speaking Countries: A Classified Bibliography." *Studies in American Drama 1945–Present* 6.2 (1991): 195–225.

Critical studies: books

Adolphs, Ulrich. *Die Tyrannei der Bilder: Sam Shepard's Dramen*. New York: Lang, 1990 [German].

Benet, Carol. *Sam Shepard on the German Stage: Critics, Politics, Myths*. New York: Lang, 1993.

Bottoms, Stephen J. *The Theatre of Sam Shepard: States of Crisis*. Cambridge University Press, 1998.

Callens, Johan. *From Middleton and Rowley's "Changeling" to Sam Shepard's "Bodyguard": A Contemporary Appropriation of a Renaissance Drama*. Lewiston, NY: Edwin Mellen, 1997.

Chocrón, Isaac. *El Teatro de Sam Shepard: de Imágenes a Personajes*. Caracas, Venezuela: Monte Avila, 1991 [Spanish].

DeRose, David J. *Sam Shepard*. New York: Twayne, 1992.

Graham, Laura J. *Sam Shepard: Theme, Image, and the Director*. New York: Lang, 1995.

Hart, Lynda. *Sam Shepard's Metaphorical Stages*. Westport, CT: Greenwood Press, 1987.

Krekel, Michael. *Von Cowboys bis True West: Sam Shepard's Dramen*. New York: Lang, 1986 [German].

McGhee, Jim. *True Lies: The Architecture of the Fantastic in the Plays of Sam Shepard*. New York: Lang, 1993.

Mottram, Ron. *Inner Landscapes: The Theater of Sam Shepard*. Columbia: University of Missouri Press, 1984.

Patraka, Vivian M., and Mark Siegel. *Sam Shepard*. Boise State University Press, 1985.

Perry, Frederick J. *A Reconstruction-Analysis of "Buried Child" by Playwright Sam Shepard*. Lewiston, NY: Edwin Mellen, 1992.

Taav, Michael. *A Body Across the Map: The Father–Son Plays of Sam Shepard*. New York: Lang, 1999.

Wade, Leslie A. *Sam Shepard and the American Theatre*. Westport, CT: Greenwood Press, 1997.

Collections

Callens, Johan (ed.). *Sam Shepard: Between the Margin and the Center*. Parts I and II. New York: Harwood Academic, 1998.

King, Kimball (ed.). *Sam Shepard: A Casebook*. New York: Garland Publishing, 1988.

Marranca, Bonnie (ed.). *American Dreams: The Imagination of Sam Shepard*. New York: Performing Arts Journal Publications, 1981.

Sam Shepard and Contemporary American Drama. Spec. issue of *Modern Drama* 36 (1993): 1–166.

Wilcox, Leonard (ed.). *Rereading Shepard: Contemporary Critical Essays on the Plays of Sam Shepard*. New York: St. Martin's Press, 1993.

Critical studies: book sections

Auerbach, Doris. *Sam Shepard, Arthur Kopit, and the Off-Broadway Theater*. Boston: Twayne, 1982.

Bertin, Michael (ed.). *The Play and its Critics: Essays for Eric Bentley*. Lanham, MD: University Press of America, 1986.

Bigsby, C. W. E. *A Critical Introduction to Twentieth-Century American Drama*, vol. III: *Beyond Broadway*. Cambridge University Press, 1985.

Modern American Drama 1945–1990. Cambridge University Press, 1992.

Blumenthal, Eileen. *Joseph Chaikin: Exploring at the Boundaries of Theater*. New York: Cambridge University Press, 1984.

Bock, Hedwig, and Albert Wertheim (eds.). *Essays on Contemporary American Drama*. Munich: Hueber, 1981.

Brater, Enoch (ed.). *The Theatrical Gamut: Notes for a Post-Beckettian Stage* (Ann Arbor: University of Michigan Press, 1995).

Burwick, Frederick, and Walter Page (eds.). *Aesthetic Illusion: Theoretical and Historical Approaches*. Berlin: de Gruyter, 1990.

Callens, Johan (ed.). *American Literature and the Arts*. Brussels: VUB, 1991.

Chénetier, Marc (ed.). *Critical Angles: European Views of Contemporary American Literature*. Carbondale: Southern Illinois University Press, 1986.

Cohn, Ruby. *New American Dramatists: 1960–1990*. Revised edn. New York: Grove Press, 1991.

Debusscher, Gilbert, and Henry Schvey (eds.). *New Essays on American Drama*. Amsterdam: Rodopi, 1989.

Demastes, William. *Beyond Naturalism: A New Realism in American Theatre*. Westport, CT: Greenwood Press, 1988.

Demastes, William (ed.). *Realism and the American Dramatic Tradition*. Tuscaloosa: University of Alabama Press, 1996.

Friedman, Alan Warren, Charles Rossman, and Dina Scherzer (eds.). *Beckett Translating/Translating Beckett*. University Park, PA: Pennsylvania University Press, 1987.

Ganz, Arthur. Afterword to *Realms of the Self: Variations on a Theme in Modern Drama*. New York University Press, 1980.

Geis, Deborah. *Monologue in Contemporary American Drama*. Ann Arbor: Michigan University Press, 1993.

Gerould, Daniel (ed.). *Melodrama*. New York: New York Literary Forum, 1980.

Grabes, Herbert, Winifred Fluck, and Jürgen Schlaeger (eds.). *REAL: Yearbook of Research in English and American Literature*, vol. IX. Tübingen, 1993.

Hall, Ann C. *"A Kind of Alaska": Women in the Plays of O'Neill, Pinter, and Shepard*. Carbondale: Southern Illinois University Press, 1993.

Herman, William. *Understanding Contemporary American Drama*. Columbia: University of South Carolina Press, 1987.

Kennedy, Andrew. *Dramatic Dialogue: The Duologue of Personal Encounter*. New York: Cambridge University Press, 1983.

Malkin, Jeanette R. *Verbal Violence in Contemporary Drama: From Handke to Shepard*. Cambridge University Press, 1992.

Marranca, Bonnie, and Gautam Dasgupta. *American Playwrights: A Critical Survey*. New York: Drama Book Specialists, 1981.

Maufort, Marc (ed.). *O'Neill and the Emergence of American Drama*. Atlanta: Rodopi, 1989.

  Staging Difference: Cultural Pluralism in American Theatre and Drama. New York: Lang, 1995.

McDonough, Carla J. *Staging Masculinity: Male Identity in Contemporary American Drama*. Jefferson, NC: MacFarland Press, 1997.

McNamara, Brook, Jerry Rojo, and Richard Schechner. *Theatres, Spaces, Environments: Eighteen Projects*. New York: Drama Book Specialists, 1975.

Michel, Pierre, Diana Phillips, and Eric Lee (eds.). *Belgian Essays on Language and Literature*. Liège: Liège Language and Literature, 1991.

Orr, John. *Tragicomedy and Contemporary Culture: Plays and Performance from Beckett to Shepard*. Ann Arbor: University of Michigan Press, 1991.

Parker, Dorothy (ed.). *Essays on Modern American Drama: Williams, Miller, Albee and Shepard*. University of Toronto Press, 1987.

Raben, Estelle Manette. *Major Strategies in Twentieth-Century Drama: Apocalyptic Vision, Allegory and Open Form*. New York: Lang, 1989.

Robinson, Marc. *The Other American Drama*. New York: Cambridge University Press, 1994.

Roudané, Matthew. *American Drama since 1960: A Critical History*. New York: Twayne, 1996.

Schlueter, June (ed.). *Feminist Rereadings of Modern American Drama*. Rutherford, NJ: Farleigh Dickinson University Press, 1989.

Simard, Rodney. *Postmodern Drama: Contemporary Playwrights in America and Britain*. Lanham, MD: University Press of America, 1984.

Vanden Heuvel, Michael. *Performing Drama/Dramatizing Performance: Alternative Theater and the Dramatic Text*. Ann Arbor: University of Michigan Press, 1991.

Webster, Duncan. *Looka Yonder: The Imaginary America of Populist Culture*. London: Routledge, 1988.

Wilmeth, Don B., and Christopher Bigsby (eds.). *The Cambridge History of American Theatre*, vol. III. Cambridge University Press, 2000.

INDEX

CAMBRIDGE COMPANIONS TO LITERATURE